NORTHWEST
BUDGET
TRAVELER

DEAR BOSS,
DON'T
GO
ANYWHERE
WITHOUT ME!
THIS IS
FOR
PLANNING ONLY
— THE MANAGER

NORTHWEST
BUDGET
TRAVELER

NORTHWEST
BUDGET
TRAVELER

Cheap Eats,

Cheap Sleeps,

Affordable

Adventure

NANCY LESON

SASQUATCH BOOKS
SEATTLE

Printed in the United States
Distributed in the United States by Sasquatch Books
Distributed in Canada by Raincoast Books Ltd.

1st edition.

01 00 99 98   6 5 4 3 2 1

ISSN: 1097-6027
ISBN: 1-57061-126-2

Some of the material in this book first appeared in a previously published title, *Northwest Cheap Sleeps* ©1992, 1995

Copyeditor: Sherri Schultz
Proofreader: Sharon Vonasch
Interior design & composition: Kate Basart
Cover design: Karen Schober
Cover photographs:
    TOP: ©1998 Paul McGuirk/Graphistock
    BOTTOM: ©1998 Lars Topelmann/Graphistock

Special Sales

Best Places® guidebooks are available at special discounts on bulk purchases for corporate, club, or organization sales promotions, premiums, and gifts. Special editions, including personalized covers, excerpts of existing guides, and corporate imprints, can be created in large quantities for specific needs. For more information, contact your local bookseller or Special Sales, Best Places Guidebooks, 615 Second Avenue, Suite 260, Seattle, Washington 98104, (800)775-0817.

Best Places®. Reach for it first.

SASQUATCH BOOKS
615 Second Avenue
Seattle, WA 98104
(206)467-4300
books@sasquatchbooks.com
www.sasquatchbooks.com

Contents

About Best Places® Guidebooks

Northwest Budget Traveler is part of the Best Places® guidebook series, which means it's written by and for locals who enjoy getting out and exploring the region. It's written for smart, adventurous people of all ages—people who know it's not necessary to pay top dollar to revel in a four-star experience. When we're traveling on the cheap, we look for independently owned establishments of good value, touched with local history, run by lively individuals, and graced with natural beauty. Every place listed is not only inexpensive but recommended.

Best Places® guidebooks, which have been published continuously since 1975, represent one of the most respected regional travel series in the country. Each guide is written completely independently: no advertisers, no sponsors, no favors. Our reviewers know their territory, work incognito, and seek out the very best a region has to offer. Because we accept no free meals, accommodations, or other complimentary services, we are able to provide tough, candid reports and describe the true strengths, foibles, and unique characteristics of each establishment listed.

Note: Readers are advised that the reviews in this edition are based on information available at press time and are subject to change. The editors welcome information conveyed by users of this book, as long as they have no financial connection with the establishment concerned. A report form is provided at the end of the book, and feedback is also welcome via email: books@sasquatchbooks.com.

Acknowledgments

As a Best Places editor, restaurant critic, and travel writer, I dine in the finest restaurants in the Northwest, slumber in downy comfort in the classiest hotels, and then—with a straight face—call it "work." Needless to say, if I were given a buck each time someone sighed and told me, "I wish I had *your* job!" I could retire to a suite at Seattle's Four Seasons Olympic Hotel and spend the rest of my days wrapped in a plush terrycloth robe, ordering room service.

If I sound as if I'm bragging, I am. But whenever I pull up to a swanky inn in my 1984 Subaru with the dried dog-slobber on the windows and make the valet wonder, "How can she *afford* this place?" there's an honest answer: I can't.

For those like me who travel the high-end road on someone else's dime and save the four-star wonders for those rare splurges, and for the traveler longing to explore the Northwest with a slender wallet in hand, I proudly present *Northwest Budget Traveler*. Here is the bargain companion to the venerable *Northwest Best Places* guide and your answer to finding the best in cheap eats, cheap sleeps, and affordable adventures in Oregon, Washington, and British Columbia.

Whether you're looking for inexpensive lodgings in Portland or a free wine-tasting in the Willamette Valley, a cheap-eats tour of Seattle's Pike Place Market or a weekend getaway near the Olympic rainforests, a bargain shopper's view of downtown Vancouver or a hot springs soak in the Kootenays, we'll show you how—and where to get the most bang for your vacation buck.

Far from a solo effort, *Northwest Budget Traveler* owes much to the adventuresome spirit and professional expertise of the many writers who packed their overnight bags, camping gear, AAA maps, laptops, and notebooks; jumped into their cars; and headed out in search of the best places not-a-lot-of-money can buy. Traveling on the cheap is always an adventure—as everyone who toes the thin line between taking a vacation and making a buck can attest.

My thanks to contributors Rebekah Anderson, Rachel Bard, Sarah Campbell, Sheri Doyle, Richard Fencsak, Joan Gregory, Lisa Shara Hall, Meghan Heffernan, Bonnie Henderson, Stephanie Irving, Leslie Kelly, Randy Luvaas, Sandra McKenzie, Kerry McPhedran, Kate Rogers, Barbara Spear, Steven Threndyle, Cleve Twitchell, and Kasey Wilson for taking working vacations, sleeping around for our benefit, and agreeing to share their favorite finds and word-of-mouth discoveries with our readers.

A fond thank you to copyeditor (and inveterate budget traveler) Sherri Schultz, designer-extraordinaire Kate Basart, and managing book editor Kate Rogers, for helping transform our words into a great-looking book. A world of kudos for assistant editor Sarah Campbell, whose careful treatment of this manuscript deserves extra applause. And a very special thanks to my darling husband, Mac McCarthy, and dear friend and editor-pal Rebecca Poole Forée—my favorite traveling companions and a pair who are always there to help me remember that there's a light at the end of the tunnel.

Nancy Leson
Editor

What's Cheap?

The *Northwest Budget Traveler* provides honest recommendations on great, inexpensive restaurants and lodgings throughout Oregon, Washington, and British Columbia. It also shares hundreds of money-saving tips for savvy travelers who want to explore the region's varied and fabulous destinations.

But there's one overriding principal that all cash-conscious visitors and daytrippers should remember: **You need to ask for a deal to get it**. Below are some general tips for budget travelers to keep in mind while planning a trip and making choices on the road:

Note: The **British Columbia** *chapters quote all rates in Canadian dollars. Our price ceilings in Canada were a bit higher, but a favorable exchange rate makes traveling there a real bargain for those with U.S. dollars in their pockets.*

Access

State and city **visitors bureaus** are an exceptional source of information, including details on travel packages and discounts—many of which include airfare, car rental, and transfers. They may also be able to tell you about rail or ferry travel packages, as well as provide you with maps. Call the bureaus or visit their Web sites.

Oregon Tourism Commission
PO Box 14070
Portland, OR 97202
(800)547-7842
www.traveloregon.com

Washington State Tourism
PO Box 42500
Olympia, WA 98504
(800)544-1800
(360)586-2088
www.tourism.wa.gov

Super Natural British Columbia
Box 9830 Stn. Prov. Govt.
Victoria, BC V8W 9W5
(800)663-6000
(604)663-6000 (Vancouver only)
www.travel.bc.ca

Car rental companies usually have discounts for AAA members, as well as for airline mileage program members. Parking garages sometimes offer a discount for AAA cardholders, and, of course, AAA itself has free travel **maps** for all its members.

Exploring

As noted above, check with state and city **visitors bureaus** before you go, for extensive information on your destination. They'll send you free packets filled with brochures, coupons, and lots of ideas on what and where to explore once you arrive.

Many museums and other **major attractions** frequently have one day or evening each week when they're open for free or at a reduced rate; most have standard discounts for students and seniors. (For museums, zoos, and aquariums, also check to see if they have reciprocal arrangements for members of their counterpart in your home city.)

Discounts for theater and concert **tickets** are prevalent when you're exploring the region during off-season, especially in major cities. Vancouver, BC, even refers to the winter months as the "Entertainment Season," offering a multitude of discounts and hotel packages tied to cultural entertainment. Again, check with the visitors bureaus.

For interesting and less expensive gifts for the kids or co-workers, shop at **open markets** rather than at standard tourist outlets.

Cheap Eats

Our **cost guideline** for choosing inexpensive restaurants was based on dinner for two for $30 or less (including tax, tip, and dessert—and sometimes even alcohol). Most cheap eats fall in the $10–$20-for-two range; many spots are even less.

Other budget eating tips to remember: diners and cafes often feature daily or "blue plate" **specials** that usually include bread, salad, and dessert—all for one great, low price. At more upscale cafes and restaurants, pairing **appetizers** to make up a meal may be a better deal than ordering an entree. **Happy hours** in major cities can be a great source of filling, free (or inexpensive) munchies. At establishments that offer wine, consider bringing your own bottle and paying a **corkage fee**, which often costs less than even the cheapest vintage on their list.

Keep in mind that all prices are subject to change, places close, and owners change. Call ahead whenever possible.

Cheap Sleeps

All **prices** for lodgings are based on double-occupancy (two people, one night) during peak season, unless otherwise indicated. **Peak season** is typically Memorial Day to Labor Day, except in the case of ski resorts or other winter destinations. We did our best to include here only those budget lodgings that we could honestly recommend. On average, these places charge $35–$55; many listings, such as hostels, fire lookouts, or cabins, are even less expensive. Rates for a few places may go as high as our ceiling price of $75, but are such great deals for the area or for the facilities, that we felt compelled to recommend them anyway. And again, prices, along with ownership and management, may change; call ahead.

While **discounts** are more prevalent at upscale hotels and chains than at budget accommodations, it never hurts to ask about basic reduced-rate options: AAA, senior, and student discounts, credit card and mileage programs, corporate and group rates (the latter usually applicable for 4 or more adults), discounts for stays of three or more nights, and mid-week discounts. Carry your relevant cards with you; for corporate discounts, you don't need to look corporate, just drop the name of your company and you'll usually be rewarded.

During the **off-season** or shoulder seasons, lodgings are likely to have notable discounts—room rates sometimes drop by half. State and city visitors bureaus keep up-to-date information on seasonal discounts, as well as which establishments are participating in both off- and peak-season travel packages.

Some destinations have **reservation services** for the whole area, which can be a great source for finding a deal; we've included them whenever possible.

In general, most of the lodgings listed welcome **kids**. We make note of those that do not, but to be sure, call ahead.

Most establishments these days offer a choice of **smoking** and nonsmoking rooms or designate all rooms as nonsmoking. If you smoke and don't want to be relegated to puffing in the rain, call ahead.

Many of the listings here are smaller bed and breakfasts, older motels, and remote cabins. Not all of them are easily accessible to those with **disabilities**. If you have special needs, please make sure to call ahead.

A surprising number of the lodgings listed here do allow **pets**, though there are often many "okay, buts" involved: small pets but not large, only well-mannered ones, dogs but not cats. Whenever possible, we've specified those establishments that generally welcome pets. In cases where the owners were lukewarm, charged a steep fee, or attached too many qualifications, we did not mention a pet policy.

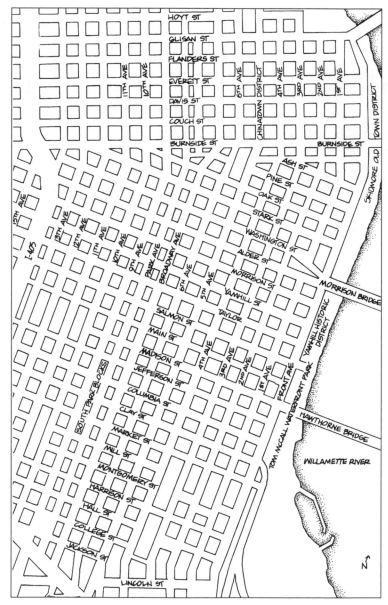

Downtown Portland

Portland

Neither big city nor cow town, Portland has a feel that's an accessible mix of comfort and creativity. No real traffic jams. No need to dress up. Sophistication is found in taste and style, and that translates to a relaxed persona: it's clear that the natural beauty of the area infuses the spirit of all who live here.

Portland's dominant color is green. Mild weather and all that rain (expect moisture from November through April) create a perpetually verdant landscape in a tree-filled city punctuated by an abundance of brilliant flowers. Central Portland is divided into east and west by the Willamette River and bounded to the north by the mighty Columbia. Residents point to the serene beauty of Mount Hood rising in the east. They gaze to the west at rambling Victorians stacked upon a series of hills blanketed in the velvety green of Forest Park—which they're quick to tell you is, at nearly 5,000 acres, the largest urban park in the nation. They relish the character of the city, from its 10 quirky bridges to its former mayor Bud Clark, who posed as a flasher in the well-known "Expose Yourself to Art" poster.

Portlanders gather at the edges of the Willamette for myriad festivals, attend twilight concerts at the zoo and in the parks, and take to the outdoors at even the slightest hint of dry weather and a bit of sun. And although they'd never admit it, they pride themselves on the long-awaited discovery of their city by the rest of the world—due at least partially to the growing fame of the local writers, artists, filmmakers, chefs, and winemakers who have brought talent and acclaim to this fair burg.

Despite census figures that put the local population at just beyond half a million (with a regional population twice that), Portland remains at heart a small town. We mean that in the kindest of ways. It's clean, it's green, and the mood is decidedly mellow; this is a place where networking is as straightforward as a trip to the grocery store. The lay of the land is easy to understand, and the city is so compact that you can ditch the car and stroll. It is in fact the neighborhoods—each with a distinct personality—that best define Portland.

Access

Portland International Airport is 20 minutes from downtown via I-205 and I-84. By cab, it can cost $30 or more, but a one-way ride is $9 on the Raz Downtowner, which picks up and drops off every half hour at major downtown hotels; (503)246-3301. **Amtrak** pulls into Old Town's Union Station with destinations north-, south-, and eastbound; (503)273-4865. Next door is **Greyhound**; (800)231-2222 or (503)243-2316. From there, you can walk a block to the Transit Mall and ride a bus into downtown at no charge; (503)238-7433.

Eighty Tri-Met **bus** lines and the **light-rail** system, MAX, make it exceptionally easy to get around the city without a car. Most buses run at 15- to 30-minute intervals throughout the week, with express service during rush hour on some routes. Many of the buses are wheelchair accessible. Travelers in the downtown core ride free anywhere in the multiblock Fareless Square, which extends from I-405 on the south and west to Hoyt Street on the north and the Willamette River on the east. Otherwise, fares are $1.05 for travel in two zones and $1.35 for three. All-day tickets are $3.25. If you're going to be in town several days and plan to travel via Tri-Met a lot, buy a book of tickets; you'll save 10 cents a ride. Tri-Met also operates the ART bus, a brightly painted public transit bus that travels Route 63 and links various city attractions. The main boarding point downtown is on SW Main Street, between SW 4th and 5th Avenues. You can purchase tickets at Tri-Met in Pioneer Square or pay cash on board buses (exact change), but MAX tickets are available only from ticket machines at each stop along the line. For more information, visit the Portland Transit Mall (SW 5th and 6th Avenues) along Pioneer Courthouse Square, the location of Tri-Met's Customer Assistance Office; (503)238-7433.

Exploring

At the slightest hint of sun, sidewalk tables appear and Portland residents set out en masse, whiling away hours in the clustered "urban villages" that dot the town, rummaging through piles of castoffs at the numerous neighborhood garage sales, sunbathing on Sauvie Island, and strolling through the gardens at Washington Park.

Once winter enshrouds the city, and early morning mists and fog nibble on the tops of the hills, the locals retreat—to bookstores such as Powell's (the country's largest), to movie houses (most shows are discounted until 6pm), and to the plentiful restaurants (there are more per capita in Portland than anywhere else in the United States). And while some head to Mount Hood to ski, others simply head to bed, leaving instructions not to be roused until the rains let up.

Downtown is home to the grassy, river-hugging expanse known as **Tom McCall Waterfront Park**, a hotbed of urban activity throughout the summer, which stretches on the west side of the Willamette from the Marquam to the Steel Bridge. At its southern end is **River-Place**, a mini-boardwalk of shops and waterfront restaurants claiming a view of the marina and boats making their way upriver. The overheated douse themselves with abandon under the Salmon Street Springs fountain. And on almost any summer weekend night, you're bound to discover something going on in the park; the Waterfront Blues Festival, the Oregon Brewers Festival, and The Bite are some of the big events. Just north, under the Burnside Bridge, you'll find **Saturday Market**, where all weekend from March through December, the smell of shish kabobs hangs in the air and artists peddle everything from jewelry to jam. Farther up the river, on Saturday mornings, the **Portland Farmers Market** brings

Festivities

In the summer and early fall months, Portland hops with concerts and festivals. Here are the biggies, many of which are free:

Rose Festival *Portland's premier festival, including parades, competitions, and*
  amusements along Waterfront Park and throughout the city
First three weeks of June ☎ *(503)227-2681*

Your Zoo and All That Jazz *Jazz under the stars at Washington Park Zoo*
Wednesdays, mid-June through mid-August ☎ *(503)226-1561*

Rhythm and Zoo Concerts *Blues and reggae at Washington Park Zoo*
Thursdays, mid-June through mid-August ☎ *(503)226-1561*

Free Live Music in the Parks *Sponsored by the Portland Parks and Recreation Bureau*
Throughout July and August ☎ *(503)823-2223*

Miller Genuine Draft Waterfront Blues Festival *Blues bash at Waterfront*
  Park near the Hawthorne Bridge
First weekend in July ☎ *(503)282-0555*

Summer Loaf Bread Celebration *Annual bread-baking festival, with demos and samples*
  at the Portland Farmers Market, under the Broadway Bridge (at the west end)
Second or third Saturday in July ☎ *(503)705-2460*

Cathedral Park Jazz Festival *Free jazz fest at Cathedral Park, under the*
  St. John's Bridge
Third weekend in July (no phone)

Oregon Brewers Festival *Free annual beer fest with swell music and $1 beer tastings,*
  at Waterfront Park
Last weekend in July ☎ *(503)778-5917*

The Bite *Pig-out benefit for Special Olympics at Waterfront Park*
Second weekend in August ☎ *(503)248-0600*

Festa Italiana *Traditional all-Italian food and arts fair at Pioneer Courthouse Square*
Usually in August ☎ *(503)223-1613*

Greek Festival *Greek eating, drinking, and dancing extravaganza at Greek Orthodox*
  Trinity Church
First weekend in October ☎ *(503)234-0484*

Gourmet Apple Tasting *Free sampling of dozens of varieties of unusual apples plus*
  cider, at Portland Nursery
First and second weekends in October ☎ *(503)231-5050*

Movie Bargains

Check out the $1 movies at the McMenamins pubs and theaters: the **Mission** (1624 NW Glisan St; (503)223-4031), the **Bagdad** (3702 Hawthorne Blvd; (503)236-9234), and the **Kennedy School** (5733 NE 33rd St; (503)249-3983). If you're 21 or over, you can sip a microbrew; bring photo ID.

Cheap movies can also be found at the **Hollywood Theatres** (NE 41st Ave and Sandy St; (503)248-6977), a vintage 1920s movie palace with worn velvet seats and balcony; the $1.50 double feature rarely includes a first run, but at that price, who cares? Check out the downtown **Guild Theatre** (SW 9th at Taylor St; (503)225-5555, ext 4610) for $2 afternoon and $3 evening flicks, and the **Valley Theatre** (9300 SW Beaverton-Hillsdale Hwy; (503)225-5555, ext 4613) for $1.50 shows.

more than 50 local vendors to Albers Mill (1200 NW Front Ave; (503)705-2460), under the Broadway Bridge.

In the downtown core, hop on one of the sleek trolleys that make up the city's light-rail system, affectionately called MAX (like the buses, light rail is free in the downtown core), and head to **Pioneer Courthouse Square** (SW Morrison St at 5th Ave), an amphitheater-style gathering place. On any sunny day of the week—particularly at lunch hour—the square is crammed with urbanites who perch on its steps to read, take in the entertainment (which might be a symphony concert or the taping of a TV show), or simply people-watch while sipping espresso. On Wednesday mornings in the summer, another branch of the Farmers Market operates in the square, selling farm-fresh produce and flowers. Under Pioneer Courthouse Square, you can travel vicariously via Powell's Travel Store and snag bus schedules at the **Tri-Met Information Center**; (503)238-7433. During the summer, midday brings a series of free mini-concerts.

A few blocks south, head for the fascinating **Niketown** (930 SW 6th Ave; (503)221-6453), where sports facts are broadcast from the sidewalk, videos play through the floor, and running shoes swim in fish tanks. Is it a shoe store, a sports museum, or Nike's answer to

Disney World? In either case, you can find less expensive shoes if you drive to Nike's super outlet store (3044 NE Martin Luther King Jr. Blvd; (503)281-5901). And since window-shopping is free, you might as well indulge your fantasies at **Pioneer Place** (SW 5th Ave at Morrison St), the city's most upscale mall, which boasts a light-filled atrium, a food court downstairs, and big-name national shops including Saks Fifth Avenue.

Head west to wander along the tree-lined Park Blocks to the **Portland Art Museum** (1219 SW Park Ave; (503)226-2811), where admission is half price from 4pm to 9pm on the first Thursday of each month. PAM also sponsors free lectures open to the public from time to time. Across the street is the **Oregon History Center** (1200 SW Park Ave; (503)222-1741), which offers a terrific Portland exhibit and the opportunity to learn about Oregon's rich history. Admission is $6 (free for seniors on Thursdays).

The **Portland Center for the Performing Arts** (1111 SW Broadway; (503)248-4335) stages Shakespearean plays, symphony concerts, and an arts and lectures series. Call to inquire about student pricing or last-minute seat deals. On the first Thursday of each month, join in the citywide **art walk**: galleries stay open late and crowds jam into the **Pearl District** (NW 10th to NW 14th Aves between

Everett and Glisan Sts). Or stop by the offices of the Metropolitan Arts Commission in the Portland Building (1120 SW 5th Ave; (503)823-5111) to pick up a guide (for a nominal fee) to the many installations of street-level art.

Literary types should scan the "Words" column in the free *Willamette Week* to see which nationally known authors are giving free readings at **Powell's** (1005 W Burnside St; (503)228-4651). Even if no readings are scheduled, you can easily spend an evening (or even days) wandering through this sprawling bookstore. Settle into the adjoining Anne Hughes Coffee Room with your stack of reading material and a cup of joe.

The **Hawthorne neighborhood** has a handful of excellent bookstores where you can spend the afternoon browsing; pick up some cheap thrills at Murder by the Book (3210 SE Hawthorne; (503)232-9995) and great deals on used or remaindered cookbooks at Powell's Books for Cooks and Gardeners (3747 SE Hawthorne; (503)235-3802). It's worth exploring this strip of Hawthorne to browse the many secondhand stores for unexpected finds and budget-priced treasures.

No part of town swings as much as the gentrified strip known as **Northwest Portland**. The primary avenues for exploration are NW 21st and 23rd Avenues, where you'll find many chichi dining spots and a maze of quirky, fun shops. NW 23rd Avenue perhaps best captures the commanding culinary spirit of Portland; once a more austere commercial route linking the industrial Northwest District with its more residential areas, the street has undergone a transition over the last 20 years that has seen folksy businesses replaced with a treasure trove of shops and restaurants. You'll find a wide range of dining options (from coffeehouses to Thai palace cuisine) as well as everything from clothing boutiques to kitschy china emporia, each with a distinct personality and array of goods.

At any time of year, you'll find twinkling white lights on the tree branches of NW 23rd. The party atmosphere continues with the crowds, ever present between 9am and 11pm; this is the one

Wine Tasting

Due in large part to the increased exposure that Oregon wines have garnered, Portland folks have developed a serious interest in learning more about the fruit of the local vine, and Saturday sampling has grown into a major sport in and around the city.

*The area's best **wine shops** and groceries offer free wine tastings on Saturdays and paid samplings (still a good deal) in the afternoon and early evening on Fridays. Among the best are Liner & Elsen (202 NW 21st Ave; (503)241-9463), Great Wine Buys (1515 NE Broadway; (503)287-2897), Mt. Tabor Fine Wine (4316 SE Hawthorne Blvd; (503)235-4444), The Cheshire Cat (1403 NE Weidler St; (503)284-5226), and the many Zupan's grocery stores.*

*If you've got a crush on grapes, though, you may want to head straight for the source: barely an hour's drive from Portland, you can visit most of Oregon's renowned wineries, whose friendly winemakers remain unassuming and unpretentious. The bucolic drive to **Yamhill County** is dotted with great picnic sites. Tasting fees vary from place to place but stay well within the budget realm, making for an informative, enjoyable, inexpensive day trip. Contact the Oregon Wine Advisory Board (1200 NW Front Ave; (503)228-8336) for a free winery guide, and see the Willamette Valley chapter for more on Oregon wineries.*

part of Portland that always hops. And if the foot traffic is constant, so is the auto action: parking can be dicey. Plan to park where you find a streetside space, and walk, walk, walk. Consider the side streets. A small pay lot is available behind the complex at NW Glisan Street, too. Or better yet, take the bus. The #15 runs from downtown Portland along W Burnside Street and turns north at NW 23rd, traveling its length north to the industrial area.

Northwest's niftiest Sunday night cheap date can be had at **L'Auberge** (2601 NW Vaughn St; (503)223-3302), one of Portland's coziest upscale restaurants. In addition to this classy joint's stellar bistro fare (which doesn't meet our budget standards, unfortunately), fabulous burgers are served with spectacular, crisp potatoes on Sundays. Dining's in the comfy bar. At 8pm, lights dim in the adjoining room and classic movies are shown ($8.25 buys a burger, fries, *and* the flick).

Those who get their thrills from the urban outdoors should head to 332-acre **Washington Park** (the entrance is at the head of SW Park Pl; (503)823-2223), also on the west side of town. Take a stroll through the International Rose Test Garden, where you can spend hours weaving among the gorgeous flowers or sequester yourself in the more private Shakespeare's Garden. Even in cooler, nonblooming months, the Rose Garden, located high on a hill overlooking the city, offers one of the best views of Portland. A short walk away you'll find the gracious, calming Japanese Gardens—proclaimed by the Japanese ambassador to be the world's loveliest this side of Japan ($6 admission charge, but worth it). Or wander onto one of the many trails that weave through the nearby **Hoyt Arboretum** (4000 SW Fairview Blvd; (503)228-TREE). Don't miss the **Crystal Springs Rhododendron Gardens** on the other side of town in Southeast Portland, just down the hill from Reed College (on SE 28th Ave at Woodstock

Blvd; (503)771-8386); in spring, blossoms burst forth with a dazzling display of colors. The gardens are free every day in fall and winter; there's a $2 admission charge Thursday through Monday, March through Labor Day.

In need of a vigorous bike ride? Pedal up the inclines of Portland's dormant volcano, **Mount Tabor**, in Southeast Portland, or through **Forest Park** on the unpaved Leif Erickson Trail. You can rent a bike from Fat Tire Farm (2714 NW Thurman St; (503)222-3276) for $5 an hour or $30 for the day. If you're in the mood for a run or a leisurely stroll, go under the Thurman Bridge to lovely McCleay Park, which leads to the Audubon Society, Pittock Mansion, and, ultimately, both Washington and Forest Parks. Across town, ice-skate at the **Lloyd Center Ice Pavilion** (953 Lloyd Center; (503)288-6073), where the whole family skates for only $7.

Portland isn't immune to the lure of music and nightlife. Two higher-end venues offer some of the best **live jazz** around—at bargain prices. At Atwater's (111 SW 5th Ave, 30th floor; (503)275-3600)—one of the city's classiest restaurants, perched at the top of the bank tower known as "Big Pink"—you can settle in at the pretty and comfortable aerial bar to catch cool jazz and the twinkliest view in town. A $5 minimum is required, but that's a sweet deal considering the quality of the music—and the quality of the drink or nibble that a five-spot can buy. Mosey on over to the very clubby lobby lounge of the Heathman Hotel (1001 SW Broadway; (503)241-4100) to catch great jazz with no cover charge in a cozy, uptown setting. The swank Brasserie Montmartre (626 SW Park Ave; (503)224-5552) is a fun late-night spot to listen to jazz while sipping a cocktail; from 11pm to closing you can munch on inexpensively priced items from the light late-night menu—say, eggs Benedict or scrambled eggs with smoked salmon. Be sure to check out the *Oregonian*'s Arts & Entertainment section each Friday to locate other budget-priced live music and club dates.

Late-night dancing to a reggae beat rocks the back room at the Red Sea Restaurant on Thursday nights ($3 cover charge); $2 on Friday or Saturday buys you calypso, world beat, or disco music (318 SW 3rd Ave; (503)241-5450). To get a taste of what Chinatown was like in the days when opium dens were the draw and the underground Shanghai tunnels were in active use, go late at night to the dark and tiny Temple Lounge at Hung Far Low (112 NW 4th Ave; (503)223-8686), where the drinks are cheap and the atmosphere mysterious. Find the hip club-crawlers at Fellini (125 NW 6th Ave; (503)243-2120), where you don't have to spend a lot of money for *la dolce vita*. Hungry after clubhopping? Suits, Gen-Xers, and infamy all mingle at Montage, a very cool late-night nosh pit (301 SE Morrison St; (503)234-1324). Try the falafel at Garbonzos (2074 NW Lovejoy St, (503)227-4196; 3433 SE Hawthorne, (503)239-6087; 6431 SW Capitol Hwy, (503)293-7335), which stays open until 1:30am.

From Portland to Seattle, drinking coffee has become the regional pastime, and why not? After all, a cup of coffee won't set you back too much, it gets you in out of the rain, and hang time is free. The growth of new java joints in Portland has been faster than that of mushrooms after the rain: you'll find at least two **coffeehouses** on almost every block in town. Among the best: Torrefazione Italia (838 NW 23rd Ave, (503)228-2528; 1403 NE Weidler St, (503)288-1608), Coffee People (533 NW 23rd Ave, (503)221-0235; various other locations), Giant Steps (1208 NW Glisan St; (503)226-2547), Java Man (1432 SW 6th Ave; (503)228-7578), and Common Grounds Coffee House (4321 SE Hawthorne Blvd; (503)236-4835).

When it comes to **dining**, native son James Beard certainly drew attention to his hometown. Over the last five years, Portland has seen a remarkable growth of restaurants—especially those that celebrate the irresistible local bounty. You don't need to spend a lot to sample some of the best Portland has to offer: even the smaller, less expensive dining options are placing emphasis on what's fresh and local. Ethnic eateries abound, making dining on a budget an international adventure.

Cheap Eats

Aztec Willie & Joey Rose Taqueria
1501 NE Broadway, Portland ☎ (503)280-8900

In one corner, an attractive bar serves up frosty margaritas; in the opposite corner, a glass-walled playroom welcomes the little ones. It's an unusual mix, but it works to attract parents in search of mealtime distraction for both themselves and their children. Like its sister taquerias, Santa Fe (831 NW 23rd Ave; (503)220-0406) and Mayas (1000 SW Morrison St; (503)226-1946), this one herds its diners down a cafeteria line offering burritos, tacos, and enchiladas—half a dozen kinds each. Try the vividly flavored chile verde taco, a chicken mole enchilada, or the chiles rellenos. No credit cards are accepted, but there is an ATM on the premises.

El Burrito Loco
1942 N Portland Boulevard (and multiple locations), Portland
☎ (503) 735-9505

The namesake creation is a fresh, floury tortilla bursting around a chile relleno, strips of tender beef, and refried beans. It's the kind of crazy concoction you occasionally *just gotta have right now*, and you might not find it anywhere else. The tacos, with chunks of pork, cilantro, tomatoes, and onion, are less filling, but they're so good and such a bargain that you'll stuff yourself on a couple anyway. Take out or sit at one of the few tables. *Hasta luego*—we know you'll be back.

Foothill Broiler
33 NW 23rd Place, Portland ☎ (503) 223-0287

Here's a genuine flame-broiler with old-fashioned cafeteria service. The burgers (available in multiple sizes) are just what you need when that cheeseburger craving hits—gooey with American cheese—and give you the chance to play dress-up at the condiment bar. Crisp fries are the requisite accompaniment. And don't miss the home-baked pies.

Fujin
3549 SE Hawthorne Boulevard, Portland ☎ (503) 231-3753

Expect Fujin to be packed, for good reason: this one-room Hawthorne neighborhood favorite captures the Chinese culinary spark now sadly missing from the dining scene. A number of the signature dishes—heavenly crispy eggplant with its seductive, creamy contrasts; plump, briny, black bean–dabbed oysters; beef or chicken packed with bitter-tangy orange rind and surprising zaps of heat—lift this spot up and over the competition. Execution is consistent, and service, while a bit brusque if the place is busy, is lightning-fast.

La Buca
2309 NW Kearney Street, Portland ☎ (503) 279-8040

Pasta is the focus of this tiny tiled and countered space nestled in a little strip mall deep in the heart of trendy Northwest Portland. Focus on inexpensive, simple fare: a bunch of straight-ahead pastas, a few super Italian-style panini, a salad or two, soup, and breads with spreads. Also look for a number of wines by the glass. Youth is in the air, and prices respect a slacker's budget.

Brewpubs

Brewpubs are big time in Portland. The Pacific Northwest began the now-ubiquitous trend toward handcrafted microbrewed beers; Oregon, also called Beervana, boasts more brewpubs per capita than any other state. Some of our faves: BridgePort (1313 NW Marshall St; (503)241-7179), BrewHouse Taproom (2730 NW 31st Ave; (503)228-5269), Widmer Brothers' Gasthaus (929 N Russell St; (503)281-3333), Ringler's (1332 W Burnside St; (503)225-0543), Hawthorne Street Ale House (3632 SE Hawthorne Blvd; (503)233-6540), and McMenamins Blue Moon Tavern (432 NW 21st Ave; (503)223-3184).

Noodles

Big, steaming, slurpy bowls of herb-infused Vietnamese noodle soups offer exotic tastes at low prices. Options range from basic beef to crab or duck versions. Try Pho Van (707 NE 82nd Ave; (503)253-2694), Pho Hung (4717 SE Powell Blvd; (503)775-3170), Pho Trang (6236 NE Sandy Blvd; (503)281-2990), and the ultra-authentic scene at Pho 54 (6852 NE Sandy Blvd; (503)281-9674).

La Macchia

2340 NW Westover, Portland ☎ (503)226-8082

Authentic Italian-style pizzas—sparsely adorned thin-crust wonders—are served in this unfussy and colorful eatery. Panini sandwiches, cappuccinos, and unpretentious service add to its charm. When weather permits, the outdoor patio is a great place to while away the afternoon with a glass of wine or enjoy live tunes in the evening.

Macheezmo Mouse

723 SW Salmon Street, Portland (and multiple locations) ☎ (503)248-0917

Once upon a time, the Mouse pioneered fast food with an ultra-healthy, flavor-packed twist: nutritionally correct, neo-Mexican, cheap and tasty stuff. But the Mouse got a bit tired over the years, and the competition moved in. Now there's good news for Mouse fans: the menu has been evolving, and more adventurous flavors have emerged. Fat is no longer totally banned (yahoo!), and the low-priced burritos, tacos, tortas, and salads now sport fresh tastes with lively seasonings—herbs and texture are back, with Thai, Mexican, and just plain quirky-good accents.

Nicholas Restaurant

318 SE Grand Avenue, Portland ☎ (503)235-5123

A constant buzz of chatter steadily emerges from a tiny storefront, while lunchtime lines snake out the door, full of hungry diners waiting to jostle their way to a table to get top-notch Lebanese fare at unbelievably low prices. But that's not all. Behind the counter, pizzas are in constant motion—tapped out, topped, paddled into the ovens, and paddled out. These aren't your typical Italianate pies, either: pay attention to the "authentic Mediterranean pizza" section of the menu, where spice is the dominant sensation.

Phil's Uptown Bento

17 NW 23rd Place, Portland ☎ (503)224-9541

Everyone with a grill and a pot serves "bento" these days—or at least the grilled skewers of chicken that are all the rage in Portland. While a butcher shop may seem an unlikely locale for bento, smack-dab in front of Phil's Uptown Market you'll find one of the best little operations around. From late morning through the afternoon, smoke spews from the grill while stick after stick of the plumpest, tastiest white-meat chicken in Portland is plopped on a massive bed of rice and doused with teriyaki and sweet-hot sauce before a box of the works is handed to the next patient person in line.

Rib Joints

The range of rib joints in Portland is impressive for both flavor and fair pricing. Pick them up to go or dine in at any of these little spots, but make sure you load up on napkins: Campbell's Bar-B-Q (8701 SE Powell Blvd; (503)777-9795), Czaba's Bar-B-Q (5907 N Lombard St; (503)240-0615), Tennessee Red's (2133 SE 11th Ave; (503)231-1710), and Doris' Cafe (325 NE Russell St; (503)287-9249).

Pizzicato

1749 SW Skyline Boulevard (and multiple locations), Portland
☎ (503) 221-8784

These gourmet pizzerias tower over their mega-chain competitors and over many local pizza places too. Credit their success to imaginative fresh ingredients (red potatoes and prosciutto, for instance) as well as respectful classics such as pepperoni. You can buy the daily special by the slice for lunch at several of the locations. The best (and cheapest) bet may be the simplest: the Margherita is little more than crust, cheese, and tomato sauce, but it's divine.

Swagat

2074 NW Lovejoy Street, Portland ☎ (503) 916-4333
4325 SW 109th Avenue, Beaverton ☎ (503) 626-3000

Stellar, mostly southern Indian fare including terrific, monster-size *dosas* (stuffed crepes), delicious naan, subtle curries, super condiments, and value-packed lunch buffets. Each location sports a different personality: one's a converted tract house that attracts the large Indian population in the Beaverton burbs, and the other's a newer urban outpost in the heart of Portland's skateboards-'n'-suits Northwest District.

Thai Touch

4806 SE Stark Street, Portland ☎ (503) 230-2875

Not everything works here; some of the sauces repeat themselves a little too often (spicy lime sauce is omnipresent). But at these low prices, it's worth trying a bunch of dishes to discover the flavor-packed winners. You won't feel as if you've died and gone to Thai heaven, but a little exploration will reward you with tasty, unusual dishes at wallet-sparing prices. Don't miss *mien cum*—big, fresh, raw spinach leaves topped with a combo of sweet, salty, sour, and spicy flavors (coconut, peanuts, lime, onions, and dried shrimp). You add a dollop of sticky sweet sauce and pop the rolled leaf in your mouth. Wow.

Cheap Sleeps

Portland offers so many great opportunities for the bargain-conscious that it's disappointing to find such a dearth of cheap sleeps. Here are a few. Let us know if you come across others. New bed and breakfasts do open regularly, but there are few rooms that fit within a tight budget; others offer locations that don't make it easy to explore Portland's wonderful food, shopping, and entertainment options.

Carriage Inn

2025 NW Northrup Street, Portland, OR 97209 ☎ (503) 224-0543

With its wood paneling and many shades of beige, this place offers rather bland decor but real-deal pricing. The elevator feels as if it won't ascend even three inches (although it does manage to climb the three floors), but the rooms are spacious (stove, oven, fridge, dishwasher, and private bath with tub and shower). It's seconds away from the stores and restaurants of Northwest Portland. For picnic or in-room dining, stop by City Market (735 NW 21st Ave; (503) 221-3007), the city's best Euro-style food emporium, for a super selection of take-away fare. Verdant McCleay and Washington Parks are within but a 20-minute stroll.

Cypress Inn

809 SW King Street, Portland, OR 97205 ☎ (503) 226-6288

Two modern two-story motel buildings sit among the stately homes on a tree-lined residential street just one block south of Burnside Street and the hopping Northwest District. The value-packed rate includes a choice of one or two queen-size beds (albeit in a quite ordinary room), free parking, and a major continental breakfast. From 6 to 10 each morning, fill up on hot and cold cereals, doughnuts, toast, muffins, juice, coffee, and tea. The quiet location is a perfect access point to downtown.

The Mallory Hotel

729 SW 15th Avenue, Portland, OR 97205 ☎ (800) 228-8657 or (503) 223-6311

The Mallory, though a bit frumpy, is a well-loved favorite in quiet surroundings on the upper edge of the downtown business area, within a comfortable walk of trendy Northwest Portland. Free parking is a plus. The rooms, whose rates approach the high end of the budget scale, are quite serviceable (if a bit small). Shade your eyes when you open the door to your room, though; some of the carpet is as green as Astroturf. The lobby and dining room sport an old-fashioned charm; Grandma would feel at home here. The dark, '50s-style Driftwood Room draws theater types and anyone else who considers the free goldfish crackers a full meal.

OREGON

Mark Spencer Hotel
409 SW 11th Avenue, Portland, OR 97205 ☎ (800) 548-3934 or (503) 224-3293

From the outside, this U-shaped, yellow-brick hotel looks pretty worn, but the remodeled interior is very clean and pleasant. Once considered a place strictly for longer stays ($930 a month translates to a mere $31 per night), the Mark Spencer is now quite a find for the short-term guest, too. The bedroom studios have handy kitchenettes.

Portland Guest House
1720 NE 15th Avenue, Portland, OR 97212 ☎ (503) 282-1402

The best deal in this charming bed and breakfast near the NE Broadway neighborhood is the back bedroom on the second floor: it's small and cozy, a door leads out to a shared balcony, and the bathroom—also shared—is right next door. It books quickly, so call well in advance to reserve. The philosophy here is come-and-go-as-you-please (when you check in, you'll be given keys for both the front door and your room). Each room has its own phone and is tastefully furnished with white carpet and antique linens and furniture. The owner doesn't live in the Guest House, but she drops in each morning to serve a fine breakfast of fresh fruit, scones, and perhaps a basil omelet. When the weather is warm, the brick courtyard out back is a pleasant place to while away the morning.

Portland International Hostel
3031 SE Hawthorne Boulevard, Portland, OR 97214 ☎ (503) 236-3380

The Hawthorne district location for Portland's only official youth hostel couldn't be better for budget travelers; within blocks are great used bookstores, good eats, and plentiful coffee and microbrew hangouts. This hostel has the familiar rules: closed between 11am and 4pm, bring your own linens (or rent theirs), and an 11pm curfew (with a 24-hour security access code). Shared showers, bunk beds, blankets, a kitchen, and two small living areas are the amenities—plus all-you-can-eat pancakes come morning. The hostel encourages groups and has one private room, good for families. In June through September, only Hostelling International members can stay here, but you can buy a HI membership ($25 for the year) when you arrive.

Columbia River Gorge & Mount Hood

M ount Hood, Oregon's highest peak—known as Wy'East to early dwellers in the area—rises to 11,285 feet, a striking centerpiece for a region blessed with geographical diversity. To the north, the Columbia River follows the path it cut through the basaltic Cascades millions of years ago, carving cliffs up to 400 feet high. In some places, the river rushes by in a flurry of swells and whitecaps; in others, federal dams have turned it into a series of lakes. Lush lands north and east of Mount Hood, on the climatic cusp between the arid desert and the moist Oregon coast, give rise to fertile orchards and farms; the southern slopes draw skiers, climbers, and sight-seekers all year round.

Exploring

As you drive east from Portland on Interstate 84, the city's outskirts persist right up to the beginning of the **Columbia River Gorge National Scenic Area**, which begins after Troutdale; (541)386-2333. If you want some sustenance before making the drive, stop by McMenamins Edgefield for a hearty breakfast or burger—and, of course, a brew (2126 SW Halsey St, Troutdale; (503)669-8610). Or join other bargain diners at Tad's Chicken 'n' Dumplings (1 mile east of Troutdale on Hwy 30; (503)666-5337).

Exit I-84 and take the old Historic Columbia River Highway (Hwy 30) for 22 miles between Troutdale and Ainsworth State Park. Almost immediately, the scenery progresses from merely interesting to most spectacular. This is the only highway listed on the National Register of Historic Places for Oregon. Along the way you'll pass a series of elegant, slender waterfalls cascading down steep precipices: Latourell, Shepperds Dell, Bridal Veil, Coopney, Mist, Wahkeena, Oneonta, Horsetail, and the 620-foot **Multnomah Falls** (the second highest in the country).

From Multnomah Falls, you can hike up **Larch Mountain** to one of the best views of the gorge (especially at sunset). The trail runs right by the top of the falls (for more information, call Multnomah Falls Lodge; (503)695-2376). You can also drive up Larch Mountain, starting from Crown Point (with a vista house 725 feet above the Columbia) off the historic highway. Oneonta Gorge, a couple of miles east of Multnomah Falls, is a narrow, dramatic cleft through which a slippery half-mile trail winds to secluded **Oneonta Falls** (for more information,

Events in the Park

Every Thursday in August, families gather at 7pm in Jackson Park (13th and May Sts, Hood River) for outdoor evening entertainment that ranges from theater to music; (541)386-2055. On Saturdays from May through October, local farmers, artists, bakers, and others sell their wares at the Farmers Market, also in Jackson Park.

call the Columbia River Gorge National Scenic Area).

Back on the main highway (I-84 and Hwy 30 join forces until Mosier), you're deep into the dramatic beauty of the gorge. Tour the **Bonneville Dam**, the oldest of the 10 dams on the river, and watch salmon in the fish ladders during the seasonal runs. At **Cascade Locks**, you can still see the locks, built to help boats across the Columbia's rapids (before dams calmed the waters). A two-hour trip on the *Columbia Gorge*, an old-fashioned stern-wheeler, costs $12.95 (three trips daily from June through September; times vary in winter) and evokes something of the river's past; (503)223-3928. Its home port is at Cascade Locks.

Salmon are not the only creatures flying through the surf of the Columbia; at the town of Hood River, **board sailors** skim across the waves like brightly colored water bugs. Here's where the wind blows east against the west-flowing current in the spring and summer months, careening down the narrow canyon formed by the gorge's basalt cliffs and making for ideal windsurfing conditions. Over two dozen local businesses in Hood River cater to the sailboard crowd; several offer lessons and rentals, and all will tell you where the winds are on any given day. The Hook and the Columbia Gorge Sailpark/Marina are favorite launching spots, although you can take off virtually anywhere land meets water.

Hood River has something for everyone, though—not just those obsessed with wind. Hikers explore the network of trails on the Columbia's cliffs; mountain bikers migrate to the Forest Service roads around Mount Hood. The region's farms (and there are 14,775 acres of them in Hood River County) are blessed with a winning combination of moisture and sun: a plenitude of **orchards and farms** sell U-pick and ready-picked fruits and vegetables, and there are festivals oriented around virtually every harvest season. Call the Hood River Chamber of Commerce, (800)366-3530 or (541)386-2000, for locations. Or drop by the Fruit Tree (4140 Westcliff Dr, Hood River; (541)386-6688) or the River Bend Country Store (2363 Tucker Rd, Hood River; (541)386-8766) for fresh produce and local specialty foods.

The **Mount Hood Railroad** (110 Railroad Ave, Hood River; (541)386-3556) makes round trips from the quaint Hood River Depot into the heart of orchard country, April through October. The four-hour trip to Parkdale is $21.95 ($13.95 for kids). If the weather's not cooperating, take a break in the Hood River Parks and Recreation Department's Aquatic Center (17th and May Sts, Hood River; (541)386-1303), which houses a recreational pool, a therapy pool (for older adults and kids under 7), and a wading pool. Join a game of aqua-volleyball, or check out the long list of classes offered. Daily rates: $2 for adults, $1.50 for kids, under 3 free. When the weather does cooperate, the roof opens.

Oenophiles sip the valley's vintages at Hood River Vineyards (4693 Westwood Dr, Hood River; (541)386-3772) or Flerchinger Vineyards (4200 Post Canyon Dr, Hood River; (541)386-2882). Or try some fabulously potent eau-de-vie at the Eve Atkins Distillery (4420 Summit Dr,

Hood River; (541)354-2550). Beer lovers should drop by the tasting room of the Full Sail Brewpub (506 Columbia St, Hood River; (541)386-2247) or quaff a cold one with pizza and a movie at the Skylight Theatre & Pub (107 Oak St, Hood River; (541)386-4888 for movie times).

The Dalles was once the largest Native American trading center in North America and the end of the overland portion of the Oregon Trail. The town vies with Astoria for the title of the oldest white settlement in the Northwest, but it's definitely *the* historic stop along this stretch. Take a quick walking tour of the town and examine the hybrid architecture (including Gothic Revival, Italianate, and American Renaissance) that lines the town's hybrid streets.

Visit the **Columbia Gorge Discovery Center** (Crate's Point, 3 miles west of The Dalles; (541)296-8600), housed in surgeon's quarters built in 1856. Located adjacent to the county historical museum, this new interpretive complex presents exhibits and educational programs documenting the geologic, natural, and anthropological history of the area; admission is $6.50 for adults, $3 for kids ages 6 to 16. Then picnic in **Celilo Park**, where Native Americans used to net and spear fish from platforms on the former Celilo Falls. (The falls once rushed with water but were slowed and eventually stayed by the Bonneville Dam.)

Take Highway 35 south from Hood River, where apple and pear trees line the roads near Parkdale and lava fields appear among the orchards. **Lolo Pass Road** is a scenic bypass drive from Hood River around the north and west sides of Mount Hood to Zig Zag on Highway 26 (the road is closed in winter); an easy and rewarding hike from this road begins at Old Maid Flat and leads to the cascading **Ramona Falls**.

Five ski areas grace the flanks of Mount Hood. The first one you reach when driving south on Highway 35 is also the oldest and the smallest (500 vertical feet). But **Cooper Spur Ski and Recreation Area** (11000 Cloud Cap Rd, Mount Hood; (541)352-7803) can be a bargain if the conditions are right. This family-owned, family-run area has a good learning hill with one T-bar and one rope tow ($5), and $15 buys a lift ticket good all day and night. The area also has a large network of cross-country ski trails.

Timberline will give you the most skiing for your dollar if you plan correctly (at the east edge of Government Camp on Highway 26, turn north on Forest Rd 50 and drive 6 miles to the ski area; (503)272-3311). Weekday tickets are $22; weekend lift tickets are $28. In summer (Timberline offers the only lift-serviced, all-summer skiing in America), tickets are $32 every day, good for the two chair lifts that carry skiers to the top of the Palmer Snowfield. The mountain is accessible to nonskiers as well in summer; take the Mile chair lift up as a foot passenger for the stunning view (around $6 round trip).

Mount Hood Meadows, (503)337-2222, has some of the best and most varied terrain in the area, accessible by nine chair lifts. Lift tickets are $32 ($5 more if you want to ski day and night). Occasionally, less expensive promotional deals may be offered; call (503)227-SNOW for a snow report. If it's a lousy

Swim the Channel

It's not the English Channel . . . but some say it feels like it. Every Labor Day, 400-plus swimmers cross the 1-mile-plus Columbia River from Washington to Oregon, just for fun; (541)386-2000.

Jazz with a View

The Mount Hood Festival of Jazz (PO Box 3024, Portland, OR 97208; (503)231-0161), which has featured such acclaimed performers as David Sanborn and Al Jarreau, is held the first weekend in August at the Mt. Hood Community College campus, with tickets running from $22 to $50 per day; order them through Ticketmaster, (503)224-4400.

ski day, return your lift ticket within 45 minutes and you'll get a voucher for another day's ticket.

Two other lift areas are **Mount Hood Skibowl Action Pass** (8700 E Highway 26, Government Camp; (503)222-2695), which has an inflatable alpine slide and a free-fall bungee tower in the summer, and **Summit Ski Area** (on Highway 26 in Government Camp; (503)272-0256), where one lift on two hills costs $10. The Snow Bunny area in Government Camp is best for sledding and tubing, even though officially it's a ski area.

From a distance, **Mount Hood** looks like the archetypal mountain—two diagonal brush strokes creating a pointed peak. Close up, the dramatic ridges and cliffs are a subtle reminder of the mountain's power. Summertime at Mount Hood finds crowds of climbers, hikers, and wilderness fans enjoying the glaciers and flowers. (Walk carefully—many Sasquatch sightings have been reported on the mountain!) The lower parts of the mountain are ablaze with rhododendrons (peaking in June) and wildflowers (peaking in July); all are easily reached from trails that spread out from Timberline Lodge. One of the best trails leads 4 1/2 miles west from Timberline to flower-studded **Paradise Park**.

What you need to climb Mount Hood is either experience or a guide. The best time to ascend is from May to early July. Most climbers take one of the south-side routes, up the Palmer and White River Glaciers. It's a technical climb, so if you're unsure of your skills, arrange for a guide from the Northwest School of Survival (PO Box 1465, Sandy, OR 97055; (503)668-8264) or the Mazamas (909 NW 19th Ave, Portland; (503)227-2345), a Portland-based climbing club that organizes climbs from May to mid-June. Climbing fees are $7 for members and $14 for nonmembers, although the club doesn't provide any equipment. You can spend the night before your climb in the club's cabin.

Hardy hikers circumnavigate the peak on the **Timberline Trail**, a 40-mile path leading through forest and over snowfield. Call the ranger station at Zig Zag for information; (503)668-1704.

Above Government Camp at the Timberline ski area, the main attraction is the Depression-era **Timberline Lodge**, a WPA project dedicated by Franklin Delano Roosevelt in 1937. Every part of the lodge—from the rough-hewn columns to the huge stone fireplace—was crafted by hand, and the lodge is filled with art: mosaics, wood carvings, paintings, and hand-loomed textiles. Even if you don't ski, drive up to the lodge (which you may recognize from Stanley Kubrick's film *The Shining*) and sit by the fire, or sip a drink in the Blue Ox Bar.

Sandy is the first town you encounter as you head west out of the Mount Hood area on Highway 26 (and the best place to stop for gas when you're going the other way; prices go up exponentially as you approach the mountain). Visit **Oral Hull Park**, designed for the blind, with its fragrant plants and splashing water (43233 Oral Hull Road, Sandy; (503)668-6195).

Cheap Eats

Big City Wraps

212 4th Street, Hood River ☎ (541) 387-5511

This lunch-only sister restaurant to the nearby Big City Chicks offers the same international flavor, but here you'll find it wrapped in a tortilla for less than five bucks. Sample the blackened caesar, with rice, chicken, and caesar salad fixings in a tomato tortilla; or the Bangkok wrap—spicy with phad Thai ingredients in a spinach tortilla. While these wraps are great on-the-go food, who'd want to eat anywhere else when the atmo here is so cool both indoors and out?

Big Horse Brew Pub

115 State Street, Hood River ☎ (541) 386-4411

Climb the stairs to this very social spot where people come (sometimes with kids) to dine on bountiful burgers, oodles of noodles (including a powerful Gorgonzola and prosciutto dish), and heaping salads. Match it all with one of their own microbrews, made downstairs, and hope for some local music playing live from the balcony.

Coffee Spot

12 Oak Street, Hood River ☎ (541) 386-1772

If you're looking for a hefty turkey, roast beef, or pastrami sandwich (and maybe an espresso to go), this is your spot. Chow down at one of the few tables, or take your meal down the hill to the park on the Columbia River.

El Sombrero

1306 12th Street, Hood River ☎ (541) 386-7300

There's nothing like a great margarita after a hot day in the sun. And El Sombrero certainly knows how to make one—not to mention all the Mexican *especiales*—enchiladas, burritos, chimichangas, and chiles rellenos—to go along with that most refreshing of drinks.

Hood River Restaurant

108 2nd Street, Hood River ☎ (541) 386-3966

Here's where you can find Hood River's favorite Chinese chow and revel in pages and pages of choices. Dinner entrees come with everything from spring rolls to wontons, but families should choose from the family page of the menu. Lunch offers especially great deals. This is your typical Chinese-American menu—not authentic, perhaps, but inexpensive and comforting.

Purple Rocks Art Bar and Cafe

606 Oak Street, Hood River ☎ (541) 386-6061

Board sailors know the best breakfast is at this popular cafe, whose (some would say, ahem, obnoxious) name evokes . . . oh, never mind. The art takes the form of sketchbooks filled with patrons' doodles, along with crayons for the kids.

Housed in a cute little cottage on Hood River's main street, this local hangout offers delicious multigrain walnut pancakes and mostly vegetarian fare (sprout and cottage cheese sandwich, lasagne, quiches, and black bean burritos).

The Dobre Deli

308 E 4th Street, The Dalles ☎ (541) 298-8239

This little deli is a good midday stop for those in The Dalles. Lunch cravings get satisfied here with good sandwiches, hearty soups (cheesy potato, ham and bean, chowders), and just the right sweet to finish it all off.

Mount Hood Country Store

6545 Cooper Spur Road, Mount Hood ☎ (541) 352-6024

A Mount Hood oasis for lunchtime munchers, this general store is home to a deli where you can find good homemade pizza by the slice, hearty homemade soups in winter (don't miss the black bean version), and freshly made deli meat and cheese sandwiches. Try their cinnamon rolls, best enjoyed with a rich Big-foot Mocha. Perch at one of the few tables upstairs, or order to go.

Mount Hood Brewpub

Highway 26, Government Camp ☎ (503) 272-3724

After you've spent a day on the mountain, the Mount Hood Brewpub is a welcome sight. Friendly servers pour a good pint of Timberline Ale (from the original pre-Prohibition recipe) and serve casual pub-style eats (sandwiches, pizzas, and pastas). Families are welcome.

Barlow Trail Inn

69580 E Highway 26, Zig Zag ☎ (503) 622-3112

If this place looks as if it's been around for over half a century, there's a good reason: it has. Zig Zaggers stop here for fried chicken, a T-bone steak, a taco salad, or breakfast—served until 11pm. You get the idea. This is one busy stop on weekends, when urban escapees come for the inn's barbecue feasts.

Michael's Bread and Breakfast

24525 E Welches Road, Welches ☎ (503) 622-5333

When you do only one thing, you usually do it well. And Michael's does only breakfast. Locals heading for a hike in the hills know to stop here for a carbo load. Good omelets, big pancakes, baked apple fritters, and bushels of other baked goods will keep you going all day long.

Elusive Trout Pub

39333 Proctor Boulevard, Sandy ☎ (503) 668-7884

The theme in Sandy's popular pub is fish and fishing. The menu reflects the slang of the former owner, who lived in hip-waders until he spawned the idea for the pub. He's since gone to the proverbial fishin' hole, but the current owners have preserved the original menu: the Keeper, Bucktail Caddis, Eastern Brookie, Red Sider, and German Brown are all names for better-than-average sandwiches. Nineteen brews are on draft. Try the ale sampler: six 5-ounce glasses of your choice.

Cheap Sleeps

McMenamins Edgefield
2126 SW Halsey Street, Troutdale, OR 97060 ☎ **(503) 669-8610**

The former Multnomah County Poor Farm, established in 1911, is now a McMenamins enterprise with a 91-room inn (complete with restaurant, sitting porches, library, brewpub, movie theater, gardens, and outdoor amphitheater where big-name bands play to crowds that can number up to 4,000). The inn is too expensive for our poor pockets, but you can spend a night in the men's or women's hostel—one large room with bunk beds and a bath down the hall—for a mere $18 (private locker included, but no breakfast).

Scandian Motor Lodge
307 Wa-Na-Pa Street (PO Box 217), Cascade Locks, OR 97014 ☎ **(541) 374-8417**

The Scandian has 30 large, woodsy rooms with bright Scandinavian colors and tiled baths (one with a sauna). A very clean upstairs room with a river view comes with a reasonable price tag ($46 in the summer). Reservations are a good idea for the summer; bring your small pet if you like.

Gorge View Bed and Breakfast
1009 Columbia Street, Hood River, OR 97031 ☎ **(541) 386-5770**

Want to touch base with Hood River's predominant windsurfing culture? Here's where the surfers like to stay. Regular bed-and-breakfast rooms toe the cheapster limit in Pat and Ann Frodel's B&B, but the "bunk room" in a renovated sun porch attracts a loyal and eclectic following, from bargain hunters to windsurfing pros. For about $35 per boardhead (May through September), you get all the interesting conversation that evolves when four strangers end up in

Fire Lookouts

The Flag Point (5,650 feet) and Fivemile Butte (4,627 feet) lookouts are still used by fire watchers (Flag Point serves as the summer home for fire scouts; Fivemile, available year-round, is staffed on an as-needed basis). When not in offical use, these crow's nests in the **Mount Hood National Forest** are available to the skilled backcountry traveler at roughly $25 per night (special-use permit required). You'll need to bring the usual amount of gear (sleeping bags, food, water, and dishes). The Forest Service provides the stove, the firewood, and the view. The length of the trek is determined by where the road becomes inaccessible by snow; you may end up with an lengthy hike (it's an eight-hour, 11-mile ski trip to Flag Point), or you may be able to drive right up to the gate for an easy jaunt to the lookout. Ask about the Forest Service's Valley View cabin near Badger Lake, also available year-round for adventure seekers. For detailed directions, applications, and information on the permit process, call the Barlow Ranger District; (541) 467-2291.

When All Else Fails

Hood River *Looks like everything's full, or you want a weeklong rental? Hood River Vacation Rental (823 Cascade Ave, Hood River, OR 97031; (541)387-3113 or www.gorge.net/business/hrvacrent/) specializes in vacation rentals—from river-front homes and in-town cottages to condominiums and B&Bs.*

Mount Hood *Try Thunderhead Lodge (PO Box 129, Government Camp, OR 97028; (503)272-3368). The management rents out privately owned condominiums complete with fully furnished kitchens. For larger groups, they can be a great deal: $89 for four people, $290 for ten. Call to see what's available. Trudie England, of England's Lodging (PO Box 9, Government Camp, OR 97028; (503)272-3350), has a number of three- and five-bedroom chalets and duplexes—great for families—that range from $75 to $500 per night, depending on the number of people and the type of accommodation. On winter weekends, there's a two-night minimum.*

one room (or share a hot tub). Breakfast may be a carbo-loading Mexican fiesta. Talk shop with Pat, a windsurfing accessories manufacturer.

Prater's Motel

1306 Oak Street, Hood River, OR 97031 ☎ (541)386-3566

A short strip of seven rooms on the main drag, Prater's boasts an unhindered view of the Columbia and Mount Adams, as well as proximity to all things Hood River. The rooms are small but versatile, clean, and very reasonably priced.

Vagabond Lodge

4070 Westcliff Drive, Hood River, OR 97031 ☎ (541)386-2992

The Vagabond is so close to the Columbia Gorge Hotel that it could almost be another wing. It's got the identical view, and the rooms are twice the size at a fraction of the cost. The front building is nothing but a nondescript highway-facing unit. The surprise is in back—three newer buildings housing riverfront rooms available for just under and over $60. Pets are allowed.

Timberline Lodge

Timberline Ski Area (6 miles from Government Camp)
Timberline, OR 97028 ☎ (800)547-1406 or (503)272-3311

For cheapskates who have a hankering to spend a night in a National Historic Monument built in 1937, here's your chance. Timberline Lodge's "chalet rooms" run about $65 for two (bunk beds, mind you), plus $15 for each additional guest. So, using a little math, in a four-person room you spend $20 apiece to stay in this grand WPA project, with its rock and timber decor, fire-warmed lobby with resident Saint Bernard, and proximity to year-round skiing. Late sleepers: beware of clomping ski boots at dawn.

Eugene & the Willamette Valley

Although it's the state's second-largest urban area, Eugene is still very much Portland's sleepy sister to the south. There's no skyline here—unless you count the grain elevator (well, okay, there's a 12-story Hilton, too)—and a Eugenean's idea of a traffic jam is when it takes more than five minutes to traverse downtown. There's always parking; people smile at you on the street; and, even at its urban heart, Eugene has more green space than pavement.

Still, this overgrown town has a sophisticated indigenous culture, from its own symphony to homegrown ballet, opera, and theater companies. There are more lectures and cultural events (courtesy of the University of Oregon) than one could possibly ever attend. There are good bookstores, the requisite number of coffeehouses, trendy brewpubs, and enough local color—from persevering hippies to backcountry loggers—to make life interesting.

The road to Eugene from Portland (and we don't mean I-5) is a destination in itself. The rich, green corridor of the Willamette Valley connects the dots of Oregon's two largest cities and acts as the perfect foil to urban sprawl. Here is the real Oregon, the Oregon of small towns and slow-talking farmers in battered pickups, the Oregon that's reserved and uncertain about strangers at first but that warms up once folks get to know you.

Some rural towns in the valley look much as they did a century ago, with covered bridges, tidy farms, and orchards that could have been transplanted from the New England countryside. Mountains frame and protect the valley and give it a warmer, drier climate than the coast. Just about everything grows here: apples, peaches, plums, walnuts, corn, peas, potatoes, cherries, blueberries . . . you get the idea.

Pressed, squeezed, left alone for a couple of months, and finally poured into a nice-looking glass, it's the grapes, though, that get all the attention. Above all, the Willamette Valley is wine country. Over the last three decades, more than 100 wineries and many more vineyards have quilted the valley, whose soil and climate are similar to those of France's cooler-weather growing areas. A few wineries sell their wines only locally, but more and more are making world-class, internationally recognized wines. While summer is usually the nicest time to venture forth, a foray out in winter months still gives a wine-curious mind and palate an opportunity to sample, discuss, and enjoy stellar wines—often with the folks who made them.

Exploring

City-hoppers whiz from Portland to Eugene on Interstate 5, which heads straight down the middle of the Willamette Valley. A more interesting and meandering route is **Highway 99W**, which parallels I-5 a little to the west and imparts a much better flavor of rural western Oregon and the valley's **wineries**. The area's most prevalent grape is pinot noir, the varietal used for the fabulous (and usually expensive) red Burgundies of France, producing silky, rich, velvety reds that are lighter and more complex than the more familiar (and ubiquitous) cabernet. Pinot gris is another Oregon superstar.

Two excellent wineries are 20 minutes west of downtown Portland: Ponzi Vineyards (14665 SW Winery Lane, Beaverton; (503)628-1227) and Cooper Mountain Vineyards (9480 SW Grabhorn Rd, Beaverton; (503)649-0027). Ponzi is one of the oldest and most recognized wineries in the state and turns out particularly fine pinot noir. Cooper Mountain is much smaller but has excellent pinot gris and good pinot noir.

Farther west, around **Forest Grove**, is another cluster of wineries. Tualatin Vineyards (10850 NW Seavey Rd, Forest Grove; (503)357-5005), now part of the large Willamette Valley Vineyards empire, produces good pinot noir and riesling. Elk Cove Vineyards (27751 NW Olson Rd, Gaston; (503)985-7760) has one of the most stunning sites in the valley, perched on a narrow ridge; pinot noir and deliciously sweet late-harvest riesling are the top wines here.

The primary wine territory starts off down Highway 99W at **Newberg**, just 30 minutes from Portland. Right on the

Wine Route Guides

The Oregon Wine Advisory Board publishes a free wineries guide; (503)228-8336. Twice a year—Memorial Day weekend and Thanksgiving weekend—many wineries not normally open to the public dust off and put out the welcome mats, offering a terrific opportunity to talk to local winemakers, nibble on food, purchase new releases, tour the facilities, and taste directly from barrels. (Some of the wineries charge a small tasting fee.) Each county wine association offers Thanksgiving and Memorial Day weekend wine-touring maps and information: Yamhill County, (503)434-5814; Polk County, (503)581-0355; and Washington County, (503)648-8198 or (503)357-5005.

Eugene's Earthy Side

Eugene's hippie legacy lives on with a plethora of environmentally friendly shopping opportunities all over town. The Saturday Market (at 8th and Oak Sts) runs from April through November and is a hub for earthy living (and buying). And if you're in town in early July, don't miss the area's oldest and wildest countercultural celebration, the Oregon Country Fair, in Veneta; (541)484-1314. For natural gardening and home-steading goods, visit Down to Earth (532 Olive St; (541)342-6820). For organic vegeta-bles, free-range meat, or alternatively packaged groceries, try L&L Market (1591 Willamette St; (541)344-3172), Red Barn Natural Grocery (357 Van Buren St; (541)342-7503), or Real Goods (77 W Broadway; (541)334-6960). But you don't have to limit yourself to shopping to join in the local zeal for organic products. Fields Restaurant and Brewpub (1290 Oak St; (541)341-6599) serves a seasonal organic microbrew, and Out of the Fog (309 3rd Ave; (541)302-8194) has an all-organic menu.

highway, you'll find Rex Hill Vineyards (30835 N Hwy 99W, Newberg; (503)538-0666), whose lovely pinot noirs from a variety of vineyards may be sampled in their fancy Napa Valley–style tasting room. Across the street is Chehalem Winery, which offers a rustic, rough-hewn contrast to the grandeur of Rex Hill. Chehalem offers a tasting room only on holiday weekends and by appoint-ment; (503)538-4700.

Down the road in **Dundee** are several places worth visiting. Argyle (691 Hwy 99W, Dundee; (503)538-8520), on the main drag, specializes in top-notch sparkling wine. Erath Vineyards Winery (Worden Hill Rd, Dundee; (800)KEW-WINE or (503)538-3318) and Sokol Blosser (5000 Sokol Blosser Lane, Dundee; (800)582-6668 or (503)864-2282), both accessed off the highway (with good, clear signage) are among the older wineries in the state and produce a wide range of wines, including fine pinot noir. Little Crabtree Park, across the road from Erath, makes a good picnic stop, as does Erath itself; there you'll find picnic tables as well as edibles to purchase. Lange Winery (18380 NE Buena Vista, Dundee; (503)538-6476), in the hills above Dundee not far from Erath, is liter-ally a basement operation; the pinot noir

and the pinot gris here are especially good.

Nearby **McMinnville** is wine-touring headquarters, having proximity to both wineries and eateries. Four top-notch producers call downtown McMinnville home—Panther Creek Cellars, (503)472-8080; Eyrie Vineyards Winery, (503)472-6315; Torii Mor Winery, (503)434-1439; and Westry Wines, (503)434-6357. South of McMinnville on 99W in **Amity**, Amity Vineyards (18150 Amity Vineyards SE, Amity; (503)835-2362) is another of the modern pioneers in Willamette Valley winemaking. The pinot noir, pinot blanc, and gewürztraminer stand out.

Bethel Heights Vineyards (6060 Bethel Heights Rd NW, Salem; (503)581-2262) offers stellar pinot noir, pinot blanc, and pinot gris from its commanding position high on a hilltop. Nearby you'll find the top-class pinot of Witness Tree Vineyards (7111 Spring Valley Rd NW, Salem; (503)538-7874). Around **Rickreall**, just west of Salem, are a few more wineries, including Eola Hills Wine Cellars (501 S Pacific Hwy W, Rickreall; (503)623-2405). Once past Rickreall, you're out of the rich-est part of the wine country.

Farther down the valley, 7 miles south of downtown Corvallis, is Tyee Wine Cel-lars (26335 Greensberry Rd, Corvallis; (503)753-8754), which produces some of the best gewürztraminer in the state. In Monroe, Broadley Vineyards (265 S 5th, Monroe; (503)847-5934) makes powerful pinot noir.

A couple of state parks provide a pleasant respite from the road (as well as inexpensive places to camp, if you're so equipped). **Champoeg State Park** (pronounced "shampooey") is a small park on the banks of the Willamette, just off I-5 and a few miles from the heart of the wine country, with fishing, boating, nature trails, and a playground. It's also a great place for biking. **Silver Falls State Park**, one of the crown jewels of the well-maintained state park system, is farther off the beaten path but worth the detour. Go east from Salem on Highway 22 to 214. This immense park, set in the forested foothills of the Cascades, has everything: sparkling waterfalls, miles of biking trails and horse trails, hiking trails, picnic and camping facilities, and even a gorgeous conference center. (Beware of summer holiday weekends; they can be a zoo.) Call the Campsite Information Center for campsite availability and reservations ($14–$20 a night); (800)452-5687.

Biking in the valley is excellent. Once outside the ring of hills surrounding Portland, you can ride a straight, flat shot down the valley by (roughly) following the Willamette River along the web of small roads that spreads between I-5 and Highway 99W. At the southern end of the valley, the relative metropolis of Eugene is cyclist-friendly, too, although motorists aren't as fond of its many blocked and one-way streets.

Whether you bike or not, when in **Eugene**, here are the musts: Hike up **Spencer's Butte**, just south of town off of Willamette Street, for sweeping urban and pastoral views of the town, valley, and its two rivers. (The two trails to the top are relatively easy.) Spend a morning at **Saturday Market**, a thriving open-air crafts and food fair and the ultimate Eugene experience: unique crafts sold by the artisans themselves, eclectic music, and inspired people-watching (held April through November at 8th and Oak Sts). Shop and eat your way through an afternoon at **Fifth Street Public Market** (5th and High Sts), where three levels of shops and upscale craft booths surround a pretty brick courtyard. Save room for a sinful *pain au chocolat* from Metropol, the city's best bakery (on the ground floor).

The **Hult Center for the Performing Arts** (at 6th Ave and Willamette St) is Eugene's world-class concert facility, with two architecturally striking halls; the 24-hour concert line is (541)342-5746. The **University of Oregon** has a lovely art museum with a permanent collection of Orientalia, a natural history museum, and several historic landmark buildings; pick up visitor information (1585 E 13th Ave; (541)346-3111) or just stroll through

U-Pick Fruits and Vegetables

Reap the rewards of the food-focused Willamette Valley! Many orchards and farms offer the chance to harvest your own fresh produce (at a fraction of the cost of buying it ready-picked). Look for U-pick signs along the highway. One great spot is Oliphant Orchards (23995 SW Hwy 99W, Sherwood; (503)625-7705), a friendly operation offering sweet and tart pie cherries, apples, peaches, plums, pears, and pumpkins in season. Pick up a copy of the "Farm Fresh Produce Guide," which covers the greater Portland area, including the upper areas of the Willamette Valley. It's free and available at Portland-area bookstores, all county chambers of commerce, county extension offices, libraries, and AAA.

the campus, along 13th Avenue between Agate and Kincaid Streets. **WISTEC**, a small but nicely conceived hands-on science and technology museum (with accompanying laser light–show planetarium), is the place to take kids on rainy afternoons (2300 Leo Harris Pkwy; (541)687-3619).

The two rivers that run through town, the **Willamette** and the **McKenzie**, provide opportunities for canoeists and rafters, both first-timers and whitewater enthusiasts. Hikers find miles of forest trails just outside the city limits. Runners love the city's several groomed, packed running trails. Run along the banks of the Willamette through **Alton Baker Park** (at the Ferry St Bridge) on the groomed Prefontaine Trail. Women will feel safer on the sloughside circuit that borders **Amazon Park** (on Hilyard St between 22nd and 34th Sts), site of spirited outdoor concerts in the summer. **Hendricks Park** (at Summit and Skyline Dr), the city's oldest, features an outstanding 10-acre rhododendron garden (best blooms in May and early June). **Skinner Butte Park** (on Cheshire St between High and Washington Sts), which skirts the Willamette, includes a lovely rose garden, several playgrounds, picnic areas, and a 12-mile bike/running path.

Cheap Eats

Etcetera
976 Highway 99W, Dundee ☎ (503)537-9340

Here's where you'll find all the area winemakers piled in for lunch. Everybody refers to this itty-bitty place as Alice's, after Alice Halstead, a longtime favorite of the wine community. Her meatloaf sandwiches are always in demand (for good reason), and her early morning scones disappear quickly. Stop here for swell picnic fixings, from salads to sandwiches and terrific, homey, just-like-Mom-made-'em desserts. Or drop by for an espresso and a cookie and watch the locals come and go.

Panadaria y Videos Gonzalez
508 E 1st Avenue, Newberg ☎ (503)538-0306

This authentic shop is really more grocery than restaurant, but it's worth knowing about. Walk through the store—past the displays of videos, canned goods, and chiles—to the back walk-up window. Little English is spoken, but the menu is printed on the wall above. Even if you overorder, it's unlikely you'll spend more than a five-spot. Feast on very authentic, very tasty *tortas* (Mexican sandwiches), tacos, and traditional dishes like menudo—tripe stew.

Alf's
1250 S Baker Street, McMinnville ☎ (503)472-7314

Whether you're suffering from nostalgia or a craving for good grease and thick shakes, this homey, old-fashioned soda shop will cure what ails you. Settle into a booth to enjoy old-time ice cream favorites or the kind of burger that may be out of fashion with the Fat Police but still really tastes the best. For top entertainment, go watch the monkeys (yup, live critters, these) cavort in their protected den.

El Ranchero

2628 NE Highway 99W, McMinnville ☏ (503) 434-9525

The many Hispanics employed by this area's farms and vineyards have developed a strong community around McMinnville, providing a plethora of high-quality, authentic south-of-the-border-style dining options with accompanying low prices. This spot offers a more expansive menu and presentation than most. Dive into the seafood, which includes ceviche and fresh seafood cocktails, and fill up with an overflowing platter of rice and beans.

Golden Valley Brewpub

980 E 4th Street, McMinnville ☏ (503) 472-2739

Who says wine-country drinks have to be wine? High ceilings and brick walls lend a casual comfort to the area's only microbrewery. The suds are pretty darn good, as is the homemade root beer. The food is solid pub fare, with pizzas, burgers, sausage sandwiches, ample appetizers, and more serious entrees such as pastas and barbecued ribs. The owner also operates Golden Valley Vineyards, so look for his wines on the menu. No cutting-edge cuisine here, nor rock-bottom prices, but you can eat well enough within your budget and enjoy a genuinely good beverage.

Kame

228 N Evans Street, McMinnville ☏ (503) 434-4326

Walking into this small Japanese restaurant immediately removes you from the small town: you're welcomed into a soothing, calm environment, a classic Asian-style space with screens and spare wooden tables and chairs. Pleasant Japanese music filters in. The menu offers typical Japanese fare at reasonable prices. Appetizers are generous and could supply enough sustenance for a light lunch. More filling options include *yakiudon*, a yummy, sticky tangle of sautéed stir-fried chicken, fresh vegetables, noodles, and sauce. The bento box of tempura—tender batter-coated shrimp and vegetables—comes with rice, soup, and some fresh vegetables for a filling, value-priced meal.

Lupita's

328 NE Evans Street, McMinnville ☏ (503) 435-4838

This funky operation dishes out *muy auténtico* road food—tacos and such—at two locations in the greater wine country area. The one in Dayton (on the main square, next to the barber shop, no phone) is worth seeking out for the fabulous *carnitas*—particularly on weekends, when you can watch as copper pots simmer with fragrant bits of pork. Taking the place of the locally famous Lupita's stand that once had chowhounds on a budget snaking around the McMinnville Wal-Mart parking lot, the new McMinnville outpost on Evans Street is more formal—a cantina offering (thankfully, finally) loads of seating.

Bombs Away Cafe

2527 NW Monroe, Corvallis ☏ (541) 757-7221

John Huyck made a name for himself when he cooked in Portland a number of years ago; now Corvallis-area residents are getting treated to his quirky, well-

Brews and Coffee in Eugene

Most Northwest college towns are chock-full of brewpubs and coffeehouses, and Eugene is no exception. Here are some of the best:

Brewpubs McMenamins High Street Brewery and Cafe (1243 High St; (541)345-4905) has a cozy atmosphere with wooden booths, Peter Max–style artwork on the walls, and the faint scent of patchouli wafting around the waitstaff—all of which make it the quintessential Eugene brewpub. You'll be humming Grateful Dead tunes over your Ruby Ale in no time. Steelhead Brewery & Cafe (188 E 5th Ave; (541)686-2739) has lots of open space and a dinner menu. For the sports enthusiast, the Wild Duck Brewery & Restaurant (169 W 6th Ave; (541)485-3825) is tuned to the games. Eugene City Brewery (844 Olive St; (541)345-8489) is a popular college hangout.

Coffeehouses Full City Coffee Roasters (842 Pearl St; (541)344-0475) is a town favorite where local painting and photography can be viewed while you sip a cappuccino. Out of the Fog (309 W 3rd Ave; (541)302-8194) offers organic coffee to the curious and local music on the weekends. Take your journal to Allan Bros. Beanery & Coffeehouse (152 W 5th Ave, (541)342-3378; 2465 Hilyard St, (541)344-0221), where a pensive crowd collects. If you're feeling adventurous, call for the open-mike schedule at Cafe Paradiso (115 W Broadway; (541)484-9933), or drop in for scheduled readings and music.

executed Mexican-influenced fare. The space is a bit funky, but since it gets overrun with the Oregon State crowd at times, it all sort of fits together. Cheapsters will want to focus on the standard options: the duck chimichangas have a following, as do the jalapeño fries. Try the red chili at your own risk, or just make sure you've got plenty of beer to kill the pain. Serious foodies focus on the daily changing fresh sheet, with upscale dishes like sorrel-Brie-potato soup and soft tacos with rock shrimp and sausage.

Ambrosia
174 E Broadway, Eugene ☎ (541)342-4141

The pizzas are wonderful here: small, crisp pies topped with rich plum tomato sauce and your choice of trendy ingredients (sun-dried tomatoes, artichoke hearts, roasted eggplant) and baked in a huge wood-burning oven. But Ambrosia is much more than a designer pizzeria; you'll also find interesting pasta dishes, fresh fish specials, and gelato that cools a dry Eugene evening.

Cafe Navarro
454 Willamette Street, Eugene ☎ (541)344-0943

Like the world beat music that plays on the sound system, Jorge Navarro's restaurant is a rich cross-cultural experience, with dishes ranging from Africa and Spain to Cuba and the Caribbean. There are no bad choices. For lunch, Navarro's version of *arroz con pollo*, with seared chicken chunks, red peppers, capers, and cilantro, is a good bet. For breakfast, the hands-down favorite is *chilaquiles*—eggs scrambled with corn tortillas, chipotle salsa, and Monterey Jack cheese.

Glenwood Restaurant Campus Cafe

1340 Alder Street, Eugene ☎ (541) 687-0355

Eugene has no lack of converted houses, and the Campus Cafe is a prime specimen with its hodgepodge of antique tables, old chairs, and even a church pew! This breakfast hot spot, voted "Best Family Restaurant" by *Eugene Weekly* readers, offers fantastic food for next to nothing. The whole-wheat waffles are a must at a whopping $2, and the skillets (scrambled eggs with vegetables and ham or bacon) are quite good. Lunch and dinner are served here too, and on weekend nights you can stop in for a microbrew and catch live music by local talent.

Keystone Cafe

395 W 5th Street, Eugene ☎ (541) 342-2075

This is the place to get back to where you once belonged. If that makes no sense to you, then Keystone is not your kind of eatery. Come here to mix and mingle with the card-carrying counterculturalists and dig into the best breakfast in town. There's an organic bakery in back and funky outside seating in nice weather.

La Tiendita & Taco Loco

764 Blair Boulevard, Eugene ☎ (541) 683-5531

From the Andean flute recordings of popular movie theme songs to the chili-emblazoned T-shirts, the atmosphere at La Tiendita is Mexican kitsch all the way. Part art gallery, part retail shop, and part restaurant, this is not your typical burrito take-out spot. The food has flair, and the menu, a combination of Mexican and Salvadoran dishes, rumbas with unusual variations on old favorites such as potato enchiladas with mole. For the brave, La Tiendita hosts an annual Habanero-eating contest. Bring on the chiles!

Mekala's

296 E 5th Avenue, Eugene ☎ (541) 342-4872

A pretty Thai restaurant with a light-filled dining area overlooking the Fifth Street Public Market courtyard (outside seating, weather permitting), Mekala's features a six-page menu with more than a dozen fiery curries and two dozen vegetarian dishes. Two standouts are the magnificent angel wings (deboned chicken wings stuffed with ground pork, glass noodles, and bean sprouts) and a flavor-packed *homoke* soufflé (shrimp, scallops, and fish in a curry-and-coconut sauce with fresh lime leaves, green pepper, and cabbage). End the meal with a dish of velvety homemade coconut ice cream.

Mona Lizza

830 Olive Street, Eugene ☎ (541) 345-1072

Part of Eugene's downtown renaissance, this pleasing restaurant with full bar offers many choices. Come for one of the wood-oven designer pizzas, a glass of the local microbrew, and a game of pool (there are a few quiet tables in the back). Come with your kids (the waitstaff is obliging, and the atmosphere is casual). Or come for more serious dining; you can choose from a diverse nouveau-Italiàn menu that features fish, chicken, meat (the baked rigatoni with homemade sausage is pure comfort food), or vegetarian fare; prices range from reasonably inexpensive to a bit beyond budget. Various renditions of the *Mona Lisa* line the walls, all painted by local artists commissioned by the restaurant.

Shiki

81 Coburg Road, Eugene ☎ (541) 343-1936

It's about time Eugene had a noteworthy Japanese restaurant, and Shiki—with its extensive sushi bar, authentic menu, and subtle service—is it. The location (a former Sizzler, plunked down in the middle of a parking lot) is the only unpromising thing about this smartly run restaurant. The menu has something for everyone, from the neophyte who wants to stay with tempura and teriyaki (the wonderful *sanshoku* bento is your choice) to those with a more adventure-some palate (the *dengaku zanmai*, portions of creamy steamed eggplant, tofu, and potato in sweet miso sauce). The sushi bar features 50 different items—cooked, smoked, and raw.

Cheap Sleeps

Flying M Ranch

23029 NW Flying M Road, Yamhill, OR 97148 ☎ (503) 662-3222

The setting, at the end of the road in the Coast Range, is terrific. The motelish bunkhouse is no bargain, but the cabins (which sleep up to six) make major economic sense. They come equipped with their own kitchens and a wood stove, but no phones or TVs. For a really large group (up to 20), check out the remote lodge on Trask Mountain (the highest peak in the Coast Range), a somewhat primitive shelter often used as an overnight spot for trail riders. For $10 a night, campers have access to all the recreational opportunities the ranch offers its guests: ponds for swimming and fishing, and miles of trails for hiking or horseback riding. The restaurant and Western bar keep 'em content.

Kelty Estate SleepyHollow

675 Highway 99W, Lafayette, OR 97127 ☎ (800) 867-3740 or (503) 864-3740

Lafayette is a sleepy little community between the Dundee area and McMinn-ville, right on the main drag of 99W. As the highway weaves through Lafayette, however, it becomes a two-lane village road with heavily enforced speed limits. Two swell rooms with private bath are available in this lovely white colonial, perhaps the most stately and attractive building in Lafayette, almost across the street from the antique center in the restored old schoolhouse. Breakfasts are always tasty—hot cooked affairs that will help fuel you before a day of wine tast-ing nearby.

Baker Street Inn

129 SE Baker Street, McMinnville, OR 97128 ☎ (800) 870-5575 or (503) 472-5575

While the outside of this 1914 cottage in a quiet residential block may be Arts and Crafts, the interior is done up in Victorian style. With only four rooms (and one separate cottage out of our price range), the feel is warm and cozy. The price-inclusive breakfast—no muffin-and-coffee scene here—is a major meal and helps keep this high-end "bargain" within the budget realm.

Best Western Vineyard Inn

2035 S Highway 99W, McMinnville, OR 97128
☎ (800) 285-6242 or (503) 472-4900

This motel's location next to the stockyards and Texaco station may not be glamorous (don't worry, you won't even know cows live next door), and the rooms may look a bit utilitarian, but the central location and swimming pool (dinky, but still useful for cooling down during the hot summer months) make this place worth knowing about.

Safari Motor Inn

345 N Highway 99W, McMinnville, OR 97128 ☎ (503) 472-5187

The Safari is right in the heart of the wine country. Accommodations here are far better than your basic bed-in-a-box: rooms are spacious and quiet, and the beds are comfortable. The former motel pool is now pushing up daisies, so if you want to cool off on a hot afternoon, head a quarter mile south on 99W to McMinnville's excellent Aquatic Center; (503)434-7309. Here you can frolic in a serious pool for a $2.50 fee.

Howell House Bed and Breakfast

212 N Knox Street, Monmouth, OR 97361 ☎ (800) 368-2085 or (503) 838-2085

Don't ask, "What's going on in Monmouth?" Instead, enjoy Howell House's location, convenient for hitting Polk County and Salem-area wineries or for launching a tour of the southern Willamette wine region. The Boylans and their four sons took a rundown 1891 rooming house and stripped off a century of changes (they even tore off the modern porch and replaced it with a Victorian one). The interior boasts richly detailed wallpapers and period antiques; there's an old coal stove, too. The immaculate high-ceilinged rooms may be small, but the breakfasts aren't. A swell parlor houses the television, if you must, but we recommend going outside to enjoy the heirloom roses, covered spa, and gazebo. And be sure to rise early enough to enjoy the hearty breakfasts, included in the price of your room.

McKenzie River Inn

49164 McKenzie River Highway, Vida, OR 97488 ☎ (541) 822-6260

In the heart of one of Oregon's most beautiful river valleys, this simple bed and breakfast, about 35 miles east of Eugene, should satisfy your longing for peace and quiet. A small orchard separates the riverfront house from the highway. Comfortable, dark furniture gives a '40s feel. Choose from one of the three bedrooms with private baths (one has a queen-size bed; the others sport twin beds) or the cottage next door, which has its own kitchen. The river runs swiftly past the doorstep; you can virtually fish from your window. For intrepid boaters, there's a public boat launch a few miles downstream. A big, hot breakfast is included with the rooms in the Inn; cottage residents cook their own morning meal.

Campus Inn
390 E Broadway, Eugene, OR 97401 ☎ (541) 343-3376

Although the Campus Inn is on the high end of our cheap sleep budgetary scale, it's worth the extra bucks. On the outside it may look like just another of the no-tell motels that dot downtown Eugene, but once you walk into the lobby you'll realize what a classy place it is. Convenient to both the university and downtown, this newer, unassuming motel has 58 units and no seasonal rate changes.

Courtesy Inn
345 W 6th Avenue, Eugene, OR 97401 ☎ (541) 345-3391

Can't leave home without Fido? For a little extra cash, the Courtesy Inn politely lets your pets take you with them when they travel. In most other respects, however, this is just an average, modestly priced motel. The location on 6th Avenue is easy to find and convenient to downtown, and the rooms are clean and nicely furnished.

Eugene International Hostel
2352 Willamette Street, Eugene, OR 97405 ☎ (541) 349-0589

It doesn't take long before a visitor begins to suspect that Eugene hasn't completely let go of the 1960s, hence the preponderance of tie-dyed clothing and all manner of organic products. Join in the spirit with a stay at this hostel, located a relaxing distance from downtown. The converted turn-of-the-century home, complete with vegetable garden and patio, can accommodate up to 20 people at a time in dormitory and private rooms. (Plan ahead if you want a room to yourself, since there are only two.) Truly the best deal in town (around $20 for a dormitory bed and $40 for a private room), rates include linen and towel rental, access to the kitchen and dining room, and continental breakfast.

Eugene Motor Lodge
476 E Broadway, Eugene, OR 97401 ☎ (541) 344-5233

Rooms at the Eugene Motor Lodge, next door to the Campus Inn, are just as comfortable and cost a little less. There's a homey feel here: a pine hutch holds the TV, and overstuffed furniture makes a pseudo-lounge area in each room. You get a mini-fridge and microwave, too. Rates range from $36 to $50, depending on the season.

Northern Oregon Coast

The northern Oregon Coast epitomizes the eternal struggle between water and land. From Astoria to Yachats—from the mouth of the Columbia River to Cape Perpetua—this rugged coastline is embossed with a series of headlands holding out against Neptune's fury, separated intermittently by expanses of sand. Numerous rivers sever the Coast Range and, finally, widen into estuaries just before emptying into the blue Pacific.

Demonstrating considerable foresight, the state of Oregon has decreed public access to all beaches sacrosanct. Many stretches of coastline, still in pristine condition, are preserved as state parks. Between the parks, however, development persists. Astoria, the largest city on the north coast, has a relatively stable population of 10,000 inhabitants, but other areas—such as Seaside and the stretch between Lincoln City and Newport—are bulging with resort hotels and related tourist concessions. Thankfully, though, most coastal towns are still hamlets of just a few hundred people.

Fishing and logging no longer dominate the coastal economy; tourism is quickly encroaching. Realizing this, many of the residents—an eclectic mix of artists, retirees, upwardly mobile surfers, blue-collar types, and entrepreneurs seeking to escape city life—are seeking a consensus on the appropriate amount of development. There is little agreement, except on two counts: that the coast's population will continue to grow, and that it rains a lot—55 to 80 inches annually.

Exploring

The Oregon Coast begins at **Fort Stevens State Park**, 10 miles west of Astoria (see "Three Spectacular State Parks" tip). But first, consider **Astoria**—the first permanent American settlement west of the Rockies, founded in 1811. Restored Victorian residences dot the steep hillside that extends up from the Columbia River. Buy the "Walking Tour of Astoria" ($3 at various outlets around town) for routes and details. The **Columbia River Maritime Museum** (1792 Marine Dr, Astoria; (503)325-2323) is the finest such museum on the West Coast; admission

Whale-Watching Week

Each year, gray whales log 12,000 miles on their round-trip voyage (which occurs between late October and mid-April) from the nutrient-rich feeding grounds in the Bering Sea to their subtropical breeding lagoons in Baja. For one week in March, Oregon State University stations about a hundred volunteers at 19 different sites along the coast; (541)867-0100. Their mission? To count whales, observe their behavior, and educate visitors on the leviathans' life and migration. Don rain gear, sweaters, boots, and binoculars and hike to the farthest tip of a headland or promontory (be aware of slippery surfaces and loose rocks). The lucky and the patient may witness a breach, three spy hops, or a courtship. Some of the best vantage points for land-based whale watching are lighthouses, which are sometimes outfitted with viewing platforms or trails leading out to the best perch.

includes a visit aboard the lightship *Columbia*. For a sweeping view of the city and the 4-mile-wide estuary of the Columbia, head up to the **Astoria Column** atop Coxcomb Hill. Hiking, running, and mountain-bike trails fan out in various directions from the parking lot.

Sea lions and seals are usually found down at the river park at the foot of Sixth Street, particularly during the winter months. The viewing pier at the foot of 14th Street shares space with the Foss Maritime tugboat fleet; it's a good place to watch the Columbia River bar and river pilots embark and disembark from oceangoing vessels just a stone's throw away in the river channel. Astoria's intelligentsia frequent Ricciardi Gallery (108 10th St, Astoria; (503)325-5450), which offers pleasing local and regional art, high-octane espresso, and engaging reading material. Parnassus Books (234 10th St, Astoria; (503)325-1363) is a good browse.

Seaside has become Oregon's most crowded beach town, with all the expected tourist accoutrements and pit stops. Along Broadway, the main drag, look for saltwater taffy, cotton candy, chocolates, and other sweets at Phillips Candies (217 Broadway, Seaside; (503)738-5402); free samples can be had at the Portland Fudge Co. (102 Broadway, Seaside; (800)338-0602 or

(503)738-0602). Surfers head for "The Point" at the south edge of town to catch the finest left-handed waves north of Santa Barbara. Cleanline Surf Company (719 1st Ave, Seaside; (503)738-7888) is a good source for ocean playthings and in-line skate rentals too.

South of Seaside, a 7-mile trail winds over Tillamook Head, high above the water—part of **Ecola State Park** (primitive camping facilities only)—and ends at Indian Beach and (farther still) Ecola Point. Beware of incoming tides and plan your water-level hikes accordingly. Sunset Empire Park and Recreation District, headquartered at Sunset Pool (1140 E Broadway, Seaside; (503)738-3311) offers lap swims ($3), a spa ($1), and a skateboard park ($3).

Cannon Beach is the Carmel of the Northwest, although the main attraction is still the wide-open, white-sand beach with its silhouette of Haystack Rock, a massive monolith that presents an excellent opportunity for low-tide exploration. During the summer, participate in the free Haystack Rock Awareness Program, a naturalist's tour of tide pools, bird life, and such (look for schedules around town). Less crowded stretches of sand are located at Chapman Point, at the north end of town (although parking is limited), and at Tolovana Park Wayside, at the south end. At low tide, you can walk all the way to **Arch Cape**, 5 miles south. Always carry a local tide table (available at many businesses), and be aware of tides on the return trip. The Cannon Beach Energy Conservation Project operates a free natural gas–powered shuttle in the Cannon Beach–Tolovana Park area year-round. Head to Osburn's Ice Creamery (240 N Hemlock, Cannon Beach; (503)436-2578) for the town's finest ice cream cones; choice picnic supplies can be purchased in the adjacent deli.

Just north of Manzanita, **Oswald West State Park** (free admission, except for camping) offers a secluded cove with a waterfall—a summer haven for surfers and kayakers. Don't miss the north coast's finest views, available along the two-mile trail to the Neahkahnie Moun-

tain summit (see "Three Spectacular State Parks" tip). Farther south, there's beachcombing galore on either the ocean or the Nehalem Bay side of the **Manzanita Peninsula**. Summer winds from the northwest afford excellent windsurfing conditions. Manzanita News and Espresso (500 Laneda Ave, Manzanita; (503)368-7450) is a good bet for a coffee jolt and take-out snacks (tasty calzones, for instance). Another java stop offering more substantial fare (say, pumpkin pancakes or a roasted veggie sandwich) is Hill House Deli & Cafe (12870 Hwy 101, Nehalem; (503)368-7933). A few miles inland, Nehalem Bay Winery (34965 Hwy 53, Nehalem; (503)368-WINE) has a tasting room where you can sample its fruit wines.

Three Spectacular State Parks

Fort Stevens State Park (10 miles southwest of Astoria; (503)861-1671) is the largest park in the state park system, with 605 campsites, a military museum and historical area, miles of paved bike paths and off-road single-track, and hiking and running trails. The South Jetty lookout tower is a prime whale- and storm-watching spot. Surf fishing can be productive off the jetty (no license required unless you're salmon fishing), and razor clamming is good on the vast expanse of the mostly empty beach (check with park officials concerning clamming regulations). Nearby Trestle Bay offers choice windsurfing conditions when the wind is blowing (which is most of the time).

Oswald West State Park (11 miles south of Cannon Beach; (503)238-7488) offers scenic beauty unsurpassed in the Northwest. The Oregon Coast Trail winds its way through the park; you can pick it up about a half mile south of the Arch Cape tunnel on the west side of Highway 101. Hike the 5 miles over Cape Falcon to Short Sands Beach, a picture-perfect cove with a creek emptying into the ocean, a waterfall, and steep, forested hillsides extending down to water level. Another option is Neahkahnie Mountain Trail, which leads to the 1,600-foot summit, offering the north coast's finest view. Oswald West's camping area (no reservations accepted) is situated a half mile down a paved trail from a parking area adjacent to Highway 101, where wheelbarrows are available for your gear.

Cape Lookout State Park (8 miles west of Tillamook on Three Capes Scenic Drive; (503)842-3182) lays claim to some of the largest old-growth cedar and hemlock in the world. A steep trail leads up from water level to the top of the cape and then hugs the headland to its tip, high above the crashing Pacific. During whale migration season, you might observe gray whales scraping off troublesome barnacles against offshore rocks. On either side of Cape Lookout, the uncrowded beach extends for miles.

Note: Be aware that many state parks charge $3 day-use fees.

Wildlife Watching

Plan a trip to the Jewell Elk Refuge (26 miles southeast of Astoria on Hwy 202; (503)755-2264), where some of the larger mammals in the Lower 48 cavort on thousands of grassy and forested acres. But drive slowly; sometimes the elk take over the roadway. Closer in, the Twilight Creek Eagle Sanctuary (8 miles east of Astoria, off Hwy 30 on Burnside Rd) is home base for 16 bald eagle pairs (they mate for life). You might spy one of these magnificent birds boldly swooping into the Columbia, ensnaring a fish in its talons, or—with the help of binoculars—watch while a mother feeds her young in a nest that can weigh as much as two tons. Depending on the time of year, hawks, ospreys, peregrine falcons, and tundra swans may be encountered.

Tillamook Bay and the surrounding countryside provide outstanding **fishing** opportunities. Anglers routinely haul 30-pound chinook salmon from the Ghost's Hole section of the bay. The Kilchis, Wilson, Tillamook, and Trask Rivers are superb salmon and steelhead streams, although more fish are taken from the Nestucca River than from any comparably sized stream in the state. The Nestucca is accessible from Highway 101 between Beaver and Pacific City. Fishing licenses are required and can be purchased at many sporting goods stores. Be aware that ever-more-restrictive regulations may prevent you from wetting your hook at certain times of the year. Purchase oysters and fresh seafood at the Pacific Oyster Company (5150 Oyster Dr, Bay City; (503)377-2323) and have a picnic on the adjacent pier. Watch cheese being made and score free samples at the Tillamook County Creamery Association (2 miles north of Tillamook on Hwy 101; (503)842-4481; no admission and open daily). Bear Creek Artichokes (11 1/2 miles south of Tillamook, Hemlock; (503)398-5411; closed in winter) features a first-class selection of fruits, veggies, and herbs.

The 22-mile **Three Capes Scenic Drive**, which begins west of Tillamook, affords spectacular vistas from atop Capes Meares, Lookout, and Kiwanda, all featuring hiking trails. It's also an excellent but hilly bicycle route, although shoulder space is minimal. Another majestic sea-

and-weather-sculpted promontory is Cascade Head, just south of Neskowin. Two little-used trails take off from the highway on the north and south sides of the headland, traversing rain forests, meadows, and rocky cliffs. In the summer, the **Sitka Center for Art and Ecology**, on the south side of Cascade Head, presents diverse workshops, concerts, and exhibits; (503)994-5485.

Once termed the "20 miracle miles," the stretch from **Lincoln City to Newport** is hardly a wonder anymore; however, there are numerous finds along this strip of almost-continuous development. Lincoln City has more tourist accommodations than any other city on the Oregon Coast. In the winter, when the place isn't as crowded, you can usually find a discounted motel room. Come summer, prices jump into the stratosphere. On Newport's north end, visit the **Yaquina Head Outstanding Natural Area** for its interpretive center, lighthouse, and easily accessible tide pools. The best beach access is at nearby Agate Beach or, farther south, the eclectic Nye Beach neighborhood. Admire two levels of oceanfront paintings and sculpture at the Newport Visual Arts Center (839 Beach Dr, Newport; (541)265-6540); admission is free. Along the Yaquina bayfront, the refurbished Hatfield Marine Science Center (2030 S Marine Science Dr, Newport; (541)867-0100) offers free marine-life displays and films. Check for field trips, some of which (such as whale-watching excursions) have a fee. Nearby, the **Oregon Coast Aquarium** (2820 SE Ferry Slip Rd, Newport; (541)867-3474) is home to a splendid collection of finny, furry, and feathery creatures, including Keiko the killer whale of *Free Willy* fame.

Beyond Newport, the coast opens up again. **Waldport** boasts the lovely Alsea River estuary, untrampled beaches at either end of town, and a city center unspoiled by tourism. Bumps and Grinds Coffeehouse (225 SW Maple St, Waldport; (541)563-5769) is a good stop. Pick up a free copy of *Inkfish Magazine* (it's published in town and is available at coffee shops and markets) for more info

about local goings-on. The beach in **Yachats** is rocky and rife with tide pools and whooshing geysers. Yachats itself is another hip, Cannon Beach–type arts community with an interesting mix of aging counterculturalists, yuppies, and tourists. It's also a prime area for harvesting sea-run smelt (savory sardinelike fish) when they congregate near the shore during mating season (April through October). The many galleries include the Earthworks Gallery (2222 N Hwy 101, Yachats; (541)547-4300) and the Backporch Gallery (4th and Hwy 101, Yachats; (541)547-4500). Orca Wholefoods (84 Beach Ave, Yachats; (541)547-4065) sells tempting salads and fresh-squeezed juices.

Cheap Eats

Lagniappe Cafe
817 Exchange Street, Astoria ☎ (503)325-5181

This garden-spot cafe, blooming in roses, geraniums, and fuchsias most of the year, is an adjunct of Clementine's B&B and is operated by the same couple. Owner/chef Judith Taylor (husband Cliff is usually working the gardens) offers unusual sandwiches such as the muffuletta, a New Orleans fave consisting of sliced sourdough layered with an olive-garlic filling, meats, and cheeses. Don't miss her cedar-plank salmon or the grilled tiger prawns skewered with oysters and veggies. In nice weather, sip espresso or savor ice cream cones and sweet treats on the outside deck. The cafe is closed January through March.

Rio Cafe
125 9th Street, Astoria ☎ (503)325-2409

The Mexican-food pipeline has reached Astoria, but instead of the usual Tex-Mex, this gaily decorated cantina offers inspired south-of-the-border cuisine. Fruit and shrimp salads are dressed with a zingy jalapeño dressing, while multiple snappy salsas are a perfect match for the huge handcrafted chips called *totopos*. Try the *pescado rojo*—a lightly breaded and grilled sole fillet coated with a fiery chile and garlic sauce.

Premier Pasta
1530 S Holladay Drive, Seaside ☎ (503)738-5062

Buy pasta by the bag or the plate at this noodle joint on the Necanicum River. A dozen herbed varieties—from spicy Cajun and lemon-dill fettuccine to myriad

Bakeries and Bagels

It's hard to live without baked goods, but until recently, frosting-encased sweet treats and deep-fried donuts were the only choices on the coast. Thankfully, a handful of craft-bread bakeries and New York–style bagel joints are now offering the good stuff.

*Try **Ben's Blest Bagels** (1448 Commercial St, Astoria; (503)325-9144) or **Bagels by the Sea** (575 S Roosevelt Dr, Seaside; (503)717-9145) for traditional, boiled-and-baked, doughy orbs in umpteen varieties. Farther south, stop at **Lincoln Beach Bagel Company** (3930 Hwy 101, Depoe Bay; (541)764-3882). Bakeries have become even more widespread. **Pacific Way Bakery & Cafe** (601 Pacific Way, Gearhart; (503)738-0245) purveys whole-grain loaves, killer cheesecake, and the coast's best baguette. Look for focaccia, muffins, croissants, and peasant loaves at the diminutive **Hane's Bakerie** (1064 S Hemlock St, Cannon Beach; (503)436-0120).*

tortellini—are yours for the asking. Order the linguine with clams or a garlic lover's sauce, or opt for the tri-colored pasta—a blend of egg, spinach, and tomato-basil noodles finished with pesto. There's also chicken marinara, feta-olive lasagne, and an Italian version of the muffuletta sandwich, an enormous concoction oozing mozzarella and layered with salami and marinated veggies. The owners are big *Seinfeld* fans; ask them about the painting of Kramer hanging in the dining room.

The Stand

220 Avenue U, Seaside ☎ (503)738-6592

Small and austerely decorated, this place nonetheless serves some seriously satisfying Tex-Mex chow. You'll appreciate the many burrito options, including a potent chile verde version packed with pork and laced with Jack cheese and a tangy green salsa. The vegetable quesadilla is fat with a cornucopia of goodies. Corn tortillas and salsas are made daily.

Pizza à fetta

231 N Hemlock Street, Cannon Beach ☎ (503)436-0333

It's easy to locate Cannon Beach's best pizza: just follow the heady aroma of garlic, oregano, provolone, and pepperoni to this pint-sized pizzeria, scrunched amid a maze of shops and galleries in the middle of downtown. The lineup ranges from a basic three-cheese pie to a white-clam concoction smothered with sun-dried tomatoes, mushrooms, cheeses, and lots of baby clams. Or create your own masterpiece with umpteen toppings including chorizo, pancetta, and a host of cheeses. For light eaters, the pizza is also offered by the slice.

Homegrown Cafe

3301 S Hemlock Street, Tolovana Park ☎ (503)436-1803

Try this healthnik eatery for green-chile stew, breakfast burritos, "veg-head" barley soup, and "tease loaf," a meatloaf lookalike concocted from brown rice, mushrooms, nuts, and herbs. Surprise! Aside from being good for you, this chow packs pizzazz. Ask the knowledgeable owners about the local music scene.

Downie's Cafe

9320 5th Street, Bay City ☎ (503) 377-2220

Take a step back to the '50s in this neighborhood cafe offering down-home service and food. The place is patronized mostly by locals, who clamor for Downie's clam chowder, a thick, creamy potion of potatoes, celery, and clam chunks. Fish 'n' chips are greasy good fun, the burgers are humongous (try the oyster burger), and the pies are yum-worthy.

Grateful Bread Bakery

34805 Brooten Road, Pacific City ☎ (503) 965-7337

In addition to robust breads and scrumptious sweet treats—carrot cake and gargantuan cinnamon rolls, to name a few—this expansive bakery offers a full breakfast and lunch menu. Opt for the gingerbread pancakes, a hangtown fry bursting with oysters, or some very cheesy New York–style pizza (the owners hail from Long Island). Enjoy your coffee and cake out on the deck, and be sure to grab a loaf of bread or a baguette for the road.

Pelican Pub & Brewery

33180 Cape Kiwanda Drive, Pacific City ☎ (503) 965-7007

The north coast's first brewpub, the Pelican is the best spot to soak up Cape Kiwanda's geographical splendor. Craft brews include Kiwanda Cream Ale, Doryman's Dark Ale, Tsunami Stout, and an unfiltered wheat brew called "Heiferweizen" (remember, this is cow country). Pub grub ranges from warm and garlicky bread sticks to beefy chili and charbroiled chicken sandwiches.

Chameleon Cafe

2145 NW Highway 101, Lincoln City ☎ (541) 994-8422

At this unassuming Highway 101 eatery, reggae and Caribbean tunes emanate from the sound system, the interior is sparsely decorated with outrageous art, and the kitchen packs a heck of a culinary punch. The intriguing menu features everything from salmon cakes with aioli and red onions to marinated eggplant sandwiches and artichoke pâté. The super-garlicky hummus is a must.

Cosmos Cafe

740 W Olive Street, Newport ☎ (541) 265-7511

Deep-blue ceilings highlighted by heavenly bodies lend the Cosmos Cafe a spacey feel, but the grub and the prices are down to earth. Look for oversize and sassy Cajun chicken burritos, or a Greek fish sandwich featuring fresh lingcod, feta, and veggies wrapped in a pita. Salads, omelets, hot and cold pastas, homemade sweet treats, and espresso are available too. The adjacent Cosmos Gallery (same address; (541)265-4049) exhibits a diverse collection of pottery, oil paintings, stained glass, and furniture.

The Taste of Newport

837 SW Bay Boulevard, Newport ☎ (541) 574-9450

Be sure to stroll the working bayfront, which is home to salty seafaring types, seafood processors, and the coast's most extensive fishing fleet. Watch boats unload rockfish, lingcod, and crab, and then sample the catch right here at the

Taste. Seafood is prepared a number of ways, and indoor and outdoor seating is available. It's a good place to bring the kids.

New Morning Coffeehouse
373 Highway 101 N, Yachats ☎ (541) 547-3848

A cross-section of Yachats society—hip locals in Gore-Tex and jeans, Eugene weekenders, and tourists—visits this pleasant roadside respite. They come for superb muffins, pies, and coffee cakes, as well as black bean chili and omelets. The congregation huddles around the homey wood stove in winter; in warm weather, folks head for the out-of-the-wind back porch to partake of evening pasta specials.

Cheap Sleeps

Clementine's Bed and Breakfast
847 Exchange Street, Astoria, OR 97103 ☎ (800) 521-6801 or (503) 325-2005

Astoria enjoys the Oregon Coast's largest collection of B&Bs, and this 1888 Italianate Victorian situated on the edge of downtown is a superb choice. Your enthusiastic and multitalented hosts, Judith and Cliff Taylor, offer a wealth of knowledge about north coast happenings (she's a master gardener and a cooking instructor; he knows his way around a kayak). Five nicely decorated rooms reflect the Taylors' attention to detail; breakfast reflects their ability to satisfy hungry guests. All the rooms have private baths and are appointed with fresh flowers from the garden. A second-floor suite features a gas fireplace and sleeps up to four guests.

Grandview Bed and Breakfast
1574 Grand Avenue, Astoria, OR 97103 ☎ (800) 488-3250 or (503) 325-0000

The view is indeed grand from this rambling Victorian structure situated on an oversize, forestlike lot a few blocks from downtown. The former home of a cannery owner, the Grandview features a tower with an open balcony, a turret, lots of bay windows, and 10 guest rooms. Anastasia's Room—cozy, pastel-colored quarters with queen bed and shared bath—is a steal. Rooms with a shared bath are discounted. All guests receive a continental breakfast with fresh fruit and juices; bagels, lox, and cream cheese; and homemade muffins. In winter, ask about "second night free" specials.

Rosebriar Hotel
636 14th Street, Astoria, OR 97103 ☎ (800) 487-0224 or (503) 325-7427

At the turn of the century, the Rosebriar was a private residence. It next became a convent and then a halfway house for the mentally ill. Now, in its finest reincarnation, the place is a rambling 11-room inn (with bargain off-season rates beginning at $49). All the guest rooms are small but beautifully furnished and meticulously clean, and include private baths. The spendier units feature fireplaces and river views. The common rooms are spacious and homey, and the grounds offer a gardenlike setting and an outside porch with a view of the Columbia River. Full breakfasts are served.

Gearhart Ocean Inn

67 N Cottage (PO Box 2161), Gearhart, OR 97138 ☎ (503) 738-7373

Eleven New England–style attached units occupy a parklike half acre just north of downtown Gearhart. The tranquil setting is a few blocks from the beach and miles from any coastal hubbub. Inside, wicker furniture, throw rugs, and colorful comforters lend a cheery ambience. Most units are suites with a kitchen, TV, and separate bedroom; others (rooms 3, 4, 5, and 6) are bargain-rate studios that sleep two or three. Room 11 can accommodate seven and rents for about $90 (in season). Ask about three-night, winter-rate specials.

Riverside Inn Bed and Breakfast

430 S Holladay Drive, Seaside, OR 97138 ☎ (800) 826-6151 or (503) 738-8254

The Riverside continues to be Seaside's best bargain for traditional-style lodging. The 11 adjacent cottages are comfortable, spacious, and clean. While the front faces bustling Holladay Drive, the rear recedes gracefully to the Necanicum River. A large riverfront deck provides opportunities for fishing, semisecluded sunbathing, or relaxing. The full breakfasts are top-notch, and the beach is just a few blocks away.

Seaside International Hostel

930 N Holladay Drive, Seaside, OR 97138 ☎ (503) 738-7911

A reconverted motel, this European-style hostel features traditional dormitory-like sleeping quarters (45 beds), shared bathroom facilities, and a large, well-equipped communal kitchen. There's an in-house espresso bar and outside

Camping

Some of the finest scenery on the Oregon Coast can be viewed from within the state parks, so consider camping. Rates are generally the same throughout the park system, beginning at $17 for an improved campsite with a parking space. The best deals (and sometimes the prettiest locations) are the rugged sites reserved for hikers and bicyclists; $4.50 buys a space as well as a hot shower (not available in all state parks). But don't overlook the yurts—rigid-walled, domed tents that can sleep up to eight. Circular in design, these comparatively upscale accommodations are outfitted with electricity and indoor lighting, a plywood floor, and a Plexiglas skylight that opens or closes with a handheld crank. They also include a bunk bed with mattress, fold-out couch, small table, electric space heater, and lockable door. All you'll need are a sleeping bag and a reservation; (800) 452-5687. Yurts cost $27.50 per night (plus a $6 reservation fee) for up to five campers; three additional persons are allowed for $5 each (prices go down in the off season). Be forewarned, though: Coastal state parks regularly fill up during the summer season, particularly on weekends. Yurts can be found in eight coastal parks. North to south, they are Fort Stevens, Nehalem Bay, Cape Lookout, Beverly Beach, South Beach, Jessie M. Honeyman, Bullards Beach, and Harris Beach.

decks, and the Necanicum River flows past the backyard. In the summer, you can expect to meet travelers from all over the world, and intermingling is encouraged. Unlike traditional hostels, you don't have to leave during the day (the place remains open), and no curfew is imposed. Dorm rates are $13 for American Youth Hostel members ($16 for nonmembers). Private rooms with baths and TVs are available, and though they cost considerably more, they're still a veritable steal.

McBee Motel Cottages

888 S Hemlock (PO Box 943), Cannon Beach, OR 97110 ☎ (503)436-2569

Most lodgings in Cannon Beach are priced somewhere west of Pluto, but these charming attached cottages offer a reasonably priced respite from the nearby, sprawling "luxury" motels. Clean and comfy units can be had for less than $50. All 10 units enjoy curly-willow furniture and homey comforters and rugs; some have kitchens and fireplaces. Pets are welcome (for a $5 surcharge). The beach is but a block away and downtown a short stroll. In the winter, inquire about midweek, three-night specials.

Brown Squirrel Hostel

44 SW Brook Street, Newport, OR 97365 ☎ (888)265-3729 or (541)265-3729

It's a given that hostels don't offer all the comforts of home, but the Brown Squirrel is a (dare we say?) quaint stopover in tourist-mad Newport. Five dorm rooms accommodate as many as 22 overnighters. Bring your own sleeping bag and take advantage of the opportunity to mingle with like-minded travelers. Rates are $13.50 per night ($6.75 for kids ages 6–14), whether or not you're an American Youth Hostel member. Couples ($25) and families ($10 per person) are welcome, but there are no private rooms. Kids 5 and under sleep free, and kitchen and laundry facilities are available to all guests. The beach is three blocks away.

Nye Beach Hotel & Cafe

219 NW Cliff Street, Newport, OR 97365 ☎ (541)265-3334

Check into this funky-comfy oceanfront hotel located a few doors down from the better-known and higher-priced Sylvia Beach Hotel. Singing canaries and cockatoos "staff" the front desk, while a piano, cactuses, and carved totems decorate the lobby and adjacent cafe. Not all of the 18 guest rooms are bargains; the oceanfront "spa" rooms are spendy. But every room comes with a private bath, gas fireplace, TV, tiny balcony, and ocean view. Appointments include beds with down comforters and lovely, Pacific-facing bent-willow loveseats. The ground-floor units, which begin at $55, offer the best bargains (and pets are allowed for an extra $10).

The Vikings

729 NW Coast Street, Newport, OR 97365 ☎ (800)480-2477 or (541)265-2477

These rustic 75-year-old cottages occupy an oceanfront bluff, while a steep but sturdy staircase leads to an untrampled beach below. All 13 cottages have color TVs; some have fireplaces and kitchens. Off-season rates begin at $50. Designed for couples, the romantic, wood-paneled Crow's Nest (room 10) is a second-story studio with a double bed, kitchen, private bath with shower, and an unbeatable Pacific panorama (and prices that creep just beyond our bargain range during the summer season).

Edgewater Cottages

3978 SW Pacific Coast Highway, Waldport, OR 97394 ☎ (541) 563-2240

Although not isolated, the Edgewater is located 2½ miles south of town on an oceanfront bluff with easy beach access. All seven cottages feature attractive wood interiors, ocean-facing sun decks, fireplaces, TVs, and kitchens, but no phones. Larger families should rent the Rustic, a two-bedroom affair that sleeps six. Alas, there are some strings attached (a four-night minimum stay in the summer; no one-night reservations any time of the year), but the hassles are worth wading through. Be sure to call in advance (for your pet, too), and leave your credit card at home.

Wayside Lodge

5773 N Highway 101, Yachats, OR 97498 ☎ (541) 547-3450

No doubt about it: This unpretentious lodging located a few miles north of Yachats is one of the coast's sweetest deals. Three low-lying, ocean-blue buildings are nestled in a thicket of shore pines, nicely sheltered from Highway 101. All seven units have a kitchen, TV, secluded deck, and ocean view. There's a grassy area out back just above the beach, and even though houses sit on either side, a feeling of privacy prevails. The screamin' deal here is Cottage 1, a single-story studio with easy beach access ($49 in season).

Southern Oregon Coast

Along large sections of the southern Oregon Coast, life goes on the way it always has—slowly. Here, miles of untouched shoreline far outnumber fast-paced commercial strips. From Yachats south to the California border, only a few towns of any size break up the 160-mile stretch of mostly wild seashore. A long succession of state parks and 50 miles of the Oregon Dunes National Recreation Area ensure that this paradise will not be subjected to the overdevelopment that has ravaged sections of the northern coast.

Small tribes of Native American hunter-gatherers first settled along this coast more than 5,000 years ago. European contact began in the late 16th century when, most historians believe, English mariner Sir Francis Drake sailed as far north as the Oregon Dunes area and became the first non-native to lay eyes on the northwest coast of North America. In his wake came other European and American seafarers led, initially, by the Spanish. Capes Ferrelo, Sebastian, and Blanco, as well as Heceta Head, are geographical reminders of these explorers' maritime forays to this area.

The Columbia River, and the Strait of Juan de Fuca farther north, became the focal points for further exploration and subsequent settlement, while the south coast remained relatively undisturbed. Perhaps because of this isolation, the folks who live here now are fiercely independent. With the exception of the stretch between Yachats and Coos Bay (a one-day, round-trip drive from Eugene), the south coast is a long way from any urban center; it remains a wild place with a singular sense of openness.

Exploring

Driving through the **Cape Perpetua Scenic Area**, a 2,700-acre slice of the Siuslaw National Forest, is an exhilarating roadside journey, jam-packed with spectacular panoramas carved out of the rocky cliffs that abut the ever-charging Pacific. Three miles south of Yachats is the Cape Perpetua Visitor

Center (PO Box 274, Yachats, OR 97498; (541)547-3289), a good place to gather information and soak up the scenery. Trails with stunning views take off from here. Some lead down to the rocky shoreline, while others, such as the Cummins Creek Loop, head up into the hills, traversing old-growth forests along the way (be aware that many national forest areas now assess day-use fees).

The next headland to the south is Heceta, named after an 18th-century Spanish explorer who sailed up the Northwest coast from Mexico. **Heceta Head Lighthouse** is the Oregon Coast's most powerful beacon and perhaps the most photographed lighthouse on the West Coast (the photo op is located about 1 mile south; look for the parking pullouts alongside Hwy 101). Situated just off Highway 101, the lighthouse itself isn't open to the public, although the former lightkeeper's residence is (it's also a part-time B&B; (541)547-3696).

Florence has transformed itself during the last quarter century from a sleepy fishing village into a tourist mecca. The revitalized Old Town has become visitor-oriented without selling out to schlock. At the Old Town Coffee Company (1269 Bay St, Florence; (541)997-7300), you can scope out the local scene. A good picnic spot is the public fishing dock on the river side of Bay Street. North of town, Sea Lion Caves (91560 Hwy 101, Florence; (541)547-3111) is a fun stop. For $6, you can descend 21 stories to a peephole into a natural cave swarming with hundreds of sea lions. On nearby Cape Mountain (turn at Herman Park Rd, off Hwy 101), there's a well-maintained equestrian trail system, a coastal rarity.

The 53-mile-long **Oregon Dunes National Recreation Area** (headquarters at 855 Hwy 101, Reedsport; (541)271-3611) begins south of Florence. Because you can catch only glimpses of this sandy wilderness from the highway, plan to stop and explore. Good departure points include the Clearwox Lake area of Jessie Honeyman State Park; the Westlake area; Threemile Road, just north of Gardiner, which leads to the north spit of the Umpqua River; North Eel campground, which has a trailhead leading to the Umpqua Scenic Dunes area; and the Horsfall Dunes area, just north of North Bend. Take an intriguing detour to the Dean Creek Elk Reserve (4 miles east of Reedsport on Hwy 38), and observe wild

Biking the Oregon Coast

Every year nearly 10,000 bicyclists pedal the Oregon Coast. If it's your turn to bike **Highway 101**, *consider choosing September for your trip: you'll enjoy the coast's sunniest weather, warmest days, and least amount of traffic. You'll also have a tail-wind if you're biking south (northwest winds are prevalent from mid-June through the end of September). Call or write for additional info (Bicycle/Pedestrian Program Manager, Oregon Department of Transportation, Room 210, Transportation Building, Salem, OR 97310; (503)378-3432).*

Challenging **mountain biking** *abounds along sections of the* **Oregon Coast Trail**, *especially at Humbug Mountain State Park and along the vertical slopes of Cape Sebastian. Steep up-and-down single-track traverses rocky cliffs and mountain meadows before diving down through lush lowlands; logging roads head off into the rugged hills along the east side of Highway 101. Ask for maps and info at Moe's Bike Shop (1397 Sherman Ave, North Bend; (541)756-7536), or stop at the Chetco Ranger District (555 5th St, Brookings; (541)469-2196).*

elk grazing on protected terrain.

The numerous lakes in the Oregon Dunes make refreshing warm-water (in season) swimming holes, and the larger lakes, such as Siltcoos, Tahkenitch, and Tenmile, are great for freshwater angling and boating. Be advised that large portions of the dunes are open to off-road recreational vehicles. Check a map to find out who's allowed where.

South of the dunes, **North Bend and Coos Bay** combine to form the largest urban area on the Oregon Coast. You can view the revitalized Coos Bay waterfront from the public pier and boardwalk adjacent to Highway 101. Score coffee drinks and fresh-baked scones at the Scenery (190 Central Ave, Coos Bay; (541)267-5600). For an exhilarating side trip and a gorgeous sunset, drive west about 10 miles to Charleston and the beach. Along the way, visit Chuck's Seafood (5055 Boat Basin Dr, Charleston; (541)888-5525) and Qualman Oyster Farms (4898 Crown Point Rd, Charleston; (541)888-3145) for fresh seafood. **Sunset Bay State Park**, with year-round camping, has a bowl-shaped cove with 50-foot-high cliffs on either side—a good spot to dip your feet or even take a swim; (541)888-4902. The water in the protected cove is perpetually calm, even during midwinter sou'westers, when a colossal surf rages a few hundred yards offshore.

Just beyond Sunset Bay on the Cape Arago Highway at **Shore Acres State Park**, see the colorful botanical gardens complex, containing a restored caretaker's house and an impeccably maintained display of native and exotic plants and flowers; (541)888-3732. At the park, there's also an enclosed shelter where you can view winter storms and watch for whales. Bring your binoculars to windy Cape Arago, which overlooks the **Oregon Islands National Wildlife Refuge**. The Oregon Coast Trail winds through all three parks. Cape Arago

Highway ends here, so double back and take Seven Devils Road south to Highway 101 just north of Bandon (a good bicycling route).

The **South Slough National Estuarine Research Center Reserve** (4 miles south of Charleston; (541)888-5558) is headquartered at an interpretive center, a good source of information, brochures, and free slough and trail maps. Hikers, canoeists, and kayakers (no motorboaters) can explore the slough and its wildlife, and experience an environment that is still untouched by civilization.

Three miles north of Bandon, **Bullards Beach State Park**, (541)347-2209, occupies an expansive area crosscut with hiking and biking trails leading to uncrowded, driftwood- and kelp-cluttered beaches. The 1896 **Coquille River Lighthouse** (open to the public) is located at the end of the park's main road. Good windsurfing beaches abound on the river and ocean side of the park.

The friendly town of **Bandon** is a selfproclaimed storm-watching hot spot and cranberry capital. Head for Old Town to buy fish 'n' chips at Bandon Fisheries (250 SW 1st St, Bandon; (541)347-4454) and take it down to the public pier, adjacent to the harbor. Sugar freaks can score at Cranberry Sweets (501 1st St, Bandon; (541)347-9475), where the staff is generous with free samples. Still more freebies can be had at Bandon Cheese (680 2nd St, Bandon; (541)347-2456). When leaving town, take Beach Loop Road (good for biking), which parallels the ocean in view of weathersculpted offshore rock formations with names such as Devil's Kitchen and Face Rock—a good alternative to Highway 101.

South of Bandon, the landscape opens to reveal sparsely forested yellow and brown hills dotted with thousands of grazing sheep. **Boice-Cope County Park** (west of Hwy 101 near Denmark) is the site of the large, freshwater Floras Lake, popular with boaters, anglers, and board sailors. The park also features an extensive trail system suitable for hiking and mountain biking (take the hike to isolated Blacklock Point).

Cape Blanco State Park (6 miles west of Hwy 101; (541)332-6774) is the westernmost piece of coastline in the Lower 48. Within the park, Cape Blanco Lighthouse (closed except for prearranged tours) is approached via a windy, narrow, and potholed road (definitely not for motor homes). The vista here is surely one of the world's more breathtaking seascapes, with its Canada-to-Mexico panorama. Blanco is the windiest station on the coast, so if the view doesn't claim your breath, surely the wind will.

Port Orford, Oregon's oldest coastal town, is a premier whale-watching location (occasionally, single whales or small groups spend all year in the quiet, kelp-protected coves found here) and a seasonal hot spot for board sailors and surfers, who head for the Battle Rock and Hubbard's Creek Beaches. Fishing fanatics should visit the Elk and Sixes Rivers for the salmon and steelhead runs. And—bonus of bonuses!—Port Orford marks the beginning of Oregon's coastal "banana belt," which reaches to the California border. This stretch enjoys the Northwest's warmest winter temperatures, along with a considerably earlier spring.

The **final 60 miles of Oregon's shore** is a can't-miss section of coastline loaded with desolate black-sand beaches, uncrowded cape-hugging trails, and kelp-strewn waters brimming with marine life. In addition to the usual harbor seals and Stellar's sea lions, tufted puffins and porpoises are sometimes visible. Stop at one of the many state parks along this stretch (possibilities include the trail up Humbug Mountain, in the state park of the same name, and the rocky vistas and isolated beaches within Cape Sebastian State Park). The photo ops are endless, and the beachcombing is superb.

The towns, however, are few and far between. In **Gold Beach**, which sits at the mouth of the Rogue River, you can rent fishing gear and clam shovels or glean local knowledge from the Rogue Outdoor Store (560 N Ellensburg Ave, Gold Beach; (541)247-7142). Hiking trails (such as the Shrader Old-Growth Trail, reachable via Jerry's Flat Road, which follows the Rogue's south shore) cut deep into the Kalmiopsis Wilderness or the Siskiyou National Forest east of town. Obtain backcountry and **jet-boat** info by calling Rogue River Reservations; (800)525-2161. For more on Gold Beach and jet-boat excursions on the Rogue, see the Rogue River & Crater Lake chapter.

Farther south in **Brookings**, Pelican Bay Seafoods (16403 Lower Harbor Rd, Brookings; (541)469-7971) is the place to soak up the Chetco Harbor ambience, rub shoulders with local fisherfolk, and scarf an order of halibut 'n' chips. Buy bagels at Home Port Bagels (1011 Chetco Ave, Brookings; (541)469-6611). Myrtlewood (which grows only on the southern Oregon Coast and in Palestine) can be seen in groves in Loeb Park (8 miles east of town on North Bank Chetco River Rd).

Cheap Eats

Blue Hen Cafe

1675 Highway 101, Florence ☎ (541)997-3907

Glass, ceramic, and plastic chickens—blue, naturally!—are everywhere in this cozy cafe. As you might expect, chicken (always Oregon-fresh fryers) dominates the menu, and it's available baked, grilled, or fried. Portions are generous: you'd be hard-pressed to polish off a "four-clack" special. The kitchen also serves some fine breakfasts, burgers, pastas, and a surprising number of vegetarian dishes, such as spinach, broccoli, and carrot lasagne and "chips Parmesan," roasted potato slices smothered in cheese. The place is packed in summer, but it's always ultra-friendly.

International C-Food Market

1498 Bay Street, Florence ☎ **(541) 997-9646**

"Catch it, cook it fresh, and keep it simple" is the plan at this sprawling seafood operation right on the Siuslaw River pier at the edge of Old Town. The fish-receiving station and the fleet are just outside the restaurant, and it's fun to watch the boats unload (a sign explains what kind of seafood), then order a fillet prepared just the way you want it. There are crab, oysters, and clams, too. Visit the attached seafood market for fresh take-out.

Bank Brewing Company

201 Central Avenue, Coos Bay ☎ **(541) 267-0963**

A bank turned microbrewery, this inviting downtown establishment features a congenial pub atmosphere with high ceilings, huge windows, and balcony seating. Sweet Wheat and Gold Coast Golden Ale top the craft-beer list, while enticing chow choices include calamari, stuffed jalapeños, mussels, clams, and hand-tossed pizzas.

Blue Heron Bistro

100 W Commercial Street, Coos Bay ☎ **(541) 267-3933**

A European-style bistro in downtown Coos Bay, where longshoremen and timber workers still hold sway, may seem unlikely; but the Blue Heron keeps customers happy with an airy atmosphere, indoor and alfresco dining, and a reasonably priced, innovative menu. There are waffles, breakfast parfaits, and strong jolts of java in the morning. Other times, look for handcrafted pastas, blackened oysters, a German sausage plate, and grilled salmon with black beans, corn relish, and salsa. Desserts are top-drawer, too.

Kum-Yon's

835 S Broadway, Coos Bay ☎ **(541) 269-2662**

Believe it: This nondescript eatery is a showcase of South Korean cuisine. Try the spicy *chap chae* (transparent noodles pan-fried with veggies and beef), *bulgoki* (thinly sliced sirloin marinated in honey and spices), or *yakitori* (Japanese-style shish kabob). The sushi, sashimi, and fried rice are fine, but not nearly as enticing. Weekends are crowded.

Andrea's

160 Baltimore Street, Bandon ☎ **(541) 347-3022**

This Old Town eatery is appointed with New Age artwork, lots of greenery, massive, comfy wooden booths, and a piano (sometimes there's even a player). Locals flock here for breakfast, which might be a steaming bowl of oatmeal topped with fresh fruit, or a massive omelet. Later in the day you'll find fried oyster sandwiches, Cajun fish salad, crepes, and charbroiled salmon. Look for the deep-dish pizza du jour. Bandon quiets down considerably in the winter, and Andrea's is open less often then.

Rubio's

1136 Chetco Avenue, Brookings ☎ (541) 469-4919

This gaudy-yellow restaurant along the Highway 101 strip is your best bet for south coast Tex-Mex. The chiles rellenos and the chile verde are top-notch choices, and the salsa is outstanding (it's available by the bottle if you need to take some on the road). For something different, try the Seafood à la Rubio, a dish combining fresh lingcod and shellfish in a jalapeño-stoked garlic and wine sauce.

Hog Wild Cafe

16158 Highway 101 S, Harbor ☎ (541) 469-8869

A pig theme runs rampant here: pig dolls, pig cups, and all manner of swinelike paraphernalia. The food is worth pigging out on, too. You'll find jambalaya, Cajun meatloaf, a prime rib sandwich, and a veggie lasagne and frittata. The "kitchen sink" pasta comes with andouille sausage, snapper, shrimp, and scallops in a zesty marinara sauce. Muffins are pig-size, and the coffee drinks sport names such as Hog Heaven (chocolate-coconut mocha). Don't overlook the cheesecake.

Cheap Sleeps

The See Vue

95590 Highway 101 S, Yachats, OR 97498 ☎ (541) 547-3227

Perched cliffside between Cape Perpetua and Heceta Head, the See Vue lives up to its name with miles of Pacific panoramas. Each of the 11 units in this cedar-shake lodging is differently appointed. The Salish, with its Northwest Native American motif, offers the sweetest deal. Other rooms are decorated with different themes (such as the Mountain Shores, with its redwood burls, and the second-story-view Crow's Nest, with nautical furnishings). Most rooms are less than $60. Your hosts can fill you in on the goings-on in Yachats and Florence, or you may prefer to meander down to the uncrowded beach a few hundred yards away.

Ocean Haven

94770 Highway 101, Florence, OR 97439 ☎ (541) 547-3583

Ocean Haven (formerly known as Gull Haven Lodge) offers a setting—high on a cliff overlooking the charging Pacific—that is perhaps as close to perfect as any lodging on the Oregon Coast. A 360-degree panorama is available from the Shag's Nest ($50), an isolated one-room cabin equipped with a fireplace, kitchenette, and private deck (you'll need to book it well in advance). For the bath, you must scamper across to the lodge 30 yards away. The lodge units aren't as good a deal, though two cedar-lined sleeping rooms with ocean views, which share a bath and a kitchen, are a bargain at $35.

Fire Lookout

*A little-known Pacific penthouse is located 21 miles northeast of Brookings. There's no indoor plumbing, electricity, or water, yet this fire lookout atop the 4,223-foot Snow Camp Mountain in the **Siskiyou National Forest** remains a very special place. Inside, there's a wood-burning stove, a single bed, and a table and chairs; a pit toilet is located outside. You bring the rest. You can drive to within sight of the lookout, but you must hike the final 200 yards to the summit. For $30, five can sleep here during the snow-free months of May through October. Reservations for a given year are taken in January—and it's popular. Contact the Forest Service (Chetco Ranger District, 555 5th St, Brookings, OR 97415; (541)469-2196) to get an application for this windy, remote getaway.*

Blackberry Inn

843 Central Avenue, Coos Bay, OR 97420 ☎ (800) 500-4657 or (541) 267-6951

The Blackberry Inn offers a different twist on the usual B&B arrangement. Guests here have the renovated 1903 Victorian home to themselves; the owners have their own residence. Breakfast is a continental affair, but a kitchen is available, and eggs and bread are supplied. There are four guest rooms; two have private baths. A night in the small but adequate Rose Room is a genuine bargain ($55 summers; $35 off season), especially in urbanized Coos Bay. Centrally located, the inn is within walking distance of most of downtown. Unfortunately, it fronts a busy thoroughfare.

Bandon Wayside Motel

1175 SE 2nd Street (Route 2, Box 385; on Hwy 42 S), Bandon, OR 97411 ☎ (541) 347-3421

This 10-unit, out-of-the-way motel occupies a parklike setting on the road to Coquille. Rooms (less than $35) are simple and clean, with an outdoor barbecue in the large backyard. Picnics are always a possibility, and the motel's quiet isolation, 2 miles from the beach, occasionally spares the visitor from the summer coastal fog. Housebroken pets are allowed at no extra charge in some units.

Sea Star Guest House and Hostel

375 2nd Street, Bandon, OR 97411 ☎ (541) 347-9632

Two lodgings in one, the Sea Star is a four-room guest house connected to a hostel by a diminutive courtyard. The guest house is considerably more lavish, so cheapsters should check into the men's and women's dorms. Here guests share bath, kitchen, dining room, laundry facilities, and a laid-back lounge (and help with the chores). Bunks are $16 a night (less for American Youth Hostel members and young kids); private rooms with shared baths go for about twice as much. The guest house features a natural-wood interior and harbor views. Skylights illuminate the two upstairs suites. In-room coffee and a TV are part of the package.

Sunset Motel

1755 Beach Loop Road (PO Box 373), Bandon, OR 97411
☎ **(800) 842-2407 or (503) 347-2453**

Everywhere along the coast, the closer you get to the ocean, the more expensive the rooms are. The Sunset is a worthwhile compromise. A clean, comfortable room with a limited view and a double bed is yours for about $50, while an oceanfront unit might be twice as much, or more. So opt for economy—you're just across Beach Loop Road from the ocean anyway, and the setting is unsurpassed. All rooms include TV, use of a sizable indoor Jacuzzi, and morning coffee.

Battle Rock Motel

136 S 6th Street (PO Box 288), Port Orford, OR 97465 ☎ **(541) 332-7331**

Although this nothin'-fancy, retro-looking motel is on the wrong (east) side of Highway 101, your room ($40 or less) is only a stone's throw from the cliffside trail of Battle Rock Wayside Park. Year-round whale watching and a wonderful stretch of uncrowded beach await. You're also within walking distance of most of Port Orford.

The Castaway

545 W 5th Street (PO Box 844), Port Orford, OR 97465 ☎ **(541) 332-4502**

This 14-room motel sits atop a site formerly occupied by Fort Orford—the Oregon Coast's oldest military installation—and the Castaway Lodge, once frequented by Jack London. All rooms enjoy ocean views (the south-facing vistas of Humbug Mountain and beyond are stunning), and rates begin in the $40 range (even less in the off season), remarkable for oceanfront lodgings. Suites—which sleep four to six and include kitchens, dining areas, and two bedrooms or a loft—are also reasonably priced. The beach, harbor, and shops are an easy stroll away.

Sea Dreamer Inn Bed and Breakfast

15167 McVay Lane, Brookings, OR 97415 ☎ **(800) 408-4367 or (541) 469-6629**

Hugs, cookies, and a friendly dog's affection can be had at this 1912 country Victorian built from local redwood. Backed by evergreens and located south of town and just a half mile from the ocean, the home looks out over ever-blooming flowers, fruit trees, and lily fields, which slope gently to beach level. There are but three rooms, two with shared bath and all enjoying Pacific vistas. The splendid interior includes a piano, a fireplace, and a formally decorated dining area where full breakfasts are served.

The Rogue River & Crater Lake

The Rogue River has been immortalized in song, literature, and film. Western author Zane Grey lived in a cabin beside its waters; Ginger Rogers had a ranch along its banks. Clark Gable loved the Rogue, and so did John Wayne. The river travels a circuitous 215-mile route across southwestern Oregon, from its headwaters west of Crater Lake National Park to its Pacific Ocean terminus at Gold Beach. Along the way it passes through Douglas fir forests, cattle ranches, pear orchards, vineyards, rugged canyons, and more than one backyard.

At the head of the Rogue is Crater Lake, all that remains of the 12,000-foot volcano called Mazama that blew its top some 6,000 years ago. The river begins here as a rushing stream, goes underground at Natural Bridge, becomes a lake behind Lost Creek Dam, and serves as a whitewater playground for rafters and kayakers. It's one long fishing hole, too. During its final 30 miles, the Rogue widens and calms as it folds into the Pacific Ocean.

Exploring

A prospector searching for gold found the treasure now known as **Crater Lake National Park** in 1853. (In 1902 it was designated a national park, the only one in Oregon.) Millions have admired this jewel, the deepest lake in the United States (1,932 feet), for its dark blue water and rugged rock walls. The visitors center and park headquarters, located at the south end of the park off Highway 62, feature a theater, information desk, and a good interpretive exhibit. Camping is available here and at other designated areas. Call the park headquarters at (541)594-2211 for information (but be forewarned: you may end up in voicemail hell and never reach a human being).

Drive or bicycle the 33-mile circuit of the lake, **Rim Drive**, which has several pullouts and viewpoints along the way. Rim Village (near park headquarters) offers the park's only facilities; beginning at the village and traveling clockwise, some of the most popular sites include Watchman Lookout, a short, easy hike to a stunning lake view, and Cleetwood Cove, a steep trail down to the water (and the only point providing access to the lake). At Cleetwood, a **tour boat** makes daily excursions out to Wizard Island and around the lake; the first tour usually leaves around 10am and costs about $10 (no reservations, just take the trail down to the dock). Continuing on,

Ancient Trees

Old-growth forests may be something of an endangered species, but near Gold Beach you can hike through one that's been preserved forever. The Frances Shrader Old-Growth Trail, named for a U.S. Forest Service employee who helped create it, offers visitors a 1-mile hike through an ancient stand of Douglas fir and Port Orford cedar. Pick up a brochure at the trailhead. To get there, take Jerry's Flat Road east from Gold Beach, on the south side of the Rogue River. After 12 miles, watch for signs on the right.

Mount Scott is the highest point in the park (8,926 feet), reached by a moderately difficult trail; **Cloudcap**, less than a mile beyond, is the highest point on the rim accessible by car. The Kerr Notch viewpoint is the best for a look at the Phantom Ship rock formation, while Sun Notch offers the best view of Wizard Island (unless you take the boat tour). In between is a turnoff to **Pinnacles Overlook**, where volcanic layers of pumice and ash have been eroded into odd-looking 80-foot-high cylindrical shapes.

Summer is the peak season at Crater Lake, but the park is open all year. Go between November and April and you'll steer clear of the entry fee ($10 per car at last report). For that matter, the cross-country skiing in winter is spectacular (but mostly advanced). At 6,000-plus feet above sea level, the area gets hundreds of inches of snow in an average winter (when only the south entrance is open). Originally built in 1909, historic **Crater Lake Lodge** was recently restored to its previous grandeur; stop in for a peek near Rim Village.

The **Rogue River** heads southwest from Crater Lake. Just past Union Creek on Highway 62, watch for Natural Bridge on the right. If you follow the trail that crosses the river and continues on the other side, you'll come to the spot where the Rogue goes underground for a few hundred feet. It's a dandy; the roar of rushing water makes it sound like a junior Niagara.

Another 10 miles west, look for the turnoff to **Prospect**. This old road, Mill Creek Drive, parallels the new highway for several miles. Mill Creek Falls is only a quarter-mile walk off the road. Backtrack a bit to another trail that leads to the aptly named Avenue of Giant Boulders. Rocks of another kind and purpose await you at **Lost Creek Dam**, a massive flood-control project completed in the mid-1970s, which resulted in the formation of Lost Creek Lake. The powerhouse and a mini-museum are open for tours in summer. Nearby **Stewart State Park** offers camping as well as day-use areas and miles of hiking trails.

Below the dam, the highway hugs the Rogue as it gently twists and turns through occasional whitewater sections. This is a popular spot for beginning **whitewater rafters**. Rafting companies spring up like mushrooms in Shady Cove, but two that have been around for a while are Rapid Pleasure, (541)878-2500, and Rogue Rafting, (541)878-2585. Figure on $45 to $55 for a three-hour river outing.

Rent a raft or a Rogue Drifter (a big burlap bag filled with Styrofoam balls) from River Trips in Gold Hill; (541)855-7238. The river from Gold Hill to the city of Rogue River is the gentlest part for floating. Just beyond, **Valley of the Rogue State Park** is a popular and often crowded camping spot.

If you want a more pampered river experience, try a **jet-boat ride**. These noisy boats propel themselves by taking water in the front end and shooting it out the back, and they can operate in just a few inches of river. Arrange a ride with Jet Boat River Excursions in Rogue River, (541)582-0800, or the older, more experienced Hellgate Excursions in Grants Pass, (541)479-7204. Rides, including dinner, run about $40 (or half that if you skip dinner).

At the mouth of the Rogue in Gold Beach, two other companies send jet boats upstream. They are Jerry's Rogue Jets, (800)451-3645 or (541)247-7601, and Mail Boat Hydro-Jets, (800)458-3511 or (541)247-7033. They charge the same prices: about $30 for a round trip to Agness, 32 miles upriver (meal extra), and $75 to $80 to Paradise Lodge, 52 miles up (meal included).

Grants Pass, population 18,000, is the largest city on the Rogue. It is the staging area for the fabled three-day rafting trips through the nationally designated Wild and Scenic part of the Rogue, a 40-mile stretch. Rafters sleep in the open or stay at wilderness lodges. These trips are far from cheap—they cost hundreds of dollars—but if you're interested, try Orange Torpedo Trips; (541)479-5061.

Finally, there's **Gold Beach**, a nice little coastal town with an unusually large number of motels and restaurants for its size. Check out the free **Rogue River Museum**, next to Jerry's Rogue Jets at the port, and you'll get a look at how this part of the world came to be. (See the Southern Oregon Coast chapter for more on Gold Beach.)

Cheap Eats

Beckie's Cafe

56484 Highway 62, Prospect ☎ (541)560-3563

Beckie's, a fixture for decades, is right across the highway from the Union Creek Resort and shares that same gorgeous Rogue River National Forest/Upper Rogue River scenery. Old-timers claim the huckleberry pie isn't what it used to be, several owners ago. But travelers and recreationists still stop here for basic eats: pie, a hot beef sandwich, or, say, a filling pork chop dinner.

Mac's Diner

22251 Highway 62, Shady Cove ☎ (541)878-6227

Doo-wop till you drop: Mac's is a paean to the '50s, with lots of neon and pictures of James Dean and Marilyn Monroe. When there's live music on weekends, some diners literally dance in the aisles. Food? The tri-tip steak isn't bad, and you might try one of the "convertibles"—hot turkey or beef sandwiches with their tops down. Whatever you do, don't miss the mashed potatoes.

Ali's Thai Kitchen

2392 N Pacific Highway, Medford ☎ (541)770-3104

When Medford-area folks are hungry for Thai food, they head for this hole-in-the-wall next door to a tire store. The atmosphere is zilch, but the food's good, it's inexpensive, and—with almost 100 menu items—there's more than enough to choose from. The spring rolls, made with glass noodles, pork, and vegetables, are grand. Ditto the phad Thai. The beef entrees (with meat that's disappointingly tough) are better ignored.

Wild River Brewing Co.

595 NE E Street, Grants Pass ☎ (541) 471-7487

Beer here! What started as a microbrewery has since grown into an appropriately noisy and decidedly decent pizza and pasta joint. Try the excellent four-cheese cannelloni spiked with spinach and sun-dried tomatoes, but avoid the mushy lasagne. While the salads are a bit ordinary, the house bread, made with malted barley and wheat, is nice.

Cheap Sleeps

Prospect Historical Hotel

391 Mill Creek Drive, Prospect, OR 97536 ☎ (800) 944-6490 or (541) 560-3664

The century-old hotel was restored in 1990 and opened as a bed and breakfast, motel, and restaurant complex. The main building houses attractive B&B-style rooms, but they carry a high tariff. For a better deal, try one of the motel rooms out back. They're pretty basic, and on the small side, but adequate for the money. Besides, who wants to hole up indoors when Prospect is home to spacious forests and clean mountain air? The hotel restaurant serves a good, inexpensive Sunday brunch and reasonably priced two-course dinners.

Union Creek Resort

56484 Highway 62, Prospect, OR 97536 ☎ (541) 560-3565 or (541) 560-3339

For the best deal, ask for a second-floor room in the resort's rather rustic lodge—if you don't mind sharing a bath. A "historic" cabin for two, with private bath, costs a little more. Families and other groups may enjoy one of the larger cabins that sleep up to six. You can't beat the scenery, which is replete with the tall trees of the Rogue River National Forest. The river itself (at this point a rushing stream not far from its headwaters) is a short walk away at the Rogue Gorge viewpoint.

Royal Coachman Motel

21906 Highway 62, Shady Cove, OR 97539 ☎ (541) 878-2481

A number of small motels dot the banks of the upper Rogue from Trail to Shady Cove. This one is about the best, with basic, adequate, clean accommodations. Some have a river view, but if you don't care about seeing the water, you can get in for less. Next door is the best restaurant in the territory, Bel Di's. It doesn't fit the budget profile, but the three-course dinners are worth splurging on (try the Louisiana stuffed prawns); (541) 878-2010.

Wolf Creek Tavern

100 Front Street, Wolf Creek, OR 97497 ☎ (541) 866-2474

Okay, so it's not on the Rogue—not even close. But the 20-mile drive north on I-5 from Grants Pass is worth the side trip for a chance to stay at this charmer (and the journey won't take long). The inn has been around for more than a century; it was used as a stagecoach stop in the 1880s, eventually acquired by the state of Oregon, and restored in 1979. There are eight guest rooms upstairs, plus one suite. Downstairs you'll find a homey parlor and a decent restaurant.

Rogue River Inn

6285 Rogue River Highway, Grants Pass, OR 97527 ☎ (541) 582-1120

In prefreeway days, the Rogue River Highway was the main road from California to points north, and it was dotted with small motels near the river. The Rogue River Inn is about the best of the few that remain. It's not right on the river, but it's close enough for something of a view. Choose from 21 rooms, and take advantage of the swimming pool—or head across the highway for a dip at Savage Rapids Park.

Rogue Valley Motel

7799 Rogue River Highway, Grants Pass, OR 97527 ☎ (541) 582-3762

Clark Gable loved this part of the Rogue River. Maybe he never stayed at the Rogue Valley Motel, but it's a fine stop between Grants Pass and the city of Rogue River for the rest of us. Just seven units; some have kitchens. There's a pool. You're across the highway from the river but close enough to see the water. The Jet Boat River Excursions dock is only a mile to the east, and there's a prime picnicking spot, Coyote Evans Wayside, nearby.

Cougar Lane Resort

04219 Agness Road, Agness, OR 97406 ☎ (541) 247-7233

Nothing fancy here, but you are on the Rogue, about an hour's drive upriver from the ocean. Lucas Lodge, across the Rogue, is nicer but more expensive. In addition to motel rooms (available from April to October), the resort offers a few cabins too. Deck seating at the adjacent restaurant makes for pleasant dining in summer and appeals to many jet-boat passengers, who disembark here from May to October for a meal.

Ireland's Rustic Lodges

1120 Ellensburg Avenue (PO Box 774), Gold Beach, OR 97444 ☎ (541) 247-7718

Ireland's is really two motels. The original eight cottages are rustic indeed, and inexpensive. They don't have an ocean view but do have attractive log walls, fireplaces, and lovely gardens. (Cottage 4 is a fave.) The newer units are not so rustic, have an ocean view, and, while still a bargain, cost a bit more.

Fire Lookout

*This lookout has only one cot, but you can fit three other people on the floor in sleeping bags. A half-mile hike offers pleasant rewards: views of the **Rogue Basin** from sheer cliffs dropping from the lookout to the west and south (be careful). As with most lookouts, the Forest Service provides the wood stove, propane refrigerator, stove, and oven, and you provide the rest. For $40 a night (three-night maximum), it's not a bad deal. For directions or reservations, call the Tiller Ranger District; (541) 825-3201.*

Paradise Lodge

52 miles up the Rogue River from Gold Beach (PO Box 456), OR 97444
☎ (800) 525-2161 or (541) 247-6022

This is the best wilderness lodge along the Wild and Scenic part of the Rogue between Grants Pass and Gold Beach. It's accessible by raft, jet boat, hiking trail, or private plane—but not by car. Most visitors arrive by jet boat, a three-hour run upriver from Gold Beach, but you can cut costs by hiking in from Marial, 4 miles upriver. You may find yourself walking through a herd of deer to get to your room, and you may have to share the room with a squirrel (so hide those nuts). Electric power runs off a generator that freaks out at the pulse of a hair dryer and is shut off altogether from 10pm to 6am: bring a flashlight! We suggest hiking in before high season begins (May or thereabouts), while rates are lower. The price of an overnight stay is at the high end of our budget scale, but the lodge remains a great deal when you factor in three squares a day.

Ashland & Beyond

The entire town of Ashland, which dates back to the Gold Rush years of the 1850s, is a historic landmark. The remarkable success of the Oregon Shakespeare Festival has transformed this once-sleepy town into the Rogue River Valley's biggest tourist attraction. The festival now draws an audience of nearly 350,000 through the nine-month season (February through October). Somehow, amazingly, the town of 19,000 still retains its soul. For the most part, it is a happy little college burg, set amid lovely ranch country, that just happens to house one of the largest theater companies in the United States.

Follow the tourists, and you too can spend more than you need to. Many inns and restaurants will charge whatever the market will bear. Follow the students (4,700 attend Southern Oregon University), actors, and locals, and you may find some bargains.

Northwest of Ashland is another Gold Rush–era town, Jacksonville. The 19th-century hotels, shops, and saloons along California Street have become a popular stage set for films, including *The Great Northfield, Minnesota Raid* and *Inherit the Wind*. Jacksonville is also the home of another top-notch outdoor event, the Britt Music Festivals.

Exploring

Medford is the biggest city in this part of the world. (In keeping with the malling of America, Medford's Rogue Valley Mall, with 80-odd stores, is your proof.) About halfway between Medford and Phoenix, you'll find the headquarters of **Harry and David** and **Jackson and Perkins**. These two mail-order giants (selling fruit and flowers, respectively) are part of a parent company called Bear Creek Corporation (2836 S Pacific Hwy, Medford; (541)776-2362). Harry and David maintains a country store in south Medford (1314 Center Dr) offering everything from fresh produce to myrtlewood pepper shakers. Free tours of the main packing plant are available most weekdays. Ask at the country store, (541)776-2277.

Nearby is **Jacksonville**, the historic 1850s Gold Rush town. Most visitors come for the **Britt Music Festivals**, held from mid-June through early September. Gold Rush–era photographer Peter Britt's former estate, on a hillside overlooking the Rogue River Valley, houses the outdoor amphitheater where concerts and musical-theater productions feature national jazz, blues, country, and

Jacksonville by Trolley

Come summertime, schoolteacher Stan Morkert leases a motorized San Francisco cable-car replica, dons dark glasses and a conductor's hat, and becomes Stan the Trolley Man, offering hour-long narrated tours of historic Jacksonville just about every day from early June to Labor Day. It's a good way to get a feel for the town and see notable sites, including the spot where gold was discovered in 1851. Look for signs at 3rd and California Streets. Fares are around $4 to $5; half price for children. Call (541)535-5617.

classical musicians for the duration of the festivals. Unfortunately, we've yet to find any way to get around the stratospheric ticket prices. The general-admission tickets are, of course, the better bargain. Occasionally there are discounted Sunday morning classical concert tickets. For a schedule, write to Britt Music Festivals, PO Box 1124, Medford, OR 97501; (541)779-0847.

Without question, the Oregon Shakespeare Festival has put **Ashland** on the national map. And yet, as locals know, there's a good deal more to the place than Bard-centric festivity. It's the dining capital of Southern Oregon, has more bed-and-breakfast inns (over 60 at last count) than gas stations, and is home to a wealth of art galleries, small theater groups, street markets, and other artistic endeavors.

Still, the center of attention is the **Oregon Shakespeare Festival** (15 S Pioneer St, Ashland, OR 97520; (541)482-4331), producing an average of 11 plays each season, in three theaters. The Angus Bowmer Theatre, named for the festival's founder, is the principal indoor venue.

Some of the more offbeat, arty plays open in the smaller Black Swan. Major Shakespearean productions are mounted outdoors on the Elizabethan stage. Indoor plays run from February through October, outdoor shows from mid-June to late September. Performances occur daily except Monday.

Tickets for the festival generally range from $26 to $45, but there are ways to cut costs. Attend one of the previews that run for about two weeks prior to the opening of each show, and tickets will cost you around 20 percent less. If you can make it to Ashland prior to June or after mid-September, look into rush tickets. If many seats remain unsold for a particular play, the festival sells rush tickets for half price during the last hour before curtain time (and only at the box office). Those looking to cut costs should try a midweek performance during off season (February through early May, or late September through October), or opt for a performance of a less popular, more obscure play. A festival membership ($50 base price) won't get you

Off-Bardway

Off-Bardway is Ashland's pet name for the part of its theater scene that isn't restricted to renditions of Shakespeare. The performances are generally less expensive and of high quality. Oregon Cabaret Theatre (1st and Hargardine Sts, Ashland, OR 97520; (541)488-2902) performs in the Old Pink Church (which isn't pink anymore). Actors' Theatre stages productions at its own playhouse (101 Talent Ave, Talent; (541)535-5250). The Southern Oregon University Theatre Arts Department puts on several plays a year by theater arts majors (on the campus; (541)552-6346).

cheaper tickets but is good for discounts at stores around town and a few other privileges. Theater enthusiasts shouldn't miss the backstage tour, which offers an intriguing two-hour look behind the scenes (about $9, starts at 10am; (541)482-4331).

To explore Ashland, concentrate your efforts on what the locals call the **Plaza** (Main St from Water to Pioneer Sts), an area with a number of good galleries. Adjacent to the Plaza is **Lithia Park**, a 99-acre beauty. The bandshell in the middle of the park is used for free outdoor con-

certs and ballet performances during summer months. Call the Chamber of Commerce for a schedule of events; (541)482-3486. Another good place to spend some time is the **Schneider Museum of Art** at Southern Oregon University (1250 Siskiyou Blvd near Hwy 66; (541)552-6245). The oft-changing exhibits feature contemporary works from regional and national artists. The **Pacific Northwest Museum of Natural History** (1500 E Main St; (541)488-1084), which opened in 1994, is noted for interactive exhibits.

Cheap Eats

Ashland Bakery and Cafe
38 E Main Street, Ashland ☎ (541)482-2117
Popular with everyone from Shakespeare buffs to author Ken Kesey, ABC (as the locals call it) is a down-home eatery just a stone's throw from the festival theaters. The menu lists a little of this, a little of that—pesto pasta, fajitas, chicken stir-fry, Greek salad, a few Asian dishes, and pizza.

Brothers
95 N Main Street, Ashland ☎ (541)482-9671
Breakfast is the most popular meal at Brothers, a deli and restaurant one block from Ashland's downtown Plaza. You'll understand why when you see the menu's list of 20 omelets along with the likes of potato pancakes, breakfast burritos, and bagels and lox. There's lunch and dinner too. Try the pesto salmon sandwich or the fajita burrito.

Geppeto's
345 E Main Street, Ashland ☎ (541)482-1138
In a town noted for expensive dinnerhouses, Geppeto's is a lower-cost alternative with something for everyone. Locals describe the menu as "Italian-Ashland." Loosely translated, that would mean a multitude of pastas, extending to fussier fare (say, chicken in currant sauce) sharing billing with veg-head favorites like Parmesan tofu patties and organic veggie burgers.

Greenleaf Deli
49 N Main Street, Ashland ☎ (541)482-2808
A popular breakfast spot with seasonal outdoor dining, the Greenleaf, located conveniently on the Plaza, offers morning fare ranging from a tofu scramble to Japanese pancakes with vegetables. Crossing cultural boundaries doesn't faze

'em here; you can also find grilled polenta and a lox and bagel platter. Yes, there's bacon and eggs too. For lunch, the place dishes up good spanakopita.

Cheap Sleeps

Phoenix Motel

510 N Main Street, Phoenix, OR 97535 ☎ (541) 535-1555

This small, older motel lies on the old highway (99) in Phoenix, about 6 miles north of Ashland. It has been remodeled and has a tidy look. There are 22 rooms (some with kitchens) and a swimming pool. If Ashland motels are heavily booked, this is the place to try.

Ashland Hostel

150 N Main Street, Ashland, OR 97520 ☎ (541) 482-9217

The Ashland Hostel's dormitory-style rooms ($14 members, $15 nonmembers) are open to all ages. If you're lucky, you and a friend can get one of the two private rooms. Hours are strict (as are rules prohibiting smoking). Guests share a common kitchen and living space. The two-story building is well maintained and pleasant. Best of all, the Shakespeare Festival theaters are only a few blocks away.

Green Springs Inn

11470 Highway 66, Ashland, OR 97520 ☎ (541) 482-0614

If you don't mind driving 17 miles up a winding mountain highway, this rustic lodge in a forested setting is one of the Ashland area's best values. The eight-room motel complex sits behind a popular rural restaurant (of the same name) that offers great fresh pasta. Rogue River Valley temperatures can top 100 degrees on some summer days, but it's almost always 10 to 15 degrees cooler up here.

Knight's Inn

2359 Ashland Street, Ashland, OR 97520 ☎ (800) 547-4566 or (541) 482-5111

You're a couple of miles away from the theater district here, but stores, restaurants, and a shopping center are nearby. (So is a freeway exit.) The motel, with 40 units, has been well maintained and doesn't look as cheap as its room rates might suggest. The pool is heated.

Ashland Clearinghouse

☎ *(800)588-0338 or (541)488-0338*

This reservation service for lodging (from Ashland to Jacksonville and beyond) mainly handles the more pricey bed and breakfasts. It's worth a call anyway, for two reasons: 1) these folks know their stuff and can make suggestions, and 2) they also represent a number of house rentals, available by the night or week. You might be able to get a good deal on a place for a party of six or eight with a several-day discount. Off season, the clearinghouse can find you some bargains at the better motels or even B&Bs, at rates as low as $55.

Manor Motel

476 N Main Street, Ashland, OR 97520 ☎ (541)482-2246

A 12-unit, single-story structure near downtown Ashland, the Manor Motel has its drawbacks: it's an older place (1940s auto court) with smallish rooms, on a busy main street. But it is reasonably well maintained, it has a garden area, and you can walk to the theaters, about a half mile away. For central Ashland, the rates are hard to beat.

Palm Motel and Houses

1065 Siskiyou Boulevard, Ashland, OR 97520 ☎ (541)482-2636

Located across the boulevard from Southern Oregon University, the Palm's 13 single-story, cabinlike units are on the cutesy side, with white walls and green trim. Out back are several two- and three-bedroom houses for rent in the summer (they're home to college students during the rest of the year). There's a small swimming pool, too.

Timbers Motel

1450 Ashland Street, Ashland, OR 97520 ☎ (541)482-4242

The Timbers may be Ashland's best older motel. You'll find it on the edge of a pie-shaped shopping center, bounded by Highways 99 and 66, and across the street from Southern Oregon University. The two-story structure has 29 clean, comfortable rooms, and there's a small swimming pool on the premises. You can walk to a number of stores and restaurants; the theater district is more than a mile away.

Bend & the Three Sisters Wilderness

Central Oregon is dominated by the drop-dead scenery of 10,000-foot Cascade peaks such as Mount Jefferson and the Three Sisters. Ancient glaciers creep downward from the summits of these dormant volcanoes until they meet vegetation at the 7,000-foot level. Below, forested slopes hiding hundreds of high-mountain lakes and unsullied alpine meadows contrast dramatically with ancient lava flows hardened to a gray-black pumice. On their eastern flank, the Cascades give way to an undulating high-desert landscape.

It's here that the central Oregon cities of Madras, Redmond, Sisters, and Bend are situated. The geography is marked by rugged rimrock canyons carved by the Deschutes and Crooked Rivers, and by human-made lakes where these and other rivers have been dammed. The Cascade summits block most of the precipitation prevalent on the west side of Oregon, so the climate is dry and sunny 300 days a year.

The bend in the Deschutes is still there, but Bend itself and its urban environs have changed dramatically with the influx of folks from Portland, Salem, Seattle, Southern California, and elsewhere. The area draws outdoor fanatics from all over: not just skiers (who come for the powder-snow slopes of Mount Bachelor) but also whitewater devotees, hikers, rock and mountain climbers, backpackers, boaters, board sailors, and road and mountain cyclists. In addition to all the rank-and-file athletes, many world-class competitors come here to train, compete, and play; they include the U.S. Nordic ski squad (to Bachelor), the top rock climbers (to Smith Rock), and the nation's best bicyclists (to July's Cascade Cycling Classic).

Exploring

Just 40 years ago, **Bend** was a smallish cowboy town located on a big curve in the Deschutes River, and its residents were a mix of farmers, ranchers, and a smattering of small-town folk. How things change! These days, a loaded ski rack (carrying a mountain bike, a sailboard or kayak, and a pair of skis) is more common than a gun rack. Even in an Old West city such as Redmond, you're as likely to meet an accountant as a cowboy (and the next person you see may well be both).

The focal point of Bend, **Drake Park**, is the logical locale for a Deschutes River stroll (the river slices through the park and forms its centerpiece, Mirror Pond), a game of Frisbee, a summer evening concert, or a picnic. Cyclists, skateboarders, and in-line skaters will pass by as you attempt to keep your edibles away from the hundreds of birds (mostly drakes) inhabiting the park's grassy slopes. Bend's best muffins and breads come from nearby Great Harvest Bread Company (835 NW Bond St, Bend; (541)389-2888). For bagels and lox, stop by Big O Bagels (1032 NW Galveston Ave, Bend; (541)383-2446). An extensive baked-goods and sandwich selection can be had at Pastries by Hans (915 NW Wall St, Bend; (541)389-9700).

One of the most popular multisport events in the country is Bend's annual **Pole, Pedal, and Paddle Race** in mid-May. This six-leg relay begins with ³/₄ mile of alpine skiing on Mount Bachelor, followed by 8 kilometers of cross-country skiing (classic or skate technique allowed). Next is a 22-mile, mostly downhill bike ride to Bend's Colorado Avenue, and then an 8-kilometer run along the Deschutes River, a 2-mile paddle on the river, and, finally, a 400-meter sprint across the grass in Drake Park. The event is open to teams, pairs, and individuals; (541)388-0002.

A foray up **Century Drive** (also known as Cascade Lakes Highway) on your road or mountain bike, on Rollerblades, or in your car is a worthwhile endeavor any time of the year. In winter, the road is plowed only to the base of Mount Bachelor, at the 6,000-foot level. Folks have been known to cross-country ski to Elk Lake (mostly downhill) and get picked up for the drive back to Bend the long way, or return via an Elk Lake Resort

The Bend Outback

Bend has some of the Northwest's best cross-country skiing conditions. You probably already know about Mount Bachelor's 56 kilometers of groomed trails, suitable for skating or traditional skiing. But there are also miles of backcountry opportunities, with trailheads located just off Century Drive. Not to be missed:

The **Meissner** area, 12 miles west of Bend, designed for beginners and intermediates (a warming shelter provides a welcome refuge 1 mile in from the parking area).

Swampy Lakes, 3 miles west of Meissner on Century Drive, offers a variety of marked trails, 2 to 10 miles in length, and five shelters that are usually stocked with wood (there are snowmobile trails on the other side of the highway).

The **Dutchman Flat** area, farther still up Century Drive and adjacent to the Mount Bachelor entrance, with trails leading into the nearby Three Sisters Wilderness. Dutchman Flat is wide open, with few obstructions, because the pumice-heavy soil cannot sustain much plant life.

In the off season, these same cross-country skiing trails make for awesome mountain biking or trail running. The areas require Sno-Park permits in the winter. For permit information and trail maps, call the Deschutes National Forest office in Bend; (541)388-2715.

snowmobile; (541)317-2994. The section of Century Drive/Cascade Lakes Highway between the base of Mount Bachelor and Elk Lake remains unplowed until Memorial Day weekend.

A dormant volcano, **Mount Bachelor** sits on the east slope—the dry side—of the Cascades, rising gracefully to an elevation of 9,065 feet. The **skiing** possibilities are so numerous at Bachelor, the mountain so huge and the powder so abundant, that you can ski in good snow throughout the winter—which lasts for seven months of the year. Depending on the snowpack, the skiing can extend into July. The **Nordic area** has its own lodge and 56 kilometers (35 miles) of groomed trails.

Additional vital stats about Bachelor: 300 inches of annual snowfall, a vertical drop of 3,100 feet, and 11 chair lifts, as well as five lodges serving 70 different downhill runs. There's even a day-care facility. **Lift tickets** cost $36 for adults. You can get three- and five-day discounts as well as "flextime point" tickets, which are good for a three-year period and geared to infrequent skiers. An adult one-day cross-country ticket costs about $10 (half that for youth). Children age 6 and under ski free anywhere on the mountain. (Downhill and cross-country ticket prices may change yearly.) Call (800)829-2442 for additional information; call the Ski Report, (541)382-7888, for up-to-date conditions. **Off season** (June through early September), the chair lift runs to the

summit, affording an impressive three-state view and unlimited hiking, trail-running, and mountain-biking ventures. Equipment rentals are available on the mountain, but you can find better prices and a superior selection in Bend.

The best place to rent downhill skiing equipment or snowboards is Skjersaa's Ski Shop (130 SW Century Dr, Bend; (541)382-2154). Sunnyside Sports (930 NW Newport Ave, Bend; (541)382-8018) and Tri-Mountain Sports (815 NW Wall St, Bend; (541)382-8330) are good sources for cross-country gear, while the latter also specializes in climbing equipment and information.

In June, the **Cascade Lakes Highway** reopens and winds into the prettiest lake region in the Northwest, the gateway to the 200,000-acre **Three Sisters Wilderness**. A number of trailheads begin from parking areas (some with fees) just off the road. Osprey Point at Crane Prairie Reservoir is a wildlife sanctuary (with a viewing deck) for osprey, bald eagles, and blue herons. The Deschutes River recreation sites, the Swampy Lakes area, the back side of Bachelor, and Todd Lake—all on national forest land—are good **mountain-biking areas**. Maps are available at the Deschutes National Forest headquarters (1645 Hwy 20 E, Bend; (541)388-2715).

Choose from an extensive bike-rental fleet (including suspension mountain bikes) and pick up riding info at Hutch's

The Museum at Warm Springs

Warm Springs is just a small bend in the road at the bottom of a rimrock canyon on Highway 26, but the Museum at Warm Springs (2189 Hwy 26, Warm Springs; (541)553-3331) is a sight to behold. Built in 1993 by three Native American tribes (Wasco, Paiute, and Warm Springs), it houses a permanent collection that includes prized heirlooms protected by tribal families for generations. The best feature of the architecturally magnificent museum is a representation of a ceremonial Wasco wedding: tule-mat lodge, wickiup and plankhouse, song chamber, and drums accompanying rhythmic hoop dancing. There are also walking trails and picnic areas.

Free Ski Bus

*The convenient **Mount Bachelor Super Shuttle** is a free ski bus that leaves the Mount Bachelor Park & Ride lot (corner of Simpson and Colorado in Bend) multiple times during the day. On busy holiday weekends as many as four buses might be operating, offering a lift to and from the mountain. Schedules are posted in the parking area.*

(725 NW Columbia St, Bend; (541)382-9253; and 820 NE 3rd St, Bend; (541)382-6248). Any of the larger lakes in this area are excellent for board sailing as well as fishing. If you're **hiking** into the Three Sisters Wilderness (no mountain bikes or mechanized vehicles are allowed), avoid the congested Green Lakes, Elk Lake, and Sisters Mirror Lake trailheads. Instead, choose the Six Lakes trailhead or, if you intend to scale the 10,358-foot South Sister (Oregon's third-highest peak and a nontechnical climb), head for the Devil's Lake parking area and the Sisters' Climbing Trail.

The route northwest from Bend to **Sisters** via Highway 20 is a pleasant sojourn through pastoral grazing fields with wonderful views of Bachelor, the Three Sisters, Black Butte, Mount Washington, Mount Jefferson, and Three-Fingered Jack. At the west end of Sisters, take Highway 242 for a drive (or bike ride) past the nation's largest llama ranch; then continue on to the Dee Wright Memorial (a castlelike, covered viewing area) and the high point of **McKenzie Pass**. The spectacular road at the 5,324-foot summit (closed to vehicles during the winter) separates the Three Sisters and Mount Washington wilderness areas.

For yet another breathtaking scene, follow Highway 20 west from Sisters to the **Metolius River** headwaters via the paved Forest Road 14 (followed by a half-mile walk on a blacktop trail). Here the crystal-clear Metolius emerges from an underground source, and is an excellent place to snap photos with 10,497-foot Mount Jefferson as a backdrop. The surrounding area offers unlimited outdoor

adventures. Visit Eurosports in Sisters (115 W Hood St, Sisters; (541)549-2471) for inspiration, maps, and rentals. Sisters Brewing Co. (291 E Cascade Ave, Sisters; (541)549-0518) provides liquid refreshments and pub grub. Farther west, on the Santiam Pass summit, **Hoodoo Ski Bowl** (Hwy 20, 42 miles west of Bend; (541)822-3799) offers free skiing the first hour of every operating day, so you can test the conditions before buying a lift ticket.

Smith Rock State Park, a half hour north of Bend on Highway 97 adjacent to the town of Terrebonne, is an internationally known rock-climbing area (day use only) centered around the majestic rock spires of the Crooked River Canyon; (541)548-7501. Peer down into the Crooked River gorge from the **Ogden Scenic Wayside** (along Hwy 97, 10 miles north of Redmond). Farther north, the dammed Metolius River forms **Lake Billy Chinook**, where sprawling Cove Palisades State Park features camping, swimming, and boating; (541)546-3412.

Twenty-five miles east of Bend on Highway 20 is the University of Oregon's **Pine Mountain Observatory** (9 miles south of Millican; (541)382-8331), the astronomy research center of the Northwest. Visiting hours are limited, so call first. A small donation is requested; bring binoculars and a flashlight, too. But even if you don't venture inside the observatory, the view from Pine Mountain is worth the drive.

Six miles south of Bend on Highway 97, the **High Desert Museum** (59800 S Hwy 97, Bend; (541)382-4754) offers interesting art and natural history exhibits, as well as entertaining outdoor wildlife demonstrations involving river otters, porcupines, and birds of prey. Two miles farther south, you can view an extinct volcanic cone and learn about the area's geology at **Lava Lands** (58201 S Hwy 97, Bend; (541)593-2421), which is open late May through October. While there, ask about lava caves to explore in the area.

Turn west at the Sunriver Resort exit to visit the free **Sunriver Nature Center &** **Observatory**, with its raptor rehabilitation area; (541)593-4394. Eight miles south of the center is **Newberry National Volcanic Monument**, (541)388-5664, Oregon's largest Ice Age volcano and the site of Paulina and East Lakes, which are hot spots for windsurfing, fishing, swimming, boating, and cross-country skiing. In the winter, the road is plowed for only the first 10 miles.

Cheap Eats

Alpenglow Cafe
1040 NW Bond Street, Bend ☎ (541) 383-7676

Breakfast is the best meal at this congenial restaurant alongside the Deschutes Brewery. Humongous cinnamon rolls and fresh-baked breads will grab your attention and taunt your taste buds. But don't miss the multiple pancake choices or the eggs Benedict—which locals claim are the best in town. Chicken-sausage pasta is a noontime favorite.

Cafe Santé
718 NW Franklin Avenue, Bend ☎ (541) 383-3530

Expect to see cyclists, Rollerbladers, and skateboarders whizzing by this inviting cafe on the edge of Drake Park, downtown Bend's recreational hot spot. The main attractions at Santé are healthy grub and a laid-back ambience. Grilled rice patties, meatless sausage scrambles, and vegetable stir-fries are some appetizing possibilities, and organic ingredients are used when available. You'll also find barbecued rock shrimp and a few pasta choices. Sidewalk tables, fruit smoothies, and craft beers make lounging easy.

Deschutes Brewery & Public House
1044 NW Bond Street, Bend ☎ (541) 382-9242

All of central Oregon seems to gather here, appreciative of the nonsmoking, family atmosphere and the tantalizing selection of craft brews such as Black Butte Porter, Obsidian Stout, and a hoppy Cascade Golden Ale (the house favorite). Pub grub includes garlic burgers, a pastrami Reuben, French onion soup, and the finest fries you'll ever taste. Dinner specials revolve around sausage plates, pasta, chicken, and fresh fish. All the items on the menu, including the condiments, are made from scratch. If you're around in the fall, take in the brewery's Oktoberfest.

Pizza, Pizza, Pizza

No matter what your recreational bent, pizza tastes darn good afterward. Here's where to find it in these parts:

John Dough's Pizza *(34 SW Century Dr, Bend; (541)382-3645): Topping choices are legion—even smoked oysters and broccoli, for Pete's sake—and pies can be ordered sans cheese at this convivial pizza joint located on the road to Bachelor and the high lakes country. The Cheese Overdose, on the other hand, comes coated with a half-dozen varieties, while the Galloping Garlic Gourmet Lite is less filling, with part-skim cheese, basil, spinach, sun-dried tomatoes, and lots of garlic.*

Stuft Pizza *(238 NE 3rd St, Bend; (541)382-4022): The 15 varieties of thick-crust pies served here, many sporting movie-star monikers, run the gamut from the Duke, featuring five different meats and a host of veggies, to the Basil Rathbone, a pizza slathered with pesto and topped with sun-dried tomatoes and two cheeses. Ask for additional garlic (no charge).*

Papandrea's Pizzeria *(325 E Hood St, Sisters, (541)549-6081; and 538 SW 4th St, Madras, (541)475-6545): For a long while, this was the only place serving decent pizza in central Oregon. The setting's nothing special, inside or out, but the pizza is a chewy, doughy, thick-crust version topped with whatever floats your boat.*

Mexicali Rose
301 NE Franklin Avenue, Bend ☎ (541)389-0149

This celebrated eatery (readers' polls proclaim it Bend's best Tex-Mex) occupies a corner slot at one of Bend's busiest intersections. Order the steak, chicken, or veggie picados, a zingy chile Colorado, or any of the dozen or so combo meals (the chicken taco/chile relleno combo is a fave), and ask for black beans.

Westside Bakery and Cafe
1005 NW Galveston Avenue, Bend ☎ (541)382-3426

A favorite haunt of skiers and backcountry enthusiasts, this chummy corner eatery is the place for fruit-filled pancakes, waffles, and croissant "scrambles." Hefty sandwiches on homemade bread make for hearty lunch fare. On your way out, grab a dozen bagels to fuel your next adventure. Expect long waits on weekend mornings.

La Siesta Cafe
8320 N Highway 97, Terrebonne ☎ (541)548-4848

Don't blink or you'll drive right by dinky Terrebonne, gateway to the world-class Smith Rock climbing venue. At La Siesta, Lycra-clad climbers rub shoulders with local ranch hands and alfalfa growers over platters of Tex-Mex chow. The usual taco-enchilada-burrito lineup is available, the salsas are fiery, and the mood's as lazy as a sunny south-of-the-border afternoon.

Cheap Sleeps

Bend Cascade Hostel
19 SW Century Drive, Bend, OR 97702 ☎ (800) 299-3813 or (541) 389-3813

Don't let appearances sway you: this large, boxy structure is warm and friendly on the inside, and it's conveniently located on Century Drive, within walking distance of the free Mount Bachelor ski shuttle (and one mile from downtown). The dormitory arrangements include 43 beds at $14 a pop and private rooms for $14 a person (discounts for American Youth Hostel members, students, and seniors; kids under 18 are half price). Pillows and blankets are provided, but bring your sleeping bag and towels. Guests have access to the kitchen, a coin-operated laundry, and lots of storage room for skis, bikes, and watercraft. The hostel closes between midmorning and late afternoon.

The Country Inn the City Bed and Breakfast
1776 NE 8th Street, Bend, OR 97701 ☎ (541) 385-7639

This two-story 1920s home in a quiet neighborhood is chock-full of knickknacks, books, videos, and board games. Outdoor enthusiasts can enjoy croquet, horseshoes, and a basketball court, and then relax in the hammock underneath the ponderosa pines or in one of the two guest rooms ($60 year-round). Evenings include teas and fruit drinks, and perhaps some chocolate chip cookies or a scrumptious fudge fest. Come mornings, there's a full breakfast.

Cultus Lake Resort
Highway 46 (PO Box 262), Bend, OR 97709
☎ Winter phone: (541) 389-3230; summer phone: (541) 389-5125, wait for beep, and then press 037244; information: (800) 616-3230

You're well into the mountains here in the Deschutes National Forest, 50 miles southwest of Bend, alongside a large lake popular with anglers, boaters, board sailors, and swimmers (yes, it's warm enough in late summer). You're also adjacent to the Three Sisters Wilderness and in the midst of an expansive trail system custom-tailored to hiking, running, or cross-country skiing. Unfortunately, this resort is open only from mid-May through mid-October. Nevertheless, catch it while you can, because the 23 cabins are reasonably priced at $52 and up. A serviceable restaurant and a small grocery store are in the handsome main lodge, while various watercraft rentals are available on the lakefront. Pets are $5 extra.

Mill Inn Bed and Breakfast
642 NW Colorado Street, Bend, OR 97701 ☎ (541) 389-9198

In its former life, this 10-room bed and breakfast served as a hotel and boardinghouse. These days it offers the most reasonable B&B rates in central Oregon. The four-bunk Locker Room, for instance, is a steal at $15 a person. Couples should opt for the Duffers Room or the Timber Room, while the High Desert Room has twin beds and a shared bath, and fetches just $40. Group rates are available (small ski teams stay here and have been known to fill the spa on the outdoor deck). Even bunk rates include a full breakfast, and there's a washer, dryer, and refrigerator, as well as ski and bike storage, for guest use.

Westward Ho Motel

904 SE 3rd Street, Bend, OR 97701 ☎ (800) 999-8143 or (541) 382-2111

Highway 97, the main north-south thoroughfare in central Oregon, cuts an unattractive swath of motels, fast-food joints, and car dealerships right through Bend. Of the numerous lodging choices, the Westward Ho, where rooms run less than $40, is the best value of the traditional-motel bunch. Most of the well-heated rooms are far enough off the highway that traffic noise isn't a problem. There's a small indoor pool and Jacuzzi for après-ski warm-ups, and enough TV channels to satisfy the addicted.

Metolius River Lodges

County Road 700 (PO Box 110), Camp Sherman, OR 97730
☎ (800) 595-6290 or (541) 595-6290

This collection of 12 rustic cabins is about 30 miles from Bend (10 miles from Sisters) and a world away from urban hassles. Nestled under a canopy of old-growth ponderosa pine, the lodges are just a cast away from the swiftly flowing Metolius River. The best deals are two duplexes, which sleep up to four. Units 2, 3, and 4 (not available in the winter) feature kitchens and fireplaces with sweet-smelling wood logs. All guests are served beverages and muffins at their door each morning. If you're looking for meticulously clean, well-appointed lodgings with a decidedly outdoorsy feel, it doesn't get any better than this. Ask about extended-stay discounts.

Breitenbush Hot Springs

PO Box 578, Detroit, OR 97342 ☎ (503) 854-3314

Slightly New Age, this old mountain spa is a favorite of folks looking for a quiet, cleansing time in the woods. Guests take soothing soaks in the two sets of temperature-regulated outdoor pools or sweat out stress in a clothing-optional outdoor steam room heated by the hot springs. Yoga, meditation, and relationship seminars take place in lodgelike meeting rooms; cross-country ski weekends and ancient-forest walks are equally inspiring (Breitenbush is located on the edge of the Mount Jefferson Wilderness). You sleep in tiny, electrically

Vacation Rentals

In Bend, house-rental arrangements are made through private owners or property management firms and can often result in good group rates. Vacation rental management companies include Central Oregon Leasing and Management (1250 NE 3rd St, Suite 200, Bend, OR 97701; (541)385-6830) and Mirror Pond Management (644 NW Broadway, Bend, OR 97701; (541)382-6766). Coldwell Banker/First Resort Realty (PO Box 4306, Sunriver, OR 97707; (800)544-0300) handles Sunriver Resort rentals, and Black Butte Ranch Corporation (Black Butte Ranch, Hwy 20, approximately 5 miles west of Sisters; (800)452-7455) handles rentals at Black Butte Ranch.

Wilderness Cabin

*In rare instances, the U.S. Forest Service has let stand small, unobtrusive, hand-built structures in wilderness areas where no signs of humanity—save hikers—are supposed to be seen. Head into the lake-splashed area of the **Three Sisters Wilderness** and you'll stumble upon a picture-perfect cabin located on the Muskrat Lake shoreline. It's a 5½-mile hike or horseback ride from the trailhead in the Cultus Lake North Unit, so you'll most likely have it to yourself. Built by a trapper earlier in this century, it includes a potbelly stove, a bunk bed, and cupboards sometimes stocked with nonperishable food. There are no rules (though you're expected to leave it clean and replace any firewood or food you use) and no disturbances. Be prepared for snow nine months of the year, lots of bugs (including pesky mosquitoes) in July and early August, and perfect conditions in September. Call the Deschutes National Forest office in Bend; (541)388-2715.*

heated cabins (those with toilets cost $10 more) or, for considerably less, tents. Meals consist of family-style, mostly organic, vegetarian fare. Bring bedding and towels, and be prepared for a half-mile walk from your vehicle to the main lodge. Those inclined to pop in just for a daytime soak should be sure to call ahead to check on space availability.

Kah-Nee-Ta Resort
100 Main Street (PO Box K), Warm Springs, OR 97761
☎ **(800) 831-0100 or (541) 553-1112**

Located in the middle of the high desert, halfway between Mount Hood and Bend, this posh and redecorated resort (with golf, tennis, hiking, horseback riding, bicycling, kayaking, and a casino) isn't for everyone traveling on a budget. Nevertheless, a large family or group of friends can stay in one of the tepees, occupying a grassy meadow, for a modest sum ($55 for three, then $5 per additional person). Bring your own bedding and an air mattress or cushion to sleep on: the tepees have concrete floors. The hot, mineral-springs pool is part of the package, although the giant water slide costs extra.

The Wallowas & the Blue Mountains

The high desert of northeastern Oregon ends east of the round-'em-up town of Pendleton. From here, you ascend into either the piney Blue Mountains or the alpine terrain of the Wallowas. These are two very different mountain ranges settled into the same blue-sky corner of the state.

The high and dry Blues, once rich in gold and timber, are now littered with ghost towns, dilapidated hot-springs resorts, and lots of wide-open valleys where hunters, hikers, fishermen, horseback riders, snowmobilers, and a slowly increasing number of cross-country skiers like to set up camp and lasso a good time.

The peaks of the Wallowas reach even higher than the Blues and are topped by the Eagle Cap Wilderness, where the mountain timber terrain turns rocky and alpine. Natural features such as glistening Wallowa Lake, at the base of the Wallowa-Whitman National Forest, and awesome Hells Canyon, the continent's deepest gorge, on the east side of the range, have kept the looming ghosts at bay. Indeed, it is quiet here—even at the height of summer.

Exploring

Pendleton, equidistant from Portland, Seattle, and Boise, is the hub of northeastern Oregon. The home of the Pendleton Round Up has become almost synonymous with saddles and wool. Hamley's Saddlery (30 SE Court St, Pendleton; (541)276-2321) is practically a local shrine—kind of an L.L. Bean of the West. They've been selling Western clothing, boots, hats, tack items, and custommade saddles since 1883. Pendleton Woolen Mills (1307 SE Court Pl, Pendleton; (541)276-6911), makers of the nationally known Pendleton Wools, gives tours Monday through Friday and sells woolen yardage and imperfect (but still warm) blankets at reduced prices. The town of Pendleton is also a key point on the historic **Oregon Trail**, which recently celebrated its 150th anniversary (see "On the Oregon Trail" tip).

Midway between Pendleton and Baker City is **La Grande**, the gateway to the Wallowas. It's also home to Eastern Oregon University and the civilized touches of a college town, such as books and well-brewed java at Sunflower Cafe and Bookstore (1114 Washington Ave, La Grande; (541)963-5242) and rosemary-garlic focaccia at A Bakery of

Kneads (109 Depot St, La Grande; (541) 963-5413).

From here, you'll want to drive east on Route 82 into the magical **Wallowas**. At the end of the road is the town of Joseph, the ancestral home of the Nez Perce leader Chief Joseph. Wallowa Lake State Park, on the edge of the Wallowa-Whitman National Forest and the Eagle Cap Wilderness, has ample room for all who wish to explore it—even in midsummer, when the pristine lake and its shores are buzzing with go-carts, sailboats, and wind surfers.

The majestic mountains, just an arm's length away, remain essentially unpeopled. Ride the **Wallowa Lake Tramway** up a steep ascent to the top of 8,200-foot Mount Howard, which has spectacular overlooks and a couple of miles of hiking trails; (541)432-5331. One of the best ways to explore the lake-laden Eagle Cap Wilderness is on foot, letting smiling llamas lug your gear (it's a long way into the wilderness area). Reserve a space with Hurricane Creek Llama Treks; (800)528-9609 or (541)432-4455.

When snow falls in the Wallowas, it's light, dry, and plentiful. There are miles and miles of quiet cross-country trails throughout the lovely highlands. Backcountry skiers seeking the best of the Wallowa winterland might want to check out the guided overnight tours with Wallowa Alpine Huts (you sleep and dine in insulated yurts); (800)545-5537 or (208)882-1955.

The continent's deepest gorge, **Hells Canyon**, is 35 miles east of Joseph. It's an awesome trench cut through sheer lava walls by the Snake River. The best view is from Hat Point near Imnaha, although you'll find McGraw Lookout more accessible. Complete a loop drive by taking paved Forest Road 39 to south Oxbow, and then following Highway 86 west to I-84. Maps of the region's roads and trails, as well as information on conditions, are available at the Wallowa Valley Ranger District in Enterprise, (541)426-5546, or at the Forest Service office just outside Halfway, (541)742-7511.

Between the steep cliffs of Hells Canyon and the fruitful southern slopes of the Wallowas is **Halfway**. It's a quiet town, the centerpiece of Pine Valley and a magnet for urban escapees seeking solace and sun, and a good jumping-off point for trips down the Snake River in Hells Canyon. River trips begin at Oxbow Dam, 16 miles east of Halfway. Hells Canyon Adventures in Oxbow provides **jet-boat tours** from Hells Canyon Dam or can help you arrange a float trip or float-and-horseback combination excursion; (800)422-3568 or (541)785-3352.

Between the Wallowas and the Elkhorns, Baker City makes a good base camp for forays into the **Blue Mountains**. The 100-mile scenic Elkhorn Loop, west of Baker, winds by numerous ghost

Pendleton Round Up

Each September the Pendleton Round Up rolls into town. It's a big event that features a legendary rodeo; call (800)457-6336 for tickets and information. Unfortunately, the festivities have become so popular that Pendleton motels routinely jack up their prices for the second week in September and typically require a four-night stay, putting even the cheapest dive out of this guidebook's price range. If your cowboy heart is set on the Round Up (but you failed to save your pennies and make reservations a year in advance), consider commuting in from accommodations in Hermiston or Milton-Freewater. Fortunately, tickets to rodeo events are often available up to the last minute. Anyway, at Round Up time, just being in Pendleton is half the fun.

On the Oregon Trail

The recent 150th anniversary of the Oregon Trail—the primary overland route to Oregon for thousands of 19th-century settlers—spurred the creation of a spate of historical sites and centers along the trail's route, which in northeast Oregon roughly parallels I-84. If you hit only one, make it the National Historic Oregon Trail Interpretive Center, 5 miles east of Baker City, where multimedia displays convincingly re-create life on the trail; (541)523-1843. West of La Grande, the Oregon Trail Interpretive Park at Blue Mountain Crossing is a great, shady picnic stop where you can walk on portions of the actual trail and see informal living-history enactments most summer weekends (exit 248 off I-84). It's open summers only, and it's free.

towns, which once boomed with people reaping the area's timber and gold. There's not much left of either these days, and most of the towns are skeletal remains, having been ravaged by fire or abandoned in despair once the natural resources were depleted. Contact the Baker Ranger District, (541)523-4476, for directions to Elkhorn Loop.

The most accessible (and the most active) ghost town is **Sumpter**, destroyed by a fire and subsequently abandoned by miners in 1917. The valley, dredged for gold three times, remains scarred with piles of very clean rocks. The last dredge machine (which cost $300,000 and mined $4.5 million worth of gold) still stands on the west side of town. Sumpter has begun to perk up a bit lately, though; a legendary flea market gets the town booming again during the weekends of Memorial Day, July 4, and Labor Day. The narrow-gauge Sumpter Valley Railroad offers history-laden excursions on the outskirts of town on summer weekends and holidays; (541)894-2268. Round-trip cost is $9 adults, $6.50 children.

Stop by **Granite** (population in the single digits), which has a general store that doubles as the local tavern, eatery, and mail stop. Fall elk-hunting season is big around here. Even less populated (zero) is Whitney, where 150 people once lived in the wide-open Whitney Valley until the train stopped coming in 1947.

Although the gold may have dwindled,

the abundance of snow in these mountains now attracts a whole new kind of prospector. Snowmobilers charge in to explore the 500 miles of groomed snow-mo trails. Cross-country skiers are gaining status here too, with a few skiers-only trails sprouting up. Tucked away in the middle of the Blues is a one-lift ski area that has a glittering reputation among powder hounds. You're deceptively high here. The base at **Anthony Lakes Ski Area** is above the 7,000-foot level. That translates into dry, light powder. There's been talk about opening up more ski terrain. Trouble is, it's 300 miles from Portland and even farther from Seattle. (No problem, say Pendletonites.) It's 20 miles to the closest accommodations, but with some prearranging, ski groups can camp out in the day lodge (for a small charge); (541)856-3277 in winter or (541)963-4599 year-round.

A number of natural hot springs bubble up in this part of Oregon. Many, such as Hot Lake and Medical Springs, were originally developed for medicinal purposes but have long since been forgotten and are now dilapidated. **Lehman Hot Springs** (PO Box 263, Ukiah, OR 97880; (541)427-3015), just east of Ukiah, is one of the few still officially open to the public. Basic A-frames are available for overnight stays in this remote territory; bring your own bedding.

The town of **John Day** is in the middle of dry cattle country. The Kam Wah

Chung Museum (adjacent to the city park; no phone), open daily in summer except Fridays, is a good stop if you're in the area. The museum includes an 1887 opium den (John Day served as a center for the Chinese community in Eastern Oregon until the early 1940s). West of town, **John Day Fossil Beds National** **Monument** offers a glimpse into the distant past, when saber-toothed tigers roamed these hills and lush subtropical forest stood in place of today's sagebrush. Get maps and brochures at the visitors center on Highway 19, 2 miles north of Highway 26 (9 miles west of Dayville); (541) 987-2333.

Cheap Eats

Como's Italian Eatery
39 SE Court, Pendleton ☎ (541) 278-9142

At this cozy little downtowner, locals stop in for pesto and artichoke sandwiches and fresh polenta dishes, which share the menu with more traditional (by American standards) pizza and pasta offerings. Open for lunch and early dinner (lunch only on Saturdays).

Great Pacific Wine & Coffee Co.
403 S Main Street, Pendleton ☎ (541) 276-1350

Situated in a refurbished 110-year-old landmark building, Great Pacific is a retail wine and coffee store that doubles as an espresso bar and deli serving bagels (from Portland Bagel Co.), homemade soups and sandwiches, freshbaked muffins and cookies, and a handful of light dinners.

Mamacita's
110 Depot Street, La Grande ☎ (541) 963-6223

Generous portions of good food and a warm, lively atmosphere have made Mamacita's a favorite local gathering spot. Prices are good (lunch or dinner can be had for under $3!); at lunch, a special Full Meal Steal varies weekly. It's kid-friendly, too, with a children's menu that doubles as a color-it-yourself placemat. Grown-ups can relax with a Mexican beer or a wine margarita.

Vali's Alpine Deli
59811 Wallowa Lake Highway, Joseph ☎ (541) 432-5691

Maggie Vali's Hungarian and German fare is legendary in these parts; dinners usually require a reservation (two seatings nightly) and always require a big appetite. The menu is prix fixe and varies by night of the week; Sunday's wiener schnitzel is exceptional. For breakfast you can expect homemade sweet doughnuts, juice, and coffee (but nothing else). Vali's closes for October and is open weekends only until Memorial Day; thereafter it's open daily except Mondays through Labor Day.

Geiser Grand Hotel Saloon

1996 Main Street, Baker City ☎ **(888) 434-7374 or (541) 523-1889**

Slip into the dark wood-paneled bar at this elegantly restored 1889 hotel in the heart of Baker City's historic downtown, and the buzz of I-84 seems far, far away. The saloon menu features such players as tiger prawns, bison wings(!), ribs, and specialty burgers—well prepared, generously portioned—accompanied by a good selection of microbrews. Inclined to splurge a little? Consider dining in luxury under the stained-glass ceiling of the adjacent Palm Court, which offers full dinners at reasonable prices.

Ferdinand's

128 Main Street, Prairie City ☎ **(541) 820-4455**

The first thing you'll notice are the elk, deer, and pronghorn antelope heads, mounted on the exposed stone wall of what was originally a butcher shop. Then turn around to meet a pair of hand-carved nymphs, part of a massive wooden bar from Italy that came around the Horn before the turn of the century. No, Dorothy, you're not in Kansas anymore. At least the menu is familiar: a good selection of microbrews on draft, build-your-own pizzas, and several pasta dishes, plus teriyaki chicken and barbecued beef ribs. Everything's made in-house, from the pizza dough to the barbecue sauce.

Cheap Sleeps

The Working Girls Hotel

17 SW Emigrant Avenue, Pendleton, OR 97801
☎ **(800) 226-6398 or (541) 276-0730**

Here's the first nonprofit hotel we've ever seen. Its mission? To bring tourism to Pendleton—and at these prices, you'll come back, Round Up or no. The hotel gets its name from its former incarnation as a bordello. The five spacious rooms in this pretty brick building each have 18-foot ceilings and antique furnishings (the television is even cleverly hidden in a vintage radio cabinet). The plumbing's still the original stuff, so you'll need to cross a hall to the bath. Continental breakfast is served, and if you stay longer, the kitchen is available for your preparations. Young children are discouraged.

Historic Union Hotel

326 N Main Street, Union, OR 97883 ☎ **(541) 562-6135**

Rumor has it Clark Gable stayed here in the '20s to fly-fish Catherine Creek. This 1921 hotel, once the centerpiece of the Grand Ronde Valley, hasn't seen visitors of his ilk for years; it was nearly condemned before Twyla and Allen Cornelius arrived from Eugene in 1996 and began a slow restoration. It still falls far short of elegant, but the individually decorated rooms are attractive and clean, with a certain charm—and you can't beat the prices ($33 to $55). Buy breakfast at Nellie's Place, off the lobby, which offers what it describes as "Home cooking—'nuf said."

Wagons and Tepees

Dive deeper into the history of the Oregon Trail and stay overnight in a canvas-topped covered wagon ($25/night) at one of two state parks off I-84: **Emigrant Springs** *(midway between Pendleton and La Grande) or* **Farewell Bend** *(northwest of Ontario, on the Idaho border). They're the real thing, but equipped with amenities no emigrant ever dreamed of: electricity and two double mattresses. Bring your own bedding and cook outside. For another perspective, try one of the four large tepees at Farewell Bend. For reservations, call (800)452-5687.*

Chandler's Bed, Bread, & Trail Inn

700 S Main Street (PO Box 639), Joseph, OR 97846
☎ (800) 452-3781 or (541) 432-9765

Ethel and Jim Chandler's comfy bed and breakfast resembles an alpine ski lodge: cedar shingles, multiangled roof lines, and plush wall-to-wall carpets. A log staircase climbs from the comfortable living rooms to a loft where five simple bedrooms share a sitting room and a kitchenette. Three of those rooms have private baths (and higher rates, which, from mid-May to mid-October, range beyond our "budget" profile). The substantial breakfast and knowledgeable hosts make this a wonderful stopover for area explorers.

The Birch Leaf Farm

47830 Steele Hill Road, Halfway, OR 97834 ☎ (541) 742-2990

Snugged up against the southern slopes of the Wallowas, Dave and Maryellen Olson's turn-of-the-century farmhouse has been updated with wraparound decks that are idyllic for whiling away a summer's afternoon. Four upstairs guest rooms—one each in ecru, coral, eggshell blue, and yellow—share baths. The yellow room is our favorite, with its view of the birches and the manicured front lawn. If Dave's cooking, enjoy a breakfast of blueberry pancakes and bacon; if Maryellen's in the kitchen, expect fancier fare. Stash the kids in the converted bunkhouse out back.

Clear Creek Farm

48212 Clear Creek Road, Halfway, OR 97834 ☎ (541) 742-2238

Clear Creek is quirky but paradisiacal, with a field of lavender, a fragrant herb and vegetable garden, a herd of bison, and an orchard filled with fruit trees. You'll find no more charming, down-home hosts than Rose and Mike Curless, and no accommodations more fun than the two multilevel, board-and-batten cabins—like backyard forts for grown-ups—behind their white farmhouse. The cabins are primitive: open windows, a walk to the bathhouse. Upstairs in the farmhouse, three homey rooms offer less adventure but more privacy. Dine in town, or prearrange a candlelight dinner with Rose.

Pine Valley Lodge

163 N Main Street, Halfway, OR 97834 ☎ (541) 742-2027

European ambience meets the rustic West at Pine Valley Lodge, housed in an eclectic collection of historic buildings arrayed along Main Street in downtown

Halfway. The main lodge building and the adjacent house (dubbed the "Blue Dog") are joined by a boardwalk through an exuberant garden; furnishings, chosen by artist-proprietors Dale and Babette Beatty, are arty and luxurious. The cost of staying here drops when you rent a suite with family or friends. Penny-pinching travelers can get in on the fun at the Bunk House (a.k.a. "Love Shack"), with its communal sleeping room and kitchenette ($25 per person). If you decide to splurge just once on your trip, consider reserving a place at Babette's dinnertime feast.

À demain Bed & Breakfast

1790 4th Street, Baker City, OR 97814 ☎ (541) 523-2509

Kristi and Pat Flanagan do their best to spoil guests at their restored Victorian home on a quiet neighborhood street a few blocks from the downtown historic district: down comforters and pillows, fresh flowers in your room, a generous breakfast (stuffed French toast is a specialty). An upstairs suite with shared bath and kitchenette is ideal (and inexpensive) for two couples traveling together; the main-floor guest room also has a private bath.

Grant House

2525 3rd Street, Baker City, OR 97814 ☎ (541) 523-6685

You'd expect a B&B run by a moonlighting school librarian to be a quiet retreat with well-stocked bookshelves. But no need to tiptoe; musical instruments are scattered about the shared living room, and guests are welcome to play them— or jam with their own. The three upstairs guest rooms, named after nearby mines, are pleasantly decorated and share a large bathroom.

Depot Inn

179 S Mill Street (PO Box 36), Sumpter, OR 97877
☎ (800) 390-2522 or (541) 894-2522

Its peeled-log exterior helps the Depot Inn blend in with the authentic mining-town ambience of Sumpter, but the boxy design gives away its true nature: it's a motel, pure and simple. Rooms are clean and nicely furnished, with two queen beds (just one in the wheelchair-accessible room). As such, they provide a pleasant base from which to explore the ghost and near-ghost towns hidden in the hills hereabouts.

Fish House Inn

110 Franklin Avenue, Dayville, OR 97825 ☎ (888) 286-3474 or (541) 987-2124

Former San Diegans Mike and Denise Smith have turned a 90-year-old Crafts-man-style home into a welcoming B&B in this remote outpost on the John Day River. Three guest rooms (one with private bath) are tucked into the attic; two larger rooms, both with private bath, are housed in a cottage a short walk across a manicured lawn. The decor is decidedly Piscean, from one room's seashell-covered reading lamp to another's salmon pink walls. Look forward to a generous breakfast in summer, something less elaborate in winter, and excellent coffee year-round.

Southeastern High Desert

T he lovely thing about southeastern Oregon is that there's a lot to look at and not much to buy, except gas (and you should buy it in Burns). Yes, this is sage land—dry, desolate cattle country—branded on the American consciousness by hundreds of Western movies.

But suddenly, just south of Burns, the geography changes dramatically. The tumbleweed terrain is transformed into the verdant marshlands that surround Harney and Malheur Lakes, marshes that are a vital stop for migrating birds. Beyond the lakes, massive Steens Mountain rises abruptly to almost 10,000 feet. East of this formidable escarpment, nothing remains of the former Alvord Lake except a vast wasteland of sunbleached borax.

Exploring

Malheur National Wildlife Refuge, 32 miles south of Burns, is one of the major bird refuges in the United States—184,000 acres of marshland and lakes. It is an important stop for migrating waterfowl in spring and fall, and is the breeding ground for magnificent sandhill cranes (with wingspans approaching 100 inches), trumpeter swans, and many other waterbirds, shorebirds, and songbirds. We recommend visiting in April, when you can experience the sandhill's courtship dance. A migratory festival in early April provides tours, entertainment, and informational exhibits. Call the ranger station in Hines for information; (541)573-7292.

You can drive through the refuge, although it's more rewarding to see it on foot or by mountain bike. Make your first stop Malheur's free museum (32 miles south of Burns, off Hwy 205;

(541)493-2612). The museum is open year-round and provides an excellent primer on the birds that frequent the refuge. Bring your binoculars.

On the south end of the refuge is the beautiful little town of **Frenchglen**—which virtually rolls up and closes come the dead of winter. This is where you'll find the only eats, sleeps, and gas around, courtesy of the Frenchglen Hotel and the neighboring Frenchglen Mercantile. Frenchglen's biggest attraction is **Steens Mountain**, the world's largest block fault, created by volcanic lava flows and glacial action. The massive mountain rises gently from the west to an elevation of 9,670 feet, and then drops sharply to the white borax expanses of the **Alvord Desert** in the east.

During the summer and early fall, the **Steens Mountain National Back Country Byway** offers a road to the summit—

a 66-mile, recently "chip-sealed" gravel loop that starts and ends at Frenchglen. It's a slow drive, so pack a picnic (stop at the Frenchglen Hotel or the Mercantile for goodies to go), and plan for an all-day excursion. The road is rough and rocky in places—particularly along a 4-mile section on the south end—with steep, narrow stretches (and no guardrails). Four-wheel-drive vehicles are recommended but not vital; RV drivers might reconsider entirely. The loop is generally open from July through October, depending on snow conditions, though sections may open earlier or later.

En route around Steens Mountain, look for **Alvord Hot Springs**, located about 100 yards east of the road, in the Alvord Desert. The springs are on the private property of the Alvord Ranch, but they're open to the respectful public. At the northeastern side of Steens, Mann Lake is reportedly loaded with Lahottan cutthroat trout. For more information on Steens, contact the Bureau of Land Management (HC 74-12533, Hwy 20, Hines, OR 97738; (541)573-4400).

The **Hart Mountain National Antelope Refuge** lies southwest of Malheur. These 275,000 acres were set aside in 1936 to provide seasonal forage for one of the West's largest herds of **pronghorn antelope**. These fleet creatures can usually be seen wandering the sagebrush lands on the east side of Hart Mountain. They range widely, so the buck you saw in the morning could be the same one you see in the evening 20 miles away. Pronghorn antelopes can be seen throughout the southeast Oregon high desert, sometimes singly but other times in herds of 50 or more. Spotting antelopes is usually more a matter of being alert to your surroundings rather than actively stalking them.

Roads between the wetlands and the base of the mountain are good places to spot Hart Mountain's **California bighorn sheep**. The best way to locate bighorn sheep is to leave the road that climbs up the mountain to the refuge headquarters and drive either north or south along the western base of the mountain. Stop frequently along the way and use 10-power binoculars, plus lots of patience, to spot bands of sheep. Watch either for movement by the sheep or for their white rump patches, which give them away in an otherwise camouflaging environment. The Hart Mountain escarpment rises 3,600 feet, so even the most powerful binoculars won't locate sheep that perch just below the mountain's rim.

Hart Mountain also provides habitat for mule deer, coyote, black-tailed jackrabbit, sage grouse, golden eagles, and red-tailed hawks. The refuge headquarters, (541)947-3315, is in room 301 of the post office in Lakeview, but most visitors stop at the field station, 65 miles northeast of Lakeview, on the Lakeview to Steens byway.

Cheap Eats

Frenchglen Mercantile
Downtown Frenchglen ☎ (541) 493-2738

Folks peruse the Frenchglen Mercantile's deli case by day and come away with such picnic fare as pasta salad or house-roasted turkey and Black Forest ham sandwiched on homemade bread. Do-it-yerselfers buy meats and cheeses by the pound and hit the Steens Mountain loop with lunch fixins' in hand. In the evening, the Mercantile's adjoining 30-seat Buckaroo Room welcomes all comers for a full-service, sit-down-and-relax-awhile dinner. Hosts Missy and Lance Litchy offer a full-service bar and—whoa, Nelly!—a real wine list, as well as a short (very short) menu featuring such reasonably priced, fussy-for-around-here entrees as grilled filet mignon, lemon-rosemary chicken, and fresh poached salmon. Closed mid-November through mid-March.

Cheap Sleeps

Best Western Ponderosa

577 W Monroe Street, Burns, OR 97720 ☎ (800) 528-1234 or (541) 573-2047

Blessed with a swimming pool to cool you off after a hot day's drive, the Ponderosa might be the best motel in this part of the state (it's virtually the only one, too). Burns is the closest sizable town to the Malheur National Wildlife Refuge. Pets are welcome (for a $10 fee); prices for two start at about $50 (and peak at about $75 for an executive suite with its own living room). A continental breakfast is part of the deal, and dinner and drinks can be had in the adjoining Pine Room.

Malheur Field Station

3 miles west of headquarters, Malheur National Wildlife Refuge
(HC 72, Box 260, Princeton, OR 97721) ☎ (541) 493-2629

Call well ahead for fall and spring reservations at the fun-but-funky Malheur National Wildlife Refuge field station. Schools and conferences often fill the place—particularly in April and May—and holiday weekends are usually booked way in advance. This old government training camp offers dorm bunks ($18 per person) as well as more accommodating two- and three-bedroom trailers (about $36 for two). The nine trailers provide comfortable living spaces with fully equipped kitchens. Either way, bring your own bedding and towels. The cafeteria-style dining room's a great bargain: seven bucks buys a breakfast that's not for the birds, a little less buys a sack lunch, and a little more fills you at dinner ($20 covers three squares). The dining room is closed October through March, but the station is open to overnighters all year, with limited accommodation in the winter months.

Diamond Hotel

PO Box 10, Diamond, OR 97722 ☎ (541) 493-1898

Twelve miles east of Highway 207, Diamond's handful of residents keep the ghosts at bay. In the early '90s, Judy and Jerry Santillie, formerly of the Frenchglen Hotel, remodeled this building and opened it to those exploring Malheur territory. Folks stop here for gas, and late in the afternoon it even doubles as a local watering hole. The five small bedrooms upstairs share two baths and two sitting areas; three have queen-size beds (and prices that go beyond our range).

Judy is a former ranch cook, and her boardinghouse-style dinners (available at a single, reserved 6:30pm seating to hotel guests) could satisfy any ranch hand. Expect such hearty fare as potatoes, green vegetables, salad, homemade bread, and all the tenderloin you can possibly eat at very reasonable prices. Open mid-March through mid-November.

McCoy Creek Inn
HC 72, Box 11, Diamond, OR 97722
☎ (541) 493-2131 (days), (541) 493-2440 (evenings)

You'll find refuge among the meadows, creeks, and streams here on this working ranch in McCoy Canyon, as do the wildlife that call "Oregon's Outback" home. The inn—a converted turn-of-the-century structure accessed by a small private road—offers three guest rooms as well as a separate guest house (the ranch's former bunkhouse), all with private bath. While the rates stretch the budget limit, they do include a full breakfast. Lunch and dinner are served by reservation only, to guests and nonguests alike. Children will be charmed by the ranch animals and are invited to help feed them; their folks will enjoy soaking in a hot tub, hiking the nearby trails, and watching for migratory birds. Closed from the end of October to April 1.

Frenchglen Hotel
General Delivery, Frenchglen, OR 97736 ☎ (541) 493-2825

This small, white-framed building that dates to 1916 is owned by the Oregon Parks Department State Wayside System. The historic inn has eight small, plain bedrooms upstairs with shared baths, renting for about $50 a night; room 2 is the largest, with a full and a twin bed. Nothing's very square or level here, and that's part of the charm. Downstairs you'll find a large, screened verandah and the dining room. Manager John Ross prepares good, simple meals for guests and drop-by visitors. The ranch-style dinner ($13 to $15) has only one seating (6:30pm sharp), and reservations are a must. Closed mid-November through February.

Frenchglen Mercantile
General Delivery, Frenchglen, OR 97736 ☎ (541) 493-2738

Opened in 1876 as the original company store for namesake rancher Pete French's outfit, the Mercantile was, in its day, the only stop for provisions in this part of the state. Things haven't changed a whole lot since. In 1995, Missy and Lance Litchy bought the place. They continue to pump gas and run the store and restaurant, in addition to providing cozy lodgings to adventure-seekers who have fallen in love with Steens Mountain but would rather spend the night in comfort than in camp. Four large guest rooms gussied up with antique furnishings and Indian artifacts offer hardwood floors and high ceilings, private baths with tile showers, and decks with views of the mountain and the refuge. Reservations are hard to come by, so call way in advance. Closed mid-November through mid-March.

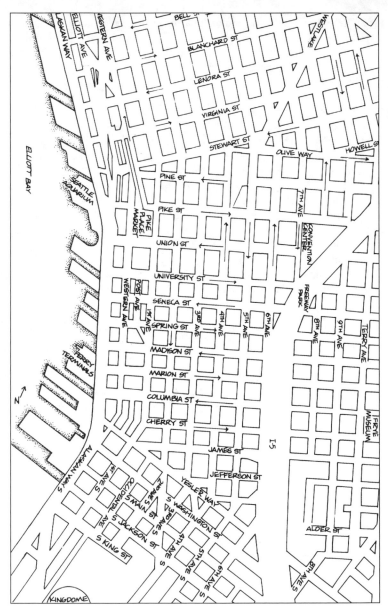

Downtown Seattle

Seattle
& the Eastside

There's something irresistible about a city where commuters travel on freeways with kayaks and bicycles on top of their cars and head for business luncheons in suits and hiking boots. Seattle offers a wonderful combination of urban amenities and access to wilderness, an enticing match that has brought the city lots of national attention. Despite the boom in the past decade, Seattle's quality of life remains very good—a fact that both natives and transplants try to keep as quiet as possible.

Seattle prides itself on cultural richness and ethnic diversity, comfortable neighborhoods, a bounty of local foods, and open, green spaces. It's a city whose theater, dance, opera, sports, and music enjoy deserved national attention, and whose inhabitants—a friendly and hardy set—exhibit a spirit not readily dampened by the fine Northwest mist. The major tourist attraction—Pike Place Market—is less for tourists than it is for locals. You haven't truly visited Seattle if you haven't stopped to sip a microbrew or a coffee at one of the city's famed establishments. A diverse nightclub scene, offering everything from grunge to R&B to country-and-western, continues to play an active role in community life. (You'd still never mistake it for New York, though—if for no other reason than the early hour at which most of the city heads off to sleep.)

Most of all, Seattle is enhanced by its proximity to all things wild and wonderful—mountains on two sides and the glimmering Puget Sound in between. Bask in a late summer evening's view—the sky turquoise and glowing orange, the Olympic Mountains casting a stark, sapphire shadow against the horizon, and a night-lit ferry heading west. You'll understand what attracts people here for vacations—and leads them to stay for life.

Access

Metro, the city's **bus** system, goes almost everywhere. Call (206)553-3000 for rider information. The bus is free until 7pm in downtown's commercial core, which is bordered by the waterfront, Interstate 5, Jackson Street to the south, and Battery Street to the north. Otherwise the fare is 85 cents within the city ($1.10 during peak hours) and $1.10 if you cross the city lines ($1.60 peak). When traveling via Metro at night, ask the driver to stop right in front of your destination—just give notice a block ahead.

Seattle-Tacoma International Airport is located 13 miles south of Seattle, barely a half-hour drive by freeway from downtown. Several Metro buses go to Sea-Tac Airport: the #174 goes from Second Avenue in downtown Seattle to the airport every half hour (a 45-minute trip), and the #194 makes a half-hour trip to Sea-Tac from the downtown bus tunnel (also every half hour). The Gray Line Airport Express, (206)626-6088, is also reasonable ($13 round trip, $7.50 one way) if you don't mind leaving from or being dropped off downtown; the shuttle stops every half hour at 10 downtown hotels. Shuttle Express, (800)487-7433 in Washington State or (206)622-1424, picks you up or drops you off at your door in Seattle or the Eastside for a somewhat higher price ($18 and up for a one-way trip); reservations are a must for departures and are a good idea for arrivals, too.

Exploring

Downtown Seattle is a good place to begin your explorations. The downtown core is bookended by two of the city's most popular attractions, Pioneer Square and Pike Place Market. In the retail core, between Third and Sixth Avenues from Stewart Street to University Street, are plenty of department stores and boutiques for window-shopping. At the glossy, centrally located mall known as **Westlake Center** (on Pine St between Fourth and Fifth Aves), upscale shops share space with a food court chock-full of cheap eats. Sixth Avenue is the headquarters for the local Planet Hollywood, Niketown, Gameworks, and other monuments to flashy consumerism.

Pioneer Square, to the south, has some of Seattle's oldest architecture, built after the fire of 1889 leveled the city. A mere $6.50 buys you an Underground Tour complete with corny humor and historical insights; (888)608-6337 or (206)682-4646. When downtown Seattle began to move northward, Pioneer Square acquired an artsy bent, housing galleries, artists' studios, and the famous Elliott Bay Book Company (101 S Main St; (206)624-6600), where free readings are held nearly

every day; call for a schedule. On the first Thursday of each month, art galleries stay open late to preview new exhibits in a free see-and-be-seen scene known (appropriately enough) as First Thursday.

A small but genuine slice of Asian culture, the **International District** is home to a number of Chinese, Japanese, Thai, Vietnamese, Philippine, and Cambodian businesses and restaurants, many of them reasonably priced. For a history of Asian immigration to the United States, including photographs and a reconstructed vintage Chinese pharmacy, visit the Wing Luke Museum (407 7th Ave S; (206)623-5124); admission is $2.50 (free on Thursdays). The International District is also a gold mine for all manner of low-cost, excellent Asian food.

The squat gray **Kingdome** watches over the International District and south Seattle like a giant clam. Construction for two new sports stadiums is under way, but the Kingdome is still the venue for the popular Seahawks and the Mariners. Tours ($5), offered mid-April through September, take you up to the highest seating level, the scoreboard, the VIP lounge, the press area, and the Royal Brougham

Sports Museum; (206)296-3126.

Today Seattle's downtown **waterfront** (Main St to Broad St along Alaskan Way) is mostly a tourist boardwalk lined with kitschy souvenir shops, harbor-tour operations, and fish 'n' chips counters. All along the waterfront, however, are opportunities to watch the busy working harbor against the stunning natural backdrop of Puget Sound. It's a worthy attraction and a fine place for an invigorating, sea-gazing stroll. Walk one direction along the waterfront and then hop aboard the waterfront **trolley** for a return ride on a quaint old streetcar that runs along Alaskan Way from Pier 70 to Main Street, a 15-minute, 85-cent ride.

Wade through the thick of the tourist boardwalk to the compact, well-designed **Seattle Aquarium** (Pier 59; (206)386-4320). There are illuminated displays and convincing re-creations of coastal and intertidal ecosystems. Follow a salmon ladder to a marvelous topside vista of Elliott Bay and the superstars of the Aquarium: the cavorting seals and the playful sea otters.

At the north end of downtown, bustling and colorful **Pike Place Market** attracts throngs of visitors in the summer and a steady stream of local devotees throughout the year. Seattleites shop the produce stands and specialty food stores as one would shop in Europe. Craftspeople—

from jewelers and quilters to T-shirt and souvenir-photo vendors—fill the other stalls, attracting the most tourists and causing the greatest traffic problems in the summer (real Seattleites don't drive through the Market). Also here is the original outlet of that now famous icon of gourmet coffee, Starbucks. Pick up a map of the Market at the information booth at First Avenue and Pike Street; (206)682-7453.

Just north and slightly east of the Market is the recently gentrified area known as **Belltown**. The streets are in various stages of development, ranging from chic stores, condominium complexes, and restaurants to little pockets of vintage Belltown, long the haunt of artists, musicians, and colorful street people. There are lots of used-clothing stores (the source of the infamous-but-on-its-way-to-defunct grunge look) and great little cafes that come and go too fast to keep up with them all. If you're ready for a splurge on a great dinner, try one of the many stylish options along First Avenue in Belltown.

The **Seattle Center** (between Denny Way and Mercer St, 1st Ave N and 5th Ave N; (206)684-8582), a 74-acre park just north of downtown, at the base of Queen Anne Hill, is the legacy of the 1962 World's Fair. Once a grounds for Indian gatherings, it's now the arts and

Cheap Tix

Discounted theater tickets for all but the most popular Seattle shows are pretty easy to come by. Many local theaters offer discounted preview tickets, decent matinee prices, and "rush" (day of show) tickets; some have special pay-what-you-will performances. Ticket/Ticket, open every day except Monday, offers same-day tickets for half price; outlets are located at Pike Place Market (First Ave and Pike St) and on the second floor of the Broadway Market (401 Broadway Ave E). You can call (206)324-2744 for general info, but you must visit Ticket/Ticket in person to find out what's available that day. (They also offer discounted dance, comedy, and concert tickets.) In summer, there are dozens of free lunchtime performances of music and local theater at various outdoor locations throughout Seattle (mostly downtown; check local newspapers for listings).

Summer Festivals

Seattle's summer begins and ends with two of the area's most popular festivals, both held at Seattle Center. The free **Northwest Folklife Festival**, *held on Memorial Day weekend, is a gathering of diverse folk-art traditions (dance, music, crafts, and food). It's the largest folk festival in the nation; (206)684-7300.* **Bumbershoot**, *held on Labor Day weekend, includes many of the same street performers you'll see at Folklife, but this multiarts festival has a considerably more frenzied feel—perhaps because of the plethora of local and national musicians who perform simultaneously during the four-day event (Sheryl Crow, David Byrne, and Beck were some recent headliners). Bumbershoot tickets are $10 per day (free for kids and $1 for seniors); (206)281-7788.*

entertainment hub of the city, and—even more significant to visitors—home of the **Space Needle**. If it's a clear day, the 520-foot elevator ride up to the observation deck provides sufficient thrills, a history mini-lesson, and a heck of a view for your $7 ($6 for seniors, $3.50 for kids).

Just southwest of the Space Needle is **Pacific Science Center**, (206) 443-2880, which features engrossing hands-on science and math exhibits for school-age children, traveling exhibits aimed at all age groups, and an IMAX theater. Also at the Seattle Center are the KeyArena (home court of the Seattle SuperSonics basketball team) and the Opera House (which accommodates the Seattle Opera and Pacific Northwest Ballet). Parking at the Seattle Center can be a problem; one way to circumvent this is to ride the 90-second **Monorail** from downtown (at Westlake Center, 400 Pine St), which drops you off at the Center House, a cavernous building with a selection of ethnic fast food.

Capitol Hill, directly east of downtown (bounded by Bellevue Ave, Pine St, E Roy St, and 15th Ave E) is the haunt of hip urbanites and punk-fashionable youth, Seattle's unofficial gay district, and the one place in town where the sidewalks are still filled after 10pm. Along the spine of this popular neighborhood lies **Broadway**, the closest Seattle comes to the spirit of New York's St. Mark's Place. Nearly written off to urban decay, Broad-

way has experienced a dramatic revival in recent decades, establishing it as the heady center for the city's trendy alternative boutique and street culture. Vintage clothing, chic apparel, espresso, and housewares predominate, as do a multitude of restaurants.

Watch boats raised and lowered at the **Hiram M. Chittenden Locks** (3015 NW 54th St; (206)783-7059) just north of downtown; more than 100,000 boats go by each year on their way to or from the "water elevator." Across the waterway, the falls generated by a **fish ladder** entice fighting salmon (sadly dwindling in number) en route to their spawning grounds in Lake Washington and Cascade streams. You can watch the fishes' progress from a viewing area with windows onto the ladder.

Fremont, the self-proclaimed "Center of the Universe," is easily reached by bus or bicycle from downtown. Here you'll find an irreverent attitude and such local artworks as the Troll (a hungry ogre under a bridge, preparing to eat a real Volkswagen). One man's trash is another's treasure at the weekly Sunday market (held at N 34th St and Evanston Ave N). Inexpensive eateries and drinkeries abound in this neighborhood—as do quirky shops and boutiques worthy of a day's browsing. RedHook (3400 Phinney Ave N; (206)548-8000), a local favorite and one of the original microbrews, opens its brewery here to the public every day for tours. Younger and older folks peacefully coexist at the brewery's appealing, smokefree Trolleyman Pub next door.

Lake Union, the body of fresh water connected to Puget Sound at the Hiram M. Chittenden Locks, is the spot for water recreation, drawing kayakers, sailors, canoeists, and others who rent traditional wooden vessels from the Center for Wooden Boats (1010 Valley St; (206)382-2628). Something of a museum, the center harbors an eclectic collection of boats; wandering is free, and rentals don't cost much. From the water, the best views of Seattle's charming houseboat communities are along Fairview Avenue E (on the east side of the lake).

Rent a canoe from the University of Washington Waterfront Activities Center, behind Husky Stadium, for $5 per hour; (206)543-9433, and paddle over to the east arm of Lake Union, through Portage Bay and the Montlake Cut, to enter the **Washington Park Arboretum**. Foster Island is a great place for a picnic and bird watching (but beware the uninhibited ducks and geese). If you can, time your visit to the Arboretum's 200-acre preserve to coincide with the blooming of the azaleas in the spring. Meet at the Arboretum Visitor Center (these folks know their plants!) for free tours on Sun-

days and for other information about the park (2300 Arboretum Dr E; (206)543-8800). The peaceful Japanese Garden ($2.50), with its pagoda, carp pond, and teahouse, is open March 1 through November 30; (206)684-4725. Spring cherry blossoms explode on the nearby campus of the **University of Washington** (UW, pronounced "U-Dub"). The park-like, accessible campus makes for a lovely stroll. On clear days, look for Mount Rainier at the end of the area on campus called Rainier Vista. The commercial strip along University Way NE (affectionately U-dubbed "The Ave") is Seattle's answer to San Francisco's Haight-Ashbury—with the requisite panhandling youth, arty cafes, musty used bookstores, and a multitude of everything a starving student might need to survive the university years.

North of the University District, a series of parks provides the city with a green necklace. Ravenna Park extends to **Green Lake** along a grassy boulevard popular with joggers and dogs. The paths around Green Lake, though overpopulated with runners, bikers, Rollerbladers, dogs, and strollers, are still a fine place to exercise your right to exercise; the lake is one of the best spots for people-watching in the city, too. In-line skates and bikes can be rented at Gregg's Greenlake Cycle (7007 Woodlawn Ave NE; (206)523-1822).

Ferry to Bainbridge Island

Riding a ferry is the best (and most inexpensive) way to enjoy the sea breeze, Seattle's skyline, and the grandeur of Puget Sound and its surrounding mountain ranges. Ferries to Bainbridge Island leave regularly from Pier 52 (Alaskan Wy and Marion St); call Washington State Ferries, (206)464-6400, for more info. Walk-on passengers pay $3.50, round trip; bringing a bike costs an extra 50¢; and a car and driver pay $5.90 each way. The island's only town, Winslow, is an easy walk from the ferry dock. With a little more time, take your bike (or car) and explore a bit more thoroughly. Look for Fay Bainbridge State Park on the island's northeast corner, with a vast view of Seattle from the beach (there are about 25 tent sites here too); Fort Ward, a prime spot for hikes and picnics; and Bloedel Reserve, a 150-acre parklike estate (reservations essential; (206)842-7631).

Film Festivals

Seattleites have acquired a reputation as serious film buffs. It's no wonder, then, that the city's film festivals garner considerable national attention as well as enthusiastic local support. The Seattle International Film Festival (various locations; (206)324-9996), held for three weeks every May and June, has been bringing an impressively wide range of movies to town for over two decades. Other festivals include the Eastside International Film Festival and the Women in Cinema Film Festival. The Seattle Art Museum runs an ongoing film series that changes throughout the year.

Green Lake Community Center (7201 E Greenlake Dr N; (206)684-0780) houses a pool and one of Green Lake's best-kept secrets: a drop-in play center ($1 per child), where tykes can tire themselves out playing in and on child-size houses, castles, cars, bikes, and such—the perfect antidote for those rainy days. Children must be supervised; open late on weekdays, closed on Sundays.

Next to Green Lake is the **Woodland Park Zoo**. For the most part, the zoo is wonderfully open, providing animals with enough room to dispel the caged-cat atmosphere. Elephants wander a replica of a Thai logging camp, while lions (not always visible) roam a modified African savannah (the antelopes and giraffes, thankfully, have their own area). Don't miss the gorillas; 5500 Phinney Avenue N, (206)684-4800.

Favorite **parks** in the city include Golden Gardens and the Shilshole Marina, just north of Ballard, with its beach and marina view. To the south, Discovery Park in the Magnolia neighborhood offers a bit of wildlife in the city, providing a home for a couple of bald eagles as well as gold-finches, red-tailed hawks, and various falcons. Take one of the trails winding through the park, go on an interpretive nature walk, or explore the remnants of Fort Lawton (a barracks house and training field), Discovery Park's former incarnation; (206)386-4236. In West Seattle, Alki Beach is packed on sunny weekend afternoons with crowds enjoying the panoramic Sound views and salty breezes.

Art and culture lovers won't feel deprived in Seattle. The **Seattle Art Museum** (100 University St; (206)654-3100) boasts highly original architecture and a fantastic African mask exhibit. Outside the museum stands the imposing profile of Jonathan Borofsky's *Hammering Man*, which has taken its place in the Seattle skyline. The **Seattle Asian Art Museum**, in Volunteer Park (14th Ave E and E Prospect St; (206)654-3100), has one of the most extraordinary collections of Asian art in the country. If used within two days, your admission ticket from either of the two Seattle art museums is good for free admission at the other; or visit on the first Thursday of the month, when both museums are free.

The Frye Art Museum (704 Terry Ave; (206)622-9250) houses some unexpected treasures from European artists, and admission is always free. Visit the recently renovated Burke Museum (NE 45th St and 17th Ave NE; (206)543-5590) on the UW campus for natural history and archaeology exhibits; admission is $5.50. For contemporary art, the UW's newly expanded art museum, the Henry Art Gallery (on the western edge of the campus at NE 41st St and 15th Ave NE; (206)543-2280) offers airy installations both temporary and permanent; it's free to high school and college students with valid ID, and to all comers each Thursday from 5pm to 8pm.

Movies are just two bucks at the UA Cinema 150 (6th Ave and Blanchard St; (206)443-9591).

For a thorough guide to what's going on around town, pick up a free copy of *The Stranger*, an alternative paper focusing on the arts and music scene and geared toward the twentysomething crowd, or *Seattle Weekly*, a more adult alternative covering the arts and local politics.

Bellevue is the booming heart of the "Eastside"—the former suburbs of Seattle, east of Lake Washington that now stand on their own. As many commuters now leave Seattle in the morning for work on the Eastside as make the traditional suburb-to-Seattle trek, causing, incidentally, some serious bridge-crossing standstills whatever the direction. This erstwhile hamlet can now rightfully be called Seattle's sister city, and boasts its own downtown skyline, an ever-growing population, and more shop-till-you-drop options than you'd care to shake a credit card at. At the core is Bellevue Place, a hotel, restaurant, and shopping complex. Nearby, the **Bellevue Square** megamall hosts Nordstrom and hundreds of other stores, but it's also one of the first malls in the country to house a museum—the Bellevue Art Museum, specializing in Northwest crafts; (425)454-6021. Admission is $3; the museum is free on Tuesdays.

The city of **Kirkland**'s comfortable downtown on Lake Washington's Moss Bay is a popular strolling ground. Art galleries, restaurants (including a number of good inexpensive options), and boutiques line the main street. Several restaurants look out over boats docked at the marina. Grab a latte and walk a block to the waterfront park, where ducks beg scraps and dodge children on the sandy beach. On Yarrow Bay, at the south end of town, lies Carillon Point, a glitzy hotel and shopping complex lining a round, red-brick courtyard with views of the lake and the Olympic Mountains in the distance. To the north, just outside of Kirkland at St. Edward State Park, spectacular rolling trails amble through old stands of Douglas fir and Western red cedar, eventually winding up on the lakefront.

The suburbs have caught up with **Woodinville**—a formerly rural outback—paving the dirt roads and lining them with strip malls. Some of the country ambience remains, however, especially to the east, where Woodinville fades into the dairy farms of the Snoqualmie Valley. Woodinville's claim to fame is **Chateau Ste. Michelle** (14111 NE 145th, Woodinville; (425)488-3300), the state's largest winery (though many other wineries and microbrewies now dot the landscape). The grapes come from Eastern Washington, but experimental vineyards are on-site, and tours of the operation, complete with tastings, run daily every half hour between 10am and 5pm. Just across the street from Ste. Michelle is **Columbia Winery** (14030 NE 145th, Woodinville; (425)488-2776), the state's oldest premium-wine company. Columbia offers tours on weekends between 10am and 4pm, and the tasting room is open daily from 10am to 7pm.

Traveling Back in Time

Throughout the year on various Saturdays and Sundays, you can take a ride on an historic Metro bus; some excursions explore the city, while others venture to such places as the quaint small town of Snohomish, north of Seattle. The Metro Employees Historic Vehicle Association sponsors day trips, with adult fares generally $6 or less. Children under 12 ride free, and there are reduced senior fares. For info on upcoming trips, listen to the recorded message at (206)633-4590.

Major Attractions—Cheaper!

*Visitors (or locals!) who plan to visit some of the major attractions around town in a short period of time should consider purchasing a **City Pass**. The Pass saves you about 50 percent on the admission for the following: the Museum of Flight, Pacific Science Center, Seattle Aquarium, Seattle Art Museum, Space Needle, and Woodland Park Zoo. Adult passes are $24, kids passes cost $15—both are valid for a week and can be purchased at any of the locations included on the City Pass.*

Once a bucolic suburban destination, **Redmond** is now known worldwide as the site of the mighty Microsoft's headquarters, but this city at the north end of Lake Sammamish is also the hub of a lot of local (and national) cycling activity. The Marymoor Velodrome in Marymoor Park is a 400-meter concrete track that was built for the 1976 Olympic trials and draws world-class bicyclists for twice-weekly races from mid-May to September. On the north shore of Lake Sammamish, the park is a huge expanse of ball fields and semiwild grassland that makes for great bird-watching. On weekends, hundreds of dog owners bring their pets to the vast and legally leashless dog run in the fields along the Sammamish River.

The center of the old coal-mining town of **Issaquah** still resembles small-town America, complete with a butcher shop, a well-respected community theater, and a working dairy. On good days, Mount Rainier appears between the hills that form the town's southern and eastern borders. The Issaquah Farmers Market, adjacent to the community center (at the intersection of First and Bush) is held from 9am to 3pm Saturdays from mid-April to mid-October. Gilman Village (on Gilman Boulevard, Issaquah; (425)392-6802) is a shopping complex with a twist: the developers refurnished old farmhouses, a barn, and a feed store, then filled them with craft and clothing shops, restaurants, and a woodworking gallery. On the edge of town, Boehm's Chocolates (255 Gilman Blvd, Issaquah; (425)392-6652) still dips its chocolates by hand; tours are available for groups (reservations are needed). **Lake Sammamish State Park**, between town and the lake, offers swimming and boat access. **Tiger Mountain**, the sprawling 13,000-acre state forest that looms to the east, is a favorite weekend destination for hikers and mountain bikers. Trails wind through alder and evergreen forests and past old coal-mine shafts.

Cheap Eats

Buca di Beppo
701 9th Avenue N, Seattle ☎ (206) 244-2288

Show up with lots of friends, the patience of Job, the appetite of a sumo wrestler, and an abundant sense of humor, and you will have so much fun you won't know what hit you. This "concept" Southern Italian restaurant is all party-down and Italian-American kitsch—from the religious icons and walls plastered with photos, to the bar decorated with Chianti bottles, to the Dean

Martin version of "That's Amore" that'll have you swaying while waiting for a table and then for your garlicky, oversize portions of family-style chow. The food's as good as it is plentiful, with foot-long pizzas, baseball-size meatballs atop mounds of spaghetti, a slab of lasagne that'd fill a shoebox, and a heap of chicken cacciatore.

Dick's Drive-In
111 NE 45th Street, Seattle (and multiple locations) ☎ (206) 632-5125

Seattle's homegrown answer to the burger-and-fries culture, Dick's is a local institution in the University District complete with horrid orange decor and paper-hatted servers cheerfully doling out Dick's Deluxe redux to the bet-you-can't-eat-just-one crowd. The food tastes better if you arrive in a car—especially one that's equipped with fins (besides, only the Queen Anne location offers seating). Hand-dipped chocolate, vanilla, and strawberry milk shakes are a treat for the ice cream lover.

El Puerco Lloron
1501 Western Avenue, Seattle ☎ (206) 624-0541

This place transports you back to that cafe in Tijuana, the one with the screaming hot pink and aquamarine walls and the bent "Cerveza Superior" tables. Belly up to the cafeteria line, place your order, and fight for a table—in warm weather, those outdoors are as hard to find as free parking spots. Try the taquitos plate, three excellent masa corn tortillas rolled around a filling and served with rice, beans, and a scallion. The chiles rellenos are fresh and bright with flavor, and the unadulterated guacamole's worth the additional splurge. Pick up lemonade or Mexican beer at the end of the counter.

Fremont Noodle House
3411 Fremont Avenue N, Seattle ☎ (206) 547-1550

Finally, a Thai restaurant whose atmosphere can compete with its food for your sensory pleasure. A short menu offers fragrant noodle-based soups and sautés and simple rice dishes spiked with various meats, seafood, and vegetables. Among the half-dozen appetizers is *mieng hahm*, a most sensually appealing starter of toasted coconut, ginger, Thai chile, peanuts, red onion and lime—all meant to be folded into the accompanying *bai cha plu* (dark green leaves). Service is swift and polite.

Gravity Bar
415 Broadway Avenue E, Seattle ☎ (206) 325-7186

Meet George Jetson. His boy Elroy. Daughter Judy. Jane, his wife. Need we say more about Seattle's slickest vegetarian restaurant and juice bar on Capitol Hill, with its conical tables of galvanized metal and green frosted glass lit from within for the ultimate Jetsons effect? Entrees are luscious, healthful, and beautifully presented: mounds of brown rice and steamed vegetables with a glistening lemon tahini sauce; chapatis rolled with hummus and fresh vegetables; miso soup with buckwheat noodles. The freshest of fresh juices can get expensive, but indulge. You'll feel like a million bucks later.

Musashi's Sushi & Grill
1400 N 45th Street, Seattle ☎ (206) 633-0212

It's cramped, crowded, and easy to find. It's one of the city's favorite you-can-afford-it Japanese restaurants, and there's often a line stretching out onto the sidewalk, so prepare to wait. The menu is limited to a few well-chosen items, plus sushi—smoked salmon and yellowtail, octopus, great California rolls—that don't cost half a week's wages for a few ethereal bites. Many loyal Wallingford neighborhood residents come for the curries, others for the chicken teriyaki, and others for the inexpensive, beautifully presented bento boxes. The congenial atmosphere is as praiseworthy as the food.

Panos Kleftiko
815 5th Avenue N, Seattle ☎ (206) 301-0393

Panos Marinos is the heart and soul (and host/chef) of this traditional Greek taverna in a small, cozy storefront a few blocks north of Seattle Center. Come with a fistful of friends and cram your table with *mezedhes* or "little dishes" (there are 25 choices, priced from $1.50–$5.25), several servings of warm pita bread (the best we've had anywhere), and a glass or three of retsina. Everything's tasty, but we especially love the *melitzanasalata* (a cold salad of roasted eggplant, tomatoes, and herbs) and the spicy meatballs. Arrive early if you have tickets to a show; Panos encourages lingering and doesn't take reservations. Open only for dinner.

Pecos Pit Barbecue
2260 1st Avenue S, Seattle ☎ (206) 623-0629

It's open only for weekday lunch, but oh what a lunch! This pit stop south of the Kingdome is worth a trip in order to give yourself over to sheer, carnivorous indulgence. Step up to the window and order your fun-on-a-bun: a sliced beef brisket, pork, Pecos beef, ham, or link sandwich. Ask them to "spike it" and you'll get a link tucked into your already meat-filled treasure. Choose from mild, medium, or hot sauce, but be warned: hot means "Whoo, hot!" Be sure to order a side of spicy baked beans before heading off to claim a picnic table.

Red Mill Burgers
312 N 67th Street, Seattle ☎ (206) 783-6362

In 1994, siblings Babe and John Shepherd opened Red Mill in a little corner shop in the Greenwood neighborhood, immediately attracting crowds of worshippers who came for one of their 18 varieties of the all-American favorite. Within months, they expanded into an adjoining space to accommodate the hordes. Now they own the building. This is not a fast-food joint, but the wait is worth it, as you'll see when you sink your teeth into a burger topped with thick slices of pepper bacon, anointed with a smoky housemade mayo, and sandwiched between a big, warm bun with the freshest of lettuce and tomatoes. Those who don't do red meat will find a terrific array of veggie and chicken burgers. Don't miss the killer onion rings. Knock 'em back with a milk shake.

Pike Place Market Cheap Eats

*This mouthwatering mecca is enough to make a droolin' fool out of anyone.
Sure, the Market is home to a ton of gorgeous produce and a world of expensive restaurants, but the stalls and shops host myriad stops for inexpensive quick eats—sure to soothe the savage stomach-growl. You won't want to miss **Piroshky Piroshky** (sweet and savory Russian pastries, fashioned while you watch); **Chicken Valley**, whose daily lunch special (a bag of excellent crispy fried chicken and jojos) costs less than $3; **Jack's Fish Spot** (seafood-rich cioppino); **Mee Sum Pastry** (oven-fresh humbao); the **Incredible Link** (Louisiana links make for fiery fun on a bun); and **World Class Chili** (what a bowl o' red!). Maps of the Market are available at the information booth at First Avenue and Pike Street; (206)682-7453.*

Saigon Bistro
1032 S Jackson Street, Seattle ☎ (206)329-4939

The light, airy Saigon Bistro is a cut above the many other cafes found along Jackson Street's Little Saigon. The open kitchen lends the room life. The menu's many options reflect the South Vietnamese style of cookery, and everything here is prepared with care. A signature dish is *bun mang vit*, the glorification of soup and salad: a light soup of noodles in duck stock on one side, and a duck and cabbage salad with sweet, pungent ginger sauce on the other. Many dishes can be ordered in cold- and hot-weather versions: with dry noodles, fragrant broth, or roll-your-own rice pancakes served with an array of fresh herbs.

Shanghai Garden
524 6th Avenue S, Seattle ☎ (206)625-1689

Owner/chef Hua Te Su attracts diners from every Chinese province with regional dishes that change seasonally. The menu is vast and filled with exotica such as black-moss-fungus soup, sautéed hog maw, and fish-head casserole. Come prepared to be wowed by anything made with pea vines or with the chef's special hand-shaved noodles. Try them in what we're sure will be the best chow mein you'll ever eat. This might be the only Chinese restaurant in town where desserts should not be missed (go for the fried ice cream).

Siam on Broadway
616 Broadway Avenue E, Seattle ☎ (206)324-0892

Among Seattle's multitude of Thai restaurants, tiny Siam wins the popularity contest, hands down. Working the woks and burners in a tiny open kitchen fronted by counter seating, a quartet of women moves with the utmost grace, portioning meats and vegetables, dipping them into salty potions. They produce, among other flavorful dishes, the city's best *tom kah gai*—the chicken soup spicy with chiles, sour with lemongrass, and soothed with coconut milk. The menu doesn't stray far from the Bangkok standards, but the dishes created by the deft hands in the kitchen are distinctive. Sit at the counter and enjoy the show, or wait for one of the (too few) tables in back.

Taco del Mar

1336 1st Avenue, Seattle (and multiple locations) ☎ **(206) 623-8741**

It started as a single Madison Street takeoff on San Francisco's Mission-style burrito shop. Now there's a Taco del Mar in every 'hood in town. Famed for their fish tacos, brothers James and John Schmidt continue their expansion (as do their gigantic burritos, once they hit your gut). Vegetarian options are available, and veg-head or no, you can choose to accent your burrito with refried or whole beans. Order a jumbo or a super (to make 'em even bigger, add guacamole, sour cream, and cheese), help yourself to a stack of napkins, and then go make a mess of yourself. You won't need to eat again for a week.

Tandoor

5024 University Way NE, Seattle ☎ **(206) 523-7477**

This little room is so bare, one suspects that the owners are conducting a sensory-deprivation experiment. Then your meal arrives. Tandoor serves exquisite and reliable Indian food with an emphasis on tandoori-style cooking. A good introduction is chicken tikka masala, tender and delicious. Also recommended is the eggplant bharta. Eggplant is roasted, mashed, and then sautéed with onions—like a dish from a fantasy dinner. The side dishes here are tasty as well: the basil and garlic naan is chewy with a hint of oil, and the rice pulao is fragrant and perfectly prepared.

Three Girls Bakery

Pike Place Market, Seattle ☎ **(206) 622-1045**

Stop by any day around noon, and the crowd around the L-shaped lunch counter will likely be three hungry locals and a couple of displaced New Yorkers deep. Sandwiches don't get a whole lot better than this, and "whole" is the operative word here, 'cause there ain't no halves, as these wisecracking architects of meat and cheese will gladly tell you. There's soup—nothing fancy, but filling and hot—and a meatloaf sandwich just like Mother used to make. Order bakery fixings at the take-out window. Open for breakfast and lunch only.

Trattoria Mitchelli

84 Yesler Way, Seattle ☎ **(206) 623-3885**

Mediocrity has never had a more appealing backdrop than this, the original "Trat" in Pioneer Square. Owner Dany Mitchell (the self-proclaimed "Papa Mitchelli") has earnestly built himself an empire of restaurants that serve good-enough Italian food. This one continues to outshine them all. Yes, the fare is often mediocre, but it's dependable, and this is a place where you can host an impromptu party in the bar or restaurant at almost any time of night (it's open till 4am). Some dishes are even quite good—say, the ravioli in garlic, the pizzas, anything made with veal, the Italian frittatas, and the cheesy omelets.

Two Bells Tavern

2313 4th Avenue, Seattle ☎ **(206) 441-3050**

Belltown's starving artists tried not to tell anyone about the excellent, cheap burgers at the funky Two Bells, but word got out and now the tavern is packed all the time with an eclectic crowd, gathering in common worship of the burger.

It's big and juicy, smothered in onions and cheese, served on a sourdough roll with your choice of side orders, including a rich, chunky potato salad. Another favorite is the hot beer-sausage sandwich. This food is so full of flavor and freshness and goes so well with the beer that you won't care about getting mustard all over your face.

Noble Court

1644 140th NE, Bellevue ☎ **(425) 641-6011**

This restaurant is a favorite with the Eastside's many Chinese residents who show up on weekends for what most consider to be the best dim sum on either side of the Lake Washington bridges. The menu ranges from standard kung pao and fried rice to the more exotic shark's fin soup, stewed abalone, and bird's-nest-with-crabmeat soup. Live tanks at the entrance display fish and crustaceans ready for a little black bean sauce.

Armadillo Barbecue

13109 NE 175th Street, Woodinville ☎ **(425) 481-1417**

Leave refinement behind when you enter this West Texas barbecue joint plopped down in the wilds of Woodinville. Brothers Bob and Bruce Gill serve up their own brand of perverse humor along with tender, lean pork and extra-moist chicken, thoroughly and powerfully smoked, with a rich hot-sauce tang, and sides of molasses-heavy beans and cakey corn bread. It all adds up to a fine Texas feast. Sit at the counter and you can jaw with the cooks, sip one of 40 beers, and order a "Snake Plate," which gives you "three bucks worth o' stuff," for $4.

Cheap Sleeps

The Bacon Mansion

959 Broadway E, Seattle, WA 98102 ☎ **(800) 240-1864 or (206) 329-1864**

Built by Cecil Bacon in 1909, this Tudor mansion is now a fine bed and breakfast, admittedly beyond our budget price range but still a good deal. Eight rooms in the main guest house (five with private baths) are appointed with antiques. The basement Garden Room (which stays pleasantly cool in summer) has a kitchenette. The unique Carriage House, a separate, two-story building, is appropriate for a small family or two couples. Rates include an expanded continental breakfast.

The College Inn Guest House

4000 University Way NE, Seattle, WA 98105 ☎ **(206) 633-4441**

Wood trim, window seats, antiques, and pastel comforters create a cozy if somewhat spartan atmosphere in this hospitable inn designed along the lines of a European pension. Housed in a renovated 1909 Tudor building, it's in the heart of the lively University District, with a cafe and rathskeller (be warned: late-night noise travels quite readily into rooms on the west side). Each room has a sink but no toilet, TV, or radio. Bathrooms reminiscent of a college dorm, with rows of showers and plenty of cold tiles (but clean at that), are found at the end of each hall. A living room is tucked away on the fourth floor, where a generous continental breakfast is served.

Green Tortoise Backpackers Guest House
1525 2nd Avenue, Seattle, WA 98101 ☎ (206) 340-1222

The no-curfew Tortoise has kitchen and laundry facilities, a common room with TV and VCR, a 24-hour check-in, and an affiliation with the laid-back travel-adventure company of the same name that squires budget travelers around the nation by bus. It also offers a variety of accommodations, all of which include breakfast: dorm-style rooms and private rooms for up to three people. There are no private bathrooms. Located in the heart of downtown, the neighborhood is a bit dicey after dark, but the cheery staff helps make the hostel a bright, welcoming sight on a dreary Seattle night.

Pacific Plaza Hotel
400 Spring Street, Seattle, WA 98104 ☎ (800) 426-1165 or (206) 623-3900

For those who care more about location and are willing to splurge for it, the downtown, mid-size Pacific Plaza is the perfect place. Rooms start at well under $100, even in summer, and include a generous continental breakfast. The ambience brings to mind a good budget hotel in a European city: long hallways; simple, comfortable rooms; and small, clean bathrooms. Light sleepers may wish to stay elsewhere, as the hotel is not air-conditioned and opening the windows invites traffic noise.

Pensione Nicols
1923 1st Avenue, Seattle, WA 98101 ☎ (800) 440-7125 or (206) 441-7125

Rates are higher here than what we usually consider budget accommodation, but the location and facilities make this an exceptional deal for Seattle. Pensione Nicols is perched just above the Pike Place Market (note that its entrance is next to an X-rated movie theater on an otherwise boutique-and-restaurant-filled block). Rooms facing this busy street can be noisy; the other rooms don't have windows, but they do have skylights and are much quieter. Ten guest rooms share four bathrooms, and a large common room on the third floor has a gorgeous view of the Market's rooftops and Elliott Bay beyond. A bountiful continental breakfast—including fresh treats from the Market—is served.

Seattle International Youth Hostel
84 Union Street, Seattle, WA 98101 ☎ (206) 622-5443

Seattle's no-nonsense, nonsmoking, no-curfew American Youth Hostel offers the comforts of hostels the world over: a cheap bed and a communal kitchen. Off season, the dormitories (male/female) are available to non-AYH members for an additional $3; $5 more gains a private room. A turn-of-the-century building at the south end of Pike Place Market, the hostel is conveniently located for exploring downtown Seattle and catching Metro buses to other neighborhoods. The area is full of character (and some characters), so it's best to keep your wits about you after dark. Lights out at 11pm.

Vincent's Guest House

527 Malden Avenue E, Seattle, WA 98112 ☎ (206) 323-7849

    Located on a quiet, tree-lined street, Vincent's is an easy walk (1 mile) or bus ride from downtown. It's an AYH, but cheapies have lauded it for its unstructured atmosphere—less rigid than most hostels, with no required chores. At its best, Vincent's looks like postcollegiate group housing—postered walls, bodies lounging everywhere (on the steps, in front of the TV)—but that's half the charm.

YMCA

909 4th Avenue, Seattle, WA 98104 ☎ (206) 382-5000

    The YMCA offers pretty much what you'd expect: a spare dorm-style room with two twin beds. Bathrooms are down the hall. Unlike the YWCA (1118 5th Ave, Seattle, WA 98101; (206)461-4888), however, it does accommodate both men and women. The Y's extensive athletic facilities, including the pool, are available to overnight guests.

Puget Sound

Puget Sound, which cuts a 100-mile-long swath between the Olympic and Cascade mountain ranges, is dotted with hundreds of fir-covered islands, seemingly endless inlets, and long stretches of sandy beaches framed by wind-twisted madrona trees. On clear days, the icy white slopes of Mount Baker and Rainier, and the jagged blue outlines of the Cascades and Olympics, frame the Sound's shimmering waters. From a handful of places, you can see them all in one graceful, stirring 360-degree turn.

Two hundred years after Captain George Vancouver poked around the waters of Puget Sound, the area has been transformed (some would say ravaged) by the industry of those who followed. No fewer than nine major cities thrive off the riches of these waters. With Interstate 5 tracing the Sound from the Canadian border to Olympia, too many travelers speed from city to city, missing the area's many delights. Seattle, the centerpiece city on Puget Sound, is beginning to touch the outer boundaries of Everett to the north and tickle the fringes of Tacoma to the south. But a number of cities around the Sound still march to a small-town drum.

Exploring

North Puget Sound

State Highway 9 ambles from the Canadian border at Sumas to Snohomish, as nice a country two-lane jaunt as you'll ever find (and a perfect alternative to the interstate). The route skirts six pretty little lakes, meanders the country wilds, and forges into the heart of timber country—with plenty of spots along the way for a picnic.

Three miles south of the Canadian border, off Highway 13, is **Lynden**—a picture-perfect, neat and tidy community sporting immaculate yards and colorful gardens lining the shady avenue into downtown. The town has adopted a Dutch theme (slightly overdone) in tribute to a community of early inhabitants. Visit the Lynden Pioneer Museum (217 Front St, Lynden; (360)354-3675) to see one of the best collections of antique vehicles and farm machinery anywhere. The museum also contains representations of historic rooms and businesses, a print shop, a barbershop, and a department store circa 1920. The curator can arrange to open the collections of privately donated Haida Indian artifacts.

Situated near Blaine, the charming **Semiahmoo Public Park** is approached (somewhat awkwardly) through the

Ferry Rides

Getting around the Puget Sound area often involves riding a Washington State Ferry, and no activity better captures the spirit of the Sound than a ferry ride—both for commuters, who rely on them for transportation, and for sightseers, who ride them to enjoy the views. The Washington State Ferries system is the largest in the country (eight routes serve 20 terminals in Puget Sound). Bellingham is the main starting point for ferry travelers heading north to British Columbia and Alaska. For a day trip, try one of the brief rides from Mukilteo (near Everett) to Clinton on Whidbey Island or from West Seattle to Vashon Island. Your fare will be much lower, and you can be sure you'll catch the ferry you want, if you leave your car behind and walk on. Summer congestion means those with cars should arrive an hour or two before the scheduled sailing, longer on a Friday or Sunday. For schedule and route information, call (800)843-3779 or (206)464-6400.

Semiahmoo Resort. From its 1½ miles of sand-spit beach (with picnic tables, fire pits, and good clam digging), you can see Point Roberts and the Canadian Gulf Islands farther west. The former cannery bunkhouses are now an interpretive center that chronicles the history of the Northwest salmon fishery.

In recent years **Bellingham**, situated where the Nooksack River flows into Bellingham Bay, has been rediscovered: the town is full of fine old houses, stately streets, lovely parks, and award-winning architecture at Western Washington University. An outdoor public art collection dots the university campus. With its unique audio-phone tour, you can listen to artists talk about their own works (Western Gallery, Western Washington University, Bellingham; (360)650-3963). The Whatcom Museum of History and Art (121 Prospect St, Bellingham; (360)676-6981), in the massive building that once housed Bellingham's City Hall, has an excellent Northwest Native American and Eskimo art exhibit, along with a collection of pioneer photographs. There's no admission charge, but donations are welcome.

Old Town, around West Holly and Commercial Streets, hosts antique and junk shops and some decent eateries. The Bellingham Farmers Market features produce (including the county's famed berry harvests), fresh seafood, herbs, flowers, and crafts. It's held on Saturdays from April through October (downtown at Railroad Ave and Chestnut St, Bellingham; (360)647-2060).

Bellingham's **Fairhaven** neighborhood, the product of a short-lived railroad boom (1889–93), has experienced a resurgence of life in its red-brick buildings and is worth exploring. The Marketplace, the grand dame and central figure among the attractive old buildings, was restored in 1988 and houses a number of interesting shops and dining options. The district is rich with diversity: craft galleries, coffeehouses, bookstores, a charming garden emporium, and a lively evening scene. Stop in at the attractive Archer Ale House for a wide selection of brews, including hard-to-find Belgian beers, and some savory Cornish pasties (1212 10th St, Bellingham; (360)647-7002).

The **Lake Whatcom Railway** (left over from the railway boom), near Wickersham on Highway 9, makes scenic summer runs using a working steam locomotive; (360)595-2218. An old electric railway is now a beautiful 5-mile-long **Interurban Trail**, popular with runners, walkers, and mountain bikers, connecting Fairhaven, Arroyo, and Larrabee State Parks at the north end of Chuckanut Drive.

The spectacular 20-mile **Chuckanut Drive** (Hwy 11), which extends from the rocky shoreline at the base of Bellingham's Chuckanut Mountain to the fertile Skagit flats (just north of Burlington), is one of the prettiest drives in the state. A narrow, winding road, it curves along the mountainside, with cliff-hanging views over the water and the San Juans. Aside from a couple of good restaurants, almost no commercial development spoils the route; however, there are a number of places to stop and admire. Teddy Bear Cove is a pretty beach on a secluded shore along Chuckanut Drive just south of the Bellingham city limits. Watch for a parking lot on the left side of the road as you drive south from Bellingham. Larrabee State Park, Washington's first state park, has beautifully sculpted sandstone along the beaches and cliffs. It also has good picnic areas and camping. A wonderful day hike leads you up to Lost Lake near the top of Chuckanut Mountain.

At the hairpin curve halfway down Chuckanut Drive near Oyster Creek Inn, a white wooden gate opens onto a dirt road that leads steeply down to the creek. Here, the **Taylor Shellfish Farm** (188 Chuckanut Dr, Bow; (360)766-6002) welcomes visitors. Park your car at the top and walk (an easy three-quarters of a mile) through the forest to the shellfish farm. Oysters (smoked, shucked, or in the shell), Dungeness crab, steamer clams, and sometimes scallops are for sale in the icy processing shed.

In **Bayview**, visit the Breazeale–Padilla Bay National Estuarine Research Reserve and Interpretive Center (1043 Bayview-Edison Rd, Bayview; (360)428-1558). Learn about the Padilla Bay estuary through displays, saltwater tanks, and a library. It's open Wednesday through Sunday. A 2-mile shoreline trail begins just a short drive south of the center. Nearby Bayview State Park is open year-round with overnight camping and beachfront picnic sites, perfect for winter bird-watching; (360)757-0227.

The gentle rolling landscape of the **Skagit Valley** is most famous for its spring bloom, when thousands of tulips and other flowers blanket the fertile fields (see the "Skagit Valley Tulip Festival" tip). **Mt. Vernon** is a working town and the population center of the valley. While not as picturesque as nearby La Conner, it makes for a pleasant stop and is home to some good restaurants and taverns. Browse in Scott's Bookstore (121 Freeway Dr, Mt. Vernon; (360)336-6181) in the historic Granary Building at the north end of town or visit the Skagit River Brewing Co. (404 S 3rd St, Mt. Vernon; (360)336-2884) for pub grub and a fresh brew. Little Mountain Park, at the southeast end of town, sports a terrific picnic spot with a knockout vista of the valley (look for migratory trumpeter swans in February).

Once not much more than a trading post for the farming and fishing communities in the Skagit Valley, **La Conner** in this century became a haven for nonconformists (Wobblies, beatniks, and

Boeing

For a glimpse at the region's industrial strengths, zoom up I-5 to Everett's Paine Field for a free weekday tour of Boeing's assembly line for 747s, 767s, and 777s. You'll behold the largest building (by volume) in the world, and learn how the planes are assembled. There are no reservations, and space for the tours is limited, so arrive early. Tickets must be picked up at the tour center on the same day, and in the summer they're usually gone by noon; (800)464-1476.

Puyallup Fair

*People don't go to the Puyallup Fair (that's "PEW-awl-lup," for the tongue-tied),
they "do the Puyallup." The granddaddy blowout of the year, the fair is officially
known as the Western Washington State Fair, but nobody calls it that. One of the
nation's largest state fairs, it takes place over the course of three-plus weeks in September.
Puyallup may not be the farm town it once was, but you'll still see plenty of pigs and
lambs, and you'll never have to ask, "Where's the beef?" Midway rides and corn on the
cob, "as-seen-on-TV" and kiddie shows—the Puyallup's got it all. Country music stars as
well as pop and jazz greats headline the entertainment roster. Go on a weekday if possible;
weekends are extremely crowded. Commercial sponsors sometimes offer midweek reduc-
tions on ticket prices. Call (253)845-1771 for exact dates and ticket information.*

bikers), always with a fair smattering of artists and writers, including Mark Tobey, Morris Graves, Guy Anderson, and Tom Robbins. Gaches Mansion (703 S 2nd St, La Conner; (360)466-4288), overlooking the main drag, is a wonderful example of American Victorian architecture filled with period furnishings, with a widow's walk that looks out on the entire Skagit Valley. Open Wednesday through Sunday, it also houses a quilt museum. The new Museum of Northwest Art (121 S 1st St, La Conner; (360)466-4446) is worth a visit, especially for its collection of Northwest glass art. Stop in at the stylish La Conner Brewing Company (117 S 1st St, La Conner; (360)466-1415) for a fine selection of ales and tasty wood-fired pizzas.

If you come into La Conner via the Conway exit off I-5, be sure to stop at Snow Goose Produce on Fir Island Road for ice cream in a homemade waffle cone. You can buy tulips here in the spring, and they stock loads of gorgeous local produce and specialty food items, as well as fresh seafood (including pre-cooked Hood Canal shrimp, a perfect snack for the drive home).

The **Pilchuck Glass School**, in nearby Stanwood, is an internationally renowned glass-art school. An open house each summer gives folks a chance to see crafts-people at work; call (206)621-8422.

Whidbey Island now qualifies as the longest island in the United States, since New York's Long Island was declared a peninsula. Boasting pretty villages, view-point parks, sandy beaches, and some scenic, rolling farmland, Whidbey makes for a great family outing. The treacherous but beautiful Deception Pass at the north end of the island has a lovely—and often crowded—state park with 2,300 acres of prime camping land, forests, and beach.

Strom's Shrimp Fountain and Grill (1480 Hwy 20, just north of Deception Pass; (360)293-2531) sells fresh seafood and shrimp for your cookout. They also grill up a mean oyster burger to go.

Whidbey's flat, relatively untrafficked roads are great for biking. A bike lane follows Engle Road 3 miles south of Coupeville to **Fort Casey**, a decommissioned fort with splendid gun mounts, beaches, and commanding bluffs. The magnificent bluff and beach at **Ebey's Landing** and Fort Ebey State Park are good spots to explore, with ancient wild-rose hedgerows (in bloom May and June), 100-year-old barns, and scraggly orchards that still mark the course of a pioneer settlement. Stop by Whidbey's Greenbank Logan-berry Farm (on Hwy 525, 5 miles south of the Hwy 20 junction; (360)678-7788) for a sample of Whidbeys Loganberry Liqueur.

Langley, at the south end of the island, evinces small-town virtues. The tidy downtown strip along First Street provides all a visitor could want: espresso, ice cream, shops, and benches overlooking Saratoga Passage. The residents like to attend first-run movies at the Clyde Theatre (213 1st St, Langley; (360)221-5525), drink pitchers of ale at the Dog House Backdoor Restaurant (230 1st St, Langley; (360)221-9996), and swap stories with Josh Hauser at Moonraker Books (209 1st St, Langley; (360)321-6962).

South Puget Sound

Glass artist Dale Chihuly, one of the Pilchuck Glass School's famous founders, is a native son of Tacoma in south Puget Sound. You'll find a mesmerizing collection of Chihuly glass in the **Tacoma Art Museum** (1123 Pacific Ave, Tacoma; (253)272-4258), displayed against muslin-screened windows and lit from behind by the sun. Admission is free on Tuesdays. The rotunda of the historic Union Station building, now a courthouse (1717 Pacific Ave, Tacoma), is graced by some spectacular work by Chihuly, too; the exhibit is an annex of the Tacoma Art Museum, open to the public at no charge during business hours. For a more practical use of glass, check out the free W. W. Seymour Botanical Conservatory in Wright Park (316 S "G" St, Tacoma). An elegant, old-fashioned hothouse dating from 1907, it contains an exotic collection of cacti, orchids, and ferns. The Washington State Historical Museum is now housed in a handsome new building just south of Union Station (1911 Pacific Ave, Tacoma; (888)238-4373). The new, much larger facility offers a state-of-the-art museum experience using interactive exhibits that talk to you when you push a button. The museum's exterior, however, was carefully designed to blend into its surroundings and complement Union Station, which was built in 1911.

In the industrial docklands near the Lincoln Avenue Bridge sprawls the **Gog-le-hi-te Wetland** (the name means "where the land and waters meet"). More than 100 species of birds inhabit this human-made estuary, which the Port of Tacoma constructed to compensate the Puyallup Indians for the wild marshes destroyed by the port. The 700-acre **Point Defiance Park** (5400 N Pearl St, Tacoma) features woodland trails, formal gardens, and a reconstruction of Fort Nisqually—a former Hudson's Bay Company outpost. Also in the park is the Point Defiance Zoo and Aquarium, (253)591-5335, which bills itself as "the Pacific Rim zoo," with specialized habitats ranging from tundra to tropical reefs. Admission is $7, but the zoo honors membership passes from many other Northwest zoos.

North, off Point Defiance, lies pastoral **Vashon Island** (served by car ferries from Point Defiance and Fauntleroy in West Seattle, and by passenger ferry from downtown Seattle). This lazy, rural island is great for biking, and the squat Point Robinson lighthouse makes a good destination (the lighthouse is open for tours on weekends only, but the grounds are open daily). The best views are from the causeway linking Vashon with Maury Island. A number of Vashon Island companies are open for tours, including the original Seattle's Best Coffee (SBC) roasting plant, (206)463-3932; Maury Island Farms with locally grown gourmet fruits, (206)463-9659; and Vashon Island Winery, (206)463-2990. Call ahead for details. Or stop by the Country Store and Garden (Valley Center, Vashon; (206)463-3655), where most island products are for sale.

At the west end of the Tacoma Narrows Bridge, **Gig Harbor**, bent like a horseshoe around its namesake bay, is home to a working fishing fleet and a spate of tourist shops. New construction nibbles away at the edges of the town, rapidly transforming it into a Tacoma suburb. On Saturdays in May through October, the Gig Harbor Farmers Market

Skagit Valley Tulip Festival

*The fertile farmlands of the Skagit Valley (between Mount Vernon and La Conner)
are painted with fields of flowers in the spring: daffodils (March 15 to April 15),
tulips (April 1 to May 10), and irises (May 15 to June 15). Vegetable stands dot
Skagit Valley roadsides in late summer and fall. The pastoral countryside is flat and ideal
for bicyclists, though two-wheelers should be aware that gridlock occurs on the small farm
lanes during the annual **Tulip Festival**, usually held in early April; call (800)4-TULIPS
for information and a map of farms.*

features locally grown produce, plants, and Northwest gifts (at the Pierce Transit Park & Ride, off Hwy 16; (253)884-2665). Beyond Gig Harbor lie less developed places such as the **Key Peninsula**, where quiet coves and forgotten towns seem dreamily lost in time. The back roads are good for biking, and Penrose State Park, (253)884-2514, is a favorite with clam diggers.

South of Tacoma, **Steilacoom**, platted by a Maine sea captain in the late 19th century, has a distinctly New England air. On weekends, long lines of visitors spill out of Bair Drug and Hardware (1617 Lafayette St, Steilacoom; (253)588-9668), a false-fronted general store now run as a small cafe. Nostalgia is clearly as big a draw as the food. But it's inexpensive and fun, especially the antique soda fountain, which still serves sarsaparilla and gooey black-and-white sundaes.

Ten miles north of Olympia, where the glacier-fed Nisqually River flows into Puget Sound, lies the **Nisqually Wildlife Refuge** (I-5 exit 114, Olympia; (360)753-9467). Woodlands, grasslands, and marshes provide a rich habitat for wildlife, especially migrating birds. Easy trails range from a half-mile walk to a 5-mile loop with photo blinds and observation decks. There's a daily fee of $2 per family.

The towering landmark of **Olympia**, seat of state government, is its neoclassical capitol building, spectacularly set on a bluff at the foot of Puget Sound. It was built to impress, and it does. Rumor has it that you could squeeze a Volkswagen

Beetle inside the rotunda's 5-ton Tiffany chandelier. Admission and daily tours are free. You can get a free tour of the governor's mansion next door, by appointment, on Wednesday afternoons; (360)586-8687.

Directly behind the capitol grounds lies the **South Capitol Neighborhood**; listed on the National Register of Historic Places, it's one of the largest historic districts in the state. Pick up a free, self-guided tour brochure at the State Capitol Visitors Center (14th Ave and S Capitol Way, Olympia; (360)586-3460). The State Capitol Museum (211 W 21st Ave, Olympia; (360)753-2580) houses a permanent exhibit that includes an outstanding collection of Western Washington Native American baskets.

Downtown Olympia remains wonderfully human in scale. Sylvester Park is a town square straight out of *The Music Man*, complete with a bandstand where free Friday lunchtime concerts are held in summer. Toward the harbor, in a new location near Percival Landing, is the lively Olympia Farmers Market, which displays produce, flowers, and crafts from all over the South Sound; open Thursday through Sunday during the growing season (700 N Capitol Way, Olympia; (360)352-9096). Percival Landing, a waterfront park, is increasingly becoming a community focal point, the site of harbor festivals of all kinds.

Art Zabel's passion is growing **rhododendrons and azaleas**, and more than 1,200 of them bloom in his 4-acre Olympia garden (2432 Bethel St NE, Olympia). Each day in May, Zabel opens his backyard to the public at no charge. His plants are not for sale, but simply for his (and our) enjoyment.

The historic heart of the whole area (Olympia, Lacey, and Tumwater) is **Tumwater Falls** (take the Brewery exit off I-5 and follow signs to the Deschutes Pkwy), where the Deschutes River flows into Capitol Lake. A pleasant walk along the river takes you past several waterfalls. This is the site of the chief local industry, the Tumwater Division of the Pabst Brewing Company, with free daily tours. If you need refreshment after strolling the falls, stop in at Desserts by Tasha Nicole (2822 Capitol Blvd SE, Olympia; (360)352-3717); the chocolate-dipped cheesecake-on-a-stick is to die for.

At **Mima Mounds Natural Area Preserve**, 12 miles south of Olympia near the village of Littlerock, thousands of inexplicable mounds, roughly 10 feet high, cover the Mima prairie. Nobody knows for sure whether they were formed by glaciers or by gophers, but they're lovely when wildflowers bloom in late spring, thick with blossoms and butterflies.

Wolf Haven International, near Tenino, is a private sanctuary for wolves that cannot be returned to the wild. Volunteer guides give tours and explain the workings of wolf society. Admission is $5 for adults, $2.50 for kids. "Howl-Ins" on summer weekend nights, when visitors howl with the wolves, cost a little bit more (3111 Offut Lake Rd, Olympia; (800)GIV-WOLF, (360)264-HOWL).

The heyday of sandstone has come and gone, but **Tenino** remembers it well. You'd never expect such a tiny town to have so many shops and houses built out of hand-hewn stone. An abandoned sandstone quarry is now a public park in which an old stone railway depot serves as a small museum. And where better to spend a hot afternoon than down at the old swimming hole? The craggy quarry pit itself has been transformed into a free swimming pool, open Wednesday through Sunday in summer.

Cheap Eats

Linda's Lunchbucket
880 E Pole Road, Lynden ☎ (360)354-3360

Two miles south of town, Linda's Lunchbucket is a direct ticket back to, say, 1962, with an $8 sirloin steak dinner and a world of housemade pies. Despite the name, Linda's is also open for breakfast and dinner, with breakfast available whenever the mood for bacon and a couple of over-easies strikes. Feast on such all-American faves as chicken-fried steak, meatloaf, and every kind of burger imaginable. Taco salads, deli sandwiches, and grilled goodies (from melts to Reubens) round out the lunch "bucket."

Boundary Bay Brewery
1107 Railroad Avenue, Bellingham ☎ (360)647-5593

In addition to its made-on-the-premises ales, Boundary Bay also serves up some fine pub grub at very reasonable prices (try the delicious lamb burger). In the separate dining room, more highfalutin' fare such as mushroom stew with polenta and chicken breast with corn salsa makes a satisfying meal, and most entrees are under $10.

Cafe Toulouse

114 W Magnolia Street, Bellingham ☎ (360) 733-8996

The tiny and popular Cafe Toulouse, open for breakfast and lunch, is known for its inventive sandwiches served on housemade bread, Greek and Provençal frittatas, huevos rancheros, soups, and pastas. This quietly remodeled corner of the old Bon Marché gets our vote as the best place in town for Sunday brunch.

Casa Que Pasa

1415 Railroad Avenue, Bellingham ☎ (360) 738-8226

Locals rave about the burritos and other Mexican fare at this casual eatery. All menu items are priced well under $10, and there are many vegetarian dishes to choose from. Don't miss the black bean soup, served up with swirls of sour cream and cilantro purée.

Colophon Cafe

1208 11th Street, Bellingham ☎ (360) 647-0092

Located in the best bookstore in town, Colophon offers table service and an outdoor wine garden on its lower level, booths and sidewalk tables above. The African peanut soup (in vegetarian and nonvegetarian versions) is justly famous—chunky with fresh tomatoes, grainy with peanuts, and pungent with ginger. Real cream pies—rich, light, and wonderful—are another house specialty.

La Patisserie

3098 Northwest Avenue, Bellingham ☎ (360) 671-3671

La Patisserie serves up soul-satisfying Vietnamese fare, including a selection of satays and their justly popular shrimp and vegetable salad rolls, sided with a peanut dipping sauce. As the name suggests, this is also a French bakery, so don't leave without sampling (or walking out with a bag of) the croissants, tarts, and other worthy pastries.

Chuck Wagon Drive Inn

800 N 4th Street, Mount Vernon ☎ (360) 336-2732

More than 50 types of burgers (including veggie options) and a few dozen variations on the milk-shake theme (hard or soft ice cream, your choice) make this a worthy stop—especially if you've got kids in tow. Baked stuffed spuds and fish 'n' chips take things beyond the burger realm, while electric trains and the largest collection of whiskey-bottle cowboys (and cowgirls) in the free world give you something to look at while you're yelling "Giddy-ap!" Eat in or take out.

The Deli Next Door

202 S 1st Street, Mount Vernon ☎ (360) 336-3886

Located in the Skagit Valley Food Co-op (where you can ogle the specialty food items and organic produce, and stock up on everything from exotic spices and teas to potted herbs), the Deli Next Door offers a super-healthy, super-tasty afternoon nosh. Everything, from salads to lasagne, is organic, with vegan options for those who just say no to meat and animal by-products.

Pacioni's Pizzeria
606 S 1st Street, Mount Vernon ☎ (360) 336-3314

The scent of fresh bread, fresh herbs, and just-pulled espresso wafts onto the street, tugging at passersby. Those who give in to temptation congregate at red-and-white-checkered tables, enjoy a friendly glass of red wine, and savor the flavors of a bubbling hot pizza. Our favorite pie: the *tricolore* (pesto, ricotta, and Roma tomatoes)—now that's Italian.

Calico Cupboard
720 S 1st Street, La Conner ☎ (360) 466-4451

It's awfully cute—Laura Ashley meets Laura Ingalls Wilder—but it's the bakery, not the ambience, that's the real reason to stop in here. Excellent carrot muffins, pecan tarts, shortbread, raspberry bars, currant scones, apple Danish, and more keep 'em lining up at the take-out counter. Hearty waffle and omelet breakfasts are offered, as is the usual soup-'n'-salad lunch fare, augmented with specials such as pot pies and black bean enchiladas. There's another Calico in Anacortes and a newer sibling in Mount Vernon.

Lucy's Mi Casita
1380 W Pioneer Way, Oak Harbor, Whidbey Island ☎ (360) 675-4800

It doesn't look like much, lined up along a strip of fast-food joints and automotive stores and decorated with old calendars, beer-bottle-cap curtains, and cutouts of flamenco dancers, but Al and Lucy Enriquez keep locals coming back with their homemade Mexican food and lively atmosphere. Upstairs is a lounge with a balcony (watch out for the 27-ounce Turbo Godzilla margarita). Don't miss the *entomatada*—a tortilla topped with tomato sauce, cheese, and onion—from Lucy's hometown of Chihuahua.

Whale & Gator Cafe
901 Grace Street, Suite B, Coupeville, Whidbey Island ☎ (360) 678-2941

The Whale & Gator serves up Southern home cooking and Cajun fare in a simple space overlooking the waterfront. The menu features everything from red beans and rice to jambalaya to catfish (served with hush puppies, natch) and chicken-fried steak. Everything's made from scratch.

The Sisters
2804 Grand Street, Everett ☎ (425) 252-0480

This place is as popular as it is funky. Soups—from exotic mulligatawny to spice-spiked gazpacho to plain old beef barley—can be outstanding. Sandwiches range from average deli stuff to more healthful concoctions, including a vegetarian burger made with chopped cashews and sunflower seeds. Fresh-squeezed lemonade will quench your thirst; a big slice of blackberry pie will cure whatever ails you.

Antique Sandwich Company
5102 N Pearl Street, Tacoma ☎ (253) 752-4069

Just a few blocks from Point Defiance Park is the Sandwich Company, a perennial favorite with students, the diaper set, and their parents. Plastic honey-filled bears adorn the shared tables; the roomy couch usually has several students curled up on it, studying and eating. Toys abound on a carpet-covered platform that doubles as a stage on open-mike Tuesdays. Peanut-butter-and-jelly sandwiches with bananas and fresh-fruit milk shakes share the menu with big-people food such as hearty homemade soups, quiches, and a variety of not-so-antique sandwiches.

Katie Downs

3211 Ruston Way, Tacoma ☎ (253) 756-0771

Katie Downs is noisy, boisterous, and fun—a tavern whose deep-dish pizza is a winner. Especially good is the Fearless pie, which recklessly matches smoked bacon and provolone with onions, spicy peperoncini, and lots and lots of fresh garlic. The pizzas can take a half hour to make and bake, so order some steamer clams to tide you over while you wait, and watch the working boats ply the waterways on Commencement Bay.

Southern Kitchen

1716 6th Avenue, Tacoma ☎ (253) 627-4282

If you have a hankering for authentic fare of the South, this is the place. Abandon all restraint and order up some pork chops smothered with gravy, or liver with lots of lovely onions. Sides include long-cooked collard greens served up in their own "pot likker," black-eyed peas, or sweet nuggets of yams. Breakfasts are great, too: pan-fried butterfish with eggs, buttery grits, home-fries, and genuine Southern-style biscuits.

The Spar

2121 N 30th Street, Tacoma ☎ (253) 627-8215

If you're looking for a waterfront view with your meal, skip the upscale restaurants on Ruston Way and head instead for the Spar, a classic Northwest tavern in gentrified Old Town. The menu features the usual burgers and such, but the Spar is known mainly for its broasted chicken and jojos (roasted potato wedges).

Dog Day Cafe and Juice Bar

17530 Vashon Highway SW, Vashon Island ☎ (206) 463-6404

At this stylish street-side cafe, you'll find espresso drinks (made with the local brew, SBC, of course) and interesting lunch fixings—say, a roasted eggplant sandwich with tapenade; a chicken sandwich with chutney and apples; a chapati roll with black beans, brown rice, and sprouts; or noodles with citrus-marinated chicken. Stroll through the craftsy mall while waiting for your order to be prepared.

Tides Tavern

2925 Harborview Drive, Gig Harbor ☎ (253) 858-3982

"Meet me at the Tides" has become such a universal invitation that this tavern perched over the harbor is often standing room only, especially on sunny days when the deck is open. People come by boat, seaplane, and car to indulge in mondo sandwiches, huge charbroiled burgers, gargantuan shrimp salads, and the (appropriately) highly touted fish 'n' chips. Pizzas are only passable.

The Fish Bowl Pub and Cafe

515 Jefferson Street SE, Olympia ☎ (360) 943-3650

Fish Tale Ales' aptly named brewpub is stocked to the gills with fish paraphernalia. The beers are the real draw, though—all Fish Tale brews are made in the adjoining facilities. For nibbles (called "Fish Food"), consider smoked oysters or oyster shooters, cheeses, the shrimp cocktail, or the antipasto plate. There's now an adjacent cafe where pizzas are baked in a wood-fired oven.

The Spar

114 E 4th Avenue, Olympia ☎ (360) 357-6444

Some 60-odd years ago, the Spar (no relation to the tavern in Tacoma) used to be known as a workingman's hangout. Today it's classless, with a volatile mixture of students, attorneys, businesspeople, artists, politicians, fishermen, tourists, and leisured retirees. The Spar's fabulous milk shakes and homemade bread pudding are locally acclaimed, although much of the menu is downright average. Willapa Bay oysters and fresh salmon are sometimes available; the prime rib dinner is popular on weekends.

Sweet Oasis

507 Capitol Way, Olympia ☎ (360) 956-0470

This spot on Capitol Way offers some delicious foods of the Mediterranean. Among the daily specials are spanakopita and Lebanese baked vegetables. Falafel, meat pies, and other traditional Mediterranean fare are available as well. The dessert pastries are housemade and very good. On Saturday nights you get a bonus: belly-dancing.

Cheap Sleeps

DeCann House

2610 Eldridge Avenue, Bellingham, WA 98225 ☎ (360) 734-9172

Within a neighborhood of historic homes overlooking Squalicum Harbor Marina, Bellingham Bay, and the San Juan Islands, this unpretentious Victorian bed and breakfast welcomes visitors to a quiet and comfortable haven offering two guest rooms. Barbara and Van Hudson maintain an extensive, current library of travel-related material and provide a log in which you can pass along your impressions to other travelers. A complete breakfast assures a cheery start to the day.

Holiday Inn Express of Bellingham

4160 Guide Meridian, Bellingham, WA 98226
☎ (800) 465-4329 or (360) 671-4800

The location on the Guide Meridian strip development just north of town is highly unprepossessing, but the hotel itself is a find, especially for time-pressed business travelers (there's a free shuttle to the airport, which is just a few miles away). Rooms are spacious and quiet, and a free continental breakfast is provided at cozy tables with a view of the pool and Jacuzzi.

The Tulip Valley Inn
2200 Freeway Drive, Mount Vernon, WA 98273 ☎ (360) 428-5969

There are times in life when a good motel room at a reasonable rate is all you're going to find, and maybe it's all you really want. The Tulip Valley Inn is just that: comfortable beds in a no-frills 40-room motel (no pool or hot tub) in the fast-growing hub of the Skagit Valley. Some units are fully handicapped-accessible; some have kitchens.

Coupeville Inn
200 NW Coveland Street (PO Box 370), Coupeville, WA 98239
☎ (800) 247-6162 or (360) 678-6668

This attractive blue-and-gray structure on Whidbey Island is a 24-unit motel, but with homey innlike touches such as historic photographs and antiques in the hallways. Budget-minded travelers should opt for a room *without* a view of the water. All the rooms are large, and everyone gets a continental-style nibble in the morning.

Mutiny Bay Resort
5856 S Mutiny Bay Road (PO Box 249), Freeland, WA 98249 ☎ (360) 321-4500

Here is one of the last old-time fishing resorts on Whidbey Island. Years ago, this was the place for wild parties. It's quieter now, with a family atmosphere. The beach chalets are nice but pricey, unless you come with a few extra friends. Instead, request one of the old fishermen's cabins. They have kitchens, although showers are in the central bathhouse. Cabin 3 is a budget honeymooner with private shower, airtight wood stove, and nicer furnishings.

Drake's Landing
203 Wharf Street (PO Box 613), Langley, WA 98260 ☎ (360) 221-3999

Pat Drake's little blue house at the working end of the Langley waterfront on Whidbey Island is a modern-day version of the respectable overnight boarding-house. The rooms are small, but each has its own private bath. Guests relax and mingle in the parlor or the upstairs sun room and deck. Coffee and juice get you started in the morning. This might not be the upscale Inn at Langley, but it's a good night's sleep in the same quaint town.

Tayberry Victorian Cottage
7406 80th Street E, Puyallup, WA 98371 ☎ (253) 848-4594

The house is a fake—a copy of the Victorian home that Puyallup pioneer Ezra Meeker built as a gift for his daughter—but it's a nice imitation. Set on the rural outskirts of Puyallup, it's also a blessedly quiet place. In summer, breakfast is served on a porch that overlooks farms in the valley below. Recently remodeled, each of the three rooms now has its own private bath, which means the rates have crept up a bit. Tayberry is only 7 miles from downtown Tacoma.

AYH Ranch/Hostel
12119 SW Cove Road, Vashon, WA 98070 ☎ (206) 463-2592

This 10-acre spread on Vashon Island has a wonderfully hokey Old West theme, and it's also wonderfully cheap. Buckaroos of all ages can sleep in a covered wagon or a Sioux-style dorm tepee, equipped with beds and a fire circle, for $12 per person. Couples and families can reserve a teepee all to themselves. All guests have access to firewood, bicycles, and do-it-yourself pancake breakfasts at no extra charge. A private bed-and-breakfast room (with bath) is available for $45. Rooms at another jointly managed lodging, the Lavender Duck B&B, may also be booked for $45 through the hostel.

No Cabbages

7712 Goodman Drive NW, Gig Harbor, WA 98332 ☎ (253) 858-7797

"Not for the terminally uptight," reads the sign near the door of this charmingly funky beachfront cottage in the woods. From your rustic four-poster bed with patchwork quilts—Grateful Dead meets *Victoria* magazine—you can look through old-fashioned casement windows at Gig Harbor below. The two knotty pine guest rooms, tucked underneath the main house, share a bath and their own outside entrance. The hostess is mellow, friendly, and a good cook to boot. Breakfast might be popovers with whipped cream, or maybe a spinach, garlic, and feta omelet.

Golden Gavel Motor Hotel

909 Capitol Way, Olympia, WA 98501 ☎ (360) 352-8533

The folks are friendly, the rooms are well maintained, and the price is good for the location—three blocks north of the capitol and four blocks south of downtown. You can walk to practically everything from here (including the bus station). Wander over to Wagner's European Bakery, just up the street, for morning espresso and good pastries.

San Juan Islands

Clustered between the Strait of Juan de Fuca and Georgia Strait are 457 islands, many of which are no more than a seagull perch (at low tide, the number increases to over 700). Some 60 islands support small communities accessible only by private boat or seaplane. Four of them—Lopez, Shaw, Orcas, and San Juan—are serviced by the Washington State Ferries system and are home to a total of 10,000 full-time residents.

Condé Nast Traveler calls the San Juan Islands one of the best-kept secrets in the United States. *Travel and Leisure* suggests avoiding the San Juans altogether in June, July, and August. We say neither is telling the entire truth. True, in the summer you can feel overwhelmed by a Coney Island atmosphere, and there might be one too many T-shirt shops. But secluded hideaways can still be found. And in the winter, tourists are scarce, while the locals settle in for a long, cold, private season. (In fact, Orcas Islanders have two nicknames for their island: Orcapulco in the summer, Orcatraz in the winter.) The magic of the islands makes them worth braving summer tourists or winter chill. Don't go seeking nirvana, but don't be surprised if you find it after all.

In the San Juans, gnarled madrona trees cling to rock outcroppings above tide pools, and giant firs stretch from the crystalline waters of Cascade Lake to the summit of Mount Constitution on Orcas. Plenty of protected coves shelter gleaming sailboats in the summer months. The islands and surrounding waters are inhabited by a wealth of wildlife, from the famous orcas to majestic bald eagles. And despite the commercialization, you need only meander down the road a piece, or travel in the autumn, to discover the true pace of this Northwest archipelago.

Access

The ferry to the San Juan Islands leaves from the shipbuilding and oil-refinery town of Anacortes, about an hour and a half north of Seattle. Getting to the San Juans on the **Washington State Ferries** in the summer is a big (though not insurmountable) problem—especially if you have a car. Bring a good book—you can expect to wait in line for hours, and there are few diversions at the terminal (although the 20-minute walk—or

5-minute bike ride—west to Washington Park is worthwhile if you have a couple of hours to kill). Unfortunately, we don't (yet) know of any way to sneak your car onto the ferry at the last minute—and if we did, it would be one secret we'd have to keep to ourselves.

Basically, if you don't like lines and refuse to get to the Anacortes ferry terminal four hours ahead of time, then by all means leave your car and bike or walk on. (With pre-arrangements, a number of lodge owners will pick you up. Island taxis can get expensive.) If you need your car, try to schedule your trip to the islands between October and May, and avoid traveling to the islands on Fridays and heading home on Sundays.

Expect to pay about $20 round trip (car and driver) plus $5 for each passenger. Once aboard, you'll find the trip undeniably scenic, but bring a picnic as ferry food is costly and unappetizing. Money-saving tip: Cars pay only westbound, so if you plan to visit more than one island, arrange to go to the farthest first and backtrack island to island for free. (Note that passengers must pay fares each way if they plan to sail to Vancouver Island, British Columbia—the final stop for many San Juan Island ferries.) For general ferry information, call (800)84-FERRY or (206)464-6400.

Exploring

The first ferry stop from Anacortes is **Lopez**—the bucolic island, the quiet island, the friendly island. Bicyclists like Lopez for its gentle inclines and for the drivers who actually wave. The island is laced with country lanes and picturesque farms with weathered barns; on the west side is sleepy Lopez. The town is small, with just a few craft shops and good restaurants. Pick up a loaf of toasted-walnut French bread (and some cappuccino bars) from Holly B's Bakery (Village Center, Lopez; (360)468-2133). If you're really hungry, add some deli meats from the Village Market and then venture to the beach at Spencer Spit State Park, 5 miles east.

At the southwest corner of the island is Shark Reef, a day park reachable by sure-footed hikers. A forested trail ends suddenly at granite cliffs high above the tide pools of the San Juan Channel. Colonies of seals and otters often reside on a small, rocky island just offshore.

The second ferry stop is **Shaw**, the smallest of the ferry-accessible islands. It's fun to watch the Franciscan nuns operate the ferry dock, but other than a campground and a grocery store run by the order, Shaw has no tourist facilities. The island is home to little more than a retreat center for nuns, a three-cow dairy, and a private enclave of residential properties whose owners want to keep it that way.

Across from Shaw is the largest island in the San Juans, **Orcas**. Explore the villages of Eastsound, Olga, and Deer Harbor. Eastsound is the most commercial, with a number of somewhat trendy restaurants. Islanders here, however, hang out at the Lower Tavern (Prune Alley, Eastsound; (360)376-4848), which serves up burgers and soups (plus darts and pool). Grab a latte and a pastry at Rose's (Northbeach Road, Eastsound; (360)376-2009), in Eastsound Square. The Orcas Homegrown Market has an interesting selection of salads-to-go, which you might consider before heading off to remote Obstruction Pass State Park, at the southwest tip of the island. A half-mile hike leads to a pretty beach. **Moran State Park** offers a spectacular setting of 5,000 wooded acres with 30 miles of trails surrounding several lakes and Mount Constitution. You can rent sailboards and small boats at Cascade Lake, swim at a supervised beach, or stay in one of the numerous campsites (see "Camping" tip). If it's too cool to swim, hike the 4.3 miles (or drive the 6½ miles) up **Mount Constitution**, the highest point in the islands at 2,400 feet. You will be well rewarded by the panorama (and maybe even a bald eagle) below you.

Beyond Moran, the sleepy hamlet of **Olga** seduces the peckish with the unforgettable cinnamon rolls and blackberry pie of the Cafe Olga (Horseshoe Hwy, Olga; (360)376-5098). Also housed in this building is Orcas Island Artworks (Horseshoe Highway, Olga; (360)376-4408), a cooperative of local artists that displays a variety of arts and crafts. On the other side of the island is the Gold Coast, which features numerous estates of old Seattle families, although only a few of the homes are visible from the road.

To get out on the water, reserve space on one of the **sea kayak trips** offered by Shearwater Adventures, (360)376-4699, or Osprey Tours, (360)376-3677. Half-day trips cost around $39 per person (beginners welcome). A few times a month, Shearwater offers a special full-moon jaunt out of Doe Bay ($35). Osprey uses kayaks handcrafted in the Aleut tradition, and they offer kids' trips that are open to children over 6; each child gets his or her own "trainer" kayak and learns about kayaking safety ($25). If a sail on a 33-foot sloop ($35) would float your boat, call Amante Sail Tours, (360)376-4231.

For an active, educational look at the San Juans' ecosystem, immerse yourself in a week of marine science activities at the island institute's family-oriented **Marine Adventure Center** based on Orcas (PO Box 358, Eastsound, WA 98245; (800)956-ORCA or (360)376-6720; www.clearwater.com/isleinst/).

The last ferry stop before British Columbia is **San Juan Island**, the county seat and definitely the most bustling of the islands. The landing is smack in the middle of **Friday Harbor**, in a town crammed with shops, galleries, grocery stores, and a large marina. The most notable attraction is the **Whale Museum** (62 1st St, Friday Harbor; (360)378-4710), which has become the base of operation for the study of the 90 or so orcas that reside in the San Juan vicinity. The museum offers exhibits as well as a short film highlighting individual whales that have been tracked over the years (admission $4).

If you're an early riser, head up to the Donut Shop (209 Spring St, Friday Harbor; (360)378-2271), which opens at 5am. Or grab a bagel at Madelyn's Yogurt and Espresso Bar (225 A St, Friday Harbor; (360)378-4545). Psst . . . locals say she has the best lattes in town. For a good picnic lunch, split one of the giant steamed sandwiches at the Cannery House (174 1st St, Friday Harbor; (360)378-2500). If you want to rub shoulders with locals, stop in at Herb's Tavern, an institution that's been doling out beer (as well as chili and burgers) for over 50 years under one name or another (80 1st St, Friday

Musical Note

For Dixieland jazz fans, Friday Harbor is the place to be on the last weekend in July. The whole town swings with well-known jazz artists performing in various locales. Suggestion: Reserve lodging far in advance (or stay on Orcas and walk over on the ferry for the events), as this has become a very popular festival. For details on bands and ticket prices, call (360)378-5509.

Winter Warmth

The location of Orcas Island's age-old, hippified Doe Bay Resort (Star Route Box 86, Olga, WA 98279; (360)376-2291) is great. The resort offers plenty of trails, two small beaches, a campground, a small store, a good vegetarian restaurant, and an outdoor mineral-spring hot tub (bathing suits optional). The minimalist cabins, however, are a bit rickety, have no screens, and could stand a lengthy visit from Mr. Clean. We suggest you stay elsewhere but enjoy the use of the hot tub during a slow winter week (for a small fee of about $5 per person).

Harbor; (360)378-7076).

The best way to see San Juan Island is to bike or drive out Roche Harbor Road, which winds its way past large farms and ranches. You can rent a bike from Island Bicycles (380 Argyle Avenue, Friday Harbor; (360)387-4941). All roads heading northwest seem to lead to **Roche Harbor**, first the site of a Hudson's Bay Company trading post in the 1800s, then the largest lime quarry in the West, and now a charming resort that's especially popular with boaters. Dally among the exquisite gardens and walk the dock as though your cruiser is tied up at slip 55. Also on the north end of the island is **English Camp**, established when ownership of the island was under dispute. The conflict led to the not-so-famous Pig War of 1859–60, so called because the sole casualty was a pig.

American Camp (on the opposite side of the island) is much more dramatic.

Allow a couple of hours there to enjoy the windswept South Beach, the longest public beach in the islands. There are picnic tables, and it's a perfect setting for beachcombing. On several Saturdays from June through August, there are historical reenactments depicting camp life in the 1860s and guided walks through the camps; call (360)378-2902 for a schedule of events.

Just beyond San Juan County Park on Mitchell Bay Road (off West Valley Road) is the first whale-watching park established in the nation. **Lime Kiln Point** has been a whale research station since 1983, and has installed underwater microphones to allow eavesdropping on unsuspecting **orcas**. The whales pass by regularly, especially in the summer months. The grassy slopes, with their wild orange poppies and westerly views toward Vancouver Island, are enough of a diversion when the whales are not.

Cheap Eats

Bay Cafe

Lopez Village, Lopez Island ☎ **(360)468-3700**

An interesting, slightly ethnic menu and reasonable prices (complete dinners at around $12, including soup and salad) make the Bay Cafe the most popular restaurant on Lopez. Reservations are a must in summer.

Gail's

Lopez Village, Lopez Island ☎ (360) 468-2150

Gail's offers tasty lunches at reasonable prices, plus a deck looking toward Fisherman Bay. Dinner is at the upper end of our budget range, but includes salad. And the well-priced wine list and live jazz several times a week make it worth the cost. The menu emphasizes seafood, with a good selection of vegetarian dishes and four homemade soups daily.

Bilbo's Festivo

North Beach Road, Eastsound, Orcas Island ☎ (360) 376-4728

Always popular, Bilbo's has great Mexican and Southwest dishes and an outside terrace. Mesquite-grilled specials such as halibut round out a menu of more standard fare including burritos and enchiladas. Islanders often opt for a round of appetizers and a couple of margaritas.

Westsound Store and Cafe

Crow Valley Road and Deer Harbor Road, Eastsound, Orcas Island ☎ (360) 376-4440

Recently purchased and renovated by the folks who used to own Bainbridge Island's famed Streamliner Diner, the Westsound Store and Cafe is now offering full breakfasts and lunches in addition to take-out and grocery items. The menu changes seasonally; breakfast might feature a wild mushroom omelet or cinnamon French toast with fresh organic strawberries, while lunch may serve up veggie wraps, grilled sandwiches, or beer-batter fish 'n' chips.

Katrina's

145 2nd Street, Friday Harbor, San Juan Island ☎ (360) 378-7290

Katrina's new location is slightly bigger than her old one, with a few more tables and chairs, but not much else has changed; she still offers wonderful, freshly made dishes such as chilled Asian noodle salad or mesquite-smoked chicken (expect to wait awhile, since it's usually just her and one or two helpers in the kitchen).

Cheap Sleeps

Unfortunately, summertime forces last-minute planners to forget price concerns and just find a room—any room. Peak-season lodging is so tight on these islands that even the tiniest room with a shared bath goes for over $75 per night. So if you're really looking for a deal during high season, we have to say we're stumped. We recommend that you go in the off season, when price ranges and availability are totally different, opening up a whole new array of choices. Below we've listed what we consider to be the best deals on the island, even if some of their prices are a little beyond our budget.

Those who insist on visiting in the summer may wish to try the lodging hotlines: for San Juan Island, (360)378-3030 or (360)376-8383; for Orcas Island, (360)376-8888. For other island information, call the islands' Chamber of Commerce, (360)378-5240.

The Island Farmhouse

Hummel Lake Road (PO Box 3114), Lopez Island, WA 98261 ☎ (360) 468-2864

Aside from campsites, this 12-acre working farm is the only resting spot that's much of a deal on Lopez. Owners Ted and Susan Sanchez have added a large room off the back of their home, with its own deck and private entry. It is generous in size and decorated à la Laura Ashley. The private bath is quite large, and there's a kitchen nook. Sit on your deck in the morning and watch the sheepdog at work on the herd of Suffolks in this pastoral setting.

Orcas Hotel

Orcas Landing (PO Box 155), Orcas Island, WA 98280
☎ (888) 672-2792 or (360) 376-4300

Most of the rooms at this turn-of-the-century inn are over our budget, but one of the tiny rooms with shared bath comes in at $69 for two, including breakfast, and a few are $79. The location, right at the ferry terminal, is convenient but busy. Off-season rates are a bargain.

Camping

For real cheap sleeps in the San Juans, try camping. Rangers suggest June or September; the weather's good, and your chances of landing a campsite are much better than in midsummer. State parks accept written reservations after January 1 and telephone reservations from Memorial Day through Labor Day.

***Lopez Island**: Spencer Spit State Park is a fir-covered slope that leads down to a sandy spit almost touching the shore of Frost Island. Of the 40 campsites, the nicest are the eight walk-ins on the beach, which have barbecues and picnic tables. Reserve through Reservations Northwest at the state-wide campsite reservations system; (800)452-5687. Odlin County Park, only 1³/4 miles from the ferry landing, has 30 sites scattered along a small beach and facing Shaw Island; there is a two-night minimum for reservations, (360)468-2496.*

***Shaw Island**: South Beach County Park, one of the smallest campgrounds in the San Juans, is at the southern end of Shaw and has only 12 sites. No reservations.*

***Orcas Island**: The mammoth Moran State Park, offering swimming, sailboarding, and canoeing, is like summer camp (and just about as crowded). The 166 campsites fill up way before most people are even thinking of summer. Reserve up to 11 months in advance by calling Reservations Northwest, (800)452-5687. A few primitive sites are available on a first-come, first-served basis to cyclists and hikers. Obstruction Pass State Park is at the southwest tip of the island. This remote campground has only nine sites and no running water, and it's a half-mile hike to the beach. We like it for these reasons. No reservations.*

***San Juan Island**: This island's best campsites are just beyond the whale-watching park at San Juan County Park. This pretty cove has only 20 campsites, so be sure to call for reservations in summer; (360)378-2992. Lakedale Campground ((800)617-CAMP or (360)378-2350) is a privately owned property of 50 acres with two lakes, fishing, swimming, boating, and about 117 campsites. You can rent canoes and rowboats.*

Vacation Rentals

A quiet week in a cabin on Lopez Island can be arranged through Lopez Island Vacation Rentals; (800)781-2882 or (360)468-3401. For rentals on Orcas Island, contact Cherie Lindholm Real Estate, (360)376-2204. The list is not huge, mind you, but a waterfront cabin on Orcas isn't a bad way to spend a week or two. You might also consider taking a two-bedroom waterfront cabin at the laid-back West Beach Resort on Orcas, (360)376-2240; when split between two couples, the weekly rate becomes affordable. San Juan Island Vacation Rentals, (800)992-1904 or (360)378-5060, handles most of the rental properties on San Juan Island, but they are considerably more pricey than those on Orcas or Lopez. Most rentals impose a weeklong minimum stay in summer.

Palmer's Chart House
Upper Road (PO Box 51), Deer Harbor, WA 98243 ☎ (360) 376-4231

A room with a private bath and a view of Deer Harbor, plus breakfast for two, for $70 per night? On Orcas Island? In summer? Don and Majean Palmer's simple daylight basement guest rooms fit the bill. The globe-trotting hosts enjoy swapping travel tales with guests. Don offers day sails on his 33-foot sloop, the *Amante*, at $35 per person.

Olympic Lights
4531-A Cattle Point Road, Friday Harbor, WA 98250 ☎ (360) 378-3186

While only one room at this charming bed and breakfast on the southern tip of San Juan Island costs under $75 (the tiny North Star room), three other rooms are $85 per night for two people, including a full breakfast, which still qualifies as one of the best deals on San Juan Island. Baths for these moderately priced rooms are shared (two full baths for four rooms). The farmhouse inn offers a great view of the Olympic Mountains and proximity to the trails and beach at American Camp.

Olympic Peninsula & Kitsap Peninsula

Geographically and historically, the clenched fist of land that is the Olympic Peninsula might as well be an island, encircled as it is by Puget Sound, Hood Canal, the Strait of Juan de Fuca, and the Pacific. Olympic National Park, a jumble of rugged peaks crowned by the 7,965-foot, glaciated Mount Olympus, occupies nearly a million acres in its middle. Highway 101 loops around the peninsula, and side roads lead to beaches, wilderness, and 589 miles of park trails. Small towns around the perimeter offer food, refreshment, amusements, and lodgings. Nearly every town has a museum with tales to tell; some, like the Makahs' cultural center at Neah Bay, are world-famous. Ancient petroglyphs along the Pacific shore also attest to life here long before Captain Vancouver laid eyes on these shores 200 years ago.

Gung-ho visitors can drive the 300-plus-mile loop around the peninsula in a day. Don't. Take time for such distractions as meadows aglow with wildflowers, temperate rain forests, rivers to raft or paddle, beaches to comb, rain-forest trails to hike, country stores to browse, and small-town life to explore. Bring rain gear and sunglasses; rainfall ranges between 200 inches per year on the west slopes of the mountains and 17 inches in the Dungeness Valley on the northeast corner of the peninsula—the rain shadow of the Olympics.

Just to the east—and geographically an appendage—lies the Kitsap Peninsula, which is still largely rural, despite harboring three big military complexes (the naval shipyard in Bremerton, the Naval Undersea Warfare Center in Keyport, and the Bangor naval submarine base). All of Kitsap's towns are on the water; so are some two dozen state and county parks, scattered along 236 miles of the peninsula's shoreline.

Exploring

Port Townsend is an ever-changing mix of quaint and quirky, with an enduring backdrop of ornate 1890s-era architecture. A stroll along **Water Street** offers a mixed bag, from china bunnies to sailing ship models to environmentally correct clothing and food. There's a connoisseur's assortment of galleries, fine shops, bookstores, and highly regarded restaurants. Marinas attract day sailors, yachts, and fishing boats, while the chunky little ferries faithfully ply their way to and from Whidbey Island. Above all this, handsome mansions on the bluff—many now converted to bed and breakfasts—preserve the aura of the 19th-century merchants and tycoons who built far above the hurly-burly of the waterfront. Port Townsend is eminently walkable but not always parkable; leave your car at the Park & Ride (Haines St and Sims Way, near Safeway) and take the free shuttle, which leaves every half hour to run uptown along Lawrence, then down to Water Street and back to the Park & Ride.

The **Historical Museum** (210 Madison St, Port Townsend; (360)385-1003) in City Hall includes the city's original courtroom, 6,000 old photos, Native American artifacts, and mementos of the Chinese community that once lived here, as well as a replica of a furbeloved Victorian bedroom and a view of the gloomy dungeon where Jack London reputedly spent a night on his way to the Klondike. The **Rothschild House** (Jefferson and Taylor Sts, Port Townsend; (360)385-4730) is an 1868 home now maintained by the Washington State Parks Commission; it's open for tours daily in summer, weekends in winter. At the end of Water Street, the Point Hudson Marina is always worth a gander to see what the boatmen are up to. Kids can use up some energy at compact **Pope Marine Park** at the end of Adams Street, where carved wooden seals loll on their huge driftwood log. Have an alfresco lunch—pick up some fish 'n' chips at the Silverwater Cafe's stand on the dock, and then settle

Shellfishing Hood Canal

Gather your own dinner, for free. Several public beaches along Hood Canal are favored by oyster gatherers and clam diggers. They include Potlatch State Park, Lilliwaup Tidelands State Park, Eagle Creek Recreational Tidelands, Twanoh State Park, Seal Rock State Park, and Bywater Bay. Get more information, and maps, from the Washington Department of Fisheries (115 General Administration Building, Olympia, WA 98504; (360)753-6600). To check on emergency regulations before gathering shellfish, call the 24-hour shellfish hotline, (360)796-3215; call the Marine Toxins Hotline, (800)562-5632, for a Red Tide update. A state regulations manual, and your license, may be picked up at any sporting goods store. Several oyster farms will sell you shucked oysters at excellent prices: Dungeness Oyster House (Dungeness Boat Ramp, Sequim; (360)683-1028), Hama Hama Oyster Company (35959 N Hwy 101, Lilliwaup; (360)877-5890), Triton Cove Oyster Farms (39521 N Hwy 101, Brinnon; (360)796-4360), and Coast Oyster Company (1570 Linger Longer Rd, Quilcene; (360)765-3474).

on a bench to admire the view—from Mount Baker to Mount Rainier.

Reach uptown by a steep stairway at Taylor and Washington Streets, heralded by the voluptuous Galatea fountain. The oldest church in the Episcopal Diocese of Olympia—a white, steepled little structure—perches on the bluff, as does an old bell tower once used to summon firemen. Foodies love Aldrich's (940 Lawrence St, Port Townsend; (360)385-0500), a grocery-cum-specialty shop with excellent deli foods, locally roasted coffee, and good budget wines. You could stock up here for a picnic at **Chetzemoka Park** (on Jackson St, between Blaine and Garfield Sts), with its playground, beach, rose arbor, and bandstand, looking out to Admiralty Inlet.

Two miles from town is **Fort Worden State Park**, a former military base that's now a recreation and cultural center. The Centrum Foundation is headquartered here, with its rich selection of seminars, plays, concerts, writers' conferences, poetry readings, and dance performances; (360)385-3102. Some events take place in the former balloon hangar, now a performing arts center. Trails, including a self-guided history walk, wind through Fort Worden's forests and meadows. Wander through old gun emplacements, camp on the beach, surf

at North Beach, or touch a three-spine stickleback at the Marine Science Center (200 Battery Way, Port Townsend; (360)385-5582). Beaches near here are great bird-watching spots.

Eight miles west of Port Townsend, make an espresso and T-shirt stop at **Railroad Park** in Discovery Bay. A row of bright shiny cabooses has come to rest on the old railroad line that once ran from Port Townsend to Port Angeles. The red, white, and blue car offers 14 flavors of ice cream; the pink Candy Depot displays 120 kinds of colorful sweets. Pull a handle and hear an old-time train whistle, and then settle at a table outside for a snack with a bay view.

At Sequim Bay, row after row of gorgeous flowers wait to be picked at **Rosemary's Garden**, south of the highway and just east of the 7 Cedars Casino (270934 Hwy 101, Sequim; (360)683-8251). It's $5 for a big bunch, and it doesn't cost a cent just to look at the flowers, browse in the gift shop, and exchange bleats with the pygmy goats. They love to be brushed, and children are supplied with brushes.

Tour the **Olympic Game Farm** (1423 Ward Rd, Sequim; (360)683-4295) to see 56 species of animals, from bison to bears—many of whom have starred in Disney movies. At the farm's petting zoo,

Port Townsend Festivals

Port Townsend is festival-happy, and at least thrice a year you're guaranteed a great free show along with modestly priced snack foods from the ubiquitous street vendors. The Rhododendron Festival (floats, royalty, bands, and all) is held the third week in May. The Wooden Boat Festival (Wooden Boat Foundation; (360)385-3628), on the first weekend after Labor Day, is centered at Point Hudson, although events take place all over town and include jazz concerts, crafts shows, and strolling entertainers. Sometimes famous vessels are in the harbor, open for tours. Uptown's August celebration is "Uptownsend"—when the Lawrence Street neighborhood puts on the Uptown Street Fair, with a parade, dancing in the street, sidewalk chalk art, and art shows. All the festive facts on these and other events are available from the Port Townsend Visitor Center (2437 Sims Way, Port Townsend, WA 98368; (360)385-2722 or ptchamber@olympus.net).

Shells and Fossils

Visit the world's beaches via a tour of a free museum, **Of Sea and Shore** *(1 Rainier Ave, Port Gamble; (360)297-2426), that occupies a mezzanine gallery above the Port Gamble General Store. It's a fascinating display of more than 14,000 shells and marine fossils from all over the globe.*

kids may meet cute four-legged kids, as well as lambs and chickens. Then walk the **Dungeness Spit**, a national wildlife refuge, to spy seals, eagles, loons, the odd gray whale, expansive views, and, if you persevere for 5 miles, a 140-year-old lighthouse. A $3-per-family fee is charged to enter the refuge; lighthouse tours are free. No pets, no fires, and no bothering the baby seals on the beach! For information, contact the U.S. Fish and Wildlife Office between Sequim and Port Angeles (Hwy 101 at Barr Rd; (360)457-8451). A wooded county park next to the refuge, (360)683-5847, offers picnic areas, views of the strait, and summer camping—no reservations, $10 fee.

Railroad Bridge Park (2151 Hendrickson Rd, Sequim), a mile north of Highway 101 at the west end of Hendrickson Road, features a restored and massive historic Burlington Northern bridge over the Dungeness River. You'll find picnic tables, views of the rushing river, woodland trails, and fishing holes. Between Sequim and Port Angeles, **Finn Hall Farm** (970 Finn Hall Rd; (360)452-9156) invites you to prowl around and into a wonderful collection of little farm- and railroad-oriented museums: a bright red 1920s-era caboose, the diminutive Agnew Depot, the Milk House, and the Browsery gift shop with lovely dried flowers and potpourri. Children may visit with the farm animals. It's all free, and open from March 1 through October; open by appointment only in the off season.)

Stroll along Railroad Avenue, on the **Port Angeles** waterfront; it comes complete with benches and espresso bars. The municipal pier has an observation tower, a sandy beach with picnic area, free summer concerts, and the Arthur D. Feiro Marine Laboratory, (360)452-9277), with hands-on exhibits about sea life. Admission is $1 for adults, 50 cents for children 6–12, free for seniors and children under 6. From the pier, or from Ediz Hook to the west, there are great views of all the harbor activity, including the comings and goings of the ferry to Victoria.

Wine lovers should make a stop at Lost Mountain Winery, up in the foothills (3174 Lost Mountain Rd, Sequim; (360)683-5229), which hosts an "open winery" in June (at other times, call ahead for an appointment). Try the roses and mead at Olympic Cellars (255410 E Hwy 101, Port Angeles; (360)683-9652), or sample the brews of the winery's own microbrewery, the Old Crab Brewing Company (tastings every day).

From Port Angeles, a 17-mile road climbs to **Hurricane Ridge**, one of the most popular routes into **Olympic National Park**. The Olympic National Park Pioneer Memorial Museum and Visitor Center (about 2 miles up; (206)452-0330 or (360)452-0329) provides the latest weather conditions; for winter ski conditions, call (360)417-4555. There's a $10 entrance fee to the national park, good for seven days. At the top, easy trails, some wheelchair-accessible, lead to spectacular viewpoints. A nature trail climbs up the wildflower-carpeted hillside to Hurricane Hill (3 miles round trip). The lodge offers ranger seminars, comestibles, and naturalist-guided snowshoe walks on winter weekends (snowshoes provided free). Kids can bring sleds and inner tubes for sliding. Hurricane

Suquamish Native Americans

The handsome Suquamish Museum (15838 Sandy Hook Rd, Suquamish; (360)598-3311) is down a cedar-lined drive off Highway 305 on the Kitsap Peninsula, just west of the Agate Pass Bridge. It rivals the Makah Cultural and Research Center in Neah Bay in dramatic displays, if not in size. See a hand-carved river canoe and award-winning videos that show a vanished way of life. Admission is $2.50 for adults, $1 for children 12 and under. A pair of evocative Indian heritage sites are nearby, across Highway 305 off Miller Road. Old Man House State Park commemorates the site of a long-gone Suquamish longhouse. The grave of Chief Sealth, for whom Seattle was named, is behind St. Peter's Catholic Church, between the park and the town of Suquamish. Come for the rousing Chief Seattle Days in August, when Native Americans remember their past with drum and dance festivities, a salmon bake, and canoe races.

Ridge is also the peninsula's only **downhill skiing area**, with two rope tows and one poma lift. (Note: The lodge is the only place in the area that rents downhill skis.) For information on cross-country and telemark skiing, drop in at Olympic Mountaineering (140 W Front St, Port Angeles; (360)452-0240).

Lake Crescent, on Highway 101, 20 miles west of Port Angeles, has many roadside pullouts for a picnic or a photo. From Barnes Point, just before Lake Crescent Lodge, walk up a shady trail to 90-foot Marymere Falls. Historic Rosemary Inn, with its idiosyncratic 75-year-old cabins, is the headquarters of the Olympic Park Institute, offering field seminars and Elderhostels on the peninsula and beyond; call or write for a catalog (111 Barnes Point Rd, Port Angeles, WA 98362; (360)928-3720).

Sol Duc Hot Springs Resort (Sol Duc Rd, Port Angeles; (360)327-3583), up a 12-mile road from Highway 101 just west of Lake Crescent, has three outdoor soaking pools, one heated swimming pool, a poolside deli, a restaurant, and a variety of cabins. It costs $6.50 to enter the pools (children free, seniors $5.50); they're open mid-May through September, weekends only in October. For a free dip, seek out the **Olympic Hot Springs**, which has no facilities and is a 2-mile hike from the end of the road (take Elwha River Rd south

from Hwy 101, then follow Boulder Creek Rd to the dead end).

There's a clutch of public and wilderness **beaches** along the Strait of Juan de Fuca between Port Angeles and the Pacific. Freshwater Bay, 10 miles west of Port Angeles off Highway 112, is a small park where tide pools teem with starfish, sea anemones, and sculpin. Just before Joyce (where there's a funny little free local museum) is Tongue Point/Salt Creek Recreation Area, with camping, a playground, cooking facilities, and a generous stretch of beach.

The first good view of the Pacific Ocean is at **Cape Flattery**, just beyond Neah Bay (66 miles from Port Angeles via Hwy 112). Hike to the ocean with dry feet on a boardwalk-style trail and come out of the trees to view ocean-carved cliffs, storm-wracked Tatoosh Island, and its gleaming lighthouse. This is a good bird-watching spot, especially in raptor-migration season. Get a list of what to look for at the **Makah Cultural and Research Center** (PO Box 160, Neah Bay, WA 98357; (360)645-2711). That's the handsome building on your left as you enter Neah Bay, where 500-year-old artifacts unearthed from a long-buried village of Makah ancestors are brilliantly displayed. It's open daily, June through mid-September; closed Mondays and Tuesdays in winter. Drop in at Washburn's General

Store for outdoor gear, groceries, a deli sandwich, and local gossip.

Lake Ozette, the state's largest natural lake, has year-round camping ($1 parking fee; $10 camping fee) and picnicking near the road's end. Explore the marshy, wooded shores of Lake Ozette by canoe, or paddle across to a campground on the western shore. (Be careful: The winds whip up quickly.) Hike the 3 miles from lake to ocean by puncheon trail (cedar slabs), pioneer-style. No permits required for day hikes; for overnights, call (206)452-0300 for a reservation and permit. At the beach, you're near the Makah Indian village archaeological dig; check out the small, informative display.

An alternative to visiting Neah Bay and Lake Ozette is to follow Highway 101 from Lake Crescent toward **Forks**. For a meal stop along Highway 101, the Hungry Bear at Beaver (2 miles east of Sappho; (360)327-3225) is more than okay—it's the only restaurant between Lake Crescent and Forks. Burgers are generous and original (try the halibut burger), doughnuts are made daily, and the wild blackberry pie really is.

At the **Forks Timber Museum** (Hwy 101, Forks; (360)374-9663), say howdy to the 10-foot, chainsaw-carved logger and stop in at the Visitor Center for free coffee and a guide to Arttrek—a free tour of nearly two dozen galleries, gift shops, and studios from La Push to the Hoh Rain Forest. West of Forks, via the La Push road, there's access to four wide **coastal beaches**. Farthest north is Rialto, which offers picnicking and smelting in season, as well as ranger-guided naturalist walks from nearby Mora Campground. You can approach the broad, sandy First Beach to the south through the Quileute village of La Push. Take the trails from the highway to reach Second and Third Beaches, which feature astonishing sea stacks, tide pools, and occasional whale sightings.

In the **Kalaloch** area, a number of short trails to wilderness beaches (a quarter mile each at most) take off from Highway 101. Northernmost **Ruby**

Whale Watching

Gray whales put on a great show when they migrate along the Pacific coast of the Olympic Peninsula on a predictable schedule: south from Alaska, late October to mid-December; north from Baja California, March to May. Better weather and better chances of sighting them close to shore occur in early spring. **Westport** *is the capital of whale watching by boat. About a dozen charters operate three-hour trips. Contact the Westport-Grayland Chamber of Commerce (2985 S Montesano, Westport, WA 98595; (800)345-6223 or (360)268-9422) for a list of charter companies. Or bring your binoculars and spy them from shore. Here are some good viewpoints (north to south):*

Cape Flattery: *Take the half-mile trail from the Makah Indian Reservation.*

Cape Alava: *Take the 3-mile trail from Lake Ozette.*

La Push: *Drive through the village and park close to the road on the south side of the Quillayute River.*

Kalaloch area: *Take the trails off Highway 101 to Ruby Beach and the numbered beaches to the south; stop at the Destruction Island overlook; walk the beach at Kalaloch Lodge.*

Point Grenville: *Take Highway 109 on the Quinault Indian Reservation (get permission).*

Westport: *Head for the whale-watching tower near the marina. Whales sometimes swim right into the harbor.*

Beach has dramatic sea stacks. Also to the north of Kalaloch Lodge and Campground are Beaches 3, 4, and 6. (The trail to Beach 5 is unmarked and quite rugged.) Beaches 1 and 2 are to the south. Prowl the tide pools of Beach 4 for an amazing assortment of intertidal creatures (don't touch, don't take). Just south of Beach 6, a side road to the east wanders for about a quarter mile through a grove of **huge western red cedars**, climaxing with a former record holder, 61 feet around. (The current "biggest cedar" is on Nolan Creek, off the Hoh River Road.)

Roads poke eastward from Highway 101 up four **rain-forest valleys**: Queets, Bogachiel, Hoh, and Quinault. The 19-mile **Hoh River Road** leads to an interpretive center in Olympic National Park, the Hall of Mosses Trail, and other trails through groves of ancient, moss-laden giants. The campground is open all year ($10 a night). The rain forest borders both the north and south shores of **Lake Quinault**. Near Lake Quinault Lodge on the south shore, visit the interpretive center and take a short loop trail to see more giants of the forest.

Kite flying on the beach is a big sport in **Ocean Shores**, further south on the Pacific coast, and the Cutting Edge Kite Co. in Nantucket Square (676 Ocean Shores Blvd, Ocean Shores; (360)289-0667) offers not only a huge selection (wind socks and wind chimes too) but also free flying lessons. A kite doctor is always on hand to make repairs.

At the south end of the Ocean Shores peninsula, the passenger ferry *Matador* makes several round trips daily to **Westport**, April to September. Feed the gulls and look for a whale during the 20-minute crossing. Rates are $8 round trip; children under 5 and bicycles are free. Board the ferry in Westport (Westhaven Dr, Float 10; (360)268-0047) or Ocean Shores (1098 Discovery Ave SE; (360)289-0414).

On the eastern side of the Olympic Peninsula is **Hood Canal**, which comes in two parts: east arm and west arm. Along the east arm, be sure to stop in at the Union Country Store (E 5130 Hwy 106, Union; (360)898-2641) for pizzas, sandwiches, and a variety of hot entrees. Eat in or take out; open every day.

Farther north, a mile and a half before Belfair, traverse the **Hood Canal–Thaler Wetlands** (E 22871 Hwy 3, Belfair; (360)275-4898). Explore the marshes, forests, river, and tidal estuary—4 miles of wide, wheelchair-accessible trails. The interpretive center offers vivid displays and interactive exhibits suitable for all ages. It's all free.

A short hop up the west arm of Hood Canal, **Hoodsport** makes a good stopping place for a burger with a water view or a bagful of groceries. At the national forest ranger station just west of Highway 101, (360)877-5254, get advice if you contemplate a side journey into the Olympics to hike up a river valley or picnic by a stream. They'll explain the backcountry fee system. Visit Hoodsport Winery (N 23501 Hwy 101, Hoodsport; (360)877-9894), where the tasting room looks out over the canal; try their rhubarb and gooseberry wines and indulge in a raspberry wine–infused chocolate truffle.

Whitney Gardens (30624 Hwy 101, Brinnon; (360)796-4411) is blindingly beautiful in May and June, with its 7 acres of rhododendrons, azaleas, shrubs, and trees—some giants. Come in fall for brilliant autumn colors. Admission is $1, children under 12 free. There's a picnic area with lovely floral views.

Near Quilcene, a 5-mile dirt road (summer only) snakes up **Mount Walker**, providing one of the best Olympic-to-Sound views on the peninsula. Drive it in June, when the rhodies are flowering exuberantly—or walk; it's a 2-mile hike, with switchbacks.

Highway 104 and the Hood Canal

Bridge connect the Olympic and Kitsap Peninsulas west of Quilcene. There are no more thriving fishermen's resorts at **Hansville**, the end-of-the-road community near Point No Point, northwest of Kingston on the **Kitsap Peninsula**. Today the town centers on the Hansville Grocery & Provisions Company (7542 NE Twin Spits Rd, Hansville; (360)638-2303), where you can stock up on food, books, local gossip, beer, wine, and videos. Nearby, the weathered remains of Captain's Landing (PO Box 113, Hansville, WA 98340; (360)638-2257) offer very basic lodgings. The housekeeping cabins strung along the shore are elderly, but you can't beat the view; bring your own linens and utensils. South of here, the stubby, 100-year-old **Point No Point Lighthouse** can be toured, but call first; (360)638-2261. Beyond, walk the sandy beach, but don't trespass on private property; stay below the high-tide line.

A neat-as-a-pin company town that lives on in spite of the closing of the company—the Pope & Talbot mill—**Port Gamble** is durably enchanting, with its maple-shaded streets lined with immaculate and authentic Victorian homes. Visit the town's past in the Port

Budget Cruising

From April through September, Sequim Bay Tours (2577 W Sequim Bay Rd, Sequim; (360)681-7408) embarks from John Wayne Marina on the 30-foot Still Water for a 2 1/2-hour voyage to both parts of the **Dungeness National Wildlife Refuge**: *Protection Island, where thousands of seabirds nest, and Dungeness Spit. No shore stops, but you'll observe seabirds in abundance, seals, maybe whales, and stunning views of the Olympics and Mount Baker. It's worth the not-quite-budget cost: $34 adults, $17 ages 6–12, kids under 5 free.*

Take a trip abroad: cruise to **Victoria** *across the Strait of Juan de Fuca, embarking from the Landing Mall in Port Angeles with Victoria Express, (360)452-8088. The cruise takes only an hour, with magnificent views of the Olympics as you reach the middle of the strait. You could leave Port Angeles at 8:10am, amuse yourself in Victoria for nine hours, and catch the 6:15pm boat back. Victoria Express makes several round trips daily, from the end of May to mid-October. Round-trip fares: $20–$25 adults, $10–$12.50 ages 5–11, kids under 5 free. Black Ball Transport (101 E Railroad Ave, Port Angeles; (360)457-4491) runs a ferry from Port Angeles to Victoria that takes walk-on passengers for a one-way fare of $6.75.*

On **Lake Crescent**, *take a 90-minute cruise on a replica of a 1920s-era paddle wheeler to view the mountains, wooded shorelines, and historic lodges while a national park interpreter explains their history and geology. Tours depart from Storm King Ranger Station on Lake Crescent, near Lake Crescent Lodge, June through September. Call Mosquito Fleet, (360)452-4520, for information and reservations. Tickets are $15 adults, $7.50 ages 6–17, kids under 5 free.*

Take a cruise between **Port Orchard and Bremerton**, *only 10 minutes apart by foot ferry. Horluck Transportation Company, (360)876-2300, runs a boat every half hour between the two. You can lunch and shop in Port Orchard, pop over to Bremerton to stroll the boardwalk, inspect the USS Turner Joy, take the harbor cruise to see the fleet, and then sail back to Port Orchard. Or vice versa. On the way you get a great view of the naval might. Fare is $1 adults, 50¢ ages 6–11; free on weekends, May through October.*

Gamble Historical Museum, (360)297-3341, half a block north of Highway 104 in the center of town. See re-creations of a ship's cabin, a sawdusty mill room, the lushly decorated lobby of the late Hotel Puget, and an Indian longhouse. Sound effects add to the illusions: waves lapping at the porthole, the buzzing of circular saws. The museum is open Memorial Day through Labor Day. The Port Gamble General Store, adjacent to the museum (1 Rainier Ave, Port Gamble; (360)297-7636), still flourishes, too. Stop in for an espresso, a sandwich, a mile-high ice cream cone, or a picnic to go. Take your lunch out to a table on the town's grassy slopes, which command fine views of the old mill and the water.

Bremerton, about 22 miles south of Port Gamble via Highway 3, is a naval city through and through. It makes the most of its waterfront and its harborful of active and mothballed vessels. Get a good view from **Overwater Park**, where a concrete promenade (familiarly, the boardwalk) runs between 1st and 4th Avenues. You'll find picnic tables, restrooms, and an observation platform. The boardwalk leads to the *USS Turner Joy*, of Gulf of Tonkin fame, open for self-guided tours from pilothouse to engine room. A moving sight is the POW memorial—a replicated cell from the "Hanoi Hilton" prison. Tours are $5 adults, $4 seniors, and $3 children 5–12. Tickets are on sale in the Ship's Store Gift Shop on the boardwalk, also the place for harbor tour tickets. Kitsap Harbor Tours, (360)377-

8924, offers a 45-minute narrated cruise around modern and retired battleships, nuclear submarines, and other warships, including the world's largest warship, a Nimitz-class aircraft carrier. The free **Bremerton Naval Museum** near the ferry terminal (130 Washington, Bremerton; (360)479-7447) tells of the swashbuckling days of sailing vessels and the history of the U.S. Navy.

Port Orchard, across Sinclair Inlet from Bremerton, is a scenic 15-minute drive from the Southworth ferry terminal. Its eight-block downtown area along arcaded Bay Street is thick with cafes, taverns, delis, and antique shops. At the two-story Olde Central Antique Mall (801 Bay St, Port Orchard; (360)895-1902), scores of entrepreneurs display such wares as Depression-era glass, quilts, and antique tools. From April to October, a **farmers market** is held along the waterfront park on Saturdays from 9am to 3pm. Wander among the gaily decorated canopies in search of herbs, scones, Hood Canal oysters and clams, just-picked flowers, and crafts galore.

See the Northwest's largest collection of modern dolls at Springhouse Dolls and Gifts (1130 Bethel Ave, Port Orchard; (360)876-0529), in a turreted pink-and-cerise Victorian-style house, a 5-minute drive from downtown Port Orchard. In addition to famous-name dolls and their friends—bears, calico kittens, Disney creatures—Springhouse has a pretty tearoom serving breakfast, lunch, teas, and espresso.

Cheap Eats

The Cellars Market
940 Water Street, Port Townsend ☎ (360) 385-7088

Descend the stairs to a tunnel-like cavern where, according to unreliable myth, Chinese laborers were smuggled in Port Townsend's lurid past. Here amid brick walls and the work of many local artists, owner Randy Unbedacht offers lunchtime fare including salads (try the crunchy pea and peanut), sandwiches, homemade soups, and lasagne or quiche by the slice. There's homemade fudge in the candy shop.

Landfall

412 Water Street, Port Townsend ☎ (360) 385-5814

Old sea dogs, young salts, and aficionados of the laid-back lunch hang out here at this faded white restaurant at the water end of Water Street—a good vantage point for watching the goings-on at the Point Hudson Marina. They serve three meals a day on weekends, breakfast and lunch on weekdays, and are justly proud of their barbecued salmon, halibut, and steaks. Seated at long wooden tables, you can also swig a brew while munching sandwiches, burgers, and several Mexican specialties.

The Public House

1038 Water Street, Port Townsend ☎ (360) 385-9708

A favorite local hangout that's big, rather bare, and high-ceilinged. When it fills up of an evening and the live music starts, things get noisy. The menu, the same for lunch and dinner, makes the most of fresh local seafood and does well by ribs, burgers, pasta, and other standbys. The list of draught beers is impressive; so is the cabinetry on the long wooden bar. Smokers will have to step outside.

Salal Cafe

634 Water Street, Port Townsend ☎ (360) 385-6532

Good news for its devotees—the Salal now serves dinner as well as breakfast and lunch. From morning Greek omelet to evening eggplant Ceylon, it's all dependably tasty and original. Settle in the cheery many-windowed back room to read the morning paper with latte in hand, or enjoy lunch with a local microbrew.

Khu Larb Thai

120 W Bell Street, Sequim ☎ (360) 681-8550

With the opening of this outpost of the venerable Port Townsend restaurant, authentic Thai cuisine inched its way westward on the peninsula. In a modest building just south of Washington Street, the family-owned establishment has gained an enthusiastic following, and dinnertimes are often crowded (parties of six or more may reserve). The menu offers a wide assortment of vegetarian dishes as well as elegantly prepared and served curries, sweet-and-sours, and Thai specialties you're unlikely to find elsewhere in these parts (try the deep-fried, spiced chicken wrapped in pandanus leaves). The fried-rice selection alone is enough to dazzle your palate.

Oak Table Cafe

292 W Bell Street, Sequim ☎ (360) 683-2179

It would be hard to find a heartier or tastier daytime repast than at this cafe, where residents bring their guests, and tourists in the know stop for fortification. The two big, bright, greenery-bedecked rooms are a scene of animated chatter amid the swift comings and goings of efficient servers bearing huge omelets, fluffy pancakes, quiches, sandwiches, soups, and salads.

Son's

206 N Sequim Avenue, Sequim ☎ (360) 683-2121

A modest fixture in downtown Sequim, Son's is a good place for a bargain lunch, dinner, or take-out, whether you're in the mood for Szechuan, Vietnamese, or American. The menu's surprisingly large, with everything cooked to order—choose from six kinds of chow mein, and many chicken, pork, beef, and seafood specialties. Steady customers swear by the pot-stickers. Son's is open 7am to 7pm; closed Sundays.

Arnel's Pacific Wine & Grill

128 Railroad Avenue, Port Angeles ☎ (360) 452-7282

Handy to the Victoria ferry and serving breakfast and lunch daily, Arnel's is a friendly, casual place. Owner-chef Arnel Alcafaras gets imaginative with his pasta dishes. Try the chicken piccata with capers, artichoke hearts, and mushrooms over linguine, or grab a take-out sandwich for the road. You can order an espresso at the walk-up window on the street.

Bonny's Bakery

215 S Lincoln Street, Port Angeles ☎ (360) 457-3585

The setting—a cleverly recycled old firehouse—is steeped in Port Angeles history. Bonny and E. J. Kelly continue to add their own culinary chapter to the record, with exquisite pastries and a line of inventive sandwiches served on homemade breads. It's a good place to relax by day over a meal or a snack, with plenty of seating indoors and out. Try the smoked salmon and cream cheese on a petite baguette, or slowly savor a napoleon and an espresso.

First Street Haven

107 E 1st Street, Port Angeles ☎ (360) 457-0352

Look carefully or you might go right by this narrow restaurant squeezed between neighboring storefronts. Weekday mornings and noontimes it's crowded with local business folk, so you may have to wait. But the service is great: before long you'll be munching your cinnamon roll or savoring your minestrone. Fresh and unusual salads, hearty sandwiches, pastas, and quiches dominate the lunch menu; the chili is great on a cold winter day.

Thai Peppers

229 N Lincoln Street, Port Angeles ☎ (360) 452-4995

Proprietor Sonthya Itti (formerly of Sequim's Khu Larb Thai) has brought Thai food to Port Angeles with splendid results. Two could happily share an appetizer of deep-fried wontons stuffed with crab, cream cheese, and scallions. Entrees such as *shu see*—tender chunks of fish swimming in a rich red curry sauce spiked with coconut milk and basil—phad Thai, or fried rice generously apportioned with fresh vegetables make for great dining. Bring a spicy meal to a refreshing close with a scoop of ginger-flavored ice cream.

Smoke House Restaurant

193161 Highway 101, Forks ☎ (360) 374-6258

At this square blue building north of Forks, salmon alder-smoked on the premises is the menu's star ingredient. Try it as an entree, in sandwiches or salads, or tossed with pasta. Liver with plenty of onions is another staple. Meals are hearty, and so is the hospitality. Cans of smoked salmon are for sale.

Billy's Bar and Grill

322 E Heron Street, Aberdeen ☎ **(360) 533-7144**

Located in Aberdeen at the south end of the Olympic Peninsula, Billy's serves the same food for lunch and dinner: seafood, chicken, steaks, and 14 hamburger choices. The meatloaf sandwich with mashed potatoes and gravy will give you strength to explore the national park—for days to come. Breakfasts are equally fortifying. Green-shaded lamps, red leather booths, dark polished wood, and the long, substantial well-stocked bar make you want to linger.

Twana Roadhouse

29473 Highway 101, Quilcene ☎ **(360) 765-6485**

Completely transformed from a sagging old cafe, the new Twana Roadhouse and adjacent Trading Post add up to a good reason to pause in Quilcene. Have breakfast, lunch, or dinner in a cheerful room where tourists and locals mingle. The menu won't dazzle, but everything is good and fresh: soups, salads, sandwiches, pizzas, and enchiladas, plus homemade pies and hand-dipped ice cream.

Old Kingston Hotel Cafe

25931 Washington Boulevard, Kingston ☎ **(360) 297-8100**

Judith Weinstock's seasonal fare bespeaks freshness, ethnic influences, and imagination, and has attracted a loyal clientele of ferry travelers and locals who crowd her funky little cafe on the north end of the Kitsap Peninsula. In the morning, sip coffee with a heavenly scone out on the porch with its view of the Seattle skyline. At lunch try the splendid soups or a grilled eggplant sandwich. At dinner, appetizers could easily serve as a light meal. Don't miss the fish stew—rich with mussels, clams, and finfish, served with basmati rice. There's a charming garden patio out back.

Aladdin's Palace Restaurant

9399 Ridgetop Boulevard NW, Suite B, Silverdale ☎ **(360) 698-6599**

Who would expect to find a gem of a Lebanese restaurant secreted in the commercial jungles of Silverdale? Begin your meal with such treats as falafel, tabbouleh, or *zahra* (deep-fried cauliflower with tahini sauce). The house salad intrigues with its mint vinaigrette. Go on to shish kabob, stuffed grape leaves, or a luscious moussaka studded with roasted garlic cloves. Arabian coffee is available, as well as baklava and other sweets.

Pot Belly Deli

724 Bay Street, Port Orchard ☎ **(360) 895-1396**

If you're hell-bent for the next antique shop, you might walk right by. But Port Orchardites know the deli well and congregate here for breakfast, lunch, and gossip. Tasty sandwiches, soups, and salads are cheerfully dispensed from the counter at the back of the narrow, brick-walled restaurant. An 1880s-era upright piano on a dais in the window is available to musical customers. Place your order at the counter, and dash off a tune while you wait for your meal.

Cheap Sleeps

Fort Flagler Hostel

10621 Flagler Road, Marrowstone Island, Nordland, WA 98358
☎ (360) 385-1288

The veteran hostel has been spiffing itself up with steady refurbishing. Dorm rooms house 14 bunk beds, and there's a living room with a wood stove, a big kitchen, a laundry room, and two baths. One room is set aside for families. Bring food and sleeping bags. The low cost of the lodgings contrasts with the scenic and recreational riches outside at Fort Flagler State Park, at the north end of Marrowstone Island. The three-way water views are sensational, and there's camping, picnicking, miles of hiking trails, fishing, crabbing (pots available), and a nature conservancy. Arrive by bike and pay less. Open March 15 through September.

Belmont Hotel

925 Water Street, Port Townsend, WA 98368 ☎ (360) 385-3007

Since 1885, this exuberantly decorated building has stood at the heart of Port Townsend's historic downtown. It's considerably more respectable now, with an acclaimed restaurant and bar downstairs and four pleasant rooms upstairs. The decor is Victorian, naturally, and all rooms have private baths. Two face the water, two the street; one has a kitchen. Children are welcome; pets are not.

Point Hudson Motel, Marina and RV Park

Point Hudson, Port Townsend, WA 98368 ☎ (800) 826-3854 or (360) 385-2828

A former Coast Guard station on the north end of town was transformed into a resort in 1970, and it keeps evolving. The 24-room oft-remodeled motel is nothing fancy, but there's lots to do just outside, including supervising the activity in the marina and walking the beach, and it's just a few blocks to downtown Port Townsend. The sprawl of peak-roofed, clapboard buildings includes a sailmaker, meeting pavilion, Chinese restaurant, bait shop, and laundry. The mood is engagingly informal. Kids and pets are welcome.

Waterstreet Hotel

635 Water Street, Port Townsend, WA 98368 ☎ (800) 735-9810 or (360) 385-5467

Unexpected pleasures are hidden away on the two top floors of the historic Hill Building. Climb the stairs from the lobby (which displays choice art from the Northwest Native Expressions Gallery) to the 16 rooms large and small—most with baths, some with lofts, some with kitchens, and a couple of pricier suites with decks and harbor views. The period furnishings are comfortable, the rooms inviting. Children and well-behaved pets are welcome.

Granny Sandy's Orchard

405 W Spruce Street, Sequim, WA 98382 ☎ (360) 683-5748

Modest prices and a dandy location, an easy walk from the shops and restaurants of sunny Sequim, are part of the attraction. So's the friendly welcome by ("Granny") Sandy and Paul Moore. The garden—where guests are invited to wander—flourishes, thanks to the couple's horticultural skills. And yes, there really is an orchard, which makes possible many a breakfast treat. One bedroom downstairs has a private bath; three upstairs share a bath.

Indian Valley Motel and Granny's Cafe

235471 Highway 101, Port Angeles, WA 98362 ☎ (360) 928-3266

For 34 years this motel has been a favorite stop for tourists looking for a good Olympic Peninsula value. The nine units are neat as a pin but innocent of frills, TV, or sample toiletries. Out back are an RV park, campsites, and a forest trail. Granny's Cafe, next door, is a down-home, out-West eatery, with regulars bantering and transient tourists joining in as they tackle the substantial meals.

Pond Motel

1425 W Highway 101, Port Angeles, WA 98363 ☎ (360) 452-8422

It's easy to miss; 1 1/2 miles west of Port Angeles, look to the right and be ready to slow down when you see the pond. Nine of the 12 well-maintained units have kitchens. You're welcome to use the barbecue, have a picnic, and wander among the gardens. The pond is stocked with ducks and fish, and a wee bridge leads to a wee island.

Van Riper's Resort

Front and Rice Streets (PO Box 246), Sekiu, WA 98381 ☎ (360) 963-2334

Van Riper's is a friendly family-run hotel, popular with fisherfolk, scuba divers, beach buffs, and, increasingly, tourists from afar who are eager to get close to western waters. In the main building, half of the 12 rooms have views of the Strait of Juan de Fuca and Sekiu's harbor—especially riveting during salmon season. The best quarters are the separate house, which sleeps six to eight; the Penthouse in the main building, which sleeps six; and a large new three-bedroom unit. All have kitchens. Closed mid-October through January, although off-season guests are sometimes accommodated; call first. No pets. For utmost economy, stay in their RV campground.

Cape Flattery Resort

Makah Tribal Center (PO Box 117), Neah Bay, WA 98357 ☎ (360) 645-3325

Two miles west of Neah Bay, a decommissioned Air Force station has been converted by the Makahs into their tribal headquarters, with lodgings available in one dorm of the enlisted men's quarters. Cost varies with the number of beds occupied; group rates are available. All rooms have baths. It's pretty basic, but it beats camping in the rain and is as close as you can get to the northwestern corner of the contiguous United States and the attractions of Cape Flattery and Hoko Beach.

Miller Tree Inn

654 E Division Street (PO Box 953), Forks, WA 98331 ☎ (360) 374-6806

Eighty years ago, a dairy farm stood on this site. The B&B is the original farm-house, updated but in a bucolic setting reminiscent of its past. The hospitality offered by Ted and Prue Miller is easygoing and considerate. Two bedrooms have private baths, two have half-baths, and two share a bath. Breakfasts are part do-it-yourself from the breakfast bar, part to-order pastries, omelets, and such. For fishermen, the Millers serve an early breakfast, suggest a guide, pack a sack lunch, and, at a lucky day's end, package and freeze the catch. No catch? They'll also serve dinner to guests who reserve.

Rain Forest Hostel

169312 Highway 101, Forks, WA 98331 ☎ (360) 374-2270

Houseparents Jim Conomos and Kay Ritchie believe firmly in the hostel con-cept: sharing accommodations, pitching in to clean up, and enjoying the fellow-ship of like-minded travelers. They offer a variety of sleeping arrangements: bunk rooms in the main house and a spacious annex, a room for families with double bed and bunks, and two trailers suitable for families or couples. All bed-ding is provided, as is use of the kitchen. Jim and Kay point guests toward the best mushroom- and berry-picking spots, hiking trails, and fishing holes. The $10 per night charge is halved for children 13 and under; tots under 5 are free.

Three Rivers Resort

7764 La Push Road, Forks, WA 98331 ☎ (360) 374-5300

Steelhead and salmon leap in the nearby Bogachiel, Soleduck, and Quillayute Rivers. Sign up for a guided fishing trip, but never mind if fish don't land in your creel. The resort has a well-stocked grocery with a little dining room annex that offers the "World-Famous River Burger" and 12 flavors of shakes. The five housekeeping cabins are no longer young, but still cozy. La Push and ocean beaches are only 10 minutes away.

La Push Ocean Park and Shoreline Resort

Front Street (PO Box 67), La Push, WA 98350 ☎ (800) 487-1267 or (360) 374-5267

You have many choices here, but reserve early at this oceanfront Quileute tribal enterprise. Its proximity to the Pacific and its many moods, coupled with easy beach access, makes it very popular. Whale and Thunderbird, with 20 motel-style units, have kitchens, electric heat, so-so but adequate furnishings, and ocean views. Other choices range from "campers' cabins" (no view, wood-burning stoves, bring your own bedding) to the more commodious cabins on the beach, which have fireplaces. Cabins and motel units sleep two to six. The resort also has RV and camping sites.

Lochaerie Resort

638 North Shore Road, Amanda Park, WA 98526 ☎ (360) 288-2215

Scattered down a steepish slope on the north shore of Lake Quinault, these five endearing cabins have weathered with considerable grace. All are named for Olympic peaks, with the earliest dating from 1926. Longtime devotees have their favorites and reserve a year ahead. Colonel Bob, the largest, sleeps six. The one-bedroom Christie (sleeps three) is closest to the lake, down the most steps, and most in demand. Linens, utensils, and firewood are provided. Guests are free to use the canoes at the dock to paddle about the lake.

Moonstone Beach Motel

4849 Pacific Street (PO Box 156), Moclips, WA 98562 ☎ (360) 276-4346

Along North Beach, where small towns welcome ocean enthusiasts, you get good value at this modest eight-unit motel, a few yards north of the bridge into town and right on the beach. Second-floor guests see a little more sea. All units have kitchens, and there's a separate six-person cabin. Plan ahead, as this place fills up fast in summer.

Sand Dollar Inn

53 Central Avenue (PO Box 206), Pacific Beach, WA 98571 ☎ (360) 276-4525

The new owners have done a commendable job of sprucing up this 50-year-old motel. Now it lives up to its location, just 300 feet from the dunes and the lovely wide beach. The eight rooms are airy, bright, and uncluttered, their brick walls gleaming with fresh white paint. All but one have full kitchens. Baths are spotless. Upstairs rooms, and some downstairs, have partial or full ocean views. A fenced garden patio in back with grill is a sun trap, just the place for a backyard barbecue. Rates are reasonable, and for a very little more you may engage the third-floor Penthouse, with its fantastic view, or one of the three family-friendly cottages across the street. Pets OK; $5 extra.

West Winds Resort Motel

2537 State Route 109, Ocean City, WA 98569 ☎ (800) 867-3448 or (360) 289-3448

Five little log-veneer cabins, plus a larger two-unit cabin, look out at lawn and trees; up above, two motel-style units view dunes and ocean, as does a house that sleeps eight. There's a mini-playground for the kids, and a "Clam Galley" where you may clean your dig. The management eases access to the beach by providing a raft to cross the creek that meanders through the dunes. All units have TV and kitchens; one cabin has a fireplace.

Vagabond House Motel

**686 Ocean Shores Boulevard (PO Box 504), Ocean Shores, WA 98569
☎ (800) 290-2899 or (360) 289-2350**

Look for the blue, peak-roofed motel a half block from the Shilo Inn, on the other, lower-cost side of Ocean Shores Boulevard. Some of the 17 rooms have refrigerators and others have kitchens. The decor may be oddly assorted, but the rooms are quiet, neat, and clean; some even afford a glimpse of the ocean. Second-floor rooms also look out to the restful green expanse of the golf course. But you don't come here for the view, you come to do all that Ocean Shores offers: beachcombing, horseback riding, kite flying, riding mopeds, and boating on Duck Lake.

Harbor Resort

871 Neddie Rose Drive, Westport, WA 98595 ☎ (360) 268-0169

A longtime fixture out at the end of the jetty, the family-run resort has recently added a row of cottages, but Mark and Kathy Dodson still refuse to get fancy. Downstairs there's a general store and a deli with a few tables, where chili, clam chowder, sandwiches, and hot dogs are always available. Some of the six rooms upstairs have kitchens and some don't (rent a couple of adjoining ones for a self-sufficient suite). Crabs and whales are major attractions. Mark will rent you a crab trap and educate fledgling crabbers. Whales sometimes come right into Westport Harbor and can be spied from the resort's ocean-facing rooms. The cottages, which can sleep up to six, cost more, but the per-person rate is still small. And you can fish from your deck.

Tokeland Hotel

100 Hotel Road, Tokeland, WA 98590 ☎ (360) 267-7006

Now that Scott and Catherine White have completed the room restoration (17 are now in service), this landmark hotel is confidently entering its second century. Bedrooms aren't too gussied up; baths are down the hall. Guests find plenty of comfortable ways to relax, whether sunning in the meadow or reading in the fireplace room off the lobby. The restaurant, open to the public, does a creditable job at a reasonable rate. You'll find down-home cooking with due deference to fresh local specialties such as oysters, crab, and cranberries. The room rate includes breakfast. Pets are not invited.

Glen Ayr Resort

2538 N Highway 101, Hoodsport, WA 98548 ☎ (800) 367-9522 or (360) 877-9522

Besides RV parking, you'll find 14 large, handsome rooms and two suites (with cooking facilities) in a two-story log and knotty pine building overlooking the canal. A rarity in a motel setting is the common room for guests, big and airy, with fireplace, pool table, card tables, and books. There's an RV park, and moorage for small boats at the motel's marina. You're free to visit the private oyster beds on Tuesdays and Thursdays—limit 10 oysters per room.

Mike's Beach Resort

38470 N Highway 101, Lilliwaup, WA 98555 ☎ (800) 231-5324 or (360) 877-5324

The activities available here could exhaust you if you tried to enjoy them all: kayaking, diving to explore the sunken vessels just offshore, snorkeling, crabbing and clamming, bird watching, and picnicking on the beach, for starters. Lodgings are almost as varied: cabins sleeping one to four, a dormitory, a youth hostel, RV spaces, and campsites. Nothing's spiffy and the cabins weren't born yesterday, but Mike Schultz and his mother manage the whole shebang with the ingenuity and helpfulness that come from 40-plus years of welcoming beach buffs.

Still Waters Bed and Breakfast

13202 Olympic Road SE, Olalla, WA 98359 ☎ (253) 857-5111

This inn on the south Kitsap Peninsula captures your heart at once. You drive up a lane beneath tall poplars and firs that look down on gnarled fruit trees, lawns, and old-fashioned gardens—a melding of nature and innkeeper Cynthia Sailer's art. A gazebo, a rose arbor, and a few tables and chairs on the grass suggest repose. So do the three comfortable, antique-furnished bedrooms. Two, with double beds, share a bath. The other, with queen, has a private bath, deck, and view of the Olympic Range. Breakfasts may be tailored to your wishes. If left to her druthers, Cynthia is likely to serve her secret-recipe French toast or German apple pancakes. Children and pets are not invited. A day spa is run in connection with the inn.

Long Beach Peninsula & Willapa Bay

En route from Seattle to the Long Beach Peninsula, you drive by the Home of the World's First Tree Farm and by the Largest Estuarine Island on the Pacific Coast. Once on the peninsula—locally proclaimed as the World's Longest Beach (we actually know a longer 60-mile stretch of beach on New York's Long Island, but never mind), you can devour the World's Largest Hamburger, break the World's Record for Kites in the Sky, or catch the World's Largest Chinook.

We haven't counted, but we suspect the residents of this 28-mile-long peninsula in southwestern Washington, 110 miles northwest of Portland and 180 miles southwest of Seattle, might also claim the world's record for most superlatives. It's easy to poke fun at this peninsula pride, as well as at the area's summertime popularity, which has spurred such illustrious attractions as bumper cars, pinball arcades, and T-shirt vendors. Still, behind all the gift shops and the tire tracks on the beach, there is plenty to explore that's wonderful and remarkable.

This southwestern elbow of Washington consists of three distinct environments: the vast beaches of the peninsula from Cape Disappointment north to Leadbetter Point; the eelgrass, shellfish, and migrating birds of Willapa Bay; and the old-growth western red cedar on Long Island.

The summer invasion of beachbound tourists doubles the prices of lodging, clogs Highway 103 (the peninsula's main artery), and crowds its only state park campground. Increasingly popular festivals make planning ahead a must for most of the summer. Instead, try visiting off-season—perhaps in spring, when the skies can just as easily be bright and sunny as wet; or in early fall, when the weather is glorious.

Exploring

The great thing about **Long Beach** is that you can do almost anything on its hard, flat sands. You can walk, run, sit, fly kites, ride horses, and even drive your car (a 25mph speed limit is strictly enforced, and some areas are off-limits, so check first).

The constant coastal winds make **kite flying** a passion. The town of Long Beach boasts three kite shops: Stormin' Norman's (205 Pacific Hwy S, Long Beach; (360)642-3482) is the oldest and stocks a huge selection of reasonably priced kites. Ocean Kites (511 Pacific Hwy S, Long Beach; (800)234-1033 or (360)642-2229) offers free kite-flying lessons, while Long Beach Kites (104 Pacific Hwy N, Long Beach; (360)642-2202) stocks kites from all over the world and sells numerous wind toys. The owners, Jim and Kay Buesing, also run the World Kite Museum (3rd St NW, Long Beach; (360)642-4020), which exhibits functional and exotic works of flying art. (Admission is $3 for families, $1 for adults, and 50¢ for kids and seniors.) Mid-August brings the International Kite Festival, during which stunt kites, home-made kites, and high-altitude kites compete for flight time; (800)451-2542.

Horseback riding on the beach is the stuff of dreams. Visit Skipper's Horse Rentals (9th St S and Beach Blvd, Long Beach; (360)642-3676) or Back Country Wilderness Outfitters (10th St S, Long Beach; (360)642-2576) for guided excursions.

Sand-Stations, a sand-sculpting contest held each year on the last weekend in July, is a beachgoing pursuit of a more artistic kind, attracting artists and gawkers from near and far. Also, don't miss the three-quarter-mile **Long Beach boardwalk**, which stretches along the dunes and the ocean, from the main beach access in town to 10th Street S. Wind-sheltered picnic tables and restrooms are available. Walk or ride your bike along the 2-mile Dune Trail, which stretches from 17th Street S to 15th Street N. Stop at Milton York (109 Pacific Hwy S, Long Beach; (360)642-2352) for saltwater taffy, ice cream, and candy. Picnic supplies can be had at Pacific Picnics (312 Pacific Hwy S, Long Beach; (360)642-2535). Other **picnic areas** include Loomis Lake State Park (6 miles north of Long Beach along Hwy 103), with wind barriers, barbecues, restrooms, and easy beach access; Moorehead County Park (just north of 273rd St in Nahcotta), a laid-back bay-side setting with tall trees, tables, and restrooms; and Riekkola Wildlife Preserve (67th Pl, off Sandridge Road), a primitive, little-used retreat.

One time-honored beach tradition, **razor clamming**, has been severely restricted recently. Call the Washington Department of Fish and Wildlife in Olympia for specific information; (360)902-2700.

The peninsula's southern tip is anchored by precipitous **Cape Disappointment**—so named by 18th-century mariner John Mears after he failed to locate the then-undiscovered Columbia River. Visitors can observe spectacular panoramas of the north jetty and the river's mouth from the viewing windows at the **Lewis & Clark Interpretive Center** at Fort Canby, (360)642-3029, which tells the story of Meriwether Lewis and William Clark's 1805–06 expedition from St. Louis to the Pacific. During winter sou'westers, unrelenting swells march in from the open Pacific like the troops of an invading army. A sometimes-steep trail leads from just inside the Fort Canby State Park entrance to **Cape Disappointment Lighthouse**, constructed in 1856. A few miles away, stalwart North Head Lighthouse, dating from 1898, is situated at the cusp of weather-beaten North Head, the Washington coast's windiest promontory. Both lighthouses are open for summer tours (a fee is charged). Also here is 1,800-acre **Fort Canby State Park**, a former military installation (established in 1862) that is now the only state park on the peninsula allowing camping. Not surprisingly, it fills up in the summer, so reserve as far ahead as possible; call (360)642-3078 for reservations and information on the lighthouses.

Ilwaco, the nearest port to the mouth of the Columbia River, is the sport-fishing hub. Charter companies, open for **fishing** primarily from May through October, will guide you on salmon, sturgeon, and bottom-fishing excursions and provide everything except a guaranteed catch. Call the Ilwaco Charter Association, (360)642-3333, for fishing-season schedules and information on charter companies. Prime freshwater angling is yours at Black Lake (between Ilwaco and Seaview), Loomis Lake (6 miles north of Long Beach along Hwy 103), and the Naselle River (east of the peninsula, near the town of Naselle). Or buy your fish at Jessie's Ilwaco Fish (West End and Port Docks, Ilwaco; (360)642-3773), take it to the nearby city park, and have a fisherman's barbecue. While in town, also check out the **Ilwaco Heritage Museum** (115 SE Lake St, Ilwaco; (360)642-3446), which presents exhibits on Native Americans, explorers, fishermen, farmers, commercial cranberry

Festivals

The peninsula offers more festivals per capita than anyplace in the Northwest. In addition to Sand-Stations in July and the International Kite Festival in August, there's a beachcomber festival, a rodeo, a "Rod Run to the End of the World," an Independence Day festival, and a jazz 'n' oyster festival, to name a few. The Long Beach Peninsula Visitor's Bureau (corner of Hwy 103 and Hwy 101, Long Beach; (800)451-2542 or (360)642-2400) is the best source of information on any of 'em. Others include:

Garlic Festival: It's chic to reek at Ocean Park's free, annual garlic-inspired get-together, held toward the end of June. Look for garlic doughnuts, garlic jam, garlic-covered chocolates, and more traditional fare such as garlic oysters, garlic steamers, and garlic-bacon burgers. There's also lots of live music, "reek-to-reek" dancing to the music of the Clove Brothers, and garlic-peeling contests and relay races.

Water Music Festival: In late October, chamber music concerts flourish everywhere, from the church in Oysterville to the community center in Ilwaco. Concert tickets run from $5–$15, but in the Water Music Festival's spirit of making good music available to all, musicians occasionally perform at no charge.

Cranberrian Fair: Headquartered at the Ilwaco Heritage Museum, this festival takes place in mid-October during the cranberry harvest (it usually lasts into early November). You can drive on Cranberry Road through acres and acres of ripe, red berries or enjoy a guided "bog tour." Any time of the year, take a free, self-guided stroll at the Cranberry Museum (2907 Pioneer Road, Long Beach), run by the Pacific Coast Cranberry Research Foundation (the museum is open on weekends from May to December).

Long Island

Crowning Long Island is 274-acre Cedar Grove, one of the last remnants of a coastal forest spared from logging, fires, and violent storms. It's a pleasant day hike. Paddle over to the island from the boat launch at the Willapa National Wildlife Refuge headquarters on Highway 101; (360)484-3482. You can camp on the island at one of five designated campgrounds (totaling 25 sites, all on a first-come, first-served basis). Bring your own boat or take a guided tour with the Shoalwater Bay Navigation Co.; (360)665-6246.

growers, and even kite flyers. There's also an on-site art gallery and cafe.

Oysterville, the peninsula's northern-most burg, is an historic town (founded in 1854) of beachworn homes and quiet streets. Ride your bike along Sandridge Road and enjoy a dozen oysters at Oysterville Sea Farms (1st and Clark Sts, Oysterville; (360)665-6585) or, in neighboring Nahcotta, at Jolly Roger Seafoods (on the Nahcotta pier; (360)665-4111). Across the way, the **Willapa Bay Interpretive Center**, (360)665-4547, offers a viewing deck and indoor exhibits on the history of the oyster industry. For even less-populated environs, head north to Stackpole Road and **Leadbetter Point State Park**, a nature lover's paradise featuring hiking, mushrooming, beachcombing,

and bird watching. Here the Willapa Bay shoreline provides a stopover for more than 100 species of birds. Deer, elk, black bears, beavers, and otters roam the forested dunes and slackwater marshes within the park's boundaries.

Other attractions include the **Willapa National Wildlife Refuge**; (360)484-3482. The most popular destination at the refuge, Long Island, in Willapa Bay, has 5,000 acres of damp coastal forests, sandy beaches, salt-grass tidal marshes, and muddy tidal flats. On the edge of the island are thriving beds of oysters, clams, and an army of crabs. Farther inland lives much varied wildlife: Roosevelt elk, black bears, river otters, and pileated woodpeckers, to name a few (see also "Long Island" tip).

Cheap Eats

Bubba's

177 SE Howerton Way, Ilwaco ☎ (360)642-8750

Bubba Kuhn is a transplanted New Yorker possessing superb pizza-making skills and a healthy dose of panache. While hand-tossing his pies, he simultaneously converses with his customers and jokes with his waiters. Garnish one of his golden-crusted creations with any number of toppings, from anchovies to artichoke hearts. Or order something unorthodox, such as the Bubba-que, featuring tangy barbecue sauce, kielbasa, chicken, and a couple of cheeses. An antipasto plate and creamy New York–style cheesecake are also worth considering.

Heron & Beaver Pub

4415 Pacific Highway S (in the Shelburne Inn), Seaview ☎ (360) 642-4142

Eating and drinking haunts don't get any cozier than this pint-size pub decorated with wood-paneled walls, stained-glass windows, booth seating, and a darling little wraparound bar. The pub shares a kitchen with the adjoining (and nationally renowned) Shoalwater restaurant, which explains why the fare is topnotch. Dip into mussel stew, share a bowl of fondue, or sample the berry cobblers. Beverages run from craft beers and single-malt scotches to a superlative wine selection.

My Mom's Pie Kitchen

4316 Pacific Highway S, Seaview ☎ (360) 642-2342

In this case, the name doesn't say it all—in addition to myriad pies, the menu at this diminutive eatery boasts a handful of sandwiches (try the meatloaf) along with crab quiches, chicken-almond potpies, and a delectable clam chowder. The pies, though, are always the attention-getters, with a lineup that includes banana cream, chocolate almond, peanut butter, pecan, rhubarb, and, of course, Mom's apple pie.

Cottage Bakery & Delicatessen

118 Pacific Highway, Long Beach ☎ (360) 642-4441

Scrunched midblock in downtown Long Beach, this is the ultimate sweet-tooth fantasy: ground zero for a sugar high. Chocolate eclairs, cupcakes overflowing with icing, bear claws, fruit turnovers, cream cheese croissants, and fancy-shaped cookies with multicolored sprinkles beckon from enormous display cases. For something more substantial, try the spicy egg salad on pumpernickel or the turkey breast layered with cranberry sauce (choose from a dozen different breads).

Dooger's

900 Pacific Highway S, Long Beach ☎ (360) 642-4224

Seafood is the house specialty here, prepared a number of ways. Your best bet is sautéed sole or prawns, grilled halibut, or a bowl of steamer clams. Fish 'n' chips are decent, and the clam chowder is, perhaps, the peninsula's finest. "Lite" dinners can be had at "light" prices, but the lunch specials (served until 4pm) are the best bargains. The pies (peanut butter and marionberry among them) are worth a look.

Pastimes Coffee & Collectibles

504 Pacific Highway S, Long Beach ☎ (360) 642-8303

The peninsula's original espresso hangout is still the best. Besides numerous coffee drinks (if you're feelin' frisky, try an espresso float) and iced sodas, Pastimes offers a fruity wild-rice salad, a quiche du jour, an almond–egg salad sandwich, and a concoction featuring pastrami, prosciutto, and provolone stuffed between slices of focaccia. Play cards, checkers, or chess; listen to occasional live music; or simply shoot the breeze with the varied clientele. There's indoor and outdoor seating and an adjoining knickknack shop.

Mario's

1904 Bay Avenue, Ocean Park ☎ (360) 665-4050

With its red-and-white-checked curtains and tablecloths and air redolent of oregano, basil, pepperoni, and provolone, this place resembles a neighborhood Italian trattoria. Most patrons come for the rigatoni or shells bathed in marinara, fettuccine with clam sauce, manicotti, or spaghetti and meatballs. The varied menu also includes a heaping antipasto plate, some appetizing pizzas, deep-fried mozzarella sticks, spumoni, and, in keeping with local custom, oyster shooters.

Cheap Sleeps

Fort Columbia Hostel

475 Route 101 (PO Box 224), Chinook, WA 98614 ☎ (360) 777-8755

Perched on Chinook Point, 6 miles from the Long Beach Peninsula and high above the water, Fort Columbia was constructed in 1893 to protect the mouth of the Columbia River from the threat of invasion. The military installation saw service during both world wars before being decommissioned in the 1950s; now one of the larger buildings, the former army hospital, has been transformed into a hostel. Don't expect anything approaching luxury, but the men's and women's quarters are handsomely decorated (in a Scottish design and a rose motif), and all guests awaken to a pancake breakfast. There's also a living room and a fully equipped kitchen. Rates are $10 for American Youth Hostel members, $13 for nonmembers; bicyclists pay $2 less. Couples can reserve the comfy private room ($26–$32). Closed October through March.

Sou'wester Lodge

Beach Approach Road at 38th Place (PO Box 102), Seaview, WA 98644
☎ (360) 642-2542

Hosts Leonard and Miriam Atkins make lodgers feel like long-awaited guests in this rambling 100-year-old house near the beach, with a variety of unusual guest quarters. Self-sufficient apartments upstairs are often frequented by artist-musician-writer types. Smaller lodgings on the main floor are available on what the Atkinses call the B&MYODB plan (bed & make your own damn breakfast). That includes kitchen privileges. There are also rustic cabins and a nostalgic assortment of classic trailers, dubbed the "TCH! TCH!" (Trailer Classics Hodgepodge) collection. Fortunate guests may be treated to chamber music or drama evenings or have the chance to participate in a "Teacup T'ink Tank" (not quite a think tank, says Len) exploring matters great and small.

Arcadia Court

N 4th and Boulevard (PO Box 426), Long Beach, WA 98631 ☎ (360) 642-2613

Modest, crisply appointed Arcadia Court has eight small-but-cozy rooms starting at $41. The principal draws are the perky flower boxes, kitchenettes (in some rooms), the picnic area out back, the location (dead-bang in the middle of the Long Beach action), and the marvelous proximity to the dunes—there they are, right behind you!

The Lighthouse Motel

12415 Pacific Highway, Long Beach, WA 98631 ☎ (360) 642-3622

Salty old trunks and ocean treasures lend a nautical feel to this nine-unit beachfront motel. Each room feels like your own cabin, and your pooch is welcome, too (for $5 extra). Some units have one bedroom and others have two, but they all have fireplaces, driftwood-inspired porches, and kitchens. Watch the sunset from your room, or take the path through the dunes to the beach. Ask about off-season specials.

Our Place at the Beach

1309 S Boulevard (PO Box 266), Long Beach, WA 98631
☎ (800) 538-5107 or (360) 642-3793

This unpretentious motel squeezed between the Long Beach commercial hoopla and the dunes has 25 rooms (some with kitchens, all with refrigerators and TVs) and some unexpected amenities: two spas, a sauna, and a well-equipped workout room. Get a room on the top floor, facing west, and you (and Fido, if you like, for $5 more) will be quite content.

Pacific View Motel

203 Bolstad Avenue (PO Box 302), Long Beach, WA 98631
☎ (800) 238-0859 or (360) 642-2415

The Pacific View's tidy yellow units on the beach-approach road have the self-contained feeling of cottages—with kitchenettes, dining nooks, and charming knotty pine interiors. To be inside one, just a stone's throw from the boardwalk and the beach, is to forget you're in a motel amid Long Beach's Coney Island–like strip. Rates vary more than at most lodgings, with July and August the spendiest months. Pets are allowed in some units.

Shakti Cove Cottages

On 253rd Place, 1 block west of Pacific Highway 103 (PO Box 385),
Ocean Park, WA 98640 ☎ (360) 665-4000

Formerly a ragtag clutch of old cabins—set on 3 forested acres just off the beaten track and within earshot of the thundering Pacific—Shakti Cove has been treated to an extensive upgrade by new "covekeepers" Celia and Liz Cavalli, who cater unobtrusively to the needs of their happy campers. If "Have pets, will travel!" is your motto, this is your place. Even oversize canines receive an open-armed welcome—as does a largely gay and lesbian clientele. Each spotlessly clean, funky-but-comfy cabin offers complete kitchen facilities, private

Summer Vacation

The key to getting a good deal anywhere on the peninsula is to simply avoid summertime. Prices plummet and everything seems affordable before May and after October. Trouble is, summer is when most people want to be here. For a list of available rental homes, phone the Long Beach Peninsula Visitor's Bureau (corner of Hwy 103 and Hwy 101, Long Beach; (800)451-2542 or (360)642-2400). You'll need to contact individual homeowners for prices, which vary widely.

bath with shower, cable TV, and private carport—to say nothing of easy access to a stunning stretch of beach. Don't expect daily maid service, and don't bother bringing provisions: Jack's Country Store (if they don't have it, you don't need it) is nearby.

Moby Dick Hotel

Sandridge Road (PO Box 82), Nahcotta, WA 98637 ☎ (360) 665-4543

The Moby Dick, which has been around since the '30s, is humble in appearance and generous in spirit. Owners Fritzi and Edward Cohen—who also own the venerable Tabard Inn in the other Washington (D.C.)—have worked hard to pretty up the interior of this nonsmoking hotel. It's a chipper place, splashed with vibrant colors and sophisticated art and punctuated with fresh flowers, hardwood floors, an upright piano, a fireplace, and put-your-feet-up couches. The rooms are simple (and all but one share a bath), but a sumptuous feast is served each morning. Outside, you'll find an oyster farm at the water's edge, dazzling gardens out front, and walking trails through Leadbetter Point State Park, a few miles up the road. For about a month each summer, a resident chef spins the local bounty into lovely, but not inexpensive, meals. The rooms, too, are spendy ($75–$85 in summer), but for sheer delightful ambience they're worth the splurge.

North Cascades

Some say the granite spires and luminous glaciers of the North Cascades—from the Canadian border to Glacier Peak—are unmatched in the lower 48 states. When the alpine flowers glow in early August or the fall colors climax in early October, head out over the North Cascades Scenic Highway and return west via Stevens Pass—the classic Cascade Loop—to behold some of Washington's finest scenery. North Cascades National Park is one of the most remote and least visited of America's national parks, and its jagged peaks, rushing streams, and exhilarating panoramas are often visible from the road. This is truly wild country—recent years have even brought wolf and brown bear sightings—but the small communities that dot the region offer a warm, rustic hospitality. Get off the highway whenever possible (many of the high trails are short day hikes) to discover pristine wilderness and blissful solitude within this craggy domain.

Exploring

The **Mount Baker Highway** (Hwy 542), which winds through the scenic, narrow valley of the North Fork of the Nooksack, ends 56 miles east of Bellingham at the **Mount Baker Ski Area** and is a stunning entree into the northern Cascade Range. The mountain seldom lacks for snow—it boasts the longest ski season in the state—and runs are predominantly intermediate, with bowls, meadows, and trails; there's also good cross-country available, and this is *the* place for snowboarders. It's open daily from mid-November through March, and weekends only in April. Tickets are about 10 bucks less on weekdays, and the beginner's rope tow is free. Reasonably priced day care is available for children (2 years and older) on weekends and holi-

days; (360)734-6771 for information, (360)671-0211 for a snow report.

As you're driving the Mount Baker Highway, be sure and stop at the fruit stand run by **Alpenglow Farms**, 1 1/2 miles east of Maple Falls, for fresh berry shakes, cider, espresso, and all manner of goodies perfect for a Northwest pantry. The little town of **Glacier** offers the last services before heading up to the ski area. Looking for a night out? Locals hang at the Holy Smoke Tavern, an old country church preaching a biker kind of gospel now; just a few miles north of Maple Falls on Kendall Road, (360)988-8333.

In summer, the snow melts on the two final miles of the highway, permitting car access to **Artist Point** and spectacular views of both Mount Baker and the geologically eccentric Mount Shuksan. Hiking from here is extensive and beautiful, especially in late summer when the foliage is turning, the wild blueberries are ripe, and the days are hot and dry. For information on hikes or other summer activities, contact the Glacier Public Service Center, (360)599-2714, or the Mount Baker Ranger Station in Sedro-Woolley, (360)856-5700.

The northernmost route *across* the Cascades is via the **North Cascades Scenic Highway** (Hwy 20), which travels east from Sedro-Woolley and cuts through **North Cascades National Park** before topping Rainy and Washington Passes and dropping into the Methow Valley. The nonprofit North Cascades Institute offers a range of field seminars that promote the park and wilderness. From kayaking and bird-watching trips to writing workshops, there's something to spark everyone's interest. They also have youth summer camps and Elderhostel programs. To find out more, contact the institute at North Cascades National Park headquarters in Sedro-Woolley (2105 Hwy 20, Sedro-Woolley, WA 98284; (360)856-5700, ext 209).

In winter, hundreds of **bald eagles** perch along the Skagit River, which runs next to Highway 20. Bring your binoculars and you might spy a number of them from highway pullouts between Rockport and Marblemount, although the best way to see them is from the river. The adventuresome may want to canoe downriver from Marblemount to Rockport (an easy 8 miles); note that while the river appears tame, it can be deceptively swift. **Rafting companies** will gladly guide you down the river in December and January, prime viewing time: watchers often spot up to 200 eagles. Trips cost around $50. Call Downstream River Runners, (800)234-4644; Northern Wilderness River Riders, (206)448-RAFT; or Orion Expeditions, (206)547-6715. Budget-minded eagle watchers can float down the Skagit for considerably less by renting their own raft. Swiftwater Sales and Rentals in Seattle, (206)547-3377, rents rafts that hold up to nine people for about $60 a day. Life vests and information on where and when to set off on the river are included with the rental. Cascadian Farm, an organic food company with a fancy highway stand just east of Concrete, makes a warm espresso stop after a day on the river.

Marblemount is the unofficial gateway to the North Cascades. Stop at the national park ranger station here for information on activities; (360)873-4500. From the town, hikers can veer southeast off Highway 20 onto the rough, 22-mile Cascade River Road, which leads to numerous trails into the park and the Glacier Peak Wilderness. The most popular is the 4-mile hike up to **Cascade Pass** (laden with blueberries come fall), which yields an exceptional view for moderate effort. The trailhead is well signed. Hoist a post-hike brew at RJ's Hideaway (5801 Hwy 20, Marblemount, (360)873-2010), where country music and taxidermy abound. Note that in winter Highway 20 is closed from just beyond Marblemount to Mazama on the east side of the range; it usually closes around November 1 and reopens in May.

Newhalem, a company town built and maintained by Seattle City Light to house workers on the Skagit Hydroelectric Project, is the last community on the west side of the North Cascades. Stop here at Ladder Creek Falls and Rock Gardens (no charge) for an inspirational walk; the falls are lit at night (electricity is in abundance up here). In the next 10 miles, you'll pass three dams—Gorge, Diablo, and Ross—all of which provide power to Seattle and were built in the 1920s by visionary engineer James Delmage Ross. **Seattle City Light's Skagit Tours** (off Hwy 20 in Diablo, 7 miles east of Newhalem; (206)684-3030) offer a fascinating 4-hour journey through this massive, his-

Darrington Bluegrass Festival

Every summer on the third weekend in July, bluegrass fans from all over the country turn their attention to the Darrington Bluegrass Festival, nestled in the Cascade foothills. Terrific foot-stomping, thigh-slapping music is played outdoors by some of the country's best musicians. Tickets are $25, and a $10 fee (per vehicle) buys an on-site camping space (no hookups, though). For more information, call the Darrington Chamber of Commerce; (360)436-1177.

toric project, including an informative video presentation, a 560-foot ride up an antique incline railway to the top of Diablo Dam, and a boat ride through the gorge of the Skagit to Ross Dam—a daring engineering achievement in its day. The tour (summers only, Thursday through Monday at 11am; reservations recommended) costs $25 (discounts for kids) and includes dinner. Those not wishing to splurge on the full tour can take the shorter 90-minute version ($5), offered three times daily, which includes the video, railway ride, and brief walking tour.

The result of the Skagit Project is **Ross Lake**, a giant pristine reservoir that extends 24 miles across the Canadian border. Since the only road access to Ross Lake is south from Hope, B.C., the best way to get to the lake—other than a 3½-mile-long hike—is on the Seattle City Light ferry from Diablo Lake. Here Seattle City Light built an outpost for crews constructing and servicing the dams on the river. The ferry makes two trips daily to Ross Dam, departing at 8:30am and 3pm, and costs $2.50 (kids $2); call the Diablo boat landing, (206)386-4393, for information. You can also launch your own canoe at Colonial Creek National Park Campground in Diablo, and paddle up the pretty lake to the dam. Pick up the phone there, and a truck ports you up and around the dam, depositing you and your gear on the shore of Ross Lake.

Between the dams and **Washington Pass** (the highest point on this route, marked by the dramatic Liberty Bell Peak), numerous hiking trails offer opportunities for day hikes (and longer). One of the shortest and most popular is the 2-mile paved path to Rainy Lake, with views of waterfalls and glaciers, which leaves from the well-signed Rainy Pass parking lot. It is here at Rainy Pass that the Canada-to-Mexico Pacific Crest Trail crosses Highway 20.

The **Mountain Loop Highway** is actually a combination of roads that circle through the Glacier Peak area. The highway offers remnants of big, mossy old-growth forests, snippets of mountain views, mining history, and terrific access for hiking and camping. The northern entrance to the loop is on Highway 530 in Darrington; it then continues southeast on Forest Service Road 20 (which is partially unpaved and closed in winter) and pushes back west on Highway 92 to its southern terminus of Granite Falls.

Traveling the loop from the north, stop at **Kennedy Hot Springs** (accessible from White Chuck River Road #23), the most popular way to enter **Glacier Peak Wilderness**, thanks to the easy terrain leading 5½ miles to natural warm pools. At Barlow Pass, you can walk or mountain bike about 4½ miles to the old mining town of Monte Cristo (circa 1890), now an eerie, overgrown ghost town. From the south side of the loop it's a short (1-mile), family hike to the well-marked **Big Four Ice Caves**—actually tunnels under a snowfield. The caves usually start to form in August and are interesting to see, but very dangerous to go into or climb on. Information on all of this and more can be obtained from the Darrington Ranger Station, a quarter mile north of town on Highway 530, (360)436-1155, or the Verlot Public Service Center, 11 miles east of Granite Falls, (360)691-7791.

Cutting across the central Cascades is **US Highway 2**, a scenic byway that passes through lower valley farmland before climbing to Stevens Pass through the upper Skykomish River gorge. The old railroad towns along the west side of US 2 offer little more than some big ice cream cones and camping provisions. But watch for circling hawks along the route, as well as the quaint Wayside Chapel just west of Sultan, which quietly urges you to "Pause, Rest, Worship." (Climbers headed to Index consider it bad form not to pause here before tackling the cliffs.) About 2 miles north of Gold Bar is lovely **Wallace Falls State Park**. The tall, skinny waterfall is visible from the highway, and the turnoff in town is well marked. Walk one of two routes to the top of the falls, and stop along the way for a picnic. Rock climbers know charming **Index** best for its challenging Town Wall, a 400-foot granite cliff just outside the tiny town (ask at the general store or the Bush House Country Inn for directions). Railroad buffs should pop into the free Pickett Historical Museum (510 Ave A, Index; (360)793-1534), which features the photographs of Lee Pickett, the official photographer for the Great Northern Railway early in this century. It's open weekends only, noon to 3pm, Memorial Day through September.

Stevens Pass—popular with Seattleites playing hooky—is a challenging downhill ski area at the top of US 2. Eleven chairs lead to over 30 runs, and the Double Diamond and Southern Cross chairs take you to some daunting expert slopes on the back side. Monday and Tuesday are the best days to go (only $20); Wednesday through Friday it's $25. Call (360)973-2441 for information and a snow report.

On the dry side of the mountains,

approximately a half hour east of the pass and just a few miles north of US 2, sits popular and breezy **Lake Wenatchee**. There's a state park at the east end of the lake, with a large, sandy public swimming beach and wooded campsites. Lakeside campsites are on only the south shore, where you'll also find the trailhead to Hidden Lake, a short, easy climb. Lake Wenatchee is one of the best family destinations in the Cascades, with easy access, plenty of activities, and proximity to the Bavarian town of Leavenworth. Ask at the ranger station on the north side of the lake for more information; (509)548-6977. Those interested in more genteel recreational activities might consider playing a round of golf or tennis at the new Kahler Glen Golf and Ski Resort (20890 Kahler Drive, Leavenworth; (800)440-2994 or (509)763-2121).

"Lederhosen-R-Us!" The town of **Leavenworth**, with its stunning alpine setting, is your next stop east on US 2. This former railroad yard and sawmill community decided a few decades back to recast itself as a Bavarian-style village, with tourism as its primary industry. The architecture in the city center features some excellent craftsmanship in the Bavarian mode. **Shopping** can be fun here: the Cuckoo Clock (725 Front St, Leavenworth; (509)548-4857) displays a neat collection of classic cuckoos and a glockenspiel that emits dancers every half hour; Tannenbaum Shoppe (735 Front St, Leavenworth; (509)548-7014) delights with hundreds of German-made nutcrackers lining the shelves; Alpen Haus (downstairs at 807 Front St, Leavenworth; (800)572-1559) offers a collection of dollhouse furniture and miniatures; and Die Musik Box (837 Front St, Leavenworth; (800)288-5883) has a dazzling array of music boxes. Doused your white T-shirt in mustard and sauerkraut? True bargain hunters will want to browse the store called "Fashion for $12.00" (905 Commercial

St, Leavenworth; (509)548-6175), a shop where everything really is $12 or less.

Popular Leavenworth events include the **Autumn Leaf Festival**, held the last weekend in September and the first weekend in October, and the **Christmas Lighting Festival**, held the first two Saturdays in December; call (509)548-5807 for details. Tour the Leavenworth National Fish Hatchery (turnoff on Fish Hatchery Rd, about 2 miles south on Icicle Rd from US 2, Leavenworth; (509)548-7641) on Icicle Creek to watch the chinook salmon run (June and July) and spawn (August and September). From here, you can follow the mile-long **Icicle Creek Interpretive Trail**, which takes a historical look at the hatchery, the spawning cycle, and the relationship between rivers and dams. Homefires Bakery, near the fish hatchery off Icicle Road (13013 Bayne Rd, Leavenworth; (509)548-7362), fires up some formidable dark German rye in its wood-burning oven; it's a great stop for cinnamon rolls and coffee. Locals meet at Gustav's (617 US Hwy 2, Leavenworth; (509)548-4509; see review in Cheap Eats) or the Leavenworth Brewery pub (636 Front St, Leavenworth; (509)548-4545) to hoist a brew. The brewpub has nine beers on tap, made on the premises (the types rotate with the seasons), and offers daily tours of the small brewery itself.

Outdoor activities abound in this area year-round; check with the Leavenworth Ranger Station (on US 2, across from McDonald's, Leavenworth; (509)548-6977) or the visitors center (on US 2 at its intersection with 9th St, Leavenworth; (509)548-5807) for information and maps on hiking, fishing, skiing, mountain biking, rafting, and horseback riding. Play golf at the scenic 18-hole Leavenworth Golf Club (on Icicle Road just past the fish hatchery, Leavenworth; (509)548-7267).

In winter, you'll find fabulous **cross-country skiing** on the golf course and at the Leavenworth Nordic Center, (509)548-

7864. Scottish Lakes Back Country Cabins, 8 miles into the backcountry west of Leavenworth, is a cluster of primitive plywood cabins at the edge of one of the nation's finest wilderness areas. You can ski the 8 miles or be carted up in a heated 12-seat Sno-Cat and ski the 3,800-foot descent home, by reservation only; contact High Country Adventures (PO Box 2023, Snohomish, WA 98291; (888)9-HICAMP or (206)844-2000).

Cashmere gives cross-mountain travelers who aren't in a Bavarian mood an alternative to stopping in Leavenworth. The main street has put up Western storefronts, and the town was named "A Tree City USA" in 1984. You can take a pleasant walking arbor tour by picking up a map at the city's Chamber of Commerce (on the corner of Division and Cottage, Cashmere; (509)782-7404). The Chelan County Historical Museum and Pioneer Village (600 Cottage Ave, Cashmere; (509)782-3230) has an extensive collection of Indian artifacts and archaeological material, and you can tour 19 historic buildings, carefully restored to reflect the style of the late 1800s. Cashmere's main claim to fame is Aplets and Cotlets—confections, made with local fruit and walnuts from an old Armenian recipe, that have been produced here for decades. You can tour the plant at Liberty Orchards and consume a few samples; tours are free and given hourly each day during most of the year (117 Mission St, Cashmere; (509)782-2191).

Wenatchee, in the heart of apple country, celebrates its good fortune with an Apple Blossom Festival during the first part of May—a good time that lasts for 11 days. Call the Wenatchee Chamber of Commerce, (509)662-4774, for information. Wenatchee's Riverfront Loop Trail on the banks of the Columbia River makes for a pleasant evening stroll—or an easy bike ride for those who want to pedal the 11-mile loop, which traverses both sides of the river (and crosses two bridges) from Wenatchee to East Wenatchee. The best place to join the trail is at the east end of 5th Street. **Ohme Gardens** (3 miles north on US 97A, Wenatchee; (509)662-5785) is a 600-foot-high promontory transformed into a natural alpine ecosystem patterned after high mountain country. It has splendid views of the valley and the Columbia River. **Rocky Reach Dam**, 6 miles north on US 97, offers a beautiful picnic and

playground area plus a fish-viewing room. Inside the dam are two large galleries devoted to the history of the region.

In winter, skiers come for the powder at **Mission Ridge** (13 miles southwest of Wenatchee; (509)663-7631). The four chairs lift downhillers to challenging and intermediate slopes. Tickets are $24 weekdays and $32 on weekends (less for kids), but call ahead and ask about special promotions.

Cheap Eats

Pueblo Viejo Family Mexican Restaurant
215 W Main, Everson ☎ (360)966-3927

Surprisingly decent Mexican fare (or a burger, if you'd rather) can be had right here, about 8 miles off the Mount Baker Highway, in tiny Everson. The worn Main Street facade belies a bright, airy space and basic south-of-the-border choices, ranging in price from $4.95 to $8.95 (most meals include rice and beans). Try the chicken quesadilla with fresh guacamole and sour cream. There's also an ice cream parlor where you can sip an espresso.

Carol's Coffee Cup
5415 Mount Baker Highway, Deming ☎ (360)592-5641

Carol's is a local institution: a pleasant little bakery/cafe, long a favorite with loggers, skiers, and hikers, who come for breakfast, lunch, and dinner. The hamburgers are fine, but the big cinnamon rolls ($1.25) and the fresh roasted turkey used in sandwiches and dinners are best. Be prepared for a long wait on summer weekends and during the peak of the Mount Baker ski season.

Milano's Restaurant & Deli
9990 Mount Baker Highway, Glacier ☎ (360)599-2863

Popular with locals and carbo-loading hikers and skiers alike, this place is really three in one—a deli, an informal Italian restaurant, and a dessert and coffee spot. The fresh pastas are great and reasonable at less than 10 bucks a pop, including salad and bread. Weekend breakfast is good too, with omelets, fresh baked goods, and crunchy homemade granola.

Good Food
5832 Highway 20, Marblemount ☎ (360)873-2771

It's only a burger and shake joint, but honestly, this is still the best dining option around, and it's open for all three squares, serving up good food at digestible prices. There are a few tables inside and out on the patio, as well as picnic tables scattered on a wide green lawn that stretches down to the river. Expect plenty of sandwich options and shakes made to order. Down the road is another purveyor of basic, low-cost food: the **Shake Mill Cafe** (Milepost 105, Hwy 20, Marblemount; (360)873-2035), where you can join locals at the counter for breakfast, lunch, or dinner.

Michelle's Country Coffee & Deli

1015 Sauk Avenue, Darrington ☎ (360) 436-0213

Darrington is the northern gateway to the Mountain Loop Highway and the Glacier Peak and Boulder River Wildernesses. Michelle's makes a fine stopping place, before or after your hike or scenic tour, for fresh sandwiches, homemade soups, and locally made fudge. You can grab a light breakfast, stop in for lunch, or take a nosh to go.

Los Flamingos

101 S Granite Avenue, Granite Falls ☎ (360) 691-7575

Classic Mexican eats in a pleasant (albeit purple) atmosphere are a great find in this historic town. You'll find large helpings of everything—except grease; try one of the many nacho options, the enchiladas suizas (chicken with verde sauce, Jack cheese, and sour cream), or the tacos Mexicana (flank steak in soft tortillas with tomato, onion, and cilantro). Margaritas, anyone?

Sky River Bakery

117 ½ W Main Street, Monroe ☎ (360) 794-7434

When headed for Stevens Pass and points beyond, consider this bright stop for a quick meal, and ignore the fast-food fungus that lines US 2 in Monroe. Fresh-baked breads, muffins, scones, cinnamon rolls, and more fill the tiny space with a warm aroma each morning (try the moist applesauce coffeecake), while savory pastries and quiche make a nice afternoon snack. Cookies, brownies, pies, and other dessert items round out the daily offerings. Sky River is just a few blocks off the strip.

Mount Index Cafe

49315 US Highway 2, Index ☎ (360) 793-0879

At this timeless roadside diner, a classic post-ski or -hike stop on US 2, the fare is basic and filling. Breakfast is served up all day, and the menu features burgers, a Reuben, and a perfectly good club, among other sandwich options and a few dinner entrees. Enjoy your selection with a beer or a glass of wine. Another roadside attraction is **Zeke's** (further west on US 2 near Gold Bar; (360)793-2287), a popular burger, fries, and shake stand.

Mexican Eats in Wenatchee

A little bit of Baja resides in Wenatchee in the form of taco vans, your best budget-dining option in orchard country. In fact, there are probably more taco vans than restaurants here, and they stay open after 9pm, when most other eateries close. The tacos are fresh, tasty, and a bargain, but—sorry, amigos!—no cerveza available to wash them down.

Best of the Wurst

220 8th Street, Leavenworth ☎ (509) 548-7580

Many say the wurst is best here . . . bratwurst, that is. The long line of dog devotees standing on the sidewalk seems to attest to the claim. The basic charbroiled menu includes sausages, chicken, and burgers (best when sided with some beer batter-dipped onion rings), all under $5 each. Order at the window and eat at one of the few patio tables, or stroll down to Waterfront Park, which fronts the Wenatchee River. If Best's line is the worst, head around the corner to **Bavarian Bar-B-Que & Sausage Haus** (226 8th St, Leavenworth; (509)548-6187), which offers a similar menu and a small beer garden.

The Gingerbread Factory

828 Commercial Street, Leavenworth ☎ (509) 548-6592

Of course it's cute—how could it be anything but? The Gingerbread is in a white gabled house, brightly decorated inside, with additional outdoor seating on a shady patio. You can stop here in the morning for espresso and baked goods, or show up for fresh, simple lunches: homemade soups, pita sandwiches, and salads. This is a fun place for kids, who will love the wonderfully chewy gingerbread cookies and adorable gingerbread houses.

Gustav's

617 US Highway 2, Leavenworth ☎ (509) 548-4509

Gustav's is one of the many Leavenworth eateries where you can sample traditional Bavarian fare—though we like it best because it tends to be a little easier on the budget than its competitors. We also like the great burgers, the sunny balcony (in summer), and the vast selection of brews. Another Germanic option is **Andreas Keller** (829 Front St, Leavenworth; (509)548-6000), with live accordion music nightly.

Los Camperos

200 8th Street, Leavenworth ☎ (509) 548-3314

A favorite choice of the local *vaqueros*, this Mexican restaurant is one of the most fun eateries in faux Bavaria. Pick a sunny day, head for the roof deck, order a margarita, and dive into one of the special salsas (lots of cabbage and jalapeños). The beans and rice are standard, but an order from the specials list (say, the enchilada *camerones*, with shrimp and salsa verde) is usually worthy of the name "special."

The Soup Cellar

725 Front Street, Leavenworth ☎ (509) 548-6300

Billing itself as the "Home of the Famous White Chili," this basement lunchery is tucked unassumingly into the hoopla and lederhosen of touristy Front Street. Sandwiches, salads, and the ubiquitous bratwurst are all to be had here, but it's the soups—five varieties made fresh daily—that are the reason to come. And what about that white chili? The rich, creamy concoction of great white Northern beans, chicken, and seasonings—topped with Jack cheese and sour cream and served with tortillas and salsa—deserves every bit of fame it gets.

EZ's Burger Deluxe

1950 N Wenatchee Avenue, Wenatchee ☎ (509) 663-1957

The best burgers around can be found on the north edge of town at this '50s-style double drive-thru. Your fresh ground is cooked to order, and the veggie burger is surprisingly satisfying.

Greathouse Springs Cafe

1505 N Miller Street, Suite 130, Wenatchee ☎ (509) 664-5162

Greathouse Springs is the noontime hot spot for local 9-to-5ers. Belly up to the sandwich bar and place your order, or have a seat at one of the cedar picnic benches. Panini—grilled focaccia combined with cheeses, meats, and seasonings *alla Italia*—are the specialty. You can show up for a light breakfast during the workweek, but the cafe's closed on weekends.

Cheap Sleeps

Wilkins Farm Bed & Breakfast

4165 South Pass Road, Everson, WA 98247 ☎ (360) 966-7616

Carmela Wilkins is the proprietor of this 120-year-old farmhouse, perhaps the least expensive B&B in the region. Three rooms share a bath, and the low prices—$22 for a single, $35 for a double—include a full breakfast. The small community of Everson, the Canadian border, and Mount Baker are all nearby.

Silver Lake Park Cabins

9006 Silver Lake Road, Sumas, WA 98295 ☎ (360) 599-2776

About 3 miles north of Mount Baker Highway lies this lovely, rustic retreat, perfect for families or groups. Sitting in a row above sparkling Silver Lake, six timber cabins are nestled among fir trees with small balconies overlooking the water. Each is equipped with a stove/oven, refrigerator, gas heater, cold water, and two or three double beds; three cabins also have stone fireplaces. Outhouses (clean and odor-free!) are nearby, while showers are available in a separate building. Park facilities also include campgrounds, a bunkhouse (sleeps

Last-Minute Leavenworth

Lodgings in the Leavenworth—Lake Wenatchee area can fill up early; if you need a last-minute reservation or are having trouble finding a good deal, try Bedfinders, (800)323-2920 or (509)548-4410, or Destinations Leavenworth, (800)962-7359 or (509)548-5802. They book cabins, hotels, B&Bs, condos, and lodges. There's also a strip of Bavarian-style no-tell motels right along US 2; they're not too exciting, but you can find rooms there in the $50–$60 range. Try Alpen Inn, (800)423-9380; Rodeway Inn, (800)693-1225; or Squirrel Tree Motel, (509)763-3157.

four), picnic areas, a boat launch, group and horse camps, and a day lodge with a small concession. Rates are $50–$60 (less for Whatcom County residents) for two, $5 for each additional adult (maximum six persons). Reservations are a must and can be made up to four months in advance, with a two-day minimum on weekends. Bring your own utensils and bedding.

Glacier Creek Lodge

10036 Mount Baker Highway (PO Box 5008), Glacier, WA 98244
☎ (360) 599-2991

On Mount Baker Highway, in the tiny town of Glacier ("Gateway to Mount Baker"), 12 cabins and 9 motel units sit among tall firs near a rushing stream. Skiers and hikers will love the proximity to slopes and backcountry—and they'll appreciate the chance to soak their tired bones in the motel's hot tub at day's end. The cabins are plain (no woodsy, rustic feeling here) but spotlessly clean, and all have some kind of kitchen facility. Barbecue areas dot the grounds, an espresso bar in the main building pumps caffeine, and the ranger station and a few restaurants are within walking distance. The helpful owners can provide lots of info about the area. Rates vary depending on the cabin and number of people; weekly discounts available. Pets allowed in some cabins. If the lodge is full, try the **Snowline Inn** (10433 Mount Baker Hwy, Glacier; (800)228-0119), a motel just up the road with rooms at $65 for two, $75 for four.

Baker Lake Resort

Milepost 20, Baker Lake Road (PO Box 100), Concrete, WA 98237
☎ (360) 757-2262

These cabins lack the charm or serenity of those at Silver Lake, with motor boats, fishermen, and a mouse or two running rampant. Still, Baker Lake offers an affordable option for families and groups, especially in the more tranquil fall and winter seasons. Eleven cabins (sleeping four to eight people) front either the 9-mile-long lake or Swift Creek, and each has a gas heater, stove, outdoor fire pit, and picnic table; six have bathrooms with shower (others use a nearby bathhouse), a fridge, dishes, and cooking utensils. Park facilities include boat rentals and a camp store. Rates range from $40–$75, with nominal extra charges for additional adults, children, or pets. Rates are discounted in the off

Mt. Baker Rentals

Don't own a vacation home? You can always rent one. Mount Baker Chalet Inc., (800)258-2405 or (360)599-2405, offers accommodations in privately owned cabins, chalets, and condos near Mount Baker Wilderness and North Cascades National Park. Located just outside the village of Glacier, these lodgings range from small, rustic A-frame cabins (perfect for a weekend à deux) to deluxe four-bedroom chalets (which sleep up to 10). Some have creek or mountain views, and all are set in wooded locations, with playgrounds, swimming pools, tennis courts, and hiking trails nearby. Rates vary, but you can get a good deal on weekly rates in summer. Also try Mount Baker Lodging, (800)709-7669 or (360)599-2453.

Ross Lake Resort

Tucked in the middle of North Cascades National Park, Ross Lake Resort offers one of the more unique lodging experiences in the state. Since it's inaccessible by road, you take the Seattle City Light ferry (see Exploring section) across Diablo Lake to Ross Dam, where a truck will transport you to the resort. All the cabins are built on log floats, and you can tie up your canoe or kayak right outside your door. No phones or food are available—just expansive views and water. The resort also rents boats and provides a water taxi and portage service around the lake. Prices and amenities vary, with great values for groups; (206)386-4437.

season. Reservations recommended, with a two-day minimum on weekends, three-day on holidays. Bring bedding and towels, and utensils if not supplied.

North Cascade Inn, Restaurant & Lounge
44628 Highway 20, Concrete, WA 98237 ☎ (800) 251-3054 or (360) 853-8870

Kids are free and the pie is perfect (sometimes we wish it were the other way around) at Larry La Plante and Einar Storaker's roadside inn. These are the two who made the Skagit Valley's Conway Tavern a success. Now they're making the North Cascades Inn the same kind of place . . . a place where people congregate. Stop in the restaurant anytime for housemade pie and coffee, or Thursdays and Sundays for prime rib. Stay in one of their 14 motel rooms ($50) and order a slice of you-know-what for breakfast. A slightly cheaper option just up the road is the **Eagles Nest Motel** (46346 Hwy 20, Concrete; (360)853-8662), with rooms starting at $38, and a laundromat.

A Cab in the Woods
Milepost 103.5, Highway 20, Rockport, WA 98283 ☎ (360) 873-4106

That's right: not "cabin," not "cat," but "cab"—as in taxi, yellow, Checker. But you won't find rude attitude or missing consonants here; the bright, shiny antique cab that marks the milepost and the five cozy cedar log cabins in a wooded setting are welcoming and perfect. Ideal as a romantic getaway or as a base for exploring North Cascades National Park, each cabin has a living area, bedroom, bathroom, fully equipped kitchen, and gas fireplace (already warming when you arrive). Number 3 is the most attractive (the new owners are gradually redoing each), decorated with lots of bright blue; extra touches include strategically placed reading lights, fresh flowers, games and magazines, and a CD player. Spend a day on the Skagit River watching eagles, and then go to sleep with the soft sounds of rain on the tin roof. A bit of a splurge at $65 ($10 for each additional adult, with four sleeping comfortably); $55 in the off season (October through April).

Clark's Skagit River Resort
5675 Highway 20, Rockport, WA 98283 ☎ (800) 273-2606 or (360) 873-2250

The Clark family has been in the resort business long enough to have worked all the bugs (but not the rabbits!) out of their 25-cabin operation. Located near the entrance to North Cascades National Park, Clark's borders the Skagit, offering plenty of possibilities to keep hikers and fishers happy. The standard cabins are cozy, clean, and authentic—in stark contrast to the newer cabins, which are a fanciful attempt to re-create, say, an Indian longhouse, a Mexican hacienda, or a mountain sawmill. Who really needs contrived atmosphere when a night in one of the standard cabins will have you expecting Bogey to tag along for some early fly fishing? Rates vary on the cabins; ask about additional adults, kids, and pets. All have kitchens, and the Eatery Restaurant is here too.

Mountain View Inn and Restaurant

32005 Mountain Loop Highway, Granite Falls, WA 98252 ☎ (360) 691-6668

These six motel rooms are dark and basic, but at $40 for a location at the base of the Cascades, they're a good value. Add friendly folks, a classic roadhouse restaurant, and a country store (offering hiking food and outdoor and fishing supplies), and who can complain? Nothing fancy at the restaurant, but solid food at solid prices; enjoy the big fireplace and read the menu that regales you with the area's mining history.

Bush House Country Inn

300 5th Street (PO Box 359), Index, WA 98256 ☎ (360) 793-2312

This bed and breakfast is a bit pricey for budget travelers—only 2 of the 11 rooms come in at $59, with the rest at $70 or (gulp) $80—but it's such a lovely place in such a quaint setting, we couldn't resist mentioning it. Built in 1898, Bush House has been carefully restored and also features a fine restaurant serving three meals daily. Rooms are warm and inviting; most share baths. Perfect for a romantic post-ski evening. The town's tavern is just across the way.

Skykomish Hotel, Restaurant & Saloon

102 Railroad Avenue (PO Box 130), Skykomish, WA 98288 ☎ (360) 677-2477

This historic 1904 lodging, reminiscent of an old boardinghouse, might be one of the most inexpensive and convenient options for skiers at Stevens Pass. Restoration continues at a slow pace, with dark halls, some worn spaces, and dormitory bathrooms. But the rooms are clean and bright, the location pleasant, and the management friendly. Prices are friendly, too, starting around $35; the good feeling extends to the adjacent restaurant, frequented by locals. A more standard motel option here is the **Sky River Inn** (333 River Dr E, Skykomish; (800) 367-8194), a few blocks away on a bank above the river, where a variety of rooms start at about $60.

Bindlestiff's Riverside Cabins

1600 US Highway 2, Leavenworth, WA 98826 ☎ (509) 548-5015

The eight cabins here are rather lackluster, basic, and small, but each has a fine wooden deck overlooking the Wenatchee River and includes a mini-fridge and continental breakfast. Downtown Leavenworth is an easy quarter-mile walk away. Doubles go for $55, while $65 is a steal for four overnighters.

Cougar Inn

Milepost 10, 23379 Highway 207, Leavenworth, WA 98826 ☎ (509) 763-3354

Most people come to this inn on Lake Wenatchee for the all-you-can-eat prime rib and seafood buffet on Friday nights. What many of them probably don't know is that if you purchase a weeknight dinner for two, you can stay in the

Fire Lookouts

*A handful of fire lookouts, originally built in the '20s and '30s, have
been maintained by local hiking and mountaineering groups. By virtue of their function,
these lodgings have amazing views and amazing fees—they're free. You'll need to bring
sleeping bags, pads, a stove, and utensils. Be aware that they're managed on a first-come,
first-served basis and are often shuttered and locked in winter. Remember, too, that these
are very special places—a slice of Northwest history—and deserve your respect. Call the
ranger station in Sedro-Woolley for information and directions, (360)856-5700.*

Park Butte Lookout, *with its close-up view of Mount Baker's Easton Glacier and surrounding mountains, seems much higher than its 4,052 feet. Bring wood for the wood
stove. The Skagit Alpine Club maintains this lookout and has priority use. The hike to the
lookout is a fairly easy 3 1/2 miles.*

Hidden Lake Lookout, *at 6,890 feet, is surrounded to the west and north by 7,000-foot
peaks and the nearby namesake lake. It's a 4-mile hike from Forest Road 1540 off Cascade Pass Road.*

Winchester Mountain, *with its panoramic view of Mount Shuksan and Mount Baker,
greets hikers a couple of miles south of the Canadian border. This lookout is maintained
by the Mount Baker Hiking Club. From the trailhead it's 2 miles to the lookout.*

Three Fingers Summit *must be the most dramatic lodging option in the Northwest. The
south summit, at 6,854 feet, affords breathtaking (and vertigo-inducing) views from all
sides. The lookout sleeps as many as eight people, though it has only one bunk. The hike
is 7 1/2 miles—long miles—and requires some knowledge of snow travel, as you'll cross a
small glacier. Call the Darrington Ranger Station in the Mount Baker–Snoqualmie
National Forest for information and directions; (360)436-1155.*

lodge that night for half price (in winter only)—and even full price ($45–$55)
ain't bad. Four of the six rooms share a bath. Also, check out one of the three
cabins that sleep four. The lake is at your doorstep, and activities abound,
including tennis, horseshoes, volleyball nets, and pedal boats. Cabins book
early in summer.

Edelweiss Hotel

843 Front Street, Leavenworth, WA 98826 ☎ **(509) 548-7015 or (509) 548-5010**

This Front Street hotel, the first building in town to go Bavarian, is now owned
by Eva Rhodes. Her son, John Rhodes, oversees the 14 rooms (5 with private
bath) and keeps the prices more than reasonable ($20–$45).

Ingall's Creek Lodge

3003 US Highway 97, Leavenworth, WA 98826 ☎ **(509) 548-6281**

Built in 1960, Ingall's Creek sports four little rooms with cable TV and private
bath. It makes a good base camp for skiing any of the 210 miles of trails in the
winter or for heading into the Enchantments via the Ingall's Creek Trail in
summer.

Mrs. Anderson's Lodging House

917 Commercial Street, Leavenworth, WA 98826
☎ (800) 253-8990 or (509) 548-6173

Adjoining a Leavenworth quilt shop, this nine-room inn has charm to spare—charm that extends to its very friendly operators. Originally opened in 1903 as a boardinghouse for sawmill workers, it's now the perfect rest stop for traveling women (although some men like it too). Rooms are minimally, crisply furnished in boardinghouse fashion but are sparkling clean. The bargain prices include a light breakfast.

Ponderosa Country Inn

11150 Highway 209, Leavenworth, WA 98826 ☎ (800) 443-3304 or (509) 548-4550

Amiable brothers Brett and Mike Robertson own this laid-back, rustic-style log inn just outside Leavenworth. Three of the five rooms (those without private bath) are priced right ($55–$65), offering couples a reasonable getaway at a top-notch B&B. It's a breezy wooded setting with a wide green lawn and a big, comfortable deck where a bonfire is lit at night (don't be surprised if one of the bros brings out his guitar). In winter, it's even cozier at $10 less.

Hillcrest Motel

2921 School Street, Wenatchee, WA 98801 ☎ (509) 663-5157

Located on Sunny Slope Hill above Wenatchee, the Hillcrest has 16 rooms that have been refurbished over the past several years, offering a variety of accommodations in the $40–$60 range. There's also an outdoor pool (summers only) and some kitchen units.

Orchard Inn

1401 N Miller Street, Wenatchee, WA 98801 ☎ (800) 368-4571 or (509) 662-3443

Smack in the middle of Wenatchee, the 103-room Orchard Inn does a good business and keeps its prices reasonable ($50–$65). A big bubble covers the heated pool in the winter, but you can swim under the stars in the summer. Pets are welcome with a deposit. Mission Ridge ski packages are available.

Methow Valley

A s it heads east across the mountains, the North Cascades Highway flirts along the granite walls of Liberty Bell Peak, elbows around the saw-toothed Early Winters Spires, and dips down into the broad, open valley of the Methow River. In the summer, deep green ponderosa pines line rocky-bottomed streams that meander through sun-baked meadows. Hikers stock up on provisions for a long trek on the Pacific Crest Trail, fly fishers cast into the Methow and Chewack Rivers, mountain bikers traverse the valley floor, and horseback riders head for the Pasayten Wilderness. RVs refuel in Winthrop, snapping photos of the Westernalia, and move on to the next camping spot.

In the winter, four-wheel-drive Jeeps and Subarus replace RVs, and cross-country skis take the place of mountain bikes. The dormant farmlands become a playground for skiers, who enjoys the crisp, blue skies and acres of squeaky-dry snow. For many Seattleites, this valley nestled below the eastern slopes of the Cascades offers a pristine and sunny respite from their dreary winter days.

Exploring

You can call it MET-how or you can call it MED-ow, but you'll never call it dull. Pick your mode of transport—mountain bike, horse, hiking boots, skis, waders, or steel-belted radials—and discover why this 50-mile-long, glacier-carved valley is every outdoor enthusiast's dream.

The first stop off the North Cascades Highway (Hwy 20) as you cross from the west is **Mazama**, which consists primarily of the Mazama Country Store; (509)996-2855. It's a general store for the '90s, where you'll find everything from Tim's Cascade Style potato chips to Patagonia jackets. Fuel up on caffeine at the very social espresso bar and gas at the pumps, if you must. In summer, check

out the outdoor barbecue. In winter, try one of the homemade soups. Next door is Mazama Mountaineering, with more high-end outdoor wear (keep your credit card in your wallet) and a climbing wall for its members (in case there isn't enough rock for you in the valley); (509)996-3802.

You can't miss **Winthrop**—it's the Western-motif town thronged with tourists. Stop at the Shafer Museum, housed in pioneer Guy Waring's 1897 log cabin on the hill behind the main street. Exhibits tell of the area's history and include old cars, a stagecoach, and horse-drawn vehicles. It is said that Waring's Harvard classmate Owen Wister came to visit in the 1880s and found some of the material for *The Virginian* here. Believable enough, perhaps, but don't be tricked into thinking the whole town is a relic. The Western storefronts, old-fashioned signs, and well-worn hitchin' posts were planned by the wife of a Twisp lumbermill operator in the early 1970s to entertain the travelers crossing the newly opened North Cascades Highway.

After you've had a big day outside, quaff a beer at the Winthrop Brewing Company (155 Riverside Ave, Winthrop; (509)996-3174; see review in Cheap Eats), a favorite local hangout right downtown. If you need to **rent equipment**—from skis to mountain bikes to fly rods or snowshoes—you're bound to find them at one of the following shops: Winthrop Mountain Sports (257 Riverside Ave, Winthrop; (509)996-2886); Sun Mountain Lodge, (509)996-2211; Jack's Hut (at the Freestone Inn), (509)996-2752; Mazama Country Inn, (509)996-2681; Mazama Mountaineering, (509)996-3802; or (for snowshoes) Mazama Country Store, (509)996-2855.

In the high waters of spring, the heat of summer, or the aspen colors of fall, **raft** the Methow or nearby Columbia via Osprey River Adventures; (509)997-4116. Lace up your hiking boots and step out on the Pacific Crest Trail for spectacular

alpine **hiking** north or south from Hart's Pass, or drop into one of the Pasayten Wilderness valleys for deep forests, fishing, and maybe a bear or two. Take a **pack trip** via horse with Early Winters Outfitting and Saddle, (509)996-2659; North Cascades Safaris, (509)996-2350; or Rocking Horse Ranch, (509)996-2768; or via llama with Pasayten Llama Packing, (509)996-2326. For a panoramic view without getting out of your car, drive east to the upper Methow Valley and turn left on **Hart's Pass Road** (via Mazama). It climbs to over 7,000 feet in 22 bumpy miles of gravel and hairpin turns, reaching Washington's highest point accessible by car, where it intersects the Pacific Crest Trail.

Fat-tire **bikers** will find ample road and trail travel in the Methow. Pedal and coast your way down Pipestone Canyon or up and over Rendezvous Hill. In early October the Methow Valley Sports Trails Association puts on the Methow Valley Mountain Bike Festival; (800)682-5787. If you've a yen for **fishing**, cast your lure over the still waters of the Methow or Chewack and perhaps hook the elusive (and endangered) Methow bull trout. And for those who like to do it all, why not register for the Mountain Triathlon, held every September? For specific information about all local activities in the

Hut-to-Hut Skiing

In the Rendezvous Hills between Winthrop and Mazama are five spartan huts operated by Rendezvous Outfitters; (800)422-3048. Each plywood hut bunks up to eight people and comes equipped with a wood stove, a propane cookstove, and basic cooking utensils. Come with just one or two others ($25 per person) and join new friends for the night, or round up eight others and reserve an entire cabin ($140 per night). Pack in your needs or have them hauled up on a snowmobile (adds a $70 surcharge to the otherwise rock-bottom rates). All the cabins are open as a warm, dry lunch stop for day skiers.

Winthrop Rhythm and Blues Fest

This three-day July festival has attracted such national performers as Mick Taylor and John Mayall, as well as the best of the local bands. Events include a New Orleans–style street dance in the boot-kick town of Winthrop and a full day of steamy blues under the blazing sun at Twin Lakes. It's a popular event with the Harley crowd; (509)996-2125.

valley, call (509)996-4000 or (509)997-2131, or stop by the forest service visitors center on Highway 20 at the west end of Winthrop (open summers only).

When the snow falls, the valley becomes a haven for **cross-country skiers**. For a mere $13 a day or $30 for three days, kick-and-glide your way around the second-largest groomed system in the United States—nearly 175 kilometers of trail that slices through feather-light snow over hill, dale, and even river (via suspension bridges). Maintained by the Methow Valley Sports Trails Association (PO Box 147, Winthrop, WA 98862; (800)682-5787 or (509)996-3287), the system links the major ski areas of Mazama, Sun Mountain, Early Winters, Rendezvous, and the smaller Methow Valley Community Trail. Depending on your route, you can ski quiet forests and meadows or link towns. Purchase passes and obtain maps at most lodgings or mountain shops, enter at the most convenient point (often the inn where you're staying), and ski your heart out.

If you're looking for the best skiing take-off points, Mazama Ski Trails, (509)996-3287, offers 35 kilometers of pleasant valley skiing starting at either Mazama Country Inn, the Mazama Ranch House, or the North Cascades Basecamp (each located on Lost River Rd in Mazama). The trails of Sun Mountain (70 kilometers) run around the lodge's namesake mountain and pamper you

with such perks as a pro shop, a rental shop, and lessons. For high-country adventure, huts to warm body and soul (see "Hut-to-Hut Skiing" tip), and good access to backcountry skiing, start your adventure with Rendezvous Ski Trails (45 kilometers; contact the local ranger station on Hwy 20 in Twisp, (509)997-2131, for backcountry information).

For **alpine skiing** without the hype, crowds, and cost, drive to Loup Loup Ski Bowl (PO Box 1686, Omak, WA 98841; (509)826-2720), just off Highway 20 between Twisp and Okanogan. Two poma lifts access surprisingly challenging runs. The lodge has a homespun feel, and you can stash your brown-bag lunch and gear without fear. You'll share the slopes with old-timers who will never make the fashion pages of *Ski* magazine—but they'll ski your Lycra pants off. Nice prices, too.

When you're tired of bumping shoulders with tourists and cowboy wannabes in Winthrop, continue 8 short miles south to **Twisp**. Here is where Methow Valley residents come for horse food, auto parts, and groceries. Tucked away in this utilitarian town is the Confluence Gallery (104 Glover St, Twisp; (509)997-2787), which houses the best arts and crafts in the valley. There are excellent breads and sweet Cinnamon Twisps at the Cinnamon Twisp Bakery (116 Glover St, Twisp; (509)997-5030). At the city park you can swim in the pool for a buck, or inner-tube the river for free.

Cheap Eats

Duck Brand Cantina, Bakery, and Hotel

248 Riverside Avenue, Winthrop ☎ (509) 996-2192

A replica of a frontier-style hotel, Duck Brand is a Winthrop standby for good, filling meals at decent prices—from bulging burritos to fettuccine to sprout-laden sandwiches on whole-grain breads. American-style breakfasts feature wonderful cheesy Spanish potatoes and billowing omelets. The in-house bakery produces delicious baked goods. When you're not in the mood for painfully slow service, just take the sweets to go. Upstairs are six sparsely furnished rooms, priced right.

Java Man

94 Bridge Street, Winthrop ☎ (509) 996-2182

Matt Jones had the good idea of starting an espresso stand in Winthrop, but it wasn't until his friend came up with the brilliant addition of food-to-go such as big, messy, two-fisted chile Colorado burritos that this place really started catching on. You can cop a java buzz here starting at 6am, but you'll have to wait till 11am (and get there before 5pm) to grab a wrap.

Winthrop Brewing Company

155 Riverside Avenue, Winthrop ☎ (509) 996-3174

Located in an old schoolhouse, the Brewing Company is a cozy spot where locals go to down a few. The menu offers classic pub food, from burgers to fish 'n' chips to a pasta or two. On hot days, head for the deck and the beer garden out back.

Glover Street Cafe

104 Glover Street, Twisp ☎ (509) 997-1323

This great little weekday breakfast-and-lunchery is located in downtown Twisp, in the same building as the Confluence Gallery. Check out the hefty egg-and-potato breakfasts or the lunchtime soups (maybe a seafood chowder or a Cuban black bean) .

Cheap Sleeps

Lost River Resort

672 Lost River Road, Mazama, WA 98833 ☎ (800) 996-2537 or (509) 996-2537

This place has cheap sleeps written all over it. First of all, we like the location: way at the end of the road (well, about as far as the road gets plowed in the winter, anyway). From here you can connect to Monument Creek Trail or ski up to Yellowjacket. Jim Sandon and Nancy Flowers are mighty knowledgeable

Methow Valley Vacations

Take time out and stay awhile. Methow Valley Central Reservations (PO Box 505, Winthrop, WA 98862; (800)422-3048 or (509)996-2148) is the clearinghouse for dozens of cabins in the valley, from Twisp to Mazama. Bring an armful of good friends, cabin games, and a few bags of food, and you'll be set for a long (and cheap) weekend in a place you can call your own.

about all the fun things to do. Everyone gets a wood stove and a full kitchen. The least expensive sleep is in the thin-walled duplex, but for a few bucks more, you can stay in the cabin and talk without fear of eavesdroppers.

The Farmhouse Inn

709 Highway 20 (PO Box 1055), Winthrop, WA 98862
☎ **(888) 996-2525 or (509) 996-2191**

The inn is in a charmingly restored farmhouse just outside Winthrop, two blocks from the ski trail. Three of the rooms are small (but then, so is the price); the other three have their own baths. There's a big hot tub and cable TV, and a continental breakfast is included in the rates.

River Run Inn

27 Rader Road, Winthrop, WA 98862 ☎ **(800) 757-2709 or (509) 996-2173**

Craig and Carol Lints took a longtime rental house on the banks of the Methow River, built a six-bedroom motel-style addition, connected the two with a modest indoor-pool atrium, and called it an inn. Just a half-mile stroll west of Winthrop, this board-and-batten complex on 11 acres is a pleasant alternative to the more standard motels in town. The least expensive rooms share a bath in the fairly plain house. The motel rooms open out to the river and are larger than usual (and slightly beyond our "cheap" budgetary limits).

The Virginian

808 North Cascades Highway (PO Box 237), Winthrop, WA 98862
☎ **(800) 854-2834 or (509) 996-2535**

Hitch up your mountain bike or mount your skis; here's a motel with personality. A sprawling complex with Western flair to match its name, the Virginian offers standard, cedar-lined motel rooms and moderately priced cabins (the latter are great for groups). Ski and bike trails cross the property; there's a volleyball court, an outdoor pool (summer), and a hot tub (anytime), as well as a restaurant. Some nights the Bicycle Bar really spins.

Winthrop Mountain View Chalets

Highway 20 & KOA Road (PO Box 280), Winthrop, WA 98862
☎ **(800) 527-3113 or (509) 996-3113**

Just off Highway 20, these well-situated "chalets" offer quick access to everything the valley has to offer. Don't let the nearby KOA put you off: these six attractive little cabins—designed for two people only—are not just cozy, they're even a bit romantic. Each offers pine interiors, private decks overlooking the valley, full-size baths, and thoughtful touches such as window boxes, art, and reading material. The cooking facilities fall somewhere between a kitchenette and a wet bar, so bring your favorite electric cookware to supplement. A good deal ($65) for a miniature hideaway.

Idle-a-While Motel

505 N Highway 20 (PO Box 667), Twisp, WA 98856 ☎ (509) 997-3222

On Highway 20, at the north end of Twisp, is this simple white motel with sunny yellow doors and a broad expanse of lawn (or snow). It's half the price of any equally pleasant spot in Winthrop (under $50 in summer, under $40 in winter). Idle a night or two—with your dog if you wish. You can stay in one of the standard rooms or get a cabin with a kitchenette. Relax in the hot tub or sauna, have an afternoon barbecue, or play tennis (chase your own balls—there's no fence around this court). The river is a short walk away, and ski trails run by the back of the motel in the winter.

Lake Chelan

A spectacular inland fjord, Lake Chelan has its headwaters deep in the Cascade Range, where jagged peaks rise 7,000 feet above the lake surface. From there the lake bends south and east down 55 miles of glacier-carved valley. Snowcapped mountains give way to rolling, semi-arid hills, evergreen forests to apple orchards, roadless wilderness to condos and highways. At the lake's southern end sprawls a recreational mecca centered around the tiny resort town of Chelan.

A sun paradise indeed, the lower end of the lake draws thousands of tourists annually; it's a haven for those who want to soak up the rays and play on the water. Families and young singles fill the resorts, spill over into parks, crowd the restaurants, and ply the lake with every type of watercraft imaginable. The remote upper reaches, accessible only by boat or float-plane, draw a different sort of folk—fleece-clad and boot-shod types in search of wilderness, or perhaps just a little peace and quiet.

The peak season at Chelan is summer, when days are reliably hot and dry and recreational activities are without limit. (If you're planning a summer weekend at Lake Chelan, be warned that most places fill up months in advance.) Spring is cool and quiet, with apple blossoms scenting the air; during harvesttime in the fall, the crowds diminish but the days remain warm and the hillsides are rich in color. In winter, with luck, cross-country skiers and snowmobilers can find enough snow to schuss and growl their way over the surrounding hills.

Exploring

The main attraction here is, of course, the lake; the challenge is getting near it without booking yourself into a pricey resort or time-share. Happily, some public shore remains. In town, the popular **Don Morse Memorial City Park** (just off the road to Manson on the north side of town) offers not only protected swim areas and beaches, but also family attractions galore: picnic areas, volleyball and basketball courts, playgrounds, and even "bumper boats" (kids love them). Also in town is **Riverwalk Park**, a mile-long promenade along the Chelan River, perfect for sunset strolls. On the western edge of town, off Highway 97A next to the West-

Cascade Pass

One of the most stunning hikes in the North Cascades traverses Cascade Pass, crowned with granite spires, backed by glaciated peaks, and softened with blueberry and wildflower meadows. The trail begins 20 miles outside of Marblemount (on Hwy 20, also the North Cascades Hwy), and extends 9 miles to Cottonwood Campground (23 miles up the Stehekin Valley Road). Trouble is, that puts you a good 150 miles by boat and road from your car. It is, however, possible to turn this into a great two-day loop. Here's how: Arrange your trip with another couple. Party 1 begins at the northern trailhead near Marblemount; Party 2 starts in Chelan. Party 1 hikes across the pass to Cottonwood Campground. Party 2 takes the Lady of the Lake to Stehekin, and then rides the shuttle bus up the valley to meet Party 1 at Cottonwood. Next morning, exchange car keys. Party 2 hikes to Marblemount via Cascade Pass, and Party 1 takes the shuttle bus and boat back to Chelan.

view Resort, is Lakeside Park, limited to picnicking and swimming. Or forget the beaches and head to wild and crazy Slidewaters at Chelan (102 Waterslide Dr, Chelan; (509)682-5751), offering slides and water fun for the whole family.

To avoid the town altogether, turn off Highway 97A west of Chelan onto S Lakeshore Drive and go 10 miles to **Lake Chelan State Park**—a huge campground in a beautiful setting, with plenty of swimming and picnic areas (see "Camping" tip). On the other side of the lake, in Manson, are picnic areas at Old Mill Park and swimming at tiny Manson Bay Park.

Boatless but yearning for an **on-the-water experience**? Watercraft aplenty are available at Chelan Boat Rentals Inc. (1210 W Woodin Ave, Chelan; (509)682-4444) and Ship 'n' Shore Watercraft & Boat Rentals and Moorage (1230 W Woodin Ave, Chelan; (509)682-5125). If you have your own craft in tow, you'll find launches at the parks listed above, as well as at 25-Mile Creek State Park (25 miles up S Lakeshore Dr; see "Camping" tip). While you're afloat, toss a line over and try to hook one of those record-breaking salmon or lake trout.

At Chelan, recreational fun isn't limited to water sports. **Chelan Butte**, which rises 3,892 feet just south of the lake, is a world-renowned paragliding site; contact

Chelan Paragliding, (509)682-7777, for the opportunity to spread your wings and soar. Mountain bikers will find miles of Forest Service roads, as well as trails at Echo Ridge. You can hit the little white ball at Lake Chelan Golf Course (1501 Golf Course Road, Chelan; (509)682-8026) or at the 18-hole putting course at Don Morse Park. And at the betting tables and slot machines of Mill Bay Casino (Manson Hwy, Manson; (509)687-2102), you might win enough money to buy your own lakeside condo. Quieter activities include browsing the thoughtfully stocked shelves at Riverwalk Books (113 Emerson St, Chelan; (509)682-8901) and visiting St. Andrew's Episcopal Church, a 1899 log structure on Woodin Avenue.

During winter in Chelan, **snowmobiling** is fast becoming *the* sport of choice. Over 200 miles of trail have been marked and groomed for 'bilers, most of it north of town. **Skiers** will find modest downhill facilities as well as 35 kilometers of groomed cross-country trails at Echo Valley and Echo Ridge; there are also skinny-skier trails at the golf course. Lake Chelan Sports (132 E Woodin Ave, Chelan; (509)682-2629) rents ski equipment.

For maps, information, and advice about all activities, accommodations, and services in and around Chelan, stop by the **visitors center** (102 E Johnson Ave, Chelan; (800)4-CHELAN or (509)682-3503; www.lakechelan.com) and the Chelan Ranger District office (428 W Woodin Ave, Chelan; (509)682-2576 for the National Forest Service; (509)682-2549 for the National Park Service).

The best thing to do when you get to Chelan, though, is to get *out* of Chelan. That's right. Leave that crowded resort scene behind, if only for a day, and head uplake to Stehekin for some of the most gorgeous fjord scenery this side of Norway. Travel uplake on either the **Lady of the Lake II** or the **Lady Express**. Both boats are operated by the Lake Chelan Boat Company (located 1 mile south of Chelan on Hwy 97A; (509)682-2224 or (509)682-4584), and both make the trip to Stehekin daily May through October (the *Express* is the only option in the winter). A round trip on the *Lady* is an all-day journey; she leaves Chelan at 8:30am and arrives back at 6pm, with a 90-minute layover in Stehekin. For a slightly shorter trip, board the *Lady* at Fields Point Landing, 30 minutes up S Lakeshore Drive. The faster *Lady Express* also leaves Chelan at 8:30am, but is back by 2pm. To give yourself more time in Stehekin, sail on the *Express* in the morning and make your return trip on the *Lady*, affording you a three-hour layover. Call the Lake Chelan Boat Company for current schedules and rates and to make advance reservations; expect to pay around $22 for a round trip on the *Lady*, $41 on the *Express*.

At the head of the lake, surrounded by granite cliffs and deep forest, is the tiny community of **Stehekin**, which consists of the North Cascades Stehekin Lodge (located right at the boat stop, PO Box 457, Chelan, WA 98816; (509)682-4494 or (509)682-4584), a small marina, a convenience store, a restaurant, a post office, a craft store, a bakery, a primitive campground, and bike rentals. A Forest Service road extends 23 miles up the Stehekin River valley; along the way are beautiful Rainbow Falls, more campsites, and Courtney's Stehekin Valley Ranch (PO Box 36, Stehekin, WA 98816; (509)682-4677), whose reasonable rates include tent-platform accommodations, shared baths, and three ranch-style meals. The Lake Chelan Boat Company operates regular shuttle buses up and down the road.

Spend your time wandering lakeside trails and drinking in the scenery. Pedal up the forested road on a rented bike (cheaper than paying to bring your own bike on the boat), or ride one of the shuttle buses for a narrated tour. Better yet, spend a night or two in one of the campgrounds or lodgings (you can make Stehekin Lodge affordable by getting a group together and renting a housekeeping cabin). Whatever you do, however long you stay, at least make the trip. After all, there is more to life than bronzed bodies and jet-skis.

Cheap Eats

Apple Cup Cafe
804 E Woodin Avenue, Chelan ☎ (509) 682-2933

A local favorite, the Apple Cup is a pleasant and reasonably priced cafe suited to a lazy breakfast or simple lunch. During morning hours, the best bets are waffles or blintzes. The egg dishes (from fried to omelet) are varied and sound great on the menu, but can lack a little something in the execution. Lunch offerings are basic and sound—soups, sandwiches, salads, and burgers.

Espresso Cafes

If there's a dining option Chelan has down pat, it's the espresso cafe. Take a tour of the town and try a different one every morning: Flying Saucers for funky atmosphere and great muffins (116 S Emerson; (509)682-5129), Latte Da Coffee Stop Cafe for bagels and light lunches (303 E Wapato Ave; (509)682-4196), and Espress Depot (137 Woodin Ave; (509)682-8822) for pastries and central location. There's even an espresso bar with computers and Internet access at Another Story (113 Emerson St, above Riverwalk Books; (509)682-8901).

Goochi's
104 E Woodin Avenue, Chelan ☎ (509)682-2436

To eat cheaply at this trendy pub, you have to stick to the salad, pasta, or burger selections. But your dollars will buy lots of atmosphere, a broad choice of microbrews on tap, and live music on the weekends. Located in an historic building across from Campbell's Resort and graced with a century-old cherry-wood bar, Goochi's is a scene, but a fun and harmless one.

Peter B's Bar & Grill
114/116 E Woodin Avenue, Chelan ☎ (509)682-1031

Located at the back of the Riverfront Shops Building, Peter B's has a lively, upscale atmosphere, with pleasant views over Riverwalk Park from its upstairs tables. Lunch and dinner selections range from ambitious pasta dishes to steaks, salads, and burgers. Nothing sensational, but all reasonably priced, which in Chelan is saying a lot.

El Vaquero
75 W Wapato Way, Manson ☎ (509)687-3179

At their friendly, unpretentious spot in Manson, the Viveros family will happily serve you authentic Mexican fare without charging resort prices. Low on atmosphere but high on flavor, El Vaquero offers everything from burritos to fajitas, as well as a wealth of *huevos*, *pollos*, *carnes*, and *camarones* dishes (eggs, chicken, meat, and prawns, for you monolingual types). There are even burgers and a child's plate. Well worth the 15-minute drive to Manson (via Manson Hwy on the east side of the lake).

Cheap Sleeps

Apple Inn Motel
1002 E Woodin Avenue, Chelan, WA 98816 ☎ (509)682-4044

Don't be put off by its location on Chelan's main thoroughfare (aka Hwy 97A) or its nine-block distance from the lake. Behind that standard-motel facade is one of Chelan's sweetest deals—a friendly (especially to your wallet) retreat from the madcap lake scene. The original building in front houses comfortable, knotty pine–paneled rooms, some with kitchenette and living room. A little more money buys you more conveniences—bigger beds, newer plumbing, and maybe a wet bar. But you'll find *us* surrounded by knotty pine. Or maybe relaxing in the hot tub or pool.

Midtowner Motel

721 Woodin Avenue (PO Box 1722), Chelan, WA 98816 ☎ (509)682-4051

Okay, so it's the motel of motels. But with 45 well-maintained units (all with refrigerator and microwave, six with fully equipped kitchens, some wheelchair accessible, some allowing pets) and perks such as a nifty indoor/outdoor pool, Jacuzzi, sauna, and laundry, who's to gripe? You're seven blocks from the lake on a busy thoroughfare (Hwy 97A), but you have everything you and your family need, plus friendly managers who will shuttle you to the *Lady of the Lake II* ferry. The Midtowner may not warm the cockles of your heart, but it'll serve your needs and then some, while leaving you plenty of pocket change.

Mom's Montlake

823 Wapato Avenue SE, Chelan, WA 98816 ☎ (509)682-5715

If you don't mind staying in somewhat cramped quarters and being out of the main loop, then it's time to go home to Mom's. Located just off E Woodin Avenue (Hwy 97A), about eight blocks from the lake, Mom's offers a sheltered, summer camp–like atmosphere at ten small units (four with kitchens), surrounded by tree-shaded grass and parking areas. You won't find frills (and Mom's doesn't allow smoking), but kids are welcome, and you can barbecue under the trees, pet Mom's dog (but not your own—they stay home), and pretend you're in the quiet old Chelan of yesteryear.

Camping

Given Chelan's reliable weather, camping is a great and affordable way to spend your nights here. You have plenty of options, but keep in mind that sites at the lower end of the lake fill up as fast as motel rooms. Reservations are a must.

*One of the most popular spots is **Lake Chelan State Park**, 10 miles up the lake on S Lakeshore Drive (Hwy 971), with 144 campsites (tent and RV), great facilities, a swimming area, boat launches, and a stargazing dock. At the end of Lakeshore Drive is woodsy **25-Mile Creek State Park**, with both tent and RV sites as well as a boat launch and marina store. For both parks, call (800)233-0321 for information; (800)452-5687 for reservations. On the other side of the lake, next to Don Morse Memorial City Park, is **Lakeshore RV Park**; (509)682-8023. Contact the Chelan visitors center, (800)4-CHELAN, for information about these and other campgrounds.*

*Along the lakeshore toward **Stehekin** are several primitive campsites, accessible only by boat. Make arrangements through the Lake Chelan Boat Company, (509)682-2224 or (509)682-4584, for the Lady of the Lake II to drop you off and pick you up at one of these primo spots. Or pitch your tent in a campground along the Stehekin River valley; both the Lake Chelan Boat Company and the Forest Service operate shuttle buses up and down the valley road from Stehekin. For information about Forest Service campsites and shuttle buses, contact the Chelan Ranger District office; (509)682-2576.*

Parkway Motel

402 N Manson Road (PO Box 1237), Chelan, WA 98816 ☎ (509) 682-2822

A great bet for families, this motel is located across a busy thoroughfare from the lakeshore Don Morse Memorial City Park. Owners Barry and Jacque De Paoli have done more than just introduce a national-park theme for the names and decor of the rooms—they've conscientiously upgraded the rustic, knotty-pine interiors and tiled baths without compromising their warmth and character. The front rooms (all nonsmoking) have kitchens, living rooms with hideabeds, and picnic tables on the broad front lawn. The small sleeping rooms in the rear of the motel are cramped but can be joined to front units to create a big two-bedroom affair. Couples should book the upstairs studio unit near the office; it offers both privacy and balcony views.

Mount Rainier & the South Cascades

Three volcanoes battle for attention in the South Cascades. Mount St. Helens, the most recently verbal one, erupted on May 18, 1980, leaving a huge, gaping scar on its north side (and scattering a temporary haze of ash on surrounding towns). Mount Rainier's majestic, glacier-covered peak (reaching 14,411 feet high) is *the* symbol of home for many Northwesterners, who joke nervously that it will be the next to rumble. Mount Adams stands peacefully to the south—a shorter (12,276 feet), well-mannered kid brother to Rainier. While a few hearty souls aspire to climb one or all of these, most weekenders use them for photo backdrops, or take a short hike hoping to catch glimpses of a black bear, a marmot, or the vibrant wildflowers that explode over alpine meadows in late summer. Less surefooted vista seekers head to majestic Snoqualmie Falls, or spend time hiking and skiing near the less challenging and more accessible Snoqualmie Pass, an hour east of Seattle on Interstate 90.

Exploring

The town of **Snoqualmie** is worth a stop on the way to the waterfall, especially if you're a railroad fanatic. State Route 202, or Railroad Avenue, is lined with the husks of historic old Northwest railroad cars waiting to be restored. In town is the Snoqualmie Railroad Depot (38625 SE King St, Snoqualmie; (425)888-3030, or information line (425)746-4025), built in 1890. On summer weekends you can hop on an old-fashioned train bound for North Bend; the 50-minute round trip costs $6. You can check out railroad memorabilia inside the depot too.

Just beyond the town of Snoqualmie is

Washington's biggest tourist attraction, **Snoqualmie Falls**. This spectacular waterfall cascades 270 feet in a rush of thunderous water and billows of mist (it's higher than Niagara Falls, and the waterpower runs an electrical plant hidden in the rock). There's an observation deck and some (fairly steep) hiking trails. Alert to David Lynch fans: Remember the waterfall that began every episode of the TV series *Twin Peaks*? This is it.

If shopping excites you more than nature, head for the 50 shops in the Factory Stores of America **outlet mall** (exit 31 off I-90, intersection of Hwy 202,

North Bend; (425)888-4505). You'll find the best lattes nearby in North Bend (plus sandwiches and pastries) at George's Bakery (127 W North Bend Way, North Bend; (425)888-0632).

In summer, the ski runs of the South Cascades thaw into mountain meadows, and melting snows unveil crystalline lakes and hiking trails galore. But it's winter that really draws the crowds. At the top of **Snoqualmie Pass** is the ski-resort quad formerly called Snoqualmie, Alpental, Ski Acres, and Hyak. For decades, these four areas have been referred to collectively as "The Pass," but after a buyout in 1997, the collective name was changed to **The Summit at Snoqualmie**, and the individual resort names have been changed as well. Call (206)236-7277 for information or (425)434-7669 for an operator at the mountain. For snow conditions, contact (206)236-1600 or check out the Web site at www.summit-at-snoqualmie.com.

The resorts, though small, are extremely popular (especially on weekends and at night) due to their proximity to Seattle. The wide-open slopes of The Summit West are a great place to learn to ski or snowboard. The challenging slopes of Alpental at The Summit are known as the home mountain of Olympic gold medalist Debbie Armstrong. The Summit Central has a number of bump runs, and The Summit East, the smallest of the four areas, is your best bet if you want to avoid the lines and try telemark turns. The Summit Central and The Summit East are connected by a groomed 20-kilometer cross-country loop around Mount Catherine (with a warming hut), and Summit Central's lower trail system has 1 1/2 kilometers of lit trails for night cross-country skiing on Tuesday and Saturday nights. Lift tickets Monday through Friday cost $20. By the weekend, lift tickets peak at $32. Summit Central gives you the most runs for your money.

Save gas and avoid snow perils by taking the I-90 Ski Bus up to Snoqualmie Pass. On Saturdays and Sundays, the bus leaves from four locations in Seattle and the Eastside for about $20 round trip. It operates in conjunction with the Seattle Times Ski School, but you don't need to take lessons to get a ride up to the pass; call the Summit Learning Center, (206)236-7277, ext 3242, for information and reservations.

In warmer months, the Summit Nordic and Mountain Bike Center, (206)236-7277, ext 3372, keeps one chair lift running for bikers and hikers. Bring your bike (or rent one of theirs) and take it up the lift to the top for some solid intermediate rides; $5 for hikers and sightseers, $9 for bikers. For picnic areas, campsites, and general information, call the Snoqualmie Pass Visitors Center; (206)434-6111.

Twenty miles east of Snoqualmie Pass is **Roslyn**, once a thriving coal-mining area whose population peaked in 1910, when 4,000 people lived here. These days, residents number a modest 936, and the equally modest turn-of-the-century homes in town have become weekend places for city folk. The former mortuary has been reincarnated as a video store and movie theater, but the main intersection still offers a cross-section of the town's former self. The historic Northwestern Improvement Company building (which once housed the miner's company store) occupies one corner, while the old brick bank across the way still operates behind the original brass bars and oak counters. Yet another visible reminder of Roslyn's yesteryears are the cemeteries, clustered on a hillside just west of downtown and worth a detour.

In the early '90s Roslyn basked in the glow of its TV alter ego, Cicely, Alaska, when it became the set for *Northern Exposure*. Fans of the now-defunct series can treat their bouts of nostalgia with a Kodak moment in front of the Roslyn Cafe mural, and follow up with a pint at the **Brick Tavern** (100 W Pennsylvania

Bonsai Tree Farm

The Mount Si Bonsai nursery (43321 Mount Si Rd, North Bend; (425)888-0350) is a pocket-size paradise right off the North Bend–Snoqualmie Road. Pull over by all the other cars (this is where hikers mounting Little Si park their vehicles), and enter through the archway into bonsai heaven—"Where getting bent out of shape is a work of art." Wandering among the rows of exquisite gnarled little pines and perfect midget maples is a positively zenlike experience. Large urns hold goldfish and water lilies, and the landscaping is soothing to the eye and spirit. Prices range from a ten-spot for a baby Japanese maple (okay, so it's not a bonsai) to prices in the hundreds for miniature twisted trees more than 50 years old. The owners wander through the rows, trimming and inspecting. Open Wednesday through Sunday.

Ave, Roslyn; (509)649-2643). Reputed to be the oldest (licensed) saloon in Washington, the Brick still has a working water-fed spittoon that runs the length of the bar. To drink the local dark lager, Roslyn Beer, at its source, head down the block to the Roslyn Brewing Company (208 W Pennsylvania Ave, Roslyn; (509)649-2232). The locals, for their part, seem relieved that Pennsylvania Avenue is no longer overrun with film crews, but are also just as pleased to prolong the increased tourism the series brought (an annual Northern Exposure Festival has been added to the odd assortment of weekend events that keep Roslyn busy all summer).

A few miles east is **Cle Elum**, another former coal-mining town that, although it doesn't have quite the charm of Roslyn, is now undergoing a modest rediscovery. It's also a good starting point for venturing into Wenatchee National Forest. The surrounding Forest Service land is laced with trails for mountain biking in the spring and summer and groomed for cross-country skiers and snowmobilers in the winter. It's the snowmobiling that draws the crowds.

In warmer weather, a better way to cover the hills (while making significantly less noise) is on horseback. Three Queens Outfitter/Guide Service, (509)674-5647, and High Country Outfitters, (888)235-0111 or (425)392-0111, lead trips in the

area. For information on the best hiking trails, contact the Cle Elum Ranger District; (509)674-4411.

Lake Cle Elum is a recreation hub for boaters. In June, the Cle Elum River just above the lake is filled with swiftly paddling racers, in brightly colored kayaks, from all over the Northwest. For access to the lake, stay at the Wish Poosh or Salmon La Sac Campgrounds, both on Highway 903 (Salmon La Sac Rd) north of Roslyn; (509)674-4411.

South on Highway 410 in the Mount Baker/Snoqualmie National Forest, **Crystal Mountain**, believed by many to have the best skiing in the state, draws outdoor enthusiasts in the summer for mountain biking and a killer up-close Mount Rainier view. Crystal has a vertical drop of 3,100 feet, full ski and snowboard services, and a fantastic, unpatrolled backcountry area. This is also an excellent place for spring skiing. Off season (late June to early September; the mountain is closed during the shoulder seasons), hikers, bikers, and sightseers can ride the chair lift to various trails (an all-day pass costs $10 for adults and $7 for kids and seniors; kids under 6 ride free). For more information, call (888)754-6199 (hotline) or (360)663-2265, or visit Crystal's Web site at www.Crystalmt.com.

In season, midweek lift tickets are no longer discounted, and adult day passes

Northwest Trek

Northwest Trek is a "zoo" where animals roam free while people tour the 600-acre grounds in rather noisy, decades-old trams. The animals don't seem to mind, and the knowledgeable guides compensate for the rickety ride. An hour-long tour passes by a large collection of native Northern beasts, from herds of elk to the lone mountain goat—but it's the bison that steal the show. Visit the park in early summer and see lots of animal babies. The less placid residents (grizzly bears, gray wolves, a cougar) can be spotted in their (fenced) living areas from a series of nature trails. The park is open daily from March through October; it's open weekends only the rest of the year. It's best to bring your own lunch. Ticket prices are $5.75 for kids and $8.25 for adults; AAA members receive a 20 percent discount, and group rates are available. The park is on State Route 161, 6 miles north of Eatonville (11610 Trek Dr E, Eatonville; (800)433-TREK).

are a whopping $35 regardless of what day you call in sick. The Alpine Inn is right on the slopes, though, and the bunk rooms here are by far the least expensive option at Crystal—you can sleep four for under $60. The Snorting Elk, a great après-ski spot, is downstairs (1 Crystal Mountain Blvd, Crystal Mountain; (360)663-2262). On the way *to* Crystal, stop at the Black Diamond Bakery (32805 Railroad Ave, Black Diamond; (360)886-2741) for breakfast, or grab one of the 26 different breads they make in the wood-fired oven to devour in the car.

Elbe, on the western approach to Mount Rainier, was once a sawmill town. It is now on the verge of becoming a museum for antique cabooses, thanks to the old train cars that line the Mountain Highway. The four-hour ride and meal on the Cascadian Dinner Train, a fully restored 1920s passenger train, is expensive. Instead, hop on the Mount Rainier Scenic Railroad for a 90-minute ride (round-trip from Elbe to tiny Mineral) that provides equally attractive scenery. Offered only in summer, the ride costs $9.50 for adults and a few bucks less for kids; (888)STEAM-11 or (360)569-2588. If you must eat on a train, try the stationary Mount Rainier Railroad Dining Company (54106 Mountain Hwy, Elbe; (360)569-2505). One car is a dining room; the other (the Sidetrack Room) is

a slightly seedy bar with a jukebox and a dance floor.

Be sure to wander behind this cluster of railcars to peek in the window of one of the smallest churches in the country. Elbe Evangelische Lutherische Kirche, an historic 1906 Lutheran church, is perched on a small patch of green grass; its 46-foot-high steeple is topped with an iron cross that contains a railroad locomotive bell. The area bishop conducts services every third Sunday, arriving by bicycle in the tradition of Elbe's early pastors.

Better eats (and sleeps) can be found a couple of miles closer to the mountain in **Ashford**. This town is also the last place to get gas (no pumps in the national park), so fill 'er up now. Fill yourself up, too, at Copper Creek Restaurant (35707 State Route 706, Ashford; (360)569-2326; closed in winter), which serves up a thick wedge of wild blackberry pie, sandwiches, burgers, and heaping plates o' fries for lunch. Dinners of pan-fried mountain trout, smoked chicken, and steaks ain't cheap—best to stop here for lunch and hit the Wild Berry Restaurant later (37718 Hwy 706 E, Ashford; (360)569-2628; see review in Cheap Eats).

A few miles before the entrance to Mount Rainier National Park on State Route 706, stop by Sweet Peaks Patisserie and Mountaineering, (360)569-2720, for some homemade cinnamon doughnuts and a latte before heading up to Longmire or Paradise (be sure to ask for a pastry that's been baked in-house). If you've forgotten your topo map or mittens, you may find those here too; there's a decent assortment of gear.

Once you pay your $10 (per carload) to pass through the Nisqually entrance, you're in **Mount Rainier National Park**. Unlimited-use, full-year passes are available to anyone for $20—a good investment if you plan to visit more than two times in a year (seniors can get a lifetime pass for $10, and disabled travelers get in free); (360)569-2211. A few miles inside the southwestern border of the park lies the little village of **Longmire**, with an inn (see National Park Inn review in Cheap Sleeps), a small wildlife museum, and a wilderness information center; (360)569-2211. Mount Rainier Guest Services handles ski touring and rentals; (360)569-2400 (ask for the ski shop). Drive carefully once past Longmire—the road is steep, and there are some nerve-wracking hairpin turns.

Ahead, however, is **Paradise**. At 5,400 feet, Paradise is the most popular destination on the mountain. On the way up you'll catch spectacular views of Narada Falls and Nisqually Glacier. The visitors center at Paradise, (360)569-2211 ext 2328, is housed in a flying saucer–like building. There's a standard cafeteria and gift shop, films and nature exhibits, and a superb view of the mountain from the observation deck. Depending on the season, you can picnic among the wild-flowers, explore some of the trails (rangers offer guided walks), let the kids slide on inner tubes in the snow-play area, try a little cross-country skiing, or even take a Park Service–guided snow-shoe tromp. The snowshoe tour lasts two hours and is free (there's a small suggested donation for equipment); there are two trips per day on weekends. Be warned that entering the ice caves (3 miles northeast of Paradise) in their deteriorating state has become extremely dangerous.

Open only during the summer months, the **Sunrise Visitor Center**, (360)569-2211, ext 2357, on Mount Rainier's north side (6,400 feet) is the closest you can drive to the peak. The old Sunrise Lodge has no overnight accommodations, but it does offer a snack bar and mountain-centric exhibits. Dozens of trails begin here, including a short one leading to the magnificent viewpoint of Emmons Glacier Canyon.

Mount Rainier, at 14,411 feet, is the most recognized symbol of natural grandeur in the Northwest. Washington residents refer to it as simply "The Mountain," and its tear-your-guts-out thrust of sheer volcanic power and beauty has been known to stop traffic on Interstate 5 in Seattle when clouds part and the stunning peak appears. One of the quickest ways to appreciate the mountain is to make an **auto loop** via Chinook or Cayuse Pass (open only May through October). Visitors with more time should get out of the car and explore Rainier's

Wildlife Watching

If you've never seen several hundred elk line up for breakfast, pack your Polaroid and head to the Oak Creek Wildlife Area (at the junction of Hwy 410 and US Hwy 12, east of Naches; (509)575-2740). On winter mornings, once the snows have pushed the herd to lower elevations, the members of a large Rocky Mountain elk herd arrive for their morning hay. Smaller groups of bighorn sheep get waited on as well, though at a different feeding station on Old Clemens Road.

flanks: 300 miles of backcountry and self-guiding nature trails lead to ancient forests, dozens of massive glaciers, waterfalls, and alpine meadows lush with wildflowers during the short summer. The 98-mile Wonderland Trail loops around the entire mountain and is a trip for hard-core hikers only—it takes a good 10 to 14 days.

Rainier is not only breathtaking, it is also a source of myths for several Native American tribes, who called it by its original name, Tahoma, and who refused to climb it out of respect for the gods they believed lived at the top. If you choose to **attempt the climb**, there are two ways to do it: with a guide service or on your own. Unless you are qualified to climb it on your own—and this is a massive, difficult, and dangerous mountain on which many people have been killed—you must climb with the guide service (climbers training for Mount Everest use Rainier as a warm-up). A number of outdoor organizations sponsor trips up the mountain; the best elevation for your dollar is with Rainier Mountaineering Inc., the concessionaire guide service (but you have to have lots and lots of dollars!); (360)569-2227 in summer, (253)627-6242 in winter). If you plan to climb with your own party, you must register at one of the ranger stations in Mount Rainier National Park; $15 per person, (360)569-2211. Generally, climbers plan trips from mid-May through early September, but the best time to go varies yearly.

All Mount Rainier **campgrounds** except one are open in summer only, and campers are limited to 14 days. None of the campgrounds accept reservations, so you may need to scramble to get a spot—they fill up quickly; (360)569-2211.

The town of **Packwood** is like the "Go" space on a Monopoly board: you inevitably pass through it if you're heading east to ski at White Pass or hike in the Goat Rocks, and it's also a convenient place to spend the night before continuing on to either Mount Rainier or Mount St. Helens. Packwood proper is not much to speak of: just a small town flanked by big mountains. But if you have some time to kill before lights-out at Hotel Packwood, take Forest Service Road 1260 (adjacent to the ranger station) to the Packwood Lake Trail for an eagle's-eye view of town and—even better—an elevated view of Rainier.

Ten miles east of Packwood is **White Pass**. Driving there is itself an education in the storied volcanic past of the South Cascades. In winter, the White Pass Ski Area, (509)672-3100, is a haven for skiers who find drier snow and less populated slopes here than at other Northwest skiing hubs. The pass has an elevation of 4,500 to 6,000 feet, and the terrain is friendly to intermediate skiers. Adult lift tickets are $19 on Monday, Tuesday, and Friday and $31 on weekends. The real deal days are Wednesday and Thursday, when ticket prices drop to $14 (children ski at reduced rates). Plan ahead, and you may be able to secure one of the privately owned Village Inn Condominiums (48933 Hwy 12, White Pass; (509)672-3131). Six people can pile into one of the standard units for $100, and for considerably less in the summer.

Come summertime, hikers replace the skiers as they show up to tromp around the extensive wilderness areas that sprawl in every direction just off US 12 and Highway 410. To the north lies the William O. Douglas Wilderness, and this is also where hard-core hikers can pick up the famed Pacific Crest Trail, following it south through the length of the **Goat Rocks Wilderness**, a jagged series of 8,000-foot crags that were once part of a much-taller volcano. The Pacific Crest Trail stretches from Canada to Mexico, so it is no small compliment that the Goat Rocks leg is considered to be one of the most dazzling sections of the trail. Hikers who don't see themselves leaving the country, take heart: there are

Wellspring: A Woodland Spa

The cottages at secluded Wellspring, in the shadow of Mount Rainier, are definitely not for budget travelers, but who can resist the chance to soak in a private outdoor cedar hot tub (one luxurious hour at $10 a head; ditto Wellspring's wood-fired sauna). If your hiking muscles are feeling extra sore (and you can afford it), owner Sunny Thompson-Ward will massage your aches away ($25 for a half hour, $45 for an hour). Call (way) ahead to reserve a time slot at Wellspring, 3 miles west of the park entrance off Highway 706 (54922 Kernahan Rd, Ashford; (360)569-2514).

countless opportunities for short hikes and not-so-grueling backpacking trips. For a thorough rundown on the possibilities (and for camping information), contact the Packwood Ranger Station, (360)494-0600, or the Naches Ranger District, (509)653-2205.

South of the older, more contained Mount Rainier, a mercurial **Mount St. Helens** stands 1,300 feet shorter today than it did two decades ago. A 5.1-magnitude earthquake on May 18, 1980, started a massive landslide on the mountain's north flank, which in turn triggered an enormous lateral blast of superheated gas, ash, and pulverized rock: after 123 years of relative quiet, the volcano had erupted. And that wasn't the end of it. The column of ash that spewed out of the mountain rose 17 miles into the sky and blocked out the sun for most of Eastern Washington. The landslide sloshed out the contents of Spirit Lake, while the lateral blast—traveling at speeds of up to 600mph—leveled thousands of acres of forest in just minutes.

Visiting the ravaged—and rejuvenating—landscape that huddles tentatively around the slopes of the volcano is still, despite the determined recovery of the land, a shocking, humbling experience. Getting a close-up peek at the gaping crater of a once nearly perfectly conal mountain is well worth the winding drive toward the blast zone. Even if you're heading to the mountain for a day trip, it's a good idea to stock up on gas, food, and water (although the many visitors centers can

help with some of these needs). Visitors are asked to buy a pass ($8 for adults, $4 for seniors and kids) if they plan to use any of the **National Volcanic Monument**'s "developed recreation sites"; (360)247-3900. (Essentially this means everyone, since these "sites" include visitors centers, viewpoints, and interpretive signs.)

The volcano can be approached from several routes, the most frequented being the **Spirit Lake Memorial Highway** (Hwy 504), which can be accessed off I-5 in Castle Rock and continues east for 51 miles, to within 5 miles of the crater. If you're an information junkie, this is the route for you: several visitors centers have sprouted along the highway like a new, posteruption species of plant. Close to the freeway, before you begin the ascent to the ridge, stop at the Cinedome (just off I-5 at the Castle Rock exit; (360)274-8000) to see the half-hour Academy Award–nominated film *The Eruption of Mount St. Helens*, projected onto a three-story-high, 55-foot-wide screen. The rumble alone, which rattles your theater seat, is worth the price of admission ($5 adults, $4 seniors and children; shows every 45 minutes).

The **Mount St. Helens Visitor Center at Silver Lake**, (360)274-2100, just a few miles east of I-5, has a walk-through volcano exhibit and an endearingly hokey short film. The center at **Coldwater Ridge** (43 miles east of I-5; (360)274-2131) is a multimillion-dollar facility with a million-dollar view of the black dome, which grows in steamy fits and starts within the crater. The focus here is on the biological resurgence of the land. Highway 504 comes to an end at the newest visitors center in the monument: the **Johnston Ridge Observatory**, (360)274-2140, named for the U.S. Geological Survey volcanologist who died in the eruption while monitoring the mountain. Appropriately, the exhibits here detail the sequence of geologic events that transformed the landscape.

For a self-guided approach, drive in from the east using Forest Service Roads 26 and 99 (usually closed in winter due to snow). Heading south from Randle, the drive to **Windy Ridge** takes over an hour, but this ascent provides the most striking views of the blast zone. Keep your fingers crossed and hope that the crater doesn't become enveloped in clouds by the time you reach Windy Ridge—which, at a distance of 4 miles, is the closest you can get by car. Better than any of the beeping, blinking exhibits is a hike (2 miles round trip) down the otherworldly Harmony Trail to Spirit Lake. It's a bit of a climb on return, but it's the only legal access to the shores of this

once-crystalline lake. As with all the trails in the monument, save yourself the $100 fine by staying on them.

If you plan on joining the 15,000 people who **climb Mount St. Helens** each year, you must begin on the southern slopes. The most popular scramble-up is the Monitor Ridge route, which begins at Climber's Bivouac—a 7- to 12-hour round trip for most climbers. A $15 permit is required, and access is limited to 100 climbers per day. Some permits can be reserved in advance, while the rest are available in a daily lottery at Jack's Restaurant near Cougar. For permit information, call (360)247-3961. Another reason to find yourself on the south side is the **Ape Cave**, a 1,900-year-old underground lava tube (use of the cave, which is open only in summer, is included in the Monument Pass fee). It's a good excursion for a cloudy afternoon when the obscured volcano might as well be in Hawaii. The walk through the cave is dark and cool—a chilly 40 degrees, even in summer—so be sure to bring a flashlight (lanterns can be rented for $2) and warm clothes.

Cheap Eats

Roslyn Cafe
201 W Pennsylvania Avenue, Roslyn ☎ (509)649-2763

Here's the type of casual eatery that every picturesque, slightly chic town deserves. It's housed in an old building with high ceilings, a counter bar, lots of neon, and a jukebox with original 78s—and full of different types of people who somehow all belong here. Dinners (in summer only) tend to be a bit fancier (and pricier)—grilled halibut with dill sauce, Chinese pepper steak. But lunch is best, when you can wrap your fist around a great burger, spoon up a fine corn chowder, or light into a Philadelphia steak sandwich. Breakfast is also worth the side trip.

Cle Elum Bakery
501 E First Street, Cle Elum ☎ (509)674-2233

A longtime local institution in the truest sense of the word (fresh bread was first served here in 1906), this bakery has one of the last brick-oven hearths in the

WASHINGTON

Northwest, and they claim it never cools. Try the Torchetti bread sticks with a newer local institution: espresso. Order a six-pack of cinnamon rolls and stash some of the great old-fashioned cake doughnuts for the road. Closed Sundays.

Naches Tavern

58411 State Route 410 E, Greenwater ☎ (360) 663-2267

After a particularly satisfying day of skiing at Crystal, stop in for a juicy chili burger and some deep-fried mushrooms at this Greenwater country tavern. The fireplace is as long as a wall and roars all winter long, warming skiers, loggers, hunters, and locals, all of whom rub shoulders and get along just fine here. During the week, hearty soups and thick sandwiches are doled out; weekends (Thursday through Sunday) are when the grill gets fired up. Slurp down a four-scoop milk shake, stroke the roving house pets, and then play a little pool before nodding off in front of the fire.

Scaleburgers

54109 Mountain Highway E, Elbe ☎ (360) 569-2247

On sunny days, kids with ketchup-smeared mouths, tourists, and locals buzz around the sturdy wooden picnic tables at this roadside stand across the highway from the Hobo Inn. The burgers, fried-egg sandwiches, and hot dogs are served by a bevy of cooks wedged into this absolutely tiny Lincoln Log–like cabin painted white with green trim. Try a wild mountain blackberry or butterscotch shake and order your burger "Lite" (just sauce), "Legal" (everything), or "Overload" (don't ask). Onion rings (crumbed, not battered) are decent; home-cut fries are thick but occasionally undercooked. Kids can fill up on grilled cheese and ice cream.

Wild Berry Restaurant

37718 Highway 706 E, Ashford ☎ (360) 569-2628

The Wild Berry is a perfect spot for hearty mountain fare and a brewski. Only a mile from the Nisqually entrance to Mount Rainier National Park, the Berry leans toward vegetarian food but also offers chicken and salmon dishes, big pizzas (veggies—as many as you want—are free, but "protein" is extra), a peasant pie, thick, homemade sandwiches, and a great house salad. The room's atmosphere is warm and comforting, and the portions are plentiful. The teenage service is informal, and the blackberry pie is excellent. Everything (including beer and wine) is available for take-out. The Berry also rents a **log cabin** (sleeps as many as eight) and a rustic cottage (can sleep five). Both have full kitchen facilities and a fireplace stove. Go with a group (perfect for a cross-country skiing posse) and it's a *great* deal. Well-behaved pets are welcome.

Club Cafe

13016 US Highway 12, Packwood ☎ (360) 494-5977

A bright and easy diner in the shadow of a big mountain, this cafe has the requisite number of dishes that pay homage to the Big Guy: there's the Mount Rainier (sliced beef with onions, mushrooms, and Swiss on a French roll) and the Mountain Lion (a roast turkey, ham, and beef sandwich). Five bucks buys the token Logger Burger, which in other, less forested places materializes as a bacon cheeseburger. Entrees run about $10 and cover a satisfactory range of chicken, seafood, and steak plates. You may want to make this your breakfast stop. The waffles are excellent, and the efficient, affable servers *must* be morning people. Seniors get a discount.

Packwood Pizza Parlor
13028 US Highway 12, Packwood ☎ (360) 494-5400

Eating here feels like eating at a friend's house in fifth grade: another family's baby pictures are propped on the windowsills; balloons get strapped to chairs for birthday parties; and there's even a huge rec room adjacent to the dining area, so you can shoot pool and baskets while wolfing down pizza. The menu mentions lasagne, calzones, spaghetti, and even subs and hamburgers, but when you're offered a pizza called the Mountaineer Pig Out (topped with all things meaty, and whatever else they can find), why veer off the established trail? Senior discount.

Cheap Sleeps

Wardholm West Bed and Breakfast
861 Yellowstone Road (PO Box 143), Snoqualmie Pass, WA 98068
☎ (425) 434-6540

Staying at this red chalet on a quiet road is like visiting an elderly aunt's house: depending on your room, you may have floral bedspreads and walls decorated with crocheted dolls' dresses (#4), or a more masculine and spare decor (#3). The house offers a sort of country-house clutter—do inspect the collection of nutcrackers, baby dolls, and golden-headed Shirley Temples inhabiting the stairway's shelves—but the beds are comfortable, robes are provided, and $50 a night (ask about the Pacific Crest Trail hiker's special) is hard to beat. Your continental breakfast might be brought to you in bed. Owners Peg and Bob Ward know the area; inquire about inexpensive lift tickets or fishing in nearby Lake Keechelus or Denny Creek.

Camping: Mt. St. Helens

*If you're not making Mount St. Helens a day trip, consider camping, since the only other affordable lodgings close to the monument are several unremarkable motels. On the north side, head for **Iron Creek Campground**, (800)280-2267, the only campground within the monument itself. There are 98 campsites ($10 a night, with running water and pit toilets), but it's a popular spot, so reserve early or arrive early (nearly half the sites are nonreservable: first come, first served). Another good choice is **Seaquest State Park**, near the Silver Lake Visitors Center off Highway 504 (sites start at $11). Reserve ahead of time, and don't be surprised if the line is busy; (800)452-5687. There are a handful of campgrounds south of the mountain. At the newer **Cresap Bay Campground**, you can take a dip in Swift Reservoir ($15 a night). For information on this and other south-side campgrounds, call Pacific Power and Light at (503)464-5035.*

Skiers' Cabins

The Mountaineers, Washington's venerable outdoor club, runs four
winter lodges in the Cascades. The dormitory-style cabins—at Snoqualmie Pass,
Stampede Pass, Stevens Pass, and Mount Baker—are located near (sometimes within
skiing distance) the respective ski areas. Meany Lodge, on a ridge above the Yakima River,
is the only one not adjacent to a downhill area. The large lodges hold 55 to 105 skiers.
They're open on winter weekends (except during the holidays) and some weekends in
spring and summer. Prices range from $12 at Stevens to $39 at Meany (which includes a
Sno-Cat ride to the remote lodge), and some meals may be included. Reportedly, the
Snoqualmie and Meany lodges are better for families (though you're encouraged to leave
toddlers at home). Nighttime activities can include folk dancing, games, and slide shows.
Reservations are required and open about a month in advance for each lodge; call as far in
advance as possible. For reservations or membership information (members get a better
deal), contact the Mountaineers, 300 3rd Ave W, Seattle, WA 98119; (206)284-8484;
www.mountaineers.org/climb.

Hobo Inn

54106 Mountain Highway E (PO Box 10), Elbe, WA 98330 ☎ (360) 569-2500

We like this place, if only because it's fun to stay in a caboose. So what if it's
right on the road to Rainier and rooms are $70 during high season—squeeze in
four and you've got a genuine train experience. Some cars have hot tubs (for an
extra $10), and kids will like the small booths that are tucked up in a loft. Eat
breakfast in the train next door (not cheap) or, better yet, grab a couple of
Scaleburgers from the stand across the street and hit the mountain.

National Park Inn
(Mount Rainier Guest Services)

**6 miles inside the Park's southwest entrance, Longmire
(PO Box 108, Ashford, WA 98304) ☎ (360) 569-2275**

The only two lodges located within Mount Rainier National Park are the Paradise Inn and the National Park Inn. You can't get any closer to Mount Rainier
than these lodges, unless you stay in a tent. Paradise really no longer qualifies as
a cheap sleep (which is too bad, since we love the location and the lobby's huge
fireplace), and the modest National Park Inn is borderline on the cheap scale,
but we still recommend its least expensive rooms ($64), some of which have
tree-branch bed frames and wrought-iron lamps. Be aware that at both places,
the least expensive rooms are very small and bathrooms are shared. Summer
rooms book up *many* months in advance—plan ahead. Only National stays open
year-round.

Whittaker's Bunkhouse

30205 State Route 706 E, Ashford, WA 98304 ☎ (360) 569-2439

"The place to stop on the way to the top" is Whittaker's motto, and they're not
kidding. This hikers' and skiers' hangout is named after world-famous climber
Lou Whittaker. Built in 1912 as a loggers' and mill workers' bunkhouse, it's now
a clean, simple hostel-like spot to rest up for some serious (or not-so-serious)

Mount Tahoma Ski Huts

Just off Highway 7 is Western Washington's first hut-to-hut ski system.
The Mount Tahoma Scenic Ski Trails Association (MTTA) has cut almost 90 miles of
cross-country trails through a spectacular area south and west of Mount Rainier National
Park. There are two eight-person huts in the South District (built by MTTA members)
and one 12-person hut in the Central District. The reservation policy limits you to a three-
night maximum at each hut (and a $25-per-person-per-night refundable deposit for
damage and usage). Reservations are taken on a first-come, first-served basis between
December 15 and April 1. (PO Box 206, Ashford, WA 98304; (360)569-2451.)

hiking. For the cheapest sleeps, bring your sleeping bag and grab a bunk in the bunk room ($20); or splurge on a room with a private bath ($80 buys a room that sleeps four or five).

Cowlitz River Lodge

13069 US Highway 12 (PO Box 488), Packwood, WA 98361 ☎ (360)494-4444

With its vaguely alpine entryway, this lodge is best suited for a winter stay—when you might actually be inclined to lounge in front of the lobby fireplace, and when a warm, clean room is really all you want after a long day of skiing. In summer, the place loses some of its appeal; the rooms seem bland and less inviting. The lodgekeepers contend that you can watch deer and elk graze in the "meadow" out back, but to the casually observing guest, the meadow more resembles a deserted Little League field. Still, there's an outdoor hot tub, cable TV, and a continental breakfast, although late sleepers beware: the coffee and doughnuts are stowed promptly at 9:30am, and you won't see either if you show up late.

Hotel Packwood

104 Main Street (PO Box 130), Packwood, WA 98361 ☎ (360)494-5431

A couple of motels in town may have more modern appliances, but this spartan lodge with a wraparound porch (open since 1912) remains a favorite. Hey, if it was good enough for Theodore Roosevelt—who reportedly snoozed here once—it's good enough for us. Two can stay in a bunk room (which has a view of Rainier) for $25, or fork out all of $30 for a double, shared-bath room; a double with private bath is $38. Many of the seven shared-bath rooms have cast-iron beds, and all have cable TV and the homey aroma of wood-fired heat.

Columbia River Gorge & Mount Adams

Mother Nature pulled out all the stops here. Basalt columns, white-water rivers, snow-covered peaks, alpine lakes, lava tubes, and the windy gorge provide a panoply of sights and outdoor activities unparalleled in the Northwest. In addition, the sheer bulk of Mount Adams (at 12,276 feet, the second-highest peak in the state) casts a welcome rain shadow over the area. It's not unusual to leave Portland on a rainy day and emerge an hour later into a breezy, sun-drenched playland. This is nirvana for the recreation-obsessed vacationer who can never pack enough into a day (and who doesn't mind packing the mosquito repellent). On the other hand, the less ambitious can spend the day sipping microbrews and contemplating views of snowcapped volcanoes—and then spend the evening at the Goldendale Observatory gazing at the celestial scenery.

Exploring

Although the Oregon side of the Columbia River Gorge gets more attention, serious boardheads can check out the scene at several **windsurfing** sites along the Washington side of the gorge, where the wind really blows. To see the hottest surfers dodging barges, doing endos on waves, and tacking on a dime, take Highway 14 and look for parked vehicles at Swell City or the nearby fish hatchery, about 4 miles west of Bingen; Doug's Beach, a few miles east of Lyle; or farther east at Maryhill State Park and Roosevelt Park. Most board shops across the water in Hood River, Oregon, provide 1- or 2-day lessons.

Just west of Stevenson off Highway 14, stop by the **Columbia Gorge Interpretive** Center (990 SW Rock Creek Dr, Stevenson; (509)427-8211) for a history of the Gorge, including a slide show that re-creates the Gorge's cataclysmic formation, Native American fishing platforms, and a 37-foot-high replica of a 19th-century fish wheel.

Drive north on Highway 141 from White Salmon to the **Mount Adams Wilderness**. Legend has it that when Mount St. Helens took a fancy to Mount Adams, the jealous Mount Hood bashed Adams on the head and flattened his top for good. (Who knows what part Mount Hood played when Mount St. Helens lost her top?) En route to Mount Adams, you can see hundreds of acres of beautiful purple echinacea fields along the backroads of the Trout Lake Valley, usually in full bloom by mid-July and harvested by mid-August. (Mid-July to early August is definitely the best time to visit if it's wildflowers you're after.) Of course, there's no better place to admire the scenery surrounding Mount Adams than from atop the volcano's massive, rounded dome. If you harbor a yen to reach Mount Adams's summit, you must obtain a permit from the Mount Adams Ranger Station (Gifford Pinchot National Forest, Trout Lake, WA 98650; (509)395-3400).

The Mount Adams area is riddled with **lava tubes**, which white settlers used as a source of ice and as a place for storing cheese in summer. Best known is **Ice Cave**, near Trout Lake, a lava tube with ice stalactites and stalagmites. You can spelunk it from end to end with a good flashlight, a hard hat, a sweater (even in the heat of the summer), and a willing-ness to squeeze through some narrow passages. The Big Lava Bed, southwest of Trout Lake, is a vast area of moss-covered lava formations. Bordering it to the northwest is Indian Heaven Wilderness, a 20,000-acre wilderness plateau studded with more than 150 lakes and ponds among subalpine forests and meadows. For information on the lave tubes, as well as outdoor activities, contact Mount Adams Ranger Station (see preceding paragraph).

Two companies offer whitewater-rafting trips from April through September on the **White Salmon National Scenic River**, down an 8-mile stretch of glacial runoff shooting through a lava gorge, with virtually continuous challenging rapids. Spring trips offer the most excitement. A 3-hour trip from BZ Corners to Northwestern Lake is available for $50 to $55 from both Phil's White

Foraging

The country bordering the Columbia River Gorge has long offered an abundance of delicious foods for the taking; Lewis and Clark noted as much in 1805, after arriving in the area half-starved. Before the Columbia was dammed, Indians caught monster-size salmon each spring; today the fish still run, though they're greatly diminished in number and size.

Picking huckleberries from the abundant fields at the base of Mount Adams is a tradition practiced by countless jam and pie lovers each year from mid-July to mid-September. The Mount Adams Ranger Station in Trout Lake offers an excellent brochure on huckleberry harvesting in the Gifford Pinchot National Forest, complete with a map of the best fields; (509)395-3400. The Trout Lake Grocery (2383 Hwy 141, Trout Lake; (509)395-2777) pays pickers per gallon and then sells the berries for a few dollars more. Most of the berries are frozen and distributed all over the country.

The hills around White Salmon are covered with orchards, including cherry, apricot, apple, and pear trees, and many farmers offer the **U-pick** option. You can tour and taste the fruits of two area **wineries**: the Charles Hooper Family Winery (9 miles north of Hwy 14, off Route 141 just north of Husum; (509)493-2324), which specializes in white riesling, and Mont Elise Vineyards (315 W Steuben St, Bingen; (509)493-3001), which consistently wins regional awards for its gewürztraminer.

Stargazing

The Goldendale Observatory (1602 Observatory Dr, Goldendale; (509)773-3141) has the largest telescope in the nation available for public use—and it's free! The observatory is open afternoons and evenings (Wednesday through Sunday in summer; Saturday and Sunday in winter). Hours vary, so call ahead.

Water Adventures in White Salmon, (800)366-2004 or (509)493-2641, and AAA Rafting in Husum, (800)866-RAFT or (509)493-2511.

The paved roads around Mount Adams and points east are ideal for **bike touring**, with little traffic, gentle grades, and stunning views. Bike from Goldendale or Trout Lake to the 5,654-acre Conboy Lake National Wildlife Refuge, (509)364-3410, a marshy oasis for waterfowl—swans, geese, ducks, and sandhill cranes—at the foot of Mount Adams. Well worth the effort of shuttling cars is the exhilarating, mostly downhill ride from Glenwood, heading east on the Glenwood-Goldendale Road and then south on Route 142 to Lyle. The route crosses above the canyons of the Klickitat River and gradually drops down into the river valley to join up with the Columbia. (If you can't swing this by bicycle, don't miss it by car.)

Just northeast of the gorge, visit the **Maryhill Museum of Art** (35 Maryhill Museum Dr, 13 miles south of Goldendale; (509)773-3733). It's housed in the 1914 mansion of financier Sam Hill, who, sadly, never lived there (his wife Mary refused to move there). Boasting spectacular Columbia River vistas, the museum (open mid-March through mid-November; $5 for adults) houses an eclectic mix of art and artifacts such as Rodin sculptures—one of the largest collections in the world—Russian icons, chess sets, and Native American baskets.

There's a small cafe, and peacocks roam the beautiful grounds. Just up the road a piece is a life-size replica of **Stonehenge**, constructed by the eccentric Hill as a memorial to the soldiers from Klickitat County who died in World War I. He was operating under the now-rejected theory that the real Stonehenge in England was a burial ground.

In the winter, you'll find 20 miles of groomed **cross-country ski trails** from three Sno-Park sites off the Wind River Road north of Carson; the first is at Oldman Pass, 25 miles north of Highway 14. For a map and information, contact the Wind River Ranger Station (1262 Hemlock Rd, Carson, WA 98610; (509)427-3200). Other ski trails from Sno-Park sites around Mount Adams include Pineside Sno-Park, 5 miles northeast of Trout Lake on Road 82, with 2 1/2- and 5-mile groomed cross-country loops; and Smith Butte Sno-Park, with access to some backcountry routes. Sno-Park passes are $7 for the day and $20 for one year. They're valid in Washington, Oregon, and some parts of Idaho and can be purchased at ranger stations.

Snowmobiles abound on the trails in the national forest; however, motorized vehicles are not allowed in the wilderness areas. There are also some groomed trails near the Flying L Ranch, (888)MT-ADAMS or (509)364-3488, in Glenwood, a wonderful overnight for couples or families, where prices for lodgings are just a bit beyond limits of this book.

Cheap Eats

Guido's

104 E Steuben Street, Bingen ☎ (509) 493-3880

The hangout for boardheads on a budget is this tiny Italian take-out spot with a handful of tables. Virginia Mahieu, her daughter, and her grown grandchildren have run every inch of this place ever since Guido himself opened it a dozen or so years ago. It's Northern Italian food diligently prepared by Virginia (lasagne, meatball sandwiches, fettuccine with a marinara; always a vegetarian option, but not many cream sauces). They're not officially open for lunch, but if you're hungry, poke your head in and you'll probably be glad you did. Desserts are worthwhile. No alcohol, but the lemonade's refreshing.

Loafer's Old World Bakery

213 W Steuben Street, Bingen ☎ (509) 493-3100

Some people call this the Bingen Bakery, but whatever you call it, it's the happeningest place in town for carbo-loaders. Chewy breads and bagels are the star items here; they're used to make the hefty sandwiches or are slathered with lox and cream cheese. The pastries and soups have a devoted following too. Doors open at 6am and usually close at 6pm, but sometimes they stay open a little later for those hankering for an evening nosh.

The Logs

1258 Highway 141, White Salmon ☎ (509) 493-1402

Here's a two-pool table tavern and restaurant that has been run by the same family since 1930. Fried chicken is their specialty at lunch or dinner, but locals also take a licking to the hickory-smoked barbecued ribs. If you don't mind smoke and don't bring up the plight of the spotted owl, you'll do just fine at this spot beside the White Salmon River.

Cheap Sleeps

Lyle Hotel

7th and Lyle Streets, Lyle, WA 98635 ☎ (509) 365-5953

The rooms here are spotless, as are the bathrooms down the hall, but the big drawback is out back. This 1905 inn is situated at the confluence of the Klickitat and Columbia Rivers, in a peaceful setting periodically interrupted by passing freight trains (you'll find complimentary earplugs in every room). Fortunately, the morning coffee is strong. Open March through December.

Bingen School Inn

Humboldt and Cedar Streets (PO Box 155), Bingen, WA 98605
☎ (509) 493-3363

No more pencils, no more books, no more teachers' dirty looks! John Newman has filled the classrooms with beds (doubles and bunks), the cafeteria with a big-screen TV, and the gymnasium with a climbing wall. Board sailors, mountain bikers, and climbers from all over the world now hang out at this hostel-like dwelling. No wonder so many big kids find themselves returning—toys in tow—to Bingen School.

Trout Lake Grocery

2383 Highway 141, Trout Lake, WA 98650 ☎ (509) 395-2777

There are two sleeping rooms above and one below this country store—the focal point of Trout Lake's social life. Lodgings are clean and basic, with queen-size beds in two rooms and three twins in the third. The upstairs guests share a bath. Hunters book a year in advance for the mid-November deer season, and foragers crowd the place in huckleberry season, but at other times you can count on an opening with little notice. You can't beat the price: all the people you can fit in a room (within reason, says the owner) for $35 a night.

Far Vue Motel

808 E Simcoe Drive (Highway 97), Goldendale, WA 98620 ☎ (509) 773-5881

Here is a motel of the best sort: new, clean, and private, with little personal touches that show it's not a chain. In addition, there's a pool, cable TV, and a view of Mount Adams or Mount Hood from every room. In the summer you need to reserve a few days in advance; at other times you can just appear. After church the locals gather at the motel's Homestead Restaurant and Lounge, reputedly the best place to eat in Goldendale.

Camping

Along the gorge off Highway 14, Horsethief Lake State Park, (509)767-1159, boasts Indian petroglyphs, a boat launch, and a dozen campsites available from April through October; farther east, Maryhill State Park, (509)773-5007, has 50 RV and 20 tent sites close to the Columbia and is open year-round. There are numerous summertime scenic campsites near Mount Adams, such as those at Takhlakh Lake and Horseshoe Lake, both of which offer breathtaking reflections of the snow-covered volcano. You can obtain a list of 26 campgrounds in Gifford Pinchot National Forest's Mount Adams Ranger District (in Trout Lake; (509)395-3400) and Wind River Ranger District (in Carson; (509)427-3200). If you'd like to be closer to town, try Guler County Park, located just behind the post office in Trout Lake, or the privately owned Elk Meadows RV Park and Campground (78 Trout Lake Creek Rd, Trout Lake; (509)395-2400). Elk Meadows has a secluded, grassy location along Trout Lake Creek, with horseshoe pits and badminton nets as well as nice walking trails that lead to the edge of the lake. It's a great place for families in the summer and hunters come fall. Closed from December through March.

Carson Hot Springs

The most basic—that is, funky—of accommodations can be found in any of the 12 tiny cabins ($40–$50) or nine hotel rooms ($30–$35) here, but that's not the draw. This weathered resort (on Wind River Hwy, 2 miles from the junction of Hwy 14 and Carson; (509)427-8292) is the place to go to slip back in time as the attendant draws the curtains around your steaming claw-footed bathtub in the dimly lit bathhouse. A soporific soak at Carson has become a requisite ingredient of many a visit to the Columbia Gorge—so plan ahead if you want a massage after you take the waters. It's suggested you reserve six to eight weeks in advance for a rub on weekends ($40 an hour). Ten dollars buys a hot mineral bath (request an extra-long tub) and an after-bath wrap (half an hour of sweating out your impurities—just try to stay awake). Baths are open from 8:45am to 7pm every day.

Yakima Valley

The Yakama Indians thrived for thousands of years in the arid Yakima Valley. They fished in the Yakima and Columbia Rivers during the spring and fall and moved to the foothills around Mount Adams to hunt for deer and other game during the summer. The first white visitors to the Yakima Valley, however, were unimpressed. Compared to the giant Douglas fir forests west of the mountains and the dramatic waters of the Columbia Gorge, the desert valley had little appeal. But with the coming of the railroad in the 1880s and the visionary construction of irrigation canals in the early 20th century, the region became almost entirely the domain of white settlers, and Native Americans were relegated to a million-acre reservation.

The economy of the Yakima Valley is driven by agriculture. Trucks roar through carrying apples, pears, beans, asparagus, and a dozen other products of the harvest, making this one of the nation's richest farming areas. And if you've ever had a stick of spearmint gum or a bottle of beer, you've helped bring economic wealth to this corner of Washington State, a prime growing area for both mint and hops.

Local wines have found national fame. There are over 25 wineries in the Yakima Valley and several more in the Tri-Cities area. The number's not surprising, according to the valley's winemakers, who proudly point out that the area's latitudinal coordinates (and thus the climate) are the same as some of France's finest winemaking regions. Touring the valley in September and October reveals the processes of harvest and winemaking and gives you a real taste of the agricultural and viticultural life.

Exploring

If you can get away from the tourist ghetto next to the freeway, the college-and-cowboy town of **Ellensburg** projects a pleasant ease. Its famous Labor Day rodeo (see "Ellensburg Rodeo" tip) draws many for its slice-of-life view of rural America.

The tranquil water of the **Yakima River** offers a perfect summer's-day float. It's an easy Class I river, so bring cold beverages, oversize inner tubes, and plenty of sunscreen, and drift on down to your favorite swimming hole or picnic area. It's also one of the state's premier catch-and-release fishing areas for trout.

Take the Scenic Route

I-82 provides an east-west thoroughfare from Yakima straight through the valley to the Tri-Cities (Richland, Kennewick, and Pasco). Take I-82 off I-90 in Ellensburg. Once you get to Yakima, abandon I-82 whenever possible in favor of more scenic routes and stopovers.

An alternative to driving I-82 between Ellensburg and Yakima is to take Canyon Road (State Hwy 821) along the Yakima River from roughly the same starting and ending points as the freeway route. The scenery along the twisted, slow-flowing river is attractive, and the route doesn't take much longer than the freeway.

Stop by the **Yakima** convention center (10 N 8th St, Yakima; (509)575-3010) for area travel literature, including a guide to winery tours and a map of produce stands and U-pick farms and orchards. Although this is wine country, it's also hops country—the area is among the world's leading producers—so one stop should be a brewery: perhaps **Grant's Brewery Pub** (32 N Front St, Yakima; (509)575-1900), in the old train station. This birthplace of Northwest microbrewing and home of Grant's Ale is a hallowed shrine for many of those who eschew light beers for the heartier flavors of hops and malt, a game of darts, and some pub grub. There's live entertainment on weekends.

As you head down the highway through Union Gap, the vista of the valley opens up and the wine country begins. A stop at the cedar-and-glass Staton Hills Winery (71 Gangl Rd, Wapato; (509)877-2112) reveals a beautiful facility with a great view and picnic area, and a wide selection of whites and reds. Near Toppenish on Highway 97, the **Yakama Nation Cultural Heritage Center** (100 Spilyi Loop, Toppenish; (509)865-2800) has a fine museum documenting the tribe's history, a restaurant, a movie theater and a large RV park. The more adventurous can spend the night in an authentic tepee ($30 a night for up to five people). **Toppenish** has transformed itself into

a tourist destination with its 40-plus Western-style historical murals covering many buildings. Wagon tours and maps are available to explain the history behind the art. A local tradition since 1932, the Pow Wow Rodeo and Indian Encampment is held yearly, July 3–6.

Exit 52 from I-82 leads to Zillah and its seven **wineries**. Covey Run Vintners (1500 Vintage Rd, Zillah; (509)829-6235) was one of the first wineries in the valley and features an expansive tasting room and picnic grounds. Bonair (500 S Bonair Rd, Zillah; (509)829-6027), a small, family-run winery, has a flair for chardonnay. At Horizon's Edge (4530 E Zillah Dr, Zillah; (509)829-6401), a spectacular view indeed stretches to the horizon from the tasting room. Hyatt Vineyards (2020 Gilbert Rd, Zillah; (509)829-6333) makes fine, dry white wines. Portteus Vineyard (5201 Highland Dr, Zillah; (509)829-6970) is an estate winery specializing in reds—cabernet, merlot, and lemberger. Zillah Oakes (1001 Vintage Valley Pkwy, Zillah; (509)829-6990), right on the highway, has a gift shop and Victorian-motif tasting room. Eaton Hill (530 Gurley Rd, Granger; (509)854-2508) is located in an old cannery. Most of these operations are open daily for tastings, tours, and sales. Winter hours are sometimes abbreviated, so call ahead.

Zillah also is home to **El Ranchito**

(1319 E 1st Ave, Zillah; (509)829-5880). This landmark features a variety of enterprises. The fast-food operation serving authentic Mexican fare is still the most popular, but the south-of-the-border gifts, cooking ingredients, folk remedies, records, tapes, magazines, and more are a browser's paradise. The on-premises bakery creates a variety of filling, colorful goodies. You've probably seen El Ranchito's tortillas, spices, and other culinary treats in your grocery store. Further down the highway, Stewart Vineyards (1711 Cherry Hill Rd, Granger; (509)854-1882) is perched on the side of Snipes Mountain in the middle of a beautiful cherry orchard that provides a fabulous blossom display in mid-April. Try a riesling or cabernet.

The importance of agriculture becomes more and more apparent as you travel east, deeper into the heart of the valley. Orchards, vineyards, and hop yards line both sides of the highway. You'll recognize the hop yards by what look like planted rows of telephone poles. In late summer, roll down your car window and inhale the aroma of delicious ripening fruit.

In Sunnyside, check out the **Yakima Valley Cheese Company** (100 Alexander Rd, Sunnyside; (509)837-6005), where Yakima Valley Gouda is made. Here you can observe the cheese-making process and hear a little about the history of this unique valley product.

Farmers in the valley since the '20s, the Tuckers of Sunnyside have now joined the wine boom with their own winery, Tucker Cellars. Their selection of varietal wines is complemented by the area's freshest in-season produce, at **Tucker Farms Fruit Stand** (70 Ray Rd, Sunnyside; (509)837-8701).

Founded in the 1930s, **Chateau Ste. Michelle** (205 W 5th Ave, Grandview; (509)882-3928) is the oldest continuing winery operation in the state. The best time to visit this facility is in early October, when guided tours reveal the remarkable production techniques involved in making red wines. The wine flows through epoxied concrete troughs and back up over the fermenting grapes. The process can be seen at other times but lacks the intoxicating aroma of fermenting cabernet and merlot.

Prosser is the birthplace of the Yakima Valley winemaking renaissance. It was here that Washington State University researcher Walter Clore predicted the suitability of wine grapes for the area's climate. And here too is the cinderblock garage where Mike Wallace founded Hinzerling Vineyard and Winery (1520 Sheridan Rd, Prosser; (509)786-2163) and brought recognition to the valley after he was profiled in *Time* in the late 1970s. Chinook Wines (Wine Country Rd, Prosser; (509)786-2725) is a small operation dedicated to handcrafting lim-

All Aboard

Rail buffs can enjoy themselves either on old-fashioned trolleys or behind a steam locomotive. Yakima Electric Railway (306 W Pine St, Yakima; (509)575-1700) offers a run on vintage trolley cars on the original line between Yakima and Selah. The trip runs 1½ hours on weekends and holidays during the summer, leaving Yakima every two hours starting at 10am. Tickets are $4 for adults, $2.50 for kids 6–12, and $3.50 for seniors. Toppenish Simcoe and Western Railroad runs its 1920s locomotive from Harrah to White Swan and back on Saturdays during the summer and fall; tickets for the 1½-hour trip are $3–$5. Schedules fluctuate, so call (509)865-1911 for details.

Ellensburg Rodeo

The oldest and biggest rodeo in these parts brings professional and amateur cow-pokes from around the country for four days of Wild West fun over Labor Day weekend. Admission is $8–$17 depending on your seat, and a family ticket for two kids and two adults is $29.95; (800)637-2444 or (509)962-7831.

ited bottlings of a few varietals. Don't miss the merlot. Down the road, the successful Hogue Cellars (at the corner of Lee and Wine Country Rds, Prosser; (509)786-4557) produces hundreds of thousands of gallons of premium wine for every palate; their "reserve" wines are particularly fine. The Hogue family has been vastly successful in other farming endeavors, including asparagus (look for jars of their delicious pickled asparagus at specialty food stores throughout the state), mint, and hops.

The **Chukar Cherry Company** (306 Wine Country Rd, Prosser; (509)786-2055) has become regionally famous for its tart dried cherries and other specialty foods. Don't miss their chocolate-covered cherries.

Columbia Crest Winery (Hwy 221, Paterson; (509)875-2061) is a 30-mile diversion south of Prosser, just above the Columbia River. The beautiful building and grounds are exceptional, and the winemaking facility is the largest north of California.

Benton City boasts a number of interesting wineries: Oakwood Cellars (Demoss Rd, Benton City; (509)588-5332), one of the newest additions to the growing number of wineries near Red Mountain; Kiona Vineyards (Sunset Rd, Benton City; (509)588-6716), the first Red Mountain winery, producing remarkable cabernet, lemberger, and a dry, sweet riesling; Blackwood Canyon (Sunset Rd, Benton City; (509)588-6249), a no-frills facility (their late-harvest wines are particularly notable); and Seth Ryan Winery (Sunset Rd, Benton City; (509)588-6780), with a

selection of fine whites and a pleasant picnic area.

The neat rows of homes and local businesses in **Richland** owe their prosperity to nuclear power. This is undeniably an historic place no matter what your political leanings. The **Hanford Science Center** (825 Jadwin Ave, Richland; (509)376-6374) presents a remarkable look at the subject. All-day free tours of the Hanford site (bring lunch) leave from the Science Center and hit the highlights of the 560-square-mile nuclear reservation, including the World War II plutonium separation and Purex plants, the now-decommissioned reactors, and the areas that have been or are in the process of being cleaned up. Tours run on selected weekends from early April through October; if you're interested, call (509)376-0557 for information and reservations.

Just across the river in north **Pasco**, Quarry Lake Vintners (2520 Commercial Ave, Pasco; (509)547-7307) welcomes visitors with fine cabernets, chardonnays, merlots, and sauvignon blancs. Preston Premium Wines (502 E Vineyard Dr, Pasco; (509)545-1990), off Highway 395, has a big tasting room and park; and Gordon Brothers Cellars (531 Levey Rd, Pasco; (509)547-6224) promises a beautiful vista and a fine merlot.

A little farther south, just off I-182 near Burbank, is Chateau Gallant (1355 S Gallant Rd, Pasco; (509)545-9570). The winery specializes in white wines and has a view of the McNary Wildlife Refuge, whose majestic flocks of waterfowl create a pastoral backdrop to your wine-tasting.

Cheap Eats

Valley Cafe

105 W 3rd Avenue, Ellensburg ☎ (509) 925-3050

Inexpensive lunches of the soup, salad, sandwich, and pasta variety are available here in the relaxed atmosphere of an old-fashioned '40s-style cafe. At dinner the menu's ante is upped (though prices stay reasonable) for steaks, seafood, and the occasional local favorite, Ellensburg lamb, best enjoyed with a glass of the local grape.

Deli di Pasta

7 N Front Street, Yakima ☎ (509) 453-0571

Owners Bob and Diane Traner have a flair for decor, making simple touches (red wooden chairs, red tablecloths, white linen napkins) seem somehow extraordinary. Fresh pastas and sauce, made on the premise, can be mixed and matched to suit your mood. The service is friendly, the coffee's fine, and the congenial atmosphere encourages many happy returnees.

Santiago's

111 E Yakima Avenue, Yakima ☎ (509) 453-1644

The high ceiling, dramatic brick walls, huge mural in the bar, and Southwestern art are festive, while the enormous skylight creates the exotic atmosphere of a Mexican courtyard (in downtown Yakima, no less). The *chalupas* and the tacos Santiago are especially popular. Steak *picado* (their version of fajitas) was on the menu long before the sizzling sirloin strips became chic everywhere else. Portions are generous.

Maria's Restaurant

310 S Frontage Road, near Wapato ☎ (509) 877-1233

A local favorite for nearly two decades, Maria Layman's little Mexican cafe is an unpretentious eatery with homemade *everything* (including the tortillas). Lunch and dinner prices start at $6; daily specials are always worth consideration. When the weather's warm, snag a table outside. Located off Highway 97 between Union Gap and Wapato.

Branding Iron Restaurant

61311 Highway 97, near Toppenish ☎ (509) 865-5440

When it's busy, patrons spill over into the banquet rooms at this 24-hour eatery. The lunch buffet draws a crowd, as do the homemade soups and enormous cinnamon rolls. Menu favorites include luncheon specials (three of them, served weekdays for only $3.75), as well as many Mexican options.

Squeeze Inn Restaurant and Lounge

611 1st Avenue, Zillah ☎ (509) 829-6226

As the name implies, the place is small—but its reputation for steaks and prime rib is large. Expect basic American fare at breakfast, lunch, and dinner. Consider splurging on the worth-it prime rib meals (starting at $12.95), or opt for less expensive fare—there's plenty to choose from.

Spaghetti Establishment

2107 4th Avenue, Kennewick ☎ (509) 586-6622

The kids will be entranced by the model trains running on overhead tracks amid the modern faux-Italian-schmaltz decor. Mom and Dad (and the rest of us) will like the fact that the pasta dinners at this family-friendly establishment even include dessert, all for a mere $5–$11.

Atomic Ale Brew Pub and Eatery

1015 Lee Boulevard, Richland ☎ (509) 965-5465

A variety of microbrews and wines are offered to wash down a diverse lunch and dinner menu. Pizza—hot, fresh, and cheesy from the wood-fired oven—is a house specialty. Lunches start at about five bucks and dinners—including seafood and steaks—start at about twice that.

Vannini's Italian Restaurant

1026 Lee Boulevard, Richland ☎ (509) 946-4525

If you knew Vannini's in Yakima, you'll recognize Vannini's in Richland. Devin and Aaron Burks partnered with Lesley Vannini to offer Northern and Southern Italian cuisine in an intimate setting: a renovated railroad dining car. Tables are small (naturally) and candlelit. Expect pastas, seafood, steaks, and more. The three-cheese tortellini smothered in pesto sauce and tossed with sun-dried tomatoes and walnuts is a standout. Local and Italian wines are available, and kids get a discount on real Italian sodas. Pasta specials are a bargain at lunch.

Cheap Sleeps

Oxford Suites

1701 Terrace Heights Drive, Yakima, WA 98901
☎ (800) 404-7848 or (509) 457-9000

Each of the 100-plus "suites" set along the Yakima Greenway facing the river has a deck from which you can watch the world stroll, float, and Rollerblade by. Though the least expensive (studio) rooms fudge the budget limit a bit, the morning buffet breakfast and evening hors d'oeuvres are complimentary, and kids under 12 stay free. Who can complain? All rooms come equipped with a VCR, microwave, small fridge, and sofa bed (where a third adult can sleep for a paltry $7). The small gift shop is open 24 hours a day.

Rio Mirada Motor Inn
1603 Terrace Heights Drive, Yakima, WA 98901 ☎ (509) 457-4444

The Rio Mirada has an outdoor pool—always a plus during the Yakima Valley's hot summers—but even better, the Yakima River is right out back, and you can fall asleep to the murmur of nature flowing past your room. You're adjacent to the Yakima Greenway, which boasts 10 miles of paved pathway for biking, skating, or strolling. The greenway also has two playgrounds and passes both Washington's Fruit Place (with its visitors center and gift shop) and the Yakima Arboretum and its interpretive center.

Sunnyside Inn Bed and Breakfast
800 E Edison Avenue, Sunnyside, WA 98944 ☎ (509) 839-5557

The Sunnyside Inn offers the best of B&B accommodations, coupled with the advantages of a hotel *and* a great price. Ten cheery, individually decorated rooms provide a cozy touch, with amenities such as color TVs, phones, air conditioning, and huge private baths; all but two have Jacuzzis, and all have showers—even the 1919 bathroom. A full breakfast is included. Weekend rates are a bit higher.

Apple Valley Motel
903 Wine Country Road, Grandview, WA 98930 ☎ (509) 882-3003

On the west end of downtown Grandview, this little gem is the perfect spot for those who want to spend the night in a clean, quiet, simple room. A small pool offers a chance for a spring or summer dip, although the attraction here is being right smack in the middle of wine country with a bargain place ($30!) to hit the rack when the sun goes down. Kitchenettes are available.

Wine Country Inn
1106 Wine Country Road, Prosser, WA 99350 ☎ (509) 786-2855

Perched on the bank of the Yakima River, this 100-year-old home has been converted to a charming B&B with four guest rooms and an adjoining restaurant (which serves lunch Monday through Saturday, dinner Wednesday through Saturday, and Sunday brunch). Relax under the huge oak tree by the river, or admire the crafts and art in the gallery.

Nendel's Inn
615 Jadwin Avenue, Richland, WA 99352 ☎ (800) 547-0106 or (509) 943-4611

There's nothing fancy about Nendel's, but you can get a clean room for a fair price with a moderate amount of style. Standard motel-chain amenities are available here, but you can find them at a dozen other places along George Washington Way as well. What makes this motel special is its location—it's convenient to restaurants and shops, and it's just a hop off the freeway to the Tri-Cities wineries.

Spokane & the Palouse

Long before the Nez Perce, Cayuse, Umatilla, and Coeur d'Alene Indian tribes roamed the regions, thousands of years of near-constant winds deposited rich dust on the rounded volcanic mounds, creating the rolling hills of southeast Washington. French fur trappers named the area the Palouse, which means "waves of blowing grass." These days, it's not grass but wheat that the wind moves. Dust from plowed fields makes for fiery orange sunsets throughout the summer and fall.

Spring comes quickly to the Palouse. Warm April winds blow across the hills, sweeping away the snow and revealing a carpet of tender green winter wheat. Mallards paddle about in shallow ponds, grazing on new wheat shoots; red-winged blackbirds sing from cattails and fence posts.

North is Spokane, Washington's biggest city east of the Cascades. It has small-town charm, but with some big-city trappings. There's a move under way to revitalize downtown with a new Nordstrom and the renovation of the historic Davenport Hotel. Well-kept neighborhoods radiate from the city's core, which features the handsome Riverfront Park.

Exploring

While **Spokane** has a reputation as a somewhat sleepy burg, it's a growing town and an attractive place to visit. **Cultural events** include performances by the award-winning Spokane Civic Theatre (1020 N Howard St, Spokane; (509)325-2507) and the professional company, Interplayers Ensemble (174 S Howard St, Spokane; (509)455-PLAY); attend a weekend matinee and save a few dollars. Second-run movies are just a buck at the art-deco Fox Theater (1005 W Sprague Ave, Spokane; (509)624-0105) and the Garland (924 W Garland Ave, Spokane; (509)327-1050).

Bing Crosby's memorabilia is housed at Gonzaga University's Crosby Student Center (502 E Boone Ave, Spokane; (509)328-4220, ext 4297), the late crooner's gift to his alma mater. There's no charge to see lots of gold records, an Oscar, and more. Bing grew up at 508 E Sharp Avenue (a block away).

Cheney Cowles Museum (2316 W First Ave, Spokane; (509)456-3931) has an art gallery and exhibits focusing on the area's early pioneer and mining history. Admission is $4; half price on Wednesdays. A nearby children's museum

Spokane Wine-tasting

While few grapes grow this far north, Spokane has a thriving wine industry. There are a half-dozen vintners, each with welcoming tasting rooms, where samples and tours are free. You can easily make a day out of sampling every varietal from sauvignon blanc to cabernet. Arbor Crest's Cliff House (4705 N Fruithill Rd, Spokane; (509)927-9894) offers the most scenic picnicking in the area, high on a bluff overlooking the Spokane Valley. The grounds burst with flowers in the summer. Latah Creek (13030 E Indiana Ave, Spokane; (509)926-0164) has a well-stocked gift shop and a friendly staff. Winemaker Mike Conway is usually around to answer questions. Caterina Winery (905 N Washington, Spokane; (509)328-5069) is located on the ground floor of an historic dairy, and the oak barrels sit in a cool room that was once used to make ice cream for Carnation. Worden's Washington Winery (7217 W 45th, Spokane; (509)455-7835) was the city's first winery and has a wall full of medals that testify to the quality of its releases. Mountain Dome Winery, (509)928-2788, is a family-run affair in the foothills of Mount Spokane that specializes in French-style sparklers; tastings and tours are by appointment only. Finally, Knipprath Cellars (163 S Lincoln St, Spokane; (509)624-9132) has a convenient downtown location and makes such unusual (for Washington) releases as pinot noir and port. All wineries participate in a spring barrel-tasting event each May around the time of the Spokane Lilac Festival and throw open-house parties during Thanksgiving weekend with complimentary eats and entertainment.

features plenty of chances to get messy while being artistic.

Riverfront Park, developed from old railroad yards for Expo '74, is the pleasant heart of Spokane's downtown core. The park is now an airy place full of meandering paved paths and playgrounds for the kids. Skip the cheesy rides in the summer and check out the overgrown Radio Flyer slide near the Opera House. There's also an IMAX theater and a beautifully restored 1909 carousel that is as tempting for the grown-ups as the kids; (800)336-PARK or (509)625-6000.

Cyclists, joggers, walkers, and skaters use the scenic **Centennial Trail**, which stretches from Riverfront Park some 30 miles to Coeur d'Alene. Spokane's annual Bloomsday Run, a 7.6-mile race held during the lilac season on the first Sunday in May, is one of the largest road races in the country: it draws about 60,000 participants, many of whom simply walk the course. Also in May is the Spokane Lilac Festival, (509)326-3339, a week-long celebration that includes a

talent show, ball, and a popular torch-light parade.

The city plays **golf** with a passion, and more than a dozen courses are often open from late March through late November. Two of the most beautiful public courses are Indian Canyon, (509)747-5353, and the challenging Creek at Qualchan, (509)448-9317. At city courses, playing 18 holes costs around $22. Some links offer summer twilight rates, when you can pony up $10 and play from 7:30pm until dark.

There's a plethora of lakes near Spokane, most of which have public beaches. One of the best is the spacious, sandy beach at the edge of **Coeur d'Alene City Park**, just across the state border in Idaho on Lake Coeur d'Alene, only a half hour's drive from Spokane.

From November to March, when snow often blankets the city, **cross-country skiers** can traverse Nordic trails, groomed by the city's parks department, at golf courses including Downriver, Esmeralda, Hangman, and the hilly Indian Canyon.

WASHINGTON

Skiers can also take advantage of the nearby Mount Spokane Nordic Area, where gliding the 17 kilometers of groomed trails is free but driving vehicles requires a Sno-Park pass, available for $20 at REI (1125 N Monroe St, Spokane; (509)328-9900). There are also separate snowmobile trails. Just up the road is the Mount Spokane Ski Area (31 miles north on Hwy 206, Spokane; (509)238-6281), which has gone steadily downhill under current management, though diehards will still find some challenging runs.

You can take in the commanding views of the rolling farmland of the Palouse from the top of **Steptoe Butte**, 47 miles south of Spokane. Sunrise and sunsets are photo-op heaven. This spot is a favorite with amateur astronomers, and it can get downright crowded on a clear night.

Founded in 1890 as a land-grant university, **Washington State University** made Pullman (75 miles south of Spokane) more of a lively college town than a gathering place for farmers. Activities naturally center around the campus. Visitors can arrange for all sorts of free tours—one is through the university creamery, which produces the famous Cougar Gold cheese. Call WSU Information at (509)335-3564. Or you can pick up a campus map and visit the Museum of Fine Arts Center, the Museum of Anthropology, or the Jewett Observatory (the observatory is not always open, so call ahead; (509)335-8518). The university hosts a full slate of athletic events, theater performances, and other entertainment at the 12,000-seat Beasley Performing Arts Coliseum. For tickets and an events calendar, call G&B Select-a-Seat; (800)325-SEAT.

Palouse Falls gushes over a basalt cliff higher than Niagara Falls and drops 198 feet into a steep-walled basin. The remote **Palouse Falls Park** has 105 acres of camping and picnicking areas and hiking trails. The falls are raging from late winter to early summer. By the way, don't take those warning signs about rattlesnakes lightly. The park is located on Highway 261, off Highway 26 about 120 miles southwest of Spokane.

At the southwest corner of the Palouse, the **Juniper Dunes Wilderness** is all that remains of an ecosystem that once stretched over nearly 400 square miles south to the Snake and Columbia Rivers. Protected under the 1984 Washington Wilderness Act, the 7,140-acre wilderness includes some of the biggest sand dunes (up to 130 feet high and a quarter mile wide) and largest natural

Birding

*North of the city limits and straddling the Little Spokane River is the **Little Spokane River Natural Area**, (509)456-3964, part of Riverside State Park. There are two canoe launches and trails where walkers can watch great blue herons, an occasional bald eagle, and waterfowl among the clumps of yellow iris.*

*The **Dishman Hills Natural Area** is a 400-acre preserve in the Spokane Valley with a network of trails through mixed habitats. Nearly 400 plant species and 100 species of birds have been spotted here. It's wise to pick up a detailed topographic map at Northwest Map Service (525 W Sprague Ave, Spokane; (509)455-6981), since it's easy to get lost on the preserve. Take I-90 east from Spokane to the Sprague Avenue exit, go east 1½ miles to Sargent Road, turn right, and continue for a half mile.*

*Forty-five minutes south of Spokane, the **Turnbull National Wildlife Refuge** is a 15,000-acre area dotted with pothole lakes and ponds that attract migrating waterfowl in the spring and fall; (509)235-4723. There's a small admission fee for vehicles. The 5-mile auto route takes you near several large ponds where the waterfowl viewing is excellent.*

Cheney Rodeo

The annual Cheney Rodeo offers roping, bronco riding, barrel racing, and bull riding with plenty of pros and lots of horseflesh. The bleachers are close to the action, and for munching there's corn on the cob as well as hot dogs and burgers. The rodeo usually takes place the second weekend in July. Call for a schedule of events (including the rodeo parade) and ticket prices; (509)235-8480.

groves of western juniper (some 150 years old) in the state. Expect to see the same wildlife and birds you would encounter in a true desert region. Authorized camping is permitted in the wilderness, but open fires are not (backpacking stoves are OK). The most scenic portion is a 2-mile hike northeast from the parking area toward the junipers and the largest dunes (bring drinking water). For directions to the parking area and further information, contact the Bureau of Land Management (1103 N Fancher Rd, Spokane; (509)536-1200).

Walla Walla, best known as the home of the Washington State Penitentiary and the Walla Walla sweet onion, was named after a Native American phrase meaning "many waters." And Main Street was built on the Nez Perce Indian Trail, another indication of the city's ties to history. The thousands of artifacts at **Fort Walla Walla** (Myra Rd and Rose St, Walla Walla; (509)525-7703) also illuminate the past—in this case, life on a pioneer farm. It's closed in winter; admission is $2.50 for adults, $1.25 for children.

In good weather, the community of 26,000 can best be seen by bicycle. Pick up a free bike map at the Chamber of Commerce (29 E Sumac, Walla Walla; (509)525-0850). For art, the town boasts the oldest continuing symphony west of the Mississippi River and myriad cultural events at the pretty campus of Whitman College. For sheer entertainment and gluttony, this town throws a free onion festival each year in late July.

Walla Walla's wine country has gained quite a reputation among oenophiles, but the tasting rooms have a down-home appeal. Stops at Woodward Canyon Winery (Hwy 12, Lowden; (509)525-4129), Waterbrook (just south of Lowden off McDonald Rd; (509)522-1918), L'Ecole No. 41 (Hwy 12, Lowden; (509)522-1918), Canoe Ridge Vineyard

Autumn Picks

It's an annual ritual for locals to make an autumn visit to Green Bluff, a small farming community north of Spokane (take Hwy 2 to Day—Mount Spokane Rd, and then turn east). Harvest is celebrated with great zest, and the abundant produce includes apples, squash, potatoes, onions, carrots, and pumpkins. Many of the orchardists help spice up the occasion with freshly squeezed apple cider and homemade specialty foods such as jams, preserves, and honey. Those in the know go to Walter's Fruit Ranch (9807 E Day Rd, Mead; (509)238-4709), where a tractor-drawn wagon takes U-pickers deep into the orchard to pluck Delicious apples; those who prefer ready-picked fruit gather from big bins in a barnlike store. The bonus is the chance to relax with a piece of homemade apple pie, pungent with cinnamon, and hot apple cider, enjoyed on a second-story deck overlooking the orchard (in less cooperative weather, you can sit at one of the cafe tables inside). In July, Green Bluff growers sell raspberries, cherries, and peaches.

(on the southwest corner of 13th Ave and W Cherry St, Walla Walla; (509)527-0885), and, just south in the Oregon town of Milton-Freewater, Seven Hills Winery (235 E Broadway, Milton-Freewater; (541)938-7710). Call ahead, since these small wineries do not always keep regular hours.

Cheap Eats

Birkebeiner Brewing Company

35 W Main, Spokane ☎ (509)458-0854

This is one of Spokane's more pleasant brewpubs. It's smoke-free, there's occasional live entertainment with no cover, and families are welcome. Chef Dale Yates makes an effort to match his menu to the ever-changing selection of handcrafted suds. Wash down a bowl of sinus-clearing jambalaya with some apricot ale. A brew tweaked with jalapeño peppers makes a fine match for the black bean cakes drizzled with crème fraîche. There's also a surprisingly sophisticated wine list that works well with some of the spendier entrees such as venison medallions with a Madeira and wild mushroom sauce.

Scab Rock Gardens

1611 S Geiger Boulevard, Spokane ☎ (509)747-5343

Sure, it's a goofy name and a bad location east of town, but they've got the best darned plate lunch this side of Honolulu. The couple who runs this place is from Oahu, and the menu's rotating selections include a mild *katsu* curry, grilled mahi-mahi, or that luau fave, Kalua pig. All plate lunches come with a side of macaroni-potato salad just like Auntie used to make. Best of all, you can fill up with only a fiver in your wallet.

Thai Cafe

410 W Sprague Avenue, Spokane ☎ (509)838-4783

The city's first Thai restaurant is still one of the best. Start with crunchy spring rolls and then share a couple of entrees. The chicken *larb* salad has a refreshing citrus kick. *Mussamun* curry with peanuts and potatoes in a creamy rich base is a house favorite. The broccoli dish, *pad se-euew*, is a tasty break from the standard phad Thai. Owner Val Charlard greets both regulars and newcomers with an infectious smile.

Pastime Cafe

215 W Main, Walla Walla ☎ (509)525-0873

Around since 1927, the Pastime remains stubbornly old-fashioned (which means that they only recently added a nonsmoking section). But that also translates into huge platters of food for well under $10. It's Americanized Italian mostly, with super-cheesy lasagne among the big sellers. Stick with the basics—say, spaghetti with marinara sauce—and enjoy the room's quirky ambience, which includes baskets of cellophane-wrapped crackers on the table and matronly waitresses who might call you "hon." A decent selection of bottled beers, but forget about ordering wine.

Cheap Sleeps

Brown Squirrel Hostel

920 E Seventh Avenue, Spokane, WA 99204 ☎ (509) 838-5968

This sprawling Spanish colonial with a red tile roof makes a dramatic first impression. Inside, it's a bit tattered but comfortably cluttered with knickknacks donated by visitors from around the world. Retired schoolteacher Tom Baker runs the place and is a great source of information about the city's attractions (it's an easy walk to downtown). Two bedrooms are reserved for couples and families; one even has its own half-bath. Other quarters are more dormlike, with bunk beds, although there's a maximum of four people per room. There's an extra charge of $1 for the use of towels and sheets. (Most guests bring their own sleeping bags.) Visitors have the run of the ground floor, which includes two well-stocked kitchens.

Oslo's Bed and Breakfast

1821 E 39th Avenue, Spokane, WA 99203 ☎ (509) 838-3175

On a quiet residential street on the city's fashionable South Hill, Oslo's is the type of restful spot where you notice the clock ticking. Admire host Aslaug Stevenson's green thumb from the deck, where Scandinavian-style breakfast is served in warm weather. The explosion of perennial colors can also be viewed from the larger of the two guest rooms, decorated with French provincial furnishings and adjoining a bathroom with twin sinks. A smaller room also has a private bath, but it's down the hall; terrycloth robes are thoughtfully provided. A Chinese pug named Susie will likely greet you at the door.

Sicyon Gallery Bed and Breakfast

1238 Star Street, Walla Walla, WA 99362 ☎ (509) 525-2964

At the end of a tree-lined street, this eclectic gallery offers just one room, so it's often booked well in advance. But if you get in, you'll be snoozing among works from Northwest artists of all descriptions. Host Bill Piper, an art teacher at Whitman College, takes reservations on weekends only during the school year. If the sun's shining, ask to eat your morning meal in the outdoor sculpture garden. Piper might whip up his special French toast made with home-baked bread.

Weinhard Hotel

235 E Main, Dayton, WA 99328 ☎ (509) 382-4032

This sleepy little town 30 miles north of Walla Walla is famous for being home to Eastern Washington's only four-star restaurant, Patit Creek, and to dozens of historic pioneer homes. This hotel has a colorful past as a former saloon, built in the late 1800s by the nephew of beer magnate Henry Weinhard, but it was boarded up for years until it opened in 1994 as the Weinhard Hotel. The 16 guest rooms are stuffed with gorgeous antiques and boast impossibly high ceilings. Those on the ground floor are less expensive. Nice extras include a fresh fruit basket and upscale toiletries. There's also morning coffee and pastries in the lobby and live entertainment on the weekends.

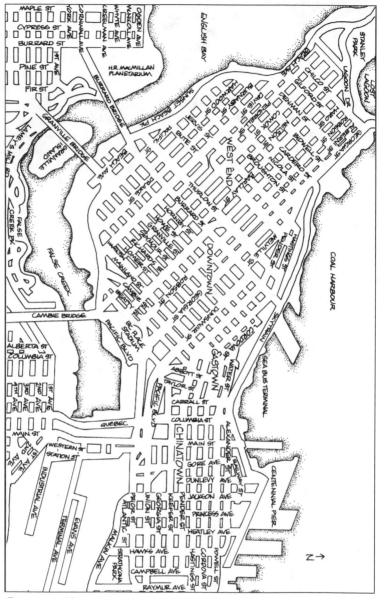

Downtown Vancouver

Vancouver

I n the international pageant of urban beauty, cities such as San Francisco, Sydney, and Hong Kong are habitual contestants. Yet many world
travelers regard Vancouver as the most irresistible of them all. Surrounded
by water and set against a stunning high-mountain backdrop, Canada's
third-largest metropolis stirs the senses. Downtown Vancouver gently
contours into the blue of English Bay, with the monumental green forests
of Stanley Park at its head. The park is a symbol of the city's pride—in its
environment, its heritage, its cosmopolitanism, and, perhaps most of all,
in its role as Canada's progressive window on the Pacific Rim.

In the mid-1860s, Vancouver was only a small coal-and-timber port on
Burrard Inlet. Today, the city is the center of a metropolitan area of close
to two million people. Canada's British Commonwealth ties have always
encouraged immigrants from Asia, but the influx has multiplied in recent
years as well-to-do Chinese from Hong Kong have moved their assets and
families out of the former Crown Colony. While there are also large and
highly visible communities of Indo-Pakistanis and southern Europeans in
this international city, a quarter of Vancouver's population is of Far Eastern descent.

Vancouver is a city of magical contradictions: from rough-and-tumble
Hastings Street, where timeworn brickwork still evokes a wild, beer-for-a-
dime seaport-town atmosphere, to trendy Robson Street, with its Japanese
noodle houses that look like something out of *Blade Runner*. Here, in one
of the oldest human habitations in North America, what people create is
still far less impressive than what nature has given us. And the myths of
the Raven, the Bear, and the Whale—the stories the Native peoples have
always told—are still woven into the landscape. In Vancouver, mystery, like
magic, abounds.

Access

To enter Canada, U.S. citizens or permanent residents do not need a passport but
must have some kind of identification, such as a driver's license, social security card, or
voter registration card. Visitors from other countries must have a valid passport.

Canadian Customs' Regional Office, (604)666-0545, can answer questions about visiting Canada.

Many U.S. citizens arrive in Vancouver via **car** from Blaine, Washington. US Interstate 5 becomes Canada Highway 99 at the border and heads northwest into the city. Note that at the city limits, the route follows secondary streets and can be somewhat confusing; follow signs for the Granville Street Bridge. Highway 99 continues north through the city to Whistler. Trans-Canada 1 approaches from the east.

Vancouver International Airport, (604)276-6101, is located south of Vancouver in the city of Richmond, approximately a 20-minute drive from downtown. An army of 150 volunteers called Green Coats are on duty from 7am to 10pm daily to assist visitors and answer questions. Need to get to or from the airport? Instead of forking over $9 for the Airporter, hop on BC Transit bus #100 for $1.50 ($2.25 if it's rush hour); for transit information, call (604)521-0400. **Rail** excursions begin in Vancouver at Pacific Central Station (1150 Station St; (604)669-3050), just south of Chinatown. Amtrak rail service to Seattle departs from Vancouver once a day; (800)872-7245. The **bus** terminals for Greyhound, Pacific Coach, and Maverick are also at the Pacific Central Station; (604)662-8074. For West Vancouver's bus schedules, call (604)985-7777.

If you travel from Sidney (on Vancouver Island) by **ferry**, you'll arrive on the mainland at Tsawwassen; pick up Highway 99 north to reach Vancouver. Other ferry routes leave from Tsawwassen or Horseshoe Bay to Nanaimo, the Gulf Islands, and the Sunshine Coast. Once you're in the city, prepare to encounter Vancouver traffic, one of the city's few negatives. **SkyTrain**, the light rail system installed for Expo 86, has provided a partial solution, with tracks from downtown Vancouver to Surrey via Burnaby and New Westminster. Or you can cross Burrard Inlet via the speedy **SeaBus**, a 400-passenger catamaran that travels from Vancouver's Waterfront Station (at Granville and Cordova Sts) to North Vancouver's Lonsdale Quay every 15 minutes; (604)261-5100.

Exploring

Canada Place, which extends into Burrard Inlet at the north end of Howe Street, has become Vancouver's landmark in much the same way the Sydney Opera House is emblematic of that Australian city. Built for Expo 86 as the Canada Pavilion, it now does multiple duty as a luxury hotel, a trade and convention center, and a cruise-ship terminal. The structure's 26-meter fiberglass "sails" make it look vaguely like a clipper ship about to leave port.

East of Canada Place along Water Street is historic **Gastown**. Its cobbled streets, shaded by trees and lined with imitation gas lamps, make it one of Vancouver's most charming neighborhoods.

Amid the art galleries, souvenir shops, restaurants, and nightclubs, keep your peepers open for the Gastown Steam Clock (at the corner of Water and Cambie Sts), the only one of its kind in the world. It operates on steam tapped from the underground pipes of nearby buildings.

The financial district is south of Canada Place between Hastings and Georgia Streets. Stop for a free tour of the Vancouver Stock Exchange at 609 Granville Street. The heart of the city's **downtown shopping district** interconnects underground shopping malls anchored by such department stores as the Bay and Eaton's. A four-block stretch on Granville Street between Robson and

Vancouver to Banff Tour

You may think your tour director is a Sasquatch, but there's only one place that guarantees it! One of the best—and least expensive—ways to see British Columbia is with Bigfoot Adventure Tours; (888)244-6673 or (604)278-8224. They'll take you by van from Vancouver to the Rocky Mountain resort of Banff, and back again if you wish, for just $95 each way. On the way, spend the night in a renovated courthouse in Kamloops, or in an old Canadian National caboose, for less than $20 per night. You'll need to find your own accommodations in Vancouver and Banff, but Hostelling International, (800)444-6111, can help find bargain beds.

Dunsmuir Streets is a pedestrian shopping and entertainment mall. Robson is the city's most fashionable (and expensive) shopping street and is lively in the evenings as people stroll, window-shop, or linger at sidewalk cafes. Anglophiles will find a plethora of British products, and compact discs are often a much better deal than in the States and elsewhere.

Robson Square (800 Robson St; (604)660-2830) is the home of a conference center that offers free films and concerts, an ice-skating rink, restaurants, and government offices. The nearby **Vancouver Art Gallery** (750 Hornby St; (604)682-5621) is housed in the imposing former law courts, and its permanent collection includes works by Picasso, Chagall, Goya, Gainsborough, and other European and North American masters. The museum's Emily Carr Gallery has collected some 200 paintings and drawings by the Vancouver Island native renowned for her depictions of indigenous West Coast cultures. Admission to the museum is by donation every Thursday from 5pm to 9pm.

The **West End**, located west of Bute Street between downtown and Stanley Park, is a residential area liberally sprinkled with restaurants and shops. Two of the most bustling areas are on Robson and Davie Streets. The stretch of Robson Street from Burrard to Denman is home to buskers, boutiques, and restaurants. Davie Street, which parallels Robson Street for six blocks to the south, has become a center for Vancouver's counterculture and a reliable spot for good cheap eats. Robson Street leads east to the dramatic **Library Square** complex at Robson and Homer Streets. Designed by world-renowned architect Moshe Safdie, the library is a miraculous structure based on the Coliseum in Rome. Across Homer Street is the Ford Theatre for the Performing Arts, also designed by Safdie.

The West End is the gateway to spectacular **Stanley Park**. A heavily forested, 1,000-acre promontory surrounded by a 10-kilometer seawall, this natural sanctuary was set aside by city fathers in 1889. Cycling and walking trails weave through groves of fir, cedar, and hemlock, connecting inland lakes and ocean beaches, restaurants, picnic grounds, a variety of sports facilities (from tennis courts to a par-3 golf course to a cricket oval), rose gardens, an outdoor amphitheater, and two small zoos. Don't miss the park's world-renowned **Vancouver Aquarium**, which has a marine-mammal center and galleries of north Pacific and tropical sea life; (604)682-1118 or (604)685-3364.

At the east end of downtown Vancouver, just beyond Gastown and adjacent to the former Expo 86 site on the north shore of False Creek, is Vancouver's **Chinatown**, the second largest in North America after San Francisco's. Wander the busy roads around Pender and Main Streets and admire streetlights decorated with golden dragons, phone booths topped with pagoda-style roofs, and ornamental signs in both Chinese and English. Then duck into one of the many bakeries for moon cakes, or visit an herbalist to discover the many amazing uses of a dried sea horse. There are free public exhibitions at the Chinese Cultural Centre (50 E Pender St; (604)687-0729). Just behind the center is the **Dr. Sun Yat-sen Classical Chinese Park and Garden** (578 Carrall St; (604)662-3207). You'll have to pay an admission fee to enter this lovely spot, the first full-scale classical Chinese garden ever built outside of China, but the adjoining park is free. On summer evenings the garden offers Enchanted Fridays, when the grounds are illuminated with lanterns, providing a soft glow for music and dancing.

Among the many other ethnic enclaves in Vancouver, each fascinating in its own way, is the **Punjabi Market** (Little India) at 49th and Main Streets. At All India Foods (6517 Main St; (604)324-1686), you'll find spices Julia Child has never heard of and the lowest milk prices around. Next door, All India Sweets offers confections and a warm and hospitable sit-down cafe.

Once just a cluster of dilapidated warehouses across the tracks from False Creek's mills and factories, **Yaletown** is now a highly desirable piece of history-crammed real estate (it was first settled in the 1890s by workers from the Canadian Pacific Railway line). In the late 1980s and early '90s, many warehouses were developed into funky cafes, bars, billiard halls, boutiques, art galleries, and condominiums. Bounded on the north by the new library on Robson Street, Yaletown has become the destination of choice for exciting and eccentric fashions—for oneself and one's home.

Granville Island, a 38-acre island of reclaimed warehouses, is now many things to many people: an artists' community, a market center with food stalls, a dining and entertainment district, an industrial site, and even a self-contained community. Wander the Granville Island **Public Market**, open daily (except Monday in the winter), and shop from colorful stalls heaped high with fresh fruits, vegetables, candy, bread, fish, and meat. Also look for the **Kids Only Market** on Cartwright Street near the entrance to the island. Kids of all ages will find games, gifts, hobbies, toys, and live entertainment.

The **Vancouver Museum** complex in Vanier Park (1100 Chestnut St; (604)736-4431) traces Vancouver's history from pre-European cultures to the late 20th century. A planetarium and observatory share the site. A few steps away is the Vancouver Maritime Museum (1905 Ogden Ave; (604)737-2211), which documents the city's growth as an international port; in the same building, take a tour of the *St. Roch*, a 1928 ketch that's now a National Historic Site, (604)666-3201; it was the first sailing vessel to navigate the Northwest Passage from west to east (in 1944).

Fondly known as the city's "golf ball," **Science World** (1455 Quebec St;

Illuminares Lantern Festival

Magic abounds every July in Trout Lake Park as families gather for the thrill of "senseless acts of beauty." At dusk, thousands of handmade lanterns are lit and paraded around the lake, and magicians, flame throwers, and stilt walkers join in the fun. Admission is free. Don't take your car, because parking will be a nightmare. The #20 Victoria bus travels downtown along Granville Street and will drop you right there. Trout Lake Park Community Centre is at 3350 Victoria Drive; call (604)257-6955 for details.

Chinatown Night Market

Every Friday, Saturday, and Sunday from the third weekend in May until the end of September, hawkers peddle their wares and services from 6:30pm to 11:30pm in Chinatown, starting at the corner of E Keefer and E Pender Streets. Hunt for bargains, sample an exotic snack, or explore your destiny with a fortune-teller at this open-air bazaar; (604)682-8998.

(604)268-6363) is housed in what was the Expo Centre at Expo 86. Now this futuristic building on the False Creek waterfront features exhibits that dazzle the senses, offering hands-on experiences that range from buzzing around a beehive to mastering the essentials of light and sound. Three main galleries explore the realms of biology, physics, and music; the fourth gallery is reserved for traveling exhibits; and the Omnimax Theatre, with one of the largest wraparound screens in the world, puts you right in the picture.

Lovers of the **performing arts** find Vancouver one of the most exciting cities on the West Coast. For information on current happenings, consult the Arts Hotline, (604)684-ARTS; the weekly *Georgia Straight*; or the two daily newspapers (see Thursday's calendar section of the *Vancouver Sun* or Friday's "Preview" section of the *Province*). Tickets are often discounted for midweek performances and matinees, and there are occasional two-for-one previews (check with individual theaters). Major touring shows—from Broadway musicals to symphony and

dance performances, as well as productions by the Vancouver Opera and Ballet British Columbia—take place at the 2,800-seat Queen Elizabeth Theatre (600 Hamilton St; (604)665-3050). The adjoining Vancouver Playhouse is home to the city's leading resident theater troupe; the two theaters share a box office (543 W 7th Ave; (604)873-3311).

After the Vancouver Playhouse, the city's best-known stage venue is the Arts Club Theatre, located in a former industrial warehouse on Granville Island (1585 Johnson St; (604)687-1644). Also on Granville Island, the Waterfront Theatre (1410 Cartwright St; (604)685-6217) features original works by British Columbia playwrights as well as entertainment suitable for children. The Vancouver East Cultural Centre (1895 Venables St; (604)254-9578), known to locals as "the Cultch," is a converted church that hosts a variety of fringe performances, from folk and jazz concerts to ethnic dance and light theater.

Summer arts events are plentiful in Vancouver too. Bard on the Beach,

Pacific National Exhibition

Better known to locals simply as PNE, one of the largest summer fairs on the North American continent runs for 17 days preceeding the Labor Day weekend in September. The PNE grounds and amusement park are just east of downtown at Exhibition Park (E Hastings and Renfrew Sts; (604)253-2311), but will move to a new site in 2000. If you want to see any of PNE's big-name concert acts, plan ahead. Accommodations—especially the budget variety—are often hard to come by in Vancouver during PNE, so be sure to reserve a room well in advance. And don't miss the Food Building for cheap eats.

(604)739-0559, presents two Shakespeare plays under a tent at Vanier Park, just west of the Burrard Street Bridge, from June to September; discounted tickets are available for 10 days before each play opens. Fans of contemporary dance should try to catch a performance at the Dancing on the Edge Festival, held each July. Always fresh and daring, some 60 to 70 shows are offered every day at adventurous venues from Vancouver's beaches to street corners; (604)689-0926. Hipsters can call (604)682-0706 for information about upcoming jazz concerts year-round as well as the annual du Maurier International Jazz Festival, which occurs in late June and early July and offers many free performances on both weekends of its two-week run.

Atop a bluff at the tip of Point Grey, Vancouver's westernmost point, is the sprawling campus of the 40,000-student **University of British Columbia**. The main public attraction here is the **Museum of Anthropology** (6393 NW Marine Dr; (604)822-5087), which boasts the world's finest collection of West Coast Indian art and artifacts, including totem poles, house posts, and longhouses. Admission is free on Tuesday from 5pm to 9pm.

A string of **beaches** extends westward from Vanier Park along the southern shore of English Bay. They include Kitsilano Beach, on Cornwall Avenue; Jericho Beach, on Point Grey Road; Locarno Beach and Spanish Banks, on NW Marine Drive; and the clothing-optional Wreck Beach, below NW

Marine Drive, near the UBC campus.

The suburb of **North Vancouver** is connected to downtown by the Lion's Gate Bridge from Stanley Park. **Lonsdale Quay** (123 Carrie Cates Ct, North Vancouver; (604)985-6261), an "open market" center, shelters three levels of shops, boutiques, and restaurants. At ground level the public market offers an array of fruits and vegetables, fish, breads, flowers, and meats. Have coffee outside in the sunshine and admire the stunning view.

Capilano River Regional Park has a famous wood-and-wire suspension bridge that traverses the canyon amid a dense rain forest. The park is free, but teetering across the 150-meter-long swinging bridge 75 meters above the river will cost you $8.95. On the other hand, for cheap thrills there's no charge to cross the Lynn Canyon Suspension Bridge (3735 Capilano Road, North Vancouver; (604)985-7474), which hangs 55 meters above the narrow canyon. For a less scary but equally dramatic experience, board the Royal Hudson Steam Train (1311 W 1st St, North Vancouver; (604)984-5246) for a round-trip ride up the rugged **Howe Sound** coastline to the logging town of Squamish, 64 kilometers to the north. Or ride the rails one way and sail on the MV *Britannia* on the way back; located at Harbour Ferries, on the north foot of Denman Street, (604)688-7246.

Well known as a ski resort, **Grouse Mountain** (6400 Nancy Greene Way, top of Capilano Rd, North Vancouver;

Salmon Spawning

Observe one of nature's great life-cycle stories for free at a federal government fish hatchery in Capilano River Regional Park (4500 Capilano Park Rd, North Vancouver; (604)666-1790). Read the information panels describing the life cycles of salmon, and then watch the juvenile Pacific salmon in the ponds. From July to December you can see the returning adult salmon jump up a series of steps. The hatchery also houses some of the oldest and tallest fir trees still standing on the Lower Mainland.

Lights! Camera! Action!

Vancouver has acquired a reputation as Hollywood North; the hit movies and TV shows filmed here include The Accused, Clueless, Jumanji, Legends of the Fall, MacGyver, *and* The X-Files. *You can pick up the BC Film Commission's Film List of projects currently in production at the BC Business Info Centre, 601 W Cordova Street, on weekdays between 8:30am and 4:30pm. Or call their hotline for film-listing updates; (604)660-3569. If you don't want to bother getting addresses, just cruise around the city—you're bound to bump into a movie crew somewhere. All you have to do is look for the big white trailers and trucks parked along the street and lots of busy folks running around in baseball caps and sneakers.*

(604)984-0661) is a different place in the summer. Just a 15-minute drive from downtown Vancouver, Grouse has something to please everyone, from energetic hikers to those who prefer relaxing strolls. The Skyride, an enclosed gondola, glides up the mountain and drops you into the center of the alpine activities. The peak chair lift will take you right to the top of the mountain for breathtaking views of the city and Washington State's San Juan Islands to the south.

Cheap Eats

Accord
4298 Main Street, Vancouver ☎ (604)876-6110

Behind white venetian blinds, this restaurant serves excellent Cantonese seafood and a handful of Chiu Chow specialties. Accord is open till the wee hours—perfect for those late evenings when Chinese food is the only thing that will do. Ask for the midnight snack menu, now available in English; the 68 half-size dishes cost between $5 and $8 each and range from deep-fried spicy baby octopus and Chinese smoked pork with gailan to clams with black bean sauce and a wonderful beef with satay sauce.

Ezogiku Noodle Cafe
1329 Robson Street, Vancouver ☎ (604)685-8606

Ramen dishes are the order of the day at this 70-seat cafe. You can order large, steaming bowls of ramen seasoned with pork, miso, or soy broth; a fried noodle dish; a curried dish; and gyozas—and that's it.

Hon's Wun Tun House
108-268 Keefer Street, Vancouver ☎ (604)688-0871

Headquartered in one of Chinatown's newer retail complexes, Hon's decor may now be urbanly chic, but the lines, noise level, rock-bottom prices, and basic menu remain the same. Soups are a major draw: basic wonton, pig's-feet, fishball, and 90 or so other variations—all in a rich, life-affirming broth. Equally noteworthy are Hon's trademark pot-stickers. Pan-fried or steamed, they come circled like wagons around a ginger-spiked dipping sauce.

JJ's Dining Room

250 W Pender Street, Vancouver ☎ (604) 443-8479

JJ's restaurant is a training ground for the Vancouver Community College downtown campus chefs' program. The budding chefs serve basic, well-prepared food; the service is enthusiastic (but sometimes slow); and the prices are cheap, cheap, cheap. The menu changes weekly, but might include entrees such as noisettes of lamb and brochettes of scallops. The Friday night buffet is a great deal at $14.95.

Milestones

1210 Denman Street, Vancouver ☎ (604) 662-3431

Mega-servings of inexpensive food (and booze) are the draw at Milestones, which, despite being a chain restaurant, manages to consistently impress with its witty takes on West Coast food trends. The breakfasts are outstanding and inexpensive, and the dinners are well prepared. Seafood pasta salads are lavish with shellfish and smoked salmon. Try the rollups—whole-wheat tortillas encasing everything from smoked chicken or spiced brisket to grilled eggplant.

Nat's New York Pizzeria

2684 W Broadway, Vancouver ☎ (604) 737-0707

Cousins Nat and Franco Bastone worked at their uncle's pizza parlor in Yonkers, where he taught them how to create thin-crusted Naples-style pizza. They learned well, and have been turning out excellent pizza ever since. Slices start at $2.10—and they're the size of half a small pizza. Order the $4.99 special (one pizza slice, a house salad, and a soft drink) till 4pm, or try the 14-inch or extra-large 16-inch Margherita pizza for about $10 and $12, respectively. Top off your order with the oven-baked garlic shavings.

Nazarre BBQ Chicken

1859 Commercial Drive, Vancouver ☎ (604) 251-1844

Rubber chickens on the turntables decorate the storefront, but only tender barbecued chicken finds its way onto your plate. The birds are basted in a mixture of rum and spices, slowly cooked on the rotisserie, and delivered with mild, hot,

Happy-Hour Food

For the price of a soft drink, you can revel in the special surroundings and enjoy all the appetizers you can eat in Vancouver's best hotels. Herons Bar in the Waterfront Centre Hotel (900 Canada Place) has complimentary hors d'oeuvres—dim sum, steamed mussels, clams, or perhaps bruschetta—on weekdays from 5pm to 7pm. Trader Vic's bar in the Westin Bayshore Hotel (1601 W Georgia St) also serves snacks such as sweet and sour spareribs, pot-stickers, or deep-fried fish every day from 5pm to 6pm. Complimentary pizza, chicken wings, calamari, or similar fare is offered Monday through Friday at the 900 West bar in Hotel Vancouver (900 W Georgia St) from 5pm to 7pm. And guests are passed a silver tray containing appetizers of sushi, caviar, smoked salmon, spanakopita, and other treats on weekdays at 5:30pm in the Wedgewood Hotel's Bacchus Lounge (845 Hornby St).

Free Dessert, Coffee, and Tea

For a free sweet, head over the Georgia Street viaduct to La Casa Gelato (1033 Venables St; (604)251-3211) for a complimentary "tasting cone" filled with soft, rich ice cream. You can even try some of La Casa's more unusual flavors, which include wasabe, cranberry, rosemary, and asparagus. Starbucks offers free samples of java in 4-ounce demitasse cups; and, hey, with 60-plus locations, it won't take long to have the equivalent of a grande coursing through your veins. If you wanna cuppa, walk through the door of Tearoom T (2460 Heather St; (604)874-8320), and you'll be offered a sampler of hot or iced tea as well as a tour.

or extra-hot garlic sauce. Order the well-priced special: half a chicken, rice, and beans. There are a few other goodies on the menu such as the vegetarian empanadas and tacos, but the chicken is your best bet. Dine at one of the four tables or take your bird to go.

Olympia Seafood Market and Grill
820 Thurlow Street, Vancouver ☎ (604) 685-0716

Olympia is first and foremost a fish market, but it whips up some of the best fish 'n' chips in the Lower Mainland. Whatever is on special in the store, which might be halibut cheeks, scallops, catfish, or calamari, is the special of the day at the 12-seat counter. The tried-and-true halibut and cod served with chips—about $7—is always available. Eat in or take out.

Planet Veg
1941 Cornwall Avenue, Vancouver ☎ (604) 734-1001

There's hope for the slender wallet at Planet Veg. This mostly Indian fast-food spot is located in the heart of health-conscious Kitsilano and serves the juiciest veggie burger in British Columbia. You can also get roti rolls (a meal in themselves), samosas, and potato salad. It's as inexpensive here as it is tasty. Inside seating is limited, so you may want to perch outdoors during the warmer months or take your meal to go.

The Red Onion
2028 W 41st Avenue, Vancouver ☎ (604) 263-0833

Head to Kerrisdale for the best double dogs in town. The wieners are the Onion's own, and so are the buns. They also make a mean cheeseburger and fries with a sour cream and dill dip. At breakfast, the muffins (blueberry, chocolate chip, or banana) and aromatic cinnamon buns are baked on the premises. You can get it all to go, too.

Sophie's Cosmic Cafe
2095 W 4th Avenue, Vancouver ☎ (604) 732-6810

Sophie's funky diner-cum-garage-sale is a fun place to visit. Don't worry about a boring wait for a table because there's plenty to look at, including Sophie's colorful lunch box and hat collections. The best dish here is the stick-to-the-ribs-style breakfast for $4.95: eggs (free-range eggs cost another 50 cents) with bacon, hash browns, toast, peanut butter, and jam. Pour a little of the homemade hot pepper sauce on the eggs to complete the meal. Other favorite foods to savor at Sophie's are the huge spicy burgers and the chocolate shakes.

Stepho's Souvlakia

1124 Davie Street, Vancouver ☎ **(604) 683-2555**

Good Greek fare is dished out in generous proportions here, including the pungent tzatziki, salads sprinkled with feta, chicken brochettes served with rice pilaf and roasted potatoes, and much more. Even though Stepho's has doubled their space, fans still have to wait in line to get in.

Subeez

891 Homer Street, Vancouver ☎ **(604) 687-6107**

Subeez has all of the urban edge that Vancouver can muster and is as much a bar and meeting place as it is a restaurant. Almost all of the furnishings in this 225-seat establishment have been recycled (the bathroom sinks are from Oakalla prison). Indulge in the burgers—lamb, turkey, or veggie—or the chicken and Brie served on focaccia. And don't skip the fab french fries with garlic mayo dip. There's an ominous 30-speaker sound system with appropriately manic music, so keep earplugs handy. The kitchen's open till 1am.

Tang's Noodle House

2805-2807 W Broadway, Vancouver ☎ **(604) 737-1278**

At Tang's you'll find locals rubbing elbows with those who have trekked in from the distant burbs for a serving of fried spicy black cod or shredded pork in garlic and sour sauce. The 100-plus options include barbecued duck, chicken, pork, or brisket; warming hot pots; and vegetarian dishes. Aficionados of incendiary fare (thoughtfully marked with an "H") shouldn't miss the wontons with spicy

Taste the Orient in Richmond

Can't afford Hong Kong? Start your Asian tour in Richmond at the Radisson President Hotel (8181 Cambie Rd, Richmond; (604)276-8181). Connected to the hotel is the President Plaza, one of five Asian-style malls (the others are Yoahan Centre, Aberdeen Centre, Parker Place, and Fairchild Square) located within a three-block radius. There is more retail space here than in Vancouver's Chinatown, and you'll find bargains galore. Don't miss the Buddhist temple in the President Plaza (the only mall in the Western Hemisphere with such a temple). After the temple's Sunday worship ceremonies, Buddhists and non-Buddhist visitors are served a free vegetarian lunch along with a dazzling view of the North Shore Mountains. Select a fish from the tanks in the T & T supermarket and they will deep-fry it for you while you shop. Or try the street food in the food courts: Singaporean curries, Vietnamese pho, Northern Chinese dim sum, Chiu Chow stir-fries, Hong Kong coffee shop—style food, and Japanese yakitori. Order a Taiwanese pearl milk tea at the Little Tea House, or head to Ten Ren Tea & Ginseng; complimentary ginger or ginseng tea is on tap here, but if you show even a slight interest, you may be invited to share a private tea ceremony. Before you leave, consider stopping at the Chinese post office to buy Chinese stamps for your postcards.

garlic and chiles. The bargain lunch specials include soup and a bowl of rice or chow mein noodles with a choice of 17 meat or vegetable toppings.

Tokyo Joe's

955 Helmcken Street, Vancouver ☎ **(604) 689-0073**

Here's the best spot in Vancouver for inexpensive sushi: prices start at $2 a roll. There's also a reasonably priced lunch box served all day with chicken teriyaki, vegetable tempura, salad, and rice. The tea is free. Eat in or take out.

Cheap Sleeps

Backpackers Youth Hostel

927 Main Street, Vancouver, BC V6A 2V8 ☎ **(604) 682-2441**

There are 15 private rooms here, and even the 18 dorm rooms contain only three or four beds apiece, but everything else (bathrooms, kitchen, dining room, TV room, laundry) in this former guest house, located on the edge of Chinatown, is shared. Don't worry about a curfew; everyone gets a front-door key. Many travelers still refer to the hostel as Vincent's Guest House.

City Centre Motor Inn

2111 Main Street, Vancouver, BC V5T 3C6 ☎ **(604) 876-7166**

The City Centre is a good option for folks who want to avoid downtown traffic. Located near the east end of the Expo 86 site, beneath the geodesic shadow of the Science World kids' museum, this modern motel is an easy walk from the Main Street SkyTrain station and a short stroll south of Chinatown. The most expensive room is about $70. Parking is free, as is the coffee served in the lobby each morning.

Hostelling International Vancouver

1515 Discovery Street, Vancouver, BC V6R 4K5 ☎ **(604) 224-3208**

Beautifully situated on Jericho Beach off Point Grey Road, this hostel is Canada's largest, and the second largest in North America. Youth hostelers accustomed to cooking in communal kitchens can do that here too, but they'll be delighted to find a budget-priced cafeteria as well. There's also a lounge with a big-screen, satellite-fed TV. Formerly the barracks of the Canadian Air Force, the hostel has 286 dormitory bunks and nine private rooms for families and couples (these must be booked two weeks in advance). Parking is $3 per day.

Kingston Hotel

757 Richards Street, Vancouver, BC V6B 3A6 ☎ **(604) 684-9024**

Guests often comment that this centrally located three-story inn reminds them of a European bed and breakfast, especially given its facade of cut granite, heavy wood, and Tudor-style windows. The 60 cozy rooms (some with private baths) have been upgraded with new furniture, carpeting, quilts, and other nice touches. Rooms with private baths have color TVs, and all units have phones. A continental breakfast is served in the small lounge downstairs. Facilities include a sauna and a coin-op laundry. There's no parking available, so management reimburses guests for the overnight rate at downtown parking garages (up to $3). The Kingston is a great value, and it even offers discounts to seniors.

The New Backpackers Hostel

347 W Pender Street, Vancouver, BC V6B 1T3
☎ (604) 688-0112 or (604) 687-9837

This hostel is more upscale than the Backpackers Youth Hostel (see earlier review) and has larger rooms. Some units have full kitchens. The location near Gastown makes this hostel a prime choice. No parking, though.

Shaughnessy Village

1125 W 12th Avenue, Vancouver, BC V6H 3Z3 ☎ (604) 736-5511

The 240-unit Shaughnessy is centrally located, making it easy to get to downtown businesses and major attractions. The one-room studios are like cabins on a cruise ship (or perhaps a comfortable motor home) with a fold-down double bed, microwave oven, fridge, color TV, and clock radio. Each room has a private bath/shower and a balcony. There are two lounges, a health club, pools, a sauna, and a restaurant. Room rates start at about $60 per day, and weekly and monthly deals are available, too; a full breakfast is included with your stay. Seniors should inquire about discounts. Underground parking is available for a fee.

Sylvia Hotel

1154 Gilford Street, Vancouver, BC V6G 2P6 ☎ (604) 681-9321

The Sylvia has gracefully accepted its role as one of Vancouver's leading senior citizens. Its ivy-cloaked stone walls, facing English Bay across Beach Avenue, only hint at the friendly warmth within. Every room is a little different, though true budget watchers might have to accept a small unit in the rear. There's room service, a restaurant, and a lounge—reportably the first cocktail bar in Vancouver (it opened in 1954), and on some winter afternoons it looks as though the original clientele is still sitting here sipping Sidecars. If the continental restaurant's prices are too steep, sate yourself with light snacks in the adjacent bistro lounge. Covered parking costs extra.

University of British Columbia (UBC), Walter Gage Residence

5961 Student Union Boulevard, Vancouver, BC V6T 2C9 ☎ (604) 822-1010

When UBC students are off campus during the summer, the university opens student residences to the traveling public—3,600 rooms in all. You can choose from three types of rooms: simple dormitory rooms (starting at $22 per night) with a bathroom down the hall; bedrooms with a bathroom, kitchen, and living room shared between six units; and one-person studios with a small private bathroom, kitchenette, TV, and phone (your best bet—and some of these units are also available during the school year). You can dine in the UBC cafeteria across the street, and for a small fee you can use the university's athletic facilities and swimming pool. Parking is free for rooms that cost more than $33; otherwise, there's a $4 per day charge.

YMCA

955 Burrard Street, Vancouver, BC V6Z 1Y2 ☎ (604) 681-0221

The college dorm-style rooms here are spartan, to say the least (with a bed, night table, desk, lamp, and closet), but they're impeccably clean. The corridors access washrooms, showers, pay phones, and a coin-op laundry. The central location (in the heart of downtown) is one good reason to stay here; free use of all Y facilities, including swimming pool, weight room, and gymnasium, is another big attraction. The building houses a small cafe serving breakfast and lunch. Women as well as men are welcome here; seniors and students get a 15 percent discount. Liquor is verboten. Parking costs extra.

YWCA Hotel/Residence

733 Beatty Street, Vancouver, BC V6B 2M4
☎ (800) 663-1424 (from BC or Alberta only) or (604) 895-5830

Although its name suggests it's for young women only, this Y welcomes everyone else, too—including couples, families, groups, and men. Built in 1995, the Y offers 155 immaculately clean and reasonably priced rooms (with fridge, sink, and mirror) on 12 floors. The units vary in size from single rooms with shared baths down the hall, to family suites that sleep five and have private baths. Rooms with private baths also have a TV. Three community kitchens are located throughout the hotel, and all are equipped with stoves, microwaves, refrigerators, toasters, and teakettles, but you have to bring your own utensils. There isn't a gym in the building, but you can work out at the YWCA Fitness Centre for free; it's eight blocks away at 535 Hornby Street and has exercise classes, a weight room, a swimming pool, a steam room, and a hot tub. The YWCA Hotel is close to theaters and sporting venues, too. Security is excellent.

Capilano RV Park

295 Tomahawk Avenue, North Vancouver, BC V7P 1C5 ☎ (604) 987-4722

If you've brought your recreational vehicle or tent to Vancouver, this is the place to park it. The Squamish Nation owns much of the North Shore waterfront and operates this first-class, 208-site camping facility on the north end of Lion's Gate Bridge, just minutes from downtown. Campsites range from about $18–$32 (with full hookup). There are showers and laundry facilities, too.

Simon Fraser University

McTaggart-Cowan Hall, Room 212, Burnaby, BC V5A 1S6 ☎ (604) 291-4503

What a deal! And what a view on top of Burnaby Mountain! From May 1 until August 31, Simon Fraser rents student accommodations to visitors. Furnished single rooms cost approximately $19 per night if you bring your sleeping bag, $32 per night if you want linens and housekeeping service. Twin rooms are available for about $49. Families or groups can rent four-bedroom townhouses complete with bathrooms and kitchen for just over $100 per night.

Victoria & Beyond

Victoria may be far from England geographically, but no place on the North American continent is more reminiscent of the Old Country than this impressive Canadian city. The imposing stone architecture of the Parliament Buildings and the Empress hotel is your first hint. The link becomes even more apparent as you walk the streets: shops display Waterford crystal, English toffee, and Scottish tartans, and cafes serve cups of Earl Grey tea or fish 'n' chips wrapped in newspaper. And yes, you can see Queen Victoria in wax, as well as replicas of her crown jewels and of Anne Hathaway's thatched cottage. Victoria's 327,000 citizens also have a spirit of their own, exemplified in spring and summer by the colorful flower baskets that line every downtown street. This is a bright and friendly garden city, displaying none of the dourness sometimes associated with Britain.

Victoria was established in 1843 when the Hudson's Bay Company built Fort Camosun as its western headquarters. The settlement was later renamed in honor of Queen Victoria and subsequently became the provincial capital of British Columbia. Timber, shipbuilding, and other industries brought considerable wealth to Victoria in the late 19th and early 20th centuries. The beautiful homes and impressive gardens that grace the city today are the legacy of this turn-of-the-century pride and prosperity. Its climate, sunnier and milder than that of either Vancouver or Seattle, soon brought steamers across the water, drawing vacationers from these cities to Victoria's refined streets and old-world airs.

Access

For **customs** information, see the Access section in the Vancouver chapter.

Most **BC Ferries** cross the Strait of Georgia between Tsawwassen on the mainland and Swartz Bay, about 28 kilometers north of Victoria on the Saanich Peninsula, eight or more times a day year-round (schedules vary seasonally); (250)669-1211. If your time is money, ante up $15 more to reserve a space and avoid a wait in line; (888)724-5223 (in British Columbia). Of the two routes from the mainland (from Tsawwassen or Horseshoe Bay), Tsawwassen–Swartz Bay's island-skimming route is the most scenic.

Washington State Ferries, (206)464-6400, link Anacortes with Sidney (via the San Juan Islands), 24 kilometers north of Victoria, twice daily in the summer and once a day in the winter; round trip $36 in summer, $30 in winter. Black Ball Transport's MV *Coho* ferry, (360)457-4491, shuttles passengers between Port Angeles, Washington, and Victoria's Inner Harbour one to four times daily, depending on the season (bicyclists take note: helmets are required by Canadian law); $27.25 one way for car and driver, $6.75 for foot passengers. *Princess Marguerite III* provides vehicle and passenger "luxury cruise" service, May through September, between Seattle and Victoria for about $80 one way for a couple with a car, $35 for a cyclist. The *Victoria Clipper*, a turbo catamaran, carries foot passengers only between Seattle and Victoria's Belleville Street four times a day from mid-May to mid-September, and once a day the rest of the year ($89–$126 round trip). Information on both boats can be found at (250)382-8100 (in Victoria), (206)448-5000 (in Seattle), or (800)888-2535 (outside Victoria and Seattle).

Exploring Victoria by **bus** is a breeze. Transit runs 40 bus routes through greater Victoria, Sooke, and Sidney (where you can catch the ferry to Vancouver). You can buy Scratch 'n' Ride day passes at many outlets, including the Tourism Victoria Travel Info-Centre (see below); passes are not sold on the bus. A $5 adult day pass gives you unlimited travel. A free pamphlet called "Explore Victoria by Bus" spells out exactly how to get to every attraction, neighborhood, and park by using public transit. A favorite route: hop aboard the #2 Oak Bay bus from downtown for a waterfront and Oak Bay village tour. Or travel by **train**: the E&B Railiner leaves Victoria around 8:15am and travels up the island to Courtenay, arriving at noon. The best part: the return trip through Goldstream Park. If you book seven days in advance, you'll save up to 40 percent.

The fastest link to Victoria (Inner Harbour) is provided by **seaplane**. In Vancouver, contact Air BC, (604)688-5515, or Helijet Airways, (604)273-1414; in Seattle, try Kenmore Air, (800)543-9595 or (425)486-1257.

Located right on the harbor, **Tourism Victoria Travel InfoCentre** (812 Wharf St; (250)382-2127) has helpful information about the city and the area.

Exploring

Within a few blocks of the flower-bedecked Inner Harbour, you can see Victoria's architectural heavyweights: the Parliament Buildings, which still serve as the province's legislative center, and the luxury Empress hotel. The **Parliament Buildings** were constructed in 1897 and are especially stunning at night, when the thousands of lights lining the historical edifices are aglow. When Parliament is not in session you can sign up for a free weekday tour, by reservation only (501 Belleville St; (250)387-3046). Just across the street is the Royal London Wax Museum (470 Belleville St; (250)388-

4461), whose 300 "timeless" wax figures are always worth a visit—and a chuckle.

A visit to Victoria wouldn't be complete without a stop at the **Empress**, the extravagant 1908 hotel where the Nixons honeymooned and New York tycoon Pierpont Morgan's family resided in the summertime (721 Government St; (250)384-8111). Even though the suites at this Francis Rattenburg–designed building are well beyond the budget traveler's price range, you should stop in for a cuppa. Not the full afternoon tea in the Tea Lobby (a pricey six-course tradition), but the more reasonably priced tea and

Harbour Cruises

It's not the QE II, but then you're no Prince Charles. Victoria Harbour Ferry Company's miniature ferryboats (each seats 12) squire passengers to and from shore points all along Victoria Harbour for about $10 per person; (250)480-0971. You can get on at any stop and take a round-trip, 40-minute cruise while viewing waterfront activity, floatplanes, seabirds, seals, and otters, among other attractions. For those trying to jam-pack their days, the $8 moonlight tour is the perfect capper. Or take a 10-minute ride up the Gorge Waterway from the Inner Harbour ($14), and then step up onto the landing dock and back into the 19th century for an afternoon of high tea and croquet at the Point Ellis House, a Victorian heritage home. For a truly inexpensive outing, hop the ferry to Fisherman's Wharf ($2.50), eat your fill of fish 'n' chips at Barb's Place (see review in Cheap Eats), and then walk back downtown.

scones in the Bengal Room, where you can sit and sup among the tiger skins. At night, a pianist even performs.

If you're a **tea** fan, stop by the Windsor House Tea Room (2540 Windsor Rd; (250)595-3135) or Point Ellice House (2616 Pleasant St; (250)380-6506; open summers only), the former home of the O'Reilly family, who served tea there to, among others, Antarctic explorer Sir Ernest Henry Shackelton and Sir John A. Macdonald, Canada's first prime minister.

Other major downtown Victoria highlights are Beacon Hill Park (a short walk from the Empress), whose resident swans are descendants of England's Royal Swannery, and **Government Street**, lined with heritage buildings full of shops stocked with English bone china and woolen goods, among other treasures. As you stroll this popular street, keep an eye out for Rogers Chocolates (913 Government St; (250)384-7021), whose divine puck-size Victoria creams wrapped in waxy pink paper are shipped to Buckingham Palace and mere mortals worldwide, and Munro's Books (1108 Government St; (250)382-2464), one of Canada's best bookstores, set in a restored 1909 heritage building.

One of the city's top attractions is the **Royal British Columbia Museum** (675 Belleville St; (250)387-3014), located between the Empress hotel and the Par-

liament Buildings. The museum hosts major traveling shows, and regular exhibits depict the province's natural and human history through lifelike dioramas, including forests, seascapes, and a turn-of-the-century townscape complete with sounds and smells. Don't miss the ceremonial longhouse and contemporary poles in **Thunderbird Park**, located behind the museum, where guest carvers often demonstrate their skills. Coin-operated lockers are available to store bags and backpacks while you explore. There's a *National Geographic*–sponsored large-format theater on the grounds of the museum. If you'll be around town for a while, inquire about the museum's two-day pass.

As hokey as it may seem, a tour on one of the **Tallyho horse-drawn carriages** offers an insightful lesson in the history of the city—one that shouldn't be missed. Two Belgian draft horses clop along to the cadence of the driver's hour-long narrated tour, complete with humorous historical anecdotes. The tour starts at the Parliament Buildings, winds through 155-acre Beacon Hill Park to the waterfront, and trots through the residential community of James Bay; (250)383-5067.

Crystal Garden (713 Douglas St; (250)381-1213) is a turn-of-the-century swimming-pool building converted into a glass conservatory with a tropical theme (lush greenery, live flamingos and macaws)—a fine place to spend a rainy day. Admission is $7, and it's open every day.

Architecture and history buffs should make a beeline to the 1889 **Craigdarroch Castle** (1050 Joan Crescent; (250)592-5323), just a short distance from downtown. Built by a wealthy industrialist, this remarkable 39-room mansion with 18 fireplaces is notable for its fine woodwork, leaded-glass windows, arches, turrets, and soaring stone walls. It's especially beautiful when adorned with Christmas decorations. Not far from Craigdarroch is the **Art Gallery of Greater Victoria** (1040 Moss St; (250)384-4101), where you'll find works by leading Canadian contemporary artists and important American and European painters, as well as an extensive collection of Asian art that includes a complete Shinto shrine from Japan. The museum's store is a wonderful place to shop.

When you complete your downtown tour, head out to Victoria's Old Town and Chinatown and into the beautiful residential communities of **James Bay**, **Ross Bay**, and **Oak Bay**. The streets that wind through these neighborhoods are lined with historic mansions surrounded by azaleas and cherry trees—a spectacular site in the springtime.

Chinatown, marked by the Gate of Harmonious Interest at Fisgard and Government Streets, offers an odd mix of Chinese restaurants and grocery shops that are slowly being encroached upon by upscale boutiques and decidedly non-Chinese coffee bars and bistros. Walk through **Fan Tan Alley**, Canada's narrowest thoroughfare. Although this is Canada's oldest Chinatown, it really isn't much to look at if you're from Vancouver. For a great Chinatown tour, call Les Chan at (250)383-7317 and ask if he can guide you to the tea shops, temples, and herbalists; he often takes visitors to a dim sum lunch at Kwong Tung, too.

Check out **Old Town**, on the docks at the northern edge of downtown Victoria. Even a century ago, this area set itself apart from Victoria's "little bit of old England" theme. This is where rollicking sailors, miners, barkeeps, and "soiled doves" worked, played, and traded when Victoria was booming, thanks to sealing, lumber, coal, and salmon. Happily, Old Town's muscular Victorian energy survived decades of stagnation before revitalization in the 1970s.

Spend some time in the funky shops along **Johnson Street** and in historic **Market Square**. Artist Bill Blair and partner Shelor Sheldan have filled the tiny, colorful shop called Hoi Polloi (on the Pandora Ave side of Market Square; (250)480-7822) with Mexican Day of the Dead curiosities, unusual art pieces (such as lobster cans turned into clocks), and a weird and artful selection of postcards.

Beacon Hill Park stretches south from the Royal British Columbia Museum along

Affordable Horticulture

The Horticulture Centre of the Pacific (505 Quayle Rd, Victoria, BC V8X 3X1; (250)479-6162), a delightful volunteer-run botanical garden and horticultural school, might be considered a poor relation when compared to the better-known and more grandly maintained Butchart Gardens. But you'll never have to fight a crowd as you walk among the flower-lined paths, examine the herb garden or fuchsia arbors, rest on a multitude of comfortable benches, and enjoy the bounty of peace and quiet available on this 100-acre preserve. Admission is only a few bucks. Take Quadra Street and head northwest to W Saanich Road (about 20 minutes from downtown Victoria).

the Strait of Juan de Fuca and is a popular destination for walkers, remote-control airplane flyers, kite flyers, sunset watchers, and bikers. A 2 1/2-kilometer path skirts the shoreline. Rent bikes from Budget Cycle Time (727 Courtney St; (250) 953-5333) or Harbour Scooter Rentals (843 Douglas St; (250)384-2133). Sports Rent (3084 Blanshard St; (250)385-7368) will rent anything sporty you forgot to pack, from kayaks to backpacks.

Fort Rodd Hill National Historic Park and **Fisgard Lighthouse National Historic Site** (603 Fort Rodd Hill Rd; (250)478-6481) are wonderful places to visit, if only to stroll the grounds. Fort Rodd, built at the end of the 19th century on the west side of Esquimalt Harbour, has three separate batteries with gun emplacements; locals find inviting places for picnics on the grassy point. The lighthouse, the first permanent light on Canada's Pacific coast, was built in 1860 and is still in operation. Sample the pub grub out this way at the Six-Mile Pub (494 Island Hwy; (250)478-3121).

One of Victoria's most impressive sights is not in the city but 21 kilometers north, on an arm of the Saanich Inlet—the renowned **Butchart Gardens** (800 Benvenuto Ave, Brentwood Bay; (250)652-4422). (It's an easy detour off the main road linking Victoria to the Swartz Bay ferry terminal. Or take bus #75, which runs along Douglas Street in Victoria and costs $2.50 one way.) This miracle of modern horticulture, spread across 50 acres of a private estate, began as the creation of Jenny Butchart, wife of cement manufacturer Robert Butchart, who took it upon herself to relandscape her husband's limestone quarry. Over the years, the Butcharts added Japanese and Italian gardens and an English rose garden, and populated them with ducks, peacocks, and trained pigeons.

Today, the place is a mecca for gardening enthusiasts from every corner of the globe (as touring maps in 12 languages will attest). Consider visiting in the evening during the summer months, when the gardens are lit with thousands of colored lights, crowds are thinner (though not by much), and entertainers give free performances. Spectacular **fireworks displays** (set to music!) are held on Saturday nights in July and August. Bring a sweater and something to sit on.

Keep in mind that there's definitely a flip side—and a less expensive one—to Victoria, too. Instead of afternoon tea at the Empress, you can knock back espresso at the Sally Cafe (704 Cormorant St; (250)381-1431; see review in Cheap Eats), timing your visit to coincide with the 10am appearance of hot-from-the-oven, big-as-your-head cinnamon buns. Eschew Butchart Gardens' hefty entry charge for the free arboreal charms of 27-acre **Ross Bay Cemetery** (east of Beacon Hill Park, overlooking Ross Bay) and the dreamy rose gardens of **Government House** (a few blocks south of Craigdarroch Castle), where volunteers happily provide the labor.

After you've strolled the Inner Harbour with all the tourists, set out for the newer **Songhees Westsong Way**. In the early

---

Beacon Hill Children's Farm

Kids of every age will get a kick out of (though hopefully not from) the baby goats, sheep, Vietnamese potbelly pigs, and other animals that call Beacon Hill Children's Farm home. A dollar donation is a small price to pay to visit this kid-friendly miniature zoo and its turtle house, aviary, duck pond, chicken yard, and petting corral. Closed in winter. In Beacon Hill Park; (250)381-2532.

Twice for the Price

Why make a day of it when you can make two? Your admission tickets at Butchart Gardens and the Royal British Columbia Museum are good for 24 hours, so if you go after noon, you can come back at no charge the next morning.

morning or late afternoon, join the commuters who walk the 2.7-kilometer waterfront path (about a mile and a half). Start near Market Square, cross the Johnson Street Bridge, and follow the signs. The best part of the walk is past Spinnaker's Pub (308 Catherine St), where you'll encounter wooden bridges and boardwalks over curving beaches, overhanging arbutus, and nesting birds. At West Bay Marina, walk up Head Street and ride bus #25 back to Market Square.

On Saturday nights in summer, drop in between 9pm and 11pm for free public stargazing at the **Dominion Astrophysical Observatory** (5071 W Saanich Rd; (250)383-0001), which is also open during the day year-round. **Christ Church Cathedral** (on the corner of Quadra and Courtney Sts), built in 13th-century Gothic style in the late 1920s, has a fine set of bells (a replica of those in Westminster Abbey, of course!). Call to see if the cathedral's campanologists plan to ring the changes; (250)383-2714.

"Victoria is a city of enthusiastic amateurs," suggests Victoria writer Peter Grant. And none are more so than the members of the **Old Cemeteries Society**, which offers year-round walking tours of Victoria's many cemeteries on Sundays (and on Tuesday and Thursday evenings in summer); $5 nonmembers, $2 members. The majority of the tours go to Ross Bay Cemetery, and with good reason: in addition to the splendid century-old trees (a virtual arboretum of London planes, pines, and yews), this cemetery offers a who's who of Victoria—or rather, a who was who. The many notable plots include that of renowned painter Emily Carr.

At night, check out the **Roxy Cine-**

gogue (2657 Quadra St; (250)382-3370), an alternative movie theater complete with old ceiling fans, drink holders, and bargain prices ("Where Movies Are a Religious Experience" is the motto over the door); or take in one of Canada's finest theater companies at the **Belfry** (1291 Gladstone Ave; (250)385-6815), a beautifully converted heritage church in the Fernwood neighborhood. In the summer, ask at downtown's Tourism Victoria Travel InfoCentre about the amateur Langham Court Theatre's occasional productions in a carriage house.

Sooke, a half-hour drive west from Victoria, is still relatively undiscovered. The village itself isn't much to look at, but nearby are excellent B&Bs, nice kayaking, glorious parks, and great wilderness for all tastes. You can bird, crab, hike, rock-climb, surf, fly-fish, scuba-dive, golf—even llama-pack in East Sooke Park. Definitely make your first stop the **Sooke Region Museum** (2070 Phillips Rd, Sooke; (250)642-6351), which is just a short distance off the main road into Sooke. The museum itself is worth a look, especially the historic cottage that describes turn-of-the-century life with the aid of free dramatized tours, but it's also the home of British Columbia's best-organized **Tourist Information Centre**, which boasts pictures (inside and out) of almost every B&B in the province. The well-informed local staff can give you information on virtually any activity or accommodation, along with tips about what not to miss. Be sure to ask about the **Galloping Goose Trail**—especially the scenic section over the trestle bridges; you can, as they say, "walk the Goose, cycle the Goose, or ride the Goose" (on horseback). Sooke Cycles (6707 Westcoast Rd, Sooke; (250)642-3123) offers half-day bike rentals for $10 and will drop you at the trailhead.

For peace and serenity, visit **East Sooke Regional Park**, an enormous (3,400-acre) semiwilderness park with great day hiking and beach walking. East Sooke's Coast Trail is one of Canada's premier day hikes, a 10-kilometer (6-mile) trip, challenging even for experienced hikers. Aylard Farm is the starting point here for easy, brief excursions out to the petroglyphs. The paved but twisty road beyond Sooke to **Port Renfrew** (literally the end of the road) goes past access points to French Beach Provincial Park, Sandcut Beach, China Beach Provincial Park (worth the hike down), and Mystic Beach. Be aware of incoming tides when hiking along these beaches. For good down-home food along the way, drop into the Country Cupboard Cafe (402 Sheringham Point, Sooke; (250)646-2323) or Shakie's roadside stand (in Jordan River, a 30-minute drive from Sooke; (250)646-2184), where regulars queue for $1.25 orders of potato wedges or the Breakfast Beachcomber's Special: two eggs, toast, and potatoes for $3.50.

The biggest news at this end of the island is the **Juan de Fuca Marine Trail**, a recently completed 72 1/2-kilometer hiking trail between Port Renfrew and China Beach that passes bathtub-size tide pools and sea lion birthing caves. Designed for all levels of hiking ability, the trail and its 30 bridges can be hiked in three days, or day trippers can step in at different access points to do day sections as short as four hours. (Unlike the very busy West Coast Trail farther north, no reservations are required, and part of the trail goes through large clearcuts—an eye-opener.) But do get good instructions, pay attention in bear season, be prepared, and tell someone where you've gone; for more info, contact BC Parks, (250)391-2300.

For guided **kayaking** right in Sooke, you can't beat the special deals and highly skilled instructors at the Ocean Kayak Institute (at Cooper's Cove, Sooke; (250)642-2159), from the third Saturday "social paddles" that end with nachos, to the free boat tryouts the third Sunday of the month between 4pm and 6pm at Cooper's Cove. They offer rentals too.

Sooke has more than its share of talented **artisans**. Not to be missed is Blue Raven Gallery (1971 Kaltasin Rd, Sooke; (250)642-3392), where Edith, Victor, and Carey Newman—a talented and fascinating family—are planning regular potlatch feast celebrations to augment their traditional and contemporary Kwagiulth native artwork; ask for details. The gallery is open daily in summer and by appointment at other times of the year.

Cheap Eats

Barb's Place

310 St. Lawrence Street, Victoria ☎ (250) 384-6515

Stick around long enough and someone in Victoria will point you to this floating take-out fish 'n' chips stand at Fisherman's Wharf in James Bay. You could opt for clam chowder or "wharf dogs," but, hey, the fish is halibut and the chips are choice.

Beacon Drive-In

126 Douglas Street, Victoria ☎ **(250) 385-7521**

Locals line up at the Beacon, just a short stroll from Beacon Hill Park, for burgers and British Columbia's best soft-serve ice cream. Summer bonus: outside tables and a "regular" breakfast that will have you wondering why you gave up crispy bacon and eggs.

Bohematea

515 Yates Street, Victoria ☎ **(250) 383-2829**

Within the brick walls of this totally retro restaurant, Bohematea's Sri Lankan chef whips up some of Victoria's finest veggie fare. Everything from a Lebanese pita bread roll to Tuscan-style rotini to pizza layered with Jack cheese and ginger pesto is served at this funky teahouse. The lengthy tea menu is impressive—and so are the huge desserts.

Cafe Mexico

1425 Store Street, Victoria ☎ **(250) 386-1425**

Mexican purists may find this more Tex-Mex than Mex, but with well-priced dinner specials, pitchers of margaritas, and all the classics from chiles rellenos to chimichangas, who cares which side of the border you're on?

Demitasse Coffee Bar

1320 Blanshard Street, Victoria ☎ **(250) 386-4442**

Java junkies consider Demitasse to be Victoria's finest coffeehouse. The artsy, bohemian atmosphere attracts a mixed crowd. Most folks go for the early-bird croissant and scrambled egg plate that can be jump-started with spicy Portuguese sausages. For lunch, dip into the hearty borscht.

Re-bar Modern Foods

50 Bastion Square, Victoria ☎ **(250) 361-9223**

Re-bar is a cheery pit stop for anyone fond of retro oilcloth and a commitment to organic, healthy fare. Lemon risotto pancakes and cinnamon-pecan-cashew buns coexist on the menu with 80 exotic fresh-squeezed fruit and veggie juices, fortified with optional electrolytes, ginkgo biloba, or bee pollen. The hard-core can order a shot of Pharoah's Sneakers—wheatgrass.

Rebecca's Food Bar

1127 Wharf Street, Victoria ☎ **(250) 380-6999**

It's tempting to eat inside this waterfront heritage building, but Rebecca's daily specials and imaginative West Coast cuisine are ideal for a picnic basket—especially if you're en route to Fort Rodd Hill park.

Sally Cafe

714 Cormorant Street, Victoria ☎ **(250) 381-1431**

Want to hang out with the locals? Head to the Sally, just east of City Hall. Healthy soups, sandwiches (try the curried chicken and apricot), salads, decadent desserts, and breakfast goodies are served on Matisse-inspired hand-painted tabletops surrounded by saffron, blue, and red walls adorned with local art.

17-Mile House

5126 Sooke Road, Victoria ☎ (250) 642-5942

You'll find lots of colorful locals at this former stage stop that also served as a school and a jail before it became a restaurant. The piano is about 150 years old (it was shipped around the Horn), and the floor tiles are circa 1940. The $29 Sunday platter of scallops, crab, shrimp, prawns, potatoes, and rice easily serves two. Drink specials include the Canterbury pint, sold for $3.95 on Fridays. Pool, darts, checkers, crib, and backgammon keep you occupied as you wait for your meal, but heed the warning on the wall: "No gambling. Play nicely."

Wah Lai Yuen

560 Fisgard Street, Victoria ☎ (250) 381-5355

For an authentic slice of Chinatown, take a seat at Wah Lai Yuen—a restaurant big on space and Formica. Chinese families come for the excellent, well-priced food. Ask your server what's good that day, and be sure to try the hot, moist buns filled with barbecued pork and the *whor wonton*—a steaming bowl of wontons, sliced barbecued pork, black mushrooms, prawns, and bok choy.

Good Life Bookstore and Cafe

2113 Otter Point Road, Sooke ☎ (250) 642-6821

You can read while you eat in this charming little house where the living room now serves as the dining room, and the two bedrooms make up the bookstore. Fresh soups, caesar salad, and an ever-changing roster of main courses are offered in the cute cafe decorated with fresh flowers. An ideal teatime table is tucked in the corner of the bookstore.

Mom's Cafe

2036 Shields Road, Sooke ☎ (250) 642-3314

Mom's dishes out real food—from hot meatloaf sandwiches with mashed potatoes for $8 to bluenose chowder served in a bread basket for $5. There are two sizes of liver and onions, too. Leave room for the homemade blackberry pie. The nonsmoking section may be healthier, but the smokers get all the great booths.

Cheap Sleeps

Backpacker's Hostel

1418 Fernwood Road, Victoria, BC V8V 4P7 ☎ (250) 386-4471

Located near downtown Victoria, this hostel offers two floors of male and female dorms and a co-ed loft on the top floor. A couple of double rooms are available for about $30 each, and there's even a honeymoon suite with a queen-size bed and a private bath (who said hostels are no fun?). The Wednesday night barbecues are a bargain.

Battery Street Guest House
670 Battery Street, Victoria, BC V8V 1E5 ☎ (250) 385-4632

Proprietor Pamela Verduyn, a gracious Dutch woman, lives in the attic of her 1898 B&B and reserves the six spacious, homey downstairs rooms for guests. Some rooms boast ocean views and two have a sink and a toilet (but no bathtub). The rest of the guests share two bathrooms. This reasonably priced guest house is located in the James Bay neighborhood, just around the corner from Beacon Hill Park.

Cherry Bank Hotel
825 Burdett Avenue, Victoria, BC V8W 1B3 ☎ (250) 385-5380

This 26-room Victorian house is a congenial spot that caters to a working-class crowd. Guest rooms lack TVs and telephones (and there are no nonsmoking rooms, which explains why the units smell of air freshener), but they're clean, comfortable, and surprisingly quiet, considering the pub and restaurant below. Some rooms have kitchenettes. In the off season, the units with private baths are quite decently priced. Breakfast is served downstairs in the old-fashioned, saloon-style Cherry Bank Spare Rib House restaurant and is included in the room rate. The hotel's game room features tables with built-in trivia games, and there is a sing-along piano bar in the pub.

Christine's Place
1408 Taunton Street, Victoria, BC V8R 1W9 ☎ (250) 595-4774

This elegant 1910 heritage home was completely gutted in 1994—and now has a cheery, bright, modern, townhouselike interior. The comfortable living area with TV, handsome book-lined dining room, and high-tech kitchen have a "model home" look about them, as do the two small guest rooms (which share a bath) and the larger suite with a private bath. Interestingly, this ever-so-much-fussier B&B is affiliated with the nearby Renouf House (see below); owner Christine Rougeau is the sister of Renouf's inexhaustible Caroline Cooper, who handles reservations—and baking duties—for both houses.

Crystal Court Motel
701 Belleville Street, Victoria, BC V8W 1A2 ☎ (250) 384-0551

Built in 1950, the Crystal Court was the first motel built in downtown Victoria—and it's still one of the city's best bargains. Centrally located, the motel is only a block from Crystal Garden, the Royal British Columbia Museum, and the Inner Harbour. Every other room has a fully equipped kitchen (for only an additional $2) stocked with everything but a casserole dish and roasting pan. All the rooms have either refrigerators or old-fashioned iceboxes, private bathrooms, color TVs, radios, and phones.

Hotel Douglas
1450 Douglas Street, Victoria, BC V8W 2G1 ☎ (250) 383-4157

Opposite City Hall in the hectic heart of the city, the old Hotel Douglas can't promise quiet, modern rooms, but it can (and does) offer spacious, clean, well-maintained accommodations with a TV, telephone, oversize closet, and bathroom. This very basic hotel also has a small cafe and a cocktail lounge with musical entertainment ranging from jazz to karaoke.

The James Bay Inn

270 Government Street, Victoria, BC V8V 2L2 ☎ (250) 384-7151

This longtime tranquil budget favorite underwent a facelift in 1992 and, with it, an upgrade that included an upgraded price. Peak season prices are high, but the rates are reasonable for rooms without a private bath from October 1 to April 30. The interior of this 1907 Edwardian manor, the last home of famed painter Emily Carr, has been completely renovated. A turn-of-the-century Victorian look, complete with reproduction antique furnishings, now extends from the lobby to the guest rooms. The Colonial Cafe serves budget-priced meals, and the James Bay Inn Pub pours ales; inn guests get a 15 percent break at both establishments.

Lilac House

252 Memorial Crescent, Victoria, BC V85 3J2 ☎ (250) 389-0252

The best thing about this authentically restored Victorian house is its location on a quiet street opposite beautiful, historic Ross Bay Cemetery, where the dearest of Victoria's dearly departed (including coal baron Robert Dunsmuir and painter Emily Carr) are buried. You will rest in peace in one of Lilac House's three guest rooms, artfully gussied up with lilac colors and tasteful antiques. Unfortunately, there's only one shared bathroom for guests, and it has a tub but no shower. Owner Gail Harris is a writer whose imagined history of the 1892 house and its inhabitants was the basis for a book of poetry and a locally produced play.

Renouf House Bed & Breakfast

2010 Stanley Avenue, Victoria, BC V8R 3X6 ☎ (250) 595-4774

What do you get when you cross Mother Jones with Martha Stewart? Why, Caroline Cooper, of course. When the surprisingly young owner of this stately 1912 heritage home isn't cooking, cleaning, or booking custom-guided tours for Intertidal Explorations (a sea kayaking and sailing company owned by Cooper and her partner, Shaen Chambers), she'll be happy to share her recipe for homemade muesli, her opinions on clearcutting and sewage disposal, and her grand store of knowledge about traversing Vancouver Island's backcountry. The Renouf, located in Victoria's Fernwood neighborhood, has four simply but prettily appointed guest rooms that share two baths, and a common room that doubles as an office/gallery. And while the B&B room rates are among the lowest in town (less than $50, including a scrumptious breakfast), the dormlike "bunk and breakfast" in the basement costs a measly $19.75 per person (same great breakfast). Two rooms with four railcar-style bunks each share a modern bathroom and a fully equipped kitchen—perfect for a group of bosom buddies on a budget. Plus, a new self-contained room with a private bath, queen-size bed, and kitchenette comes at a very reasonable rate.

Travellers Inn on Gorge

120 Gorge Road E, Victoria, BC V9A 1L3 ☎ (250) 388-6611

Yes, it's a chain hotel, but it's also right on beautiful Gorge Waterway, the units have two king-size beds, and there's complimentary coffee, juice, and continental breakfast. And believe it or not, there's also a pool, sauna, hot tub, and free covered parking.

Help with Reservations

Few tourist offices are better organized than the Tourism Victoria Travel InfoCentre (812 Wharf St; (250)382-2127). No room at any inn? The reservations hotline has the skinny on last-minute bookings; (800)663-3883. They'll even steer you to discounts and do their best to stick to your price range.

University of Victoria Housing and Conference Services

Parking Lot 5 off Sinclair Road (PO Box 1700) Victoria, BC V8W 2Y2
☎ **(250) 721-8395**

From May to August, when university students are on holiday, their campus dormitory rooms are open to visitors. Play it safe and book ahead for the single (about $32) or twin-bed rooms ($34), although some units may be available on a drop-in basis. Toilets, showers, pay phones, and a TV lounge are on every floor; there's also a laundry room in each residence building, and towel and linen service. A full breakfast is included. Guests have access to campus services.

The Vacationer

1143 Leonard Street, Victoria, BC V8V 2S3 ☎ **(250) 382-9469**

How many B&Bs let you know you're welcome to invite friends over for a visit? Anne and Henry DeVries raised their family here, and now they're raising the spirits of weary travelers with their pleasant inn. The Vacationer borders Beacon Hill Park; take a walk there or, better yet, borrow one of their bikes for a spin. Four-course breakfasts are served, too.

Victoria International Hostel

516 Yates Street, Victoria, BC V8W 1K8 ☎ **(250) 385-4511**

Victoria's youth hostel is housed in a wonderful, renovated, late 19th-century heritage property just a few steps from Wharf Street and the waterfront, in the heart of downtown. The men's and women's dormitory rooms together offer 109 rooms, with toilets and hot showers down the halls. A pair of fully equipped kitchens, a dining room, a TV lounge, a library, a game room, and a laundry round out the place. There is also lots of info here for those seeking cheap eats, travel-adventure trips, and rides (and riders) to points beyond. A night in a bunk will cost only about $19 ($15.50 for hostel members), and family rooms are available for a few bucks more per person. Beds fill up fast during the summer months, so be sure to reserve in advance.

YM-YWCA of Victoria

880 Courtney Street, Victoria, BC V8W 1C4 ☎ **(250) 386-7511**

This adult women's residence, a few blocks east of downtown, has 31 small college-style rooms with twin beds, a dresser and closet, and little else. They're clean but basic, with shared toilets and showers, and available only on a nightly basis from May through September (rooms are rented by the month the rest of the year). The building has a TV lounge, pay phones, laundry facilities, and a budget-priced cafeteria; guests are invited to use the Y's swimming pool and other athletic facilities.

Blackfish Bed & Breakfast

2440 Blackfish Road, Sooke, BC V0S 1N0 ☎ (250)642-6864

A bargain bed with an oceanfront location and a spectacular, secluded pebble beach? Could it be true? How 'bout 35 bucks for a bunk in the basement bedrooms? The rooms aren't as special as the outdoor scenery, but at these prices, who's complaining? Families with children and pets are welcome. If you have a large party, consider the nine-person cottage that rents for $125 per night—that's only $14 per person for a full house.

Dutch Retreat Country Cottage

2882 Sooke River Road, Sooke, BC V0S 1N0 ☎ (250)642-3812

Dutch hosts Mia and Ernie Van Beers offer a quaint, self-contained one-bedroom cottage overlooking Sooke River, home to many happy geese and ducks. The cottage is close to the Galloping Goose hiking and cycling trail, too. No smoking.

Mrs. Lewers Farmhouse Bed & Breakfast

5526 Sooke Road, Sooke, BC V0S 1N0 ☎ (250)642-3150

Who can resist the bucolic cherry orchard surrounding this B&B with two very private and cozy guest rooms? (Psst . . . the rooms were literally former chicken coops!) Although the bathroom is shared, you get your own farm-fresh eggs.

Vancouver Island: West Coast

Only two paved roads briefly touch Vancouver Island's western edge. But where these roads end, a natural path to adventure begins: long, sandy beaches and thriving tide pools in Pacific Rim National Park, nature trails through cedar groves on remote islands, a rain forest with natural hot springs, colonies of sea lions, and—perhaps the biggest attraction of all—migrating gray whales, whose vapor spouts trail across breathtaking and often moody skies every March and September.

At the very end of Highway 4 is Tofino, a small town built by loggers and fishermen and now populated by a number of watchful environmentalists. A sense of serenity has always encouraged a more laid-back lifestyle among the locals. Though Pacific Rim National Park has an average of 148 inches of rainfall a year (compared to Seattle's 39 inches) and only two remaining groves of old-growth forest, the park's challenging terrain is becoming a popular destination for adventurous travelers. (Even in the slack season, the area's ever-changing canvas attracts curious onlookers who are fascinated by the dramatic winter storms.) Too many tourists can be as hard on the environment as too much logging. Trouble is, the local economy needs both. Despite philosophical differences in recent times, this is one of the few areas on Vancouver Island where the residents recognize the importance of maintaining a delicate balance between the economy and the environment. They've been working hard to welcome tourism but not encourage it, to regulate logging but not end it, and to limit development but not stop it.

Access

There is no inexpensive or quick way to get to the west coast of Vancouver Island because it is not on the road to anywhere, and first you have to get to Vancouver Island. Catch a **ferry** to Nanaimo from Horseshoe Bay or Tsawwassen; (250)943-9331. The sailing from Tsawwassen is about a half hour longer. Both routes cost about $28 for the car and driver, and $6 for other passengers. Discounts are available to British Columbia students, seniors, and groups of 15 or more.

Tofino is about 322 kilometers (200 miles) from Nanaimo at the end of Highway 4. Laidlaw Coach Lines, (800)318-0818 or (250)753-4371, runs the only scheduled **bus** service on the island. A bus departs from Nanaimo once a day to Tofino and Ucluelet for about $50 round trip.

Exploring

Pacific Rim National Park, (250)726-7721, the first national marine park established in Canada, encompasses three separate areas—the West Coast Trail, Broken Islands, and Long Beach—all of which offer beautiful views of the Pacific Ocean. The **West Coast Trail**, a rugged 72-kilometer path, stretches along the southernmost portion of the park. It can be traveled only by foot (from Port Renfrew to Bamfield), and is a strenuous but spectacular five- to seven-day hike for hardy and experienced backpackers. Since the number of hikers is now limited in order to protect against overuse, reservations are necessary and can be made after March 1 by calling (250)728-1282.

Or sample the trail on a day hike from **Bamfield**, a tiny fishing village at the trail's northern end. The *Lady Rose,* (800)663-7192 or (250)723-8313, sails between Bamfield and Port Alberni every few days and is a relaxing alternative to the heavily trafficked gravel logging road

that connects the two towns (see "Barkley Sound Cruise" tip). In Bamfield you can rent boats for fishing or exploring the islands.

The Broken Islands—more than 100 islands located at the entrance to Barkley Sound—are accessible by boat only (take the *Lady Rose* from Port Alberni). This area is famous for sea lions, seals, and whales, and is very popular with anglers, skin divers, and kayakers. You can arrange island drop-offs and pickups via the *Lady Rose* .

Long Beach, on the Himwista Peninsula, is a 30-kilometer expanse of sand and rocky outcroppings backed by forest and mountains. There are many great spots for beach walks and short coastal hikes. If chasing around a little dimpled white ball is your idea of exercise, take advantage of the good golfing deals at the Long Beach Golf Course; (250)725-3332.

For more information on Pacific Rim National Park, visit the information center at the park entrance on Highway

Whale Watching

Watch the mighty gray whales feeding in the great Pacific here from March through October. You can save some bucks on all tours by traveling in groups of eight. Zodiacs (inflatable boats) offer the most exciting whale-watching excursions (the motorized rafts keep you close to the water's surface). This also means you might get wet, but rain gear is usually provided. Be forewarned: The ride can be a little rough, especially for those with back problems. For Zodiac tour info, call Remote Passages at (800)666-9833 (British Columbia only) or (250)725-3330; all tours are based in Tofino. Remote Passages also offers families a 10 percent discount on all tours, except in August. For other whale-watching companies, call the Ucluelet Chamber of Commerce, (250)726-4641.

Barkley Sound Cruise

*If Ucluelet or Bamfield (at the northern end of the West Coast Trail) is your desti-
nation, leave the car in Port Alberni and hop on the* **Lady Rose***, which carries
mail and cargo in addition to passengers; (800)663-7192 or (250)723-8313.
This stout packet freighter departs from the Harbour Quay at Argyle Street Dock in Port
Alberni and voyages through the Broken Islands in Barkley Sound to Bamfield on Tuesday,
Thursday, and Saturday (as well as Friday and Sunday from June to the end of September,
with special Sunday trips during July and August that also stop at the Broken Islands).
Round-trip fare is approximately $40 (BCAA and AAA members get a 10 percent dis-
count). From early June to late September, she sails for Ucluelet on Monday, Wednesday,
and Friday. The* Lady Rose's *five-hour cruise down Alberni Inlet and through the Broken
Islands offers breathtaking scenery—not to mention a much better way to reach these
remote towns than navigating the rough roads. You can also order breakfast and lunch on
board, and the galley food ain't bad. Kayakers can make arrangements to be dropped off
or picked up at Sechart Island.*

4, or call (250)726-4212. Or visit the **Wickaninnish Interpretive Center**, 10 kilometers north of Ucluelet off Highway 4, (250)726-4701, which has park information and interesting oceanic exhibits, including displays and films on whales. The center's expansive view can be enhanced by peering into the telescopes on the observation decks.

At the very tip of Esowitsa Peninsula sits the small town of **Tofino**. You can easily spend most of the day wandering through the town's two fine **native art galleries**: Eagle Aerie Gallery, (250)725-3235, owned by celebrated native artist Roy Vickers, and House of Himwista (which includes a gallery, restaurant, and lodging facilities; (800)899-1947 or (250)725-2017).

Although everything north of Tofino is accessible only by water or air, you don't need to bring your own boat (or plane). **Water taxis** are as ubiquitous here as taxicabs are in Manhattan. They all charge about the same fare (approximately $20 for a drop-off and pickup to nearby Meares Island, and $55 for a round trip to Hot Springs Cove, about a half hour up the coast; see below for more information about the hot springs). **Whale-watching trips** cost about $50 for a 2½-hour tour. (Lower-priced tours spend less time on the water, diminishing your chances of seeing the whales.) The best months for catching a glimpse of these magnificent marine mammals are March and April. (See "Whale Watching" tip.)

If you're an adventurous camper, pull out a map of the area, pick an island or an inlet, and ask one of the water taxis to

Best Beaches

*Long Beach, all 18 sandy kilometers of it, wins top honors for its sheer expansive-
ness. Cox and Chesterman Beaches get the prize for best breakers, while Templar
offers the most peace and MacKenzie the most warmth. Florencia Bay, aka Wreck
Bay, was once home to squatters but is now a local favorite with good tide pools and no
crowds. Note that Long Beach and Florencia Bay are within Pacific Rim National Park
and thus require the $8 day pass or the 2-hour parking fee of $3.*

Park Tips

Don't miss Pacific Rim National Park's self-guided boardwalk loop trail through the weird woods on Shorepine Bog Trail, the site of stubby, centuries-old, broccoli-like trees. Pick up the free "Hiker's Guide" at the Pacific Rim Park InfoCentre, (250)726-4212, just five minutes down the road after you turn north to Tofino from the Highway 4 junction. Better yet, buy the new Official Guide/Pacific Rim National Park Reserve or Bruce Obee's excellent Pacific Rim Explorer, loaded with history, practical tips, and such surprising tidbits as how whales procreate. To park your vehicle within park boundaries, you'll need to buy an $8 day pass from one of the dispensers throughout the park; Credit card or cash is accepted. For more Pacific Rim National Park info, tune your car radio to AM 1260 once you pass the park's sign announcing Long Beach weather and park news.

drop you off there. You can camp as long as you like, and the taxi will pick you up at a prearranged time.

Seasoned and wannabe **sea kayakers** should explore **Clayoquot Sound**. Neophyte paddlers can contact the Tofino Sea-Kayaking Company, (250)725-4222, for information on guided day trips in single or double kayaks (the intimidated can double up with an instructor). Rentals are available for experienced paddlers. (Psst . . . one of the best views in Tofino is from the rental company's tiny three-stool seaside espresso bar.) Trips range from a 2½-hour sunset paddle to a full-day excursion to Meares Island.

If you're willing to part with several more dollars, consider visiting the islands here by air instead of by water taxi: Tofino Air Lines (1st St Dock, Tofino; (250)725-4454) will drop you off on the island or cove of your choice and pick you up at a prearranged time. The company has four **floatplanes**: three of them

hold up to three passengers each and charge about $125 per 20 minutes; the other accommodates up to seven passengers and costs about $190 per 20 minutes. Therefore, if you can fill up the bigger plane and split the cost, your fare will be much less expensive. You can also cut costs by being flexible; airpool with other parties, or arrange for a drop-off with someone who is being picked up at the same place and time.

Another island highlight is a visit to **Hot Springs Cove**. The springs are reachable only by boat or floatplane, followed by an unforgettable forest hike into the 109-degree waterfalls and pools. (Combine the trip with a whale-watching cruise, and you can save a considerable amount of money.) If you can't bear to leave the springs, book one of the six self-contained units in tiny Hot Springs Lodge; (250)724-8570. You'll have to bring your own supplies and do your own cooking but, oh, the peace of it all!

Cheap Eats

Alley Way Cafe

305 Campbell Street, Tofino ☎ (250)725-3105

Craving a vegetarian burrito? Alley Way's Lore Rowland whips up a mean, big burrito and other mucho-gusto-size portions of tasty ethnic-inspired, health-conscious fare until 8pm at this funky little eatery. Breakfasts, too.

Coffee Pod

461 Campbell Street, Tofino ☎ (250)725-4246

Tofino's local version of Starbucks, the Coffee Pod dishes up atmosphere as well as breakfast and lunch. Expect eggs, ham, sausage, and bagels for breakfast, and homemade soups, burritos, and the celebrated Podwich—their take on panini—for lunch. The Pod closes at 5pm.

Common Loaf Bake Shop

180 1st Street, Tofino ☎ (250)725-3915

This perennial town meeting spot is the place to find out what's happening on the environmental front. You can pick up save-the-trees newsletters and eavesdrop—or join in—on the latest strategy discussions. Wonderful cinnamon buns and healthful peasant bread are tempting year-round; come summer, pizza's the thing and the Common Loaf is the busiest nook in town. Carry your food upstairs to the log tables and benches, and get into the relax-and-crusade mood this place inspires.

Weigh West Marine Resort

634 Campbell Street, Tofino ☎ (250)725-3277

Solid pub food is served here for lunch and dinner. It's tough to beat a cold beer, a half crab, the local color, and the waterfront setting overlooking the inlet. All patrons must be over 19.

Cheap Sleeps

Middle Beach Lodge at the Beach

200 McKenzie Road (PO Box 413), Tofino, BC V0R 2Z0 ☎ (250)725-2900

Tofino is always crowded in the summer, so bargain beds are difficult to find. Unfortunately, Middle Beach qualifies as a cheap sleep only during the month of March (a good time for storm and whale watching), but what a slice of heaven! Stay in the beautiful adult retreat (expect small rooms), and kick back with a good book in front of the rock fireplace in the lodge's wonderful lounge. From April to October, guests get a 10 percent discount for two-day stays, 15 percent for three days, and 20 percent for five days. Closed from November through February.

Travel Web Sites

Visit the site www.travel.bc.ca and you'll find more than 4,000 tourist-related British Columbia businesses, ranging from B&Bs to restaurants and kayaking operators. Linking to other sites is a snap: for example, type in llama and voilà, you'll get a list of every llama-based business in the province. You can also make reservations here through Super, Natural British Columbia Travel Reservations and Information Service; (800)663-6000.

Island Sleeps

What could be dreamier than sailing away to an island inn? Well, okay, so most of these inns are like hostels with shared showers and whatnot, but the hosts are welcoming and you can't beat the ambience. Check out Dream Isle's cabins, (250)726-7827; Neilsen Island Inn's four bedrooms, (250)726-7968; and Vargas Island Inn & Hostel's various accommodations (see review in Cheap Sleeps), (250)725-3309. Proprietors will scoop you up at their local dock.

Midori's B&B

370 Gibson Street (PO Box 582), Tofino, BC V0R 1Z0 ☎ (250) 725-2203

An international clientele tends to book this B&B's three guest rooms, each with a private bath. Guests share a common room (sorry, no fireplace) and deck. Midori's is particularly convenient if you're limited to schlepping around by bus (a bus line runs nearby, and the friendly proprietors will even pick you up at the bus stop if you let them know in advance when you're arriving).

Netty's Bed & Breakfast

2384 Lynn Road, Chesterman Beach, Tofino, BC V0R 2Z0 ☎ (250) 725-3451

Amiable Netty Cullion is reason enough to hang your hat here. Her cedar home is a short walk from the beach, and she offers a guest room with twin beds and a loft that sleeps up to four. Netty is a great resource on the Tofino community, too. If you pine for a place of your own, ask her about renting a cabin in the area. Children are welcome here; smoking is permitted only on the porch. Ask about off-season rates.

Paddler's Inn Bed and Breakfast

320 Main Street (PO Box 620), Tofino, BC V0R 2Z0 ☎ (250) 725-4222

Making this good place even better are the bookstore and espresso bar that Dorothy Baert runs downstairs in her bed-and-breakfast-cum-sea-kayaking-company headquarters on the Tofino waterfront. The five rooms in Tofino's original hotel are as basic and lovely as Tofino itself: no phones, no TVs, white cotton sheets, down comforters, shared bath. You can serve yourself from a continental breakfast bar in the kitchen, or opt for the Paddlers' Suite, where you can cook your own. Closed some winters.

Tofino Swell Lodge

341 Olsen Road (PO Box 160), Tofino, BC V0R 1Z0 ☎ (250) 725-3274

A waterfront location near the Crab Dock and a view of the inlet are this simple lodge's best attributes. Rooms are motel-like. Guests have access to a full kitchen, barbecue pit, and hot tub. Beautiful gardens decorate the landscape.

Vargas Island Inn & Hostel
Vargas Island (PO Box 267), Tofino, BC V0R 2Z0 ☎ (250) 725-3309

It will take you a couple of hours to travel to this lodging by kayak, but what a romantic way to reach your getaway. Then again, you could arrive via the 20-minute skiff ride from Tofino. The wonderfully welcoming proprietor, Marilyn Buckle, offers seven guest rooms in the main house, two A-frame cabins, a "beach studio," and camping sites. Whichever accommodation you choose, prepare to make a few sacrifices—for example, there are no showers (except in the summer). Most guests think the inconveniences are a small price to pay to experience this island's many charms. A new store is stocked with soup, fresh seafood, snacks, and the like—enough to fuel you for the duration of your stay. Hostel members get a $10 discount on the nightly rate. The inn's owners make a pickup every day at the Crab Dock just south of town, and they'll give you a ride for $15 round trip—less than the cost of a water taxi.

Vancouver Island: Inside Passage

Half a million cruise ship passengers can't be wrong. The natural setting of Vancouver Island's eastern coast, plied daily by the 20-plus Alaska-bound cruise ships whose summer homeport is Vancouver, is unabashedly spectacular: idyllic islands ringed with serene waters, snow-capped mountains rising above luxuriously forested hills, and the sparkling lights of Vancouver across the water to the east. But the mixture of fishing, industry, and the oddly crafted dose of tourism hasn't always succeeded in creating welcoming—or even interesting—towns, although the locals seem to have loosened up a bit over the past few years. Still, there's much to be gleaned from the eastern shores of the island if you look in the right places. A new highway now parallels sections of the renowned Island Highway (aka Highway 19), primarily a two-lane stretch from Nanaimo to the north. A good look at a map shows how amazingly few roads there are on Vancouver Island. If you get stuck in traffic in the summer crawl up-island north of Nanaimo, just try to think of yourself as part of the remaining slice of a wagons-north convoy.

Exploring

North of Victoria lies the **Cowichan Valley**, meaning "land warmed by the sun," a gentle stretch of farmland and forest that includes Mill Bay, Shawnigan Lake, Cowichan Bay, Duncan, Chemainus, Ladysmith, Yellow Point, and Lake Cowichan. Keep an eye out for signs to small farm **wineries** with shops, such as Cherry Point Vineyards (840 Cherry Point Rd, Cobble Hill; (250)743-1272).

Duncan is a town known mainly for its large Cowichan Indian population. The artistic Cowichans carve the totem poles that line the highway and appear through-

out town, and knit the namesake hand-crafted sweaters familiar in the Northwest. (Beware: British Columbia is loaded with pseudo-Cowichan sweaters. Chances of finding the real thing are greater here at the source.) Be sure to stop at the much-lauded **Cowichan Native Village** (200 Cowichan Way, Duncan; (250)746-8119) for a chance to try traditional food, watch carvers at work on poles or jewelry, and view the "Great Deeds" multimedia theater presentation. Admission $6, or $15 for families. On a summer evening, take in the

Hollyhock Seminar Centre

Hollyhock has great packages, especially the special spring "Open Community" program from mid-March to mid-June, which offers mini-workshops (from cooking classes to Tibetan chanting). Even if you don't think workshops on tantric loving are your thing, visit Hollyhock anyway; you'll be surprised, delighted, and amazed. The heart of Hollyhock may well be the walled garden with vegetables, sweet-scented honeysuckle, great orange Oriental poppies, sunflowers, and the startlingly white blooms of Datura stramonium, aka locoweed, which was used as a hallucinogenic by Don Juan in Tales of Power. Gardeners will cut herbs or armfuls of flowers for you, and the Garden Store is filled with local plant seeds (great inexpensive gifts), herb vinegars, and dried flowers. See the review of Hollyhock's restaurant in Cheap Eats too. Call (800)933-6339 for general information.

memorable four-hour program "Feast & Legends" ($35). Locals like the Arbutus Cafe (195 Kenneth St, Duncan; (250)746-5443) for sandwiches, burgers, and good conversation.

One of the best things about the Island Highway is driving off it whenever you can—detouring inland or to an island. Head west from Duncan to the large **Cowichan Lake** and the Honeymoon Bay Wildflower Reserve (something of a summer resort area in itself). Lake Cowichan is a resort community on Cowichan Lake with an excellent provincial campground. It's also the launching point for trips out to the West Coast's now-famous old-growth forests of Carmanagh Valley, site of much controversy between loggers and environmentalists.

When MacMillan Bloedel closed its sawmill in the town of **Chemainus**, residents of the community (known as "the little town that did") saved it from becoming a ghost town by covering it with enticing **historical murals** that make for a fun wander (especially if your legs need stretching). Grab an ice cream from Billy's Delight Ice Cream Parlour (9752 Willow St, Chemainus; (250)246-4131) and follow the yellow footsteps on the sidewalk to the murals. Continue down Oak Street to the ferry terminal, where more murals grace the walls of Old Town. On the way through **Ladysmith**, stop at the Crow and Gate Neighbor-

hood Pub (2313 Yellow Point Rd, Ladysmith; (250)722-3731) for some soul-warming English country food: flaky pasties, steak and kidney pie, and Yorkshire pudding.

You'll know you're close to Nanaimo when you spot signs telling you that 11 kilometers south is the **Bungy Zone Adrenalin Centre**; (888)668-7874, (250)716-7874, or (250)753-5867. More than 35,000 adrenaline seekers have jumped off the Zone's 43-meter bridge—North America's only legal bungee bridge—tied by the feet to a stretchy umbilical cord. A jump is definitely not cheap—$95, plus an extra charge if you want it on videotape—but watching is free. Been there, done that? Check out the zone's three new attractions: Ultimate Swing (experience speeds up to 140kmph); Flying Fox (ride a "zip line" along the canyon), and Rap Jumping (make a rapid rappel straight down from the bridge using mountaineering equipment).

If Victoria's history is genteel, **Nanaimo**'s is working-class, although its coal mines are long gone. With the help of the aforementioned bungee jumping, as well as bathtub races (an annual, internationally known event offering big prizes) and Nanaimo Bars (an addictive chocolate and butter confection), the island's second-largest city has put itself on the tourist map. Recently, it has even acquired some charm, with interesting

Nootka Sound Day Trip

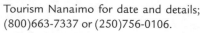

The MV Uchuck III, a nifty converted 1943 minesweeper, now chugs the West Coast inlets, carrying freight, passengers, and mail to isolated communities along Nootka Sound. The one-day round trip to Tahsis—with a 1-hour stopover—is a bargain at about $45; Government Wharf, Gold River, (250)283-2325.

boutiques in the old city's Heritage Mews (on Fitzwilliam St, near downtown Nanaimo) and intriguing restaurants such as Filthy McNasty (at the corner of Commercial and Terminal Sts, Nanaimo; (250)753-7011), known for its live jazz, lattes, and wunder-muffins, and the Olde Firehall Coffee Roasterie (#2-34 Nicol St (Island Hwy), Nanaimo; (250)754-7733; see review in Cheap Eats). Other fun shops in the retail core include the venerable Bookstore on Bastion Street (76 Bastion St, Nanaimo; (250)753-3011) and the Scotch Bakery (87 Commercial St, Nanaimo; (250)753-3521), where you can sink your teeth into a true **Nanaimo Bar**, if you haven't already sampled a free one at Tourism Nanaimo (2290 Bowen Rd, Nanaimo; (800)663-7337 or (250)756-0106). Ask there for the "ultimate" recipe as well as discount coupons for everything from golf courses to restaurants and museums.

Pipers Lagoon, northeast of downtown, includes a spit that extends into Georgia Strait and is backed by sheer bluffs that are great for bird watching. **Newcastle Island**, (250)753-5811, is an autoless wilderness island reached by ferries that leave hourly from behind Nanaimo's civic arena; it has a long shoreline trail, a trail for the handicapped, and some fine old-growth timber. Come summer, fans of the swinging big band sounds of the '30s and '40s ride the ferry to the island on one magic night in August to dance to Campa Big Band, a group of amateur and professional musicians who play to capacity crowds. If the island's campground is full, you can spill into the meadow and stay the night. Call

Tourism Nanaimo for date and details; (800)663-7337 or (250)756-0106.

The trick in Nanaimo is to escape the frightening sprawl of roads you'll hit on arrival at the ferry terminal. Your best bet is to get into the heart of Nanaimo, park your car, and explore on foot, bike, or ferry. The **waterfront walk**—from Maffeo-Sutton Park along Swy-A-Lana Marine Park (a human-made lagoon) to the Bastion (an 1853 fort)—is a pleasant diversion. The **Nanaimo District Museum** (100 Cameron Rd, Nanaimo; (250)753-1821) explores early coastal geology and offers dioramas of native life and a life-size replica of part of a coal mine. Admission is $2.

Just north of the city center, the younger, boom box–toting set hangs out on the rocky beach of **Departure Bay** in the summer; the quieter crowd, and those with young children, head farther north to **Rathtrevor Provincial Park**, where sandy shores invite sunbathers and tide pools encourage exploring. The park has a great campground, but car space is booked three days ahead in summer (try walking or bicycling there instead). Departure Bay is the place for reasonable water-sports rentals. North Island Water-Sports (2755 Departure Bay Rd, Nanaimo; (250)758-2488) rents kayaks at $40 per day for a single or $75 for a double.

Parksville and Qualicum Beach are coastal towns with broad, sweeping beaches. **Parksville** (with its fairy-tale miniature golf course and "imported" sandy beaches) is rather commercial, but it's a better choice if you're traveling with the kids. The much more low-key **Qualicum Beach** (British royalty have stayed with "friends" in the area) has huge sandbars and an interesting, walkable village worth a detour, but the beach is pebbly when the tide's in. Resorts and hotels crowd the shore, and golf courses fill all other available space.

Consider a side trip west on Highway 4 toward the paper-mill town of **Port Alberni**. The combination of oddities and natural wonders on the way make the trip worthwhile: Englishman River Falls, a provincial park with pretty hiking trails and some swimming holes; the surprisingly interesting Butterfly World (1080 Winchester Rd, Coombs; (250)248-7026), where butterflies fly free in an oversize greenhouse (open mid-March through October); Coombs Old Country Market, where goats live on the grass roof in summer (Hwy 4, Coombs; (250)248-6272); and Cathedral Grove, a wondrous slice of old-growth forest 11 kilometers west of Coombs. Be sure to park and walk, not just drive, through. "Port," as the locals call it, is a mill town now bent on tourism too, with a cherry festival in April and the Alberni Valley Museum, which offers great exhibits on local history (4255 Wallace St, in the Parks and Recreation Eco Aquatic Center, Port Alberni; (250)723-2181). For information on Port Alberni's *Lady Rose* and Vancouver Island's Pacific Rim National Park, see the Vancouver Island: West Coast chapter.

Before reaching Comox Valley, you round the bend in **Fanny Bay**. Look for the bright blue Fanny Bay Inn (7480 Island Hwy, Fanny Bay; (250)335-2323)—it's hard to miss. Known to locals as the FBI, this is the spot for general (and generally good) pub fare, such as creamy chowder with buttery garlic bread, accompanied by a good pint. Down the road a bit farther, you can catch a ferry for **Denman and Hornby Islands**, two laid-back islands where the lifestyle is reminiscent of the '60s.

Comox Valley is the pretty valley that tourism forgot. Most people mentally jump from Qualicum Beach to Campbell River, and admittedly, from the highway Comox and Courtenay look like mill towns. But real estate is booming here; it's the province's fastest-growing region, and it's also the launch point for good **skiing** at Mount Washington. In summer you can ride the ski lift to a mile above sea level and then mountain-bike down. Few people know that this ski area gets more snow than any other in British Columbia and has 35 kilometers of cross-country skiing trails as well. Lift tickets are in the $36 range all week long. On Getaway Tuesday, a lift ticket, lesson, and lunch set you back a mere $38 (yup, just $2 for lesson *and* lunch!); call (250)338-1386 for information.

Free Tours in Nanaimo

Enough free tours abound in Nanaimo to keep you entertained for days. Enjoy a walk through the Morrell Wildlife Sanctuary (1050 Nanaimo Lakes Rd; (250)753-5811). Or take one of several self-guided tours at Malaspina University College (900 5th St; (250)753-3245); choose from arboretum nature trails, Tamagawa Gardens, the art gallery and exhibition center, the bee yard, aquaculture, and the Museum of Natural History. There's also St. Jean's Custom Cannery, which cans fish, so bring your catch of the day (242 Southside Dr; (250)754-2185); the MacMillan Bloedel Harmac pulp mill (980 MacMillan Rd; (250)722-3211); and several salmon hatcheries. For more information on all these tours, call Tourism Nanaimo at (800)663-7337 or (250)756-0106.

The towns of Comox, Courtenay, and Cumberland are year-round recreational spots, with skiing in winter and water sports in summer; in milder weather, try kayaking in the harbor with Comox Valley Kayaks (1595 Comox Road, Courtenay; (250)334-BOAT). Of the three towns, **Comox** is the most pleasant. Drive out to Goose Spit for wide-open views of Comox Harbour and the snow-crested mountains sitting back on their haunches; then pass back through Comox for a beer and seafood at the Leeward Pub (649 Anderton Road, Comox; (250)339-5400) or, better yet, have tea at the delightful Filberg Lodge (61 Filberg Rd, Comox; (250)339-2715). This lumberman's home, built of local wood in the early '30s, boasts 9 acres of meadows, orchards, lawns, and specimen trees that slope down to the ocean, and is now home to the annual four-day Filberg Festival of BC Arts and Crafts in early August.

Campbell River, only halfway up the island but as far north as some ever go, is primarily a town for fisherfolk, as is evident in the amenities offered by most of its hotels: smoking, canning, and cleaning (of fish, that is), but not too many Jacuzzis. It has something of the boomtown feel that Victoria must have had when Klondike-bound gold seekers arrived there to provision in the 1890s. Between mid-July and late November, be sure to snorkel down the legendary Campbell River while the steelhead and **salmon** make their way upstream—it's an amazing event to witness. The best reasons to venture this far north are to fish and to strike out east and west—to the lovely, remote islands of Quadra and Cortes, or to **Strathcona Provincial Park**, a hub for hiking and water sports galore. Golfers can try their luck at Storey Creek Golf Club, (250)923-3673, named one of British Columbia's top courses.

Not **fishing** in Campbell River is like not skiing at Whistler. Unfortunately, chartering a boat can be prohibitively expensive. We found only one inexpensive way to fish—cast off from Discovery Pier in downtown Campbell River. It costs only $1 (summer rate) to spend the day under one of the pier's glass enclosures; you can rent equipment at the concession stand for $2 an hour. Kid stuff, you say? Resort guests were gnashing their teeth when someone at the pier hooked a 50-pounder during his lunch hour! Grab some grub at Piccadilly Fish and Chips, housed in the abandoned-looking double-decker bus across the street from Discovery Pier. Del's Drive-In (1423 Island Hwy, Campbell River; (250)287-3661)

Quadra Island

The coves and channels of Quadra Island are lovely from every angle. Hike up Chinese Mountain for a great view of the entire island. In Cape Mudge Village, you'll find the Kwagiulth Museum and Cultural Center, which displays returned potlatch artifacts; (250)285-3733. Ask about making a rubbing of ancient petroglyphs. Then lunch on fresh shrimp at Tsa-Kwa-Luten Lodge, (800)665-7745 or (250)285-2042 (reservations recommended). April Point Lodge is a luxury fishing resort for the rich and famous—General Norman Schwarzkopf, Julie Andrews, and John Wayne are a few of the notables on the guest list—that's worth visiting for at least a drink, despite the sometimes snooty attitude of the staff; (800)663-5555 or (250)285-2222. The 12-minute ferry ride back to Campbell River is a treat in itself; wait for the boat in the Landing Neighbourhood Pub at the ferry landing, a pleasant spot with stained-glass windows, pub grub and beer, and friendly folks; (250)285-3713.

is home to some great burgers.

On **Cortes Island**, two ferry rides away from Campbell River, the soul is free to expand (and does, at Hollyhock Seminar Centre, Canada's leading holistic learning center (see review in Cheap Eats and "Hollyhock Seminar Centre" tip). Many of the island's 800 residents earn their keep by farming and exporting oysters and clams around the world. At the Gorge Marina Resort you can rent scoot-ers ($12 per hour) or boats (from $17). Cortes Cafe, on Manson's Landing, operates on mail days (Monday, Wednesday, and Friday), when it offers espresso and supposedly the best soup on the island; but the atmosphere is strictly local, without much charm. Smelt Bay and Sutil Point are great spots to watch the sun set. **Quadra Island**, the stop between ferries, is lovely, too—and only 12 minutes from Campbell River (see "Quadra Island" tip).

Cheap Eats

Red Rooster Coffee Shop

8432 Trans-Canada Highway, Westholme ☎ (250) 246-9342

Seven dinner entrees priced at about eight bucks each is something to crow about in this rooster-theme restaurant. And be sure to save room for dessert: fresh cheesecake or the incredible banana cream pie.

Mom's Diner

9338 Trans-Canada Highway, Chemainus ☎ (250) 246-1461

Prepare to be mothered by Fjola Roberts when you eat at this original dining car-style diner. She serves the island's best breakfasts—and her hearty portions keep you fueled for most of the day. For only $3.50 you get eggs and a choice of bacon, sausage, or ham, plus a side of either hotcakes, hash browns, or French toast. Lunch specialties include the curry chicken (ask about the two-for-one curry chicken special offered twice a month) and the Wednesday Burger—served only on Wednesdays, natch.

Dot's Cafe

25935 N Island Highway, Nanaimo ☎ (250) 390-3331

Built in 1941, Nanaimo's first diner still serves fish 'n' chips, Greek salads, and burgers, but it's the fresh-baked pies that keep folks coming back. Dot's also offers breakfast all day long.

Olde Firehall Coffee Roasterie

#2-34 Nicol Street (Island Highway), Nanaimo ☎ (250) 754-7733

At last count, the Olde Firehall served 37 types of coffees, 27 teas, and home-made sandwiches and treats (try the Iced Chocolate if you dare). Hand-painted church pews, brick walls, and fire-hall memorabilia set the scene, and board games and newspapers are available for whiling away the time. Upstairs, you can get reasonably priced build-your-own-pasta meals at the popular **Pagliacci's**; (250)754-3443.

Cola Diner
6060 W Island Highway, Qualicum Bay ☎ (250) 757-2029

Step into the Cola Diner and step back in time to the '50s. Nostalgia buffs will enjoy the authentic decor as they sip cherry Cokes, ice cream floats, or thick, creamy shakes. Don't miss the adjacent Cola Emporium, which features a turn-of-the-century soda fountain.

Crown and Anchor Pub
6120 W Island Highway, Qualicum Bay ☎ (250) 757-9444

Just the spot to grab a pint and a tasty, inexpensive lunch or dinner. Show up on a Saturday and take advantage of the cheapster's specials: a draft, a burger, and chicken wings for only $1.49 each.

Beehive
921 Island Highway, Campbell River ☎ (250) 286-6812

At breakfast, make a beeline for a table with a view of the fishing boats docked in the marina, Discovery Passage, and the islands. You'll find everything from eggs Benedict to waffles on the menu—and the thick French toast is a particularly good bet.

The Ideal Cafe
2263 N Island Highway, Campbell River ☎ (250) 287-9055

Truckers and locals know it, and now you do too: the Ideal serves the best all-American cheap eats ($7.50 a plate, plus an extra buck for soup and dessert). Menu highlights include the fish burger, hamburger, liver and onions, roast beef sandwich, and fish 'n' chips. Portions are more than generous (half portions are available too), and the friendly staff is quite attentive.

Hollyhock Seminar Centre
Highfield Road, Cortes Island ☎ (800) 933-6339 or (250) 935-6576

Hollyhock opens its flower-strewn buffet tables to the public for breakfast ($8), lunch ($9), and dinner ($15), and the meals are more than worth the price. Eating here, says Vancouver singer Ann Mortifee, is such a beautiful experience that it becomes almost a sacrament (one that, with luck, includes oysters). Everything from crispy papadams to pungent curries and chocolate-chip cookies is served. Reservations are recommended.

Old Floathouse Restaurant, Gorge Marina Resort
Hunt Road, Cortes Island ☎ (250) 935-6631

Transplanted from Kingcomb Inlet and now landlocked at the Gorge Marina Resort, the Old Floathouse still overlooks the water. On summer evenings patrons spill out onto the deck, sipping white wine and and munching on mussels. Sharing a main course or even an appetizer is just fine with the staff, and it makes the Old Floathouse wonderfully affordable. Prices are lower in the off season.

Cheap Sleeps

Deer Lodge Motel

2529 Trans-Canada Highway, Mill Bay, BC V0R 2P0
☎ (800) 668-5011 or (250) 743-2423

This 30-room motel, with a great view overlooking Georgia Strait and the Gulf Islands, has three wings offering rooms or mini-housekeeping suites, complete with stocked kitchens and fireplaces flanked by easy chairs. The bargain beds don't come with kitchens, but they cost only about $50 ($40 if you skip breakfast).

Chemainus Hostel

9694 Chemainus Road, Chemainus, BC V0R 1K0 ☎ (250) 246-2809

A former logging company house, the Chemainus Hostel has been renovated with the budget traveler in mind ($15 a bunk for nonmembers, plus a small fee for the optional towels and linens). It's an easy walk from the Chemainus murals, the bus, and the E&N Railway, which runs between Victoria and Nanaimo. Expect a clean, bright lodging, with a separate dormitory for men and women. The kitchen is well equipped, and the front porch is a pleasant place to rest your tired dogs on warm days and nights.

Horseshoe Bay Inn

9576 Chemainus Road, Chemainus, BC V0R 1K0 ☎ (250) 246-3425

Here's a good bet for decent, inexpensive lodgings located between Duncan and Nanaimo. Just down the road from the murals and a skip away from a golf course, the Horseshoe Bay Inn is the kind of cozy, family-run place where the owners' grandchildren shyly examine the guests. Some of the rooms have a private bath; others share a bathroom with an old, large tub. The pub downstairs attracts a lively local crowd, and the adjoining restaurant serves reasonably priced fare.

Buccaneer Motel

1577 Stewart Avenue, Nanaimo, BC V9S 4E3 ☎ (250) 753-1246

The Buccaneer doesn't have the waterside setting of the more expensive Moby Dick Motel five blocks down the street, but it has ocean views and a two-story mural of a swashbuckling buccaneer (oh boy!), and it's only three blocks from the BC Ferries terminal at Departure Bay. The rooms are cheery and bright and offer fully stocked kitchenettes. Guests have access to barbecues and picnic tables, and the motel's management is quite accommodating.

Carey House Bed and Breakfast

750 Arbutus Avenue, Nanaimo, BC V9S 5E5 ☎ (250) 753-3601

Friendly proprietress Catherine Molnar offers inexpensive rooms (about $50 for two or $35 for a single lodger) with bathrooms down the hall. But don't let the lack of private bath deter you—it's a small price to pay in exchange for the reasonable rates and the opportunity to enjoy the Carey House's award-winning garden.

Nicol Street Hostel

65 Nicol Street (Island Highway), Nanaimo, BC V9R 4S7
☎ (800) 861-1366 or (250) 753-1188

Open year-round in the heart of Nanaimo, this hostel is only a 5-minute walk from the Newcastle Island ferry, and it even offers rooms for families. Their motto is "under $20 and safe, clean, and comfortable," and that's no lie. Ask about special hostel discounts at nearby businesses. Nicol Street Hostel welcomes Canadians, too—unlike the nearby **Thomson's Hostel**, (250)722-2251, which offers the quiet benefits of a country setting and free use of a canoe or kayak, but has an "international guests only" policy.

Quatna Manor

512 Quatna Road, Qualicum Beach, BC V9K 1B4 ☎ (250) 752-6685

Quatna Manor is a rarity in the world of cheap sleeps. This civilized English Tudor-style home has gorgeous grounds, a fish pond, a grape arbor, and wonderfully cushy lodgings with an elegant, Old World ambience, thanks to proprietors Bill and Betty Ross. Choose from a room with a private or shared bath (during the off season, you might be able to afford a tub of your own). A guest lounge is located on the second floor. The breakfast area is decorated with fine antiques and polished silver.

St. Andrews Lodge and Glen Cottages

3319 W Island Highway, Qualicum Beach, BC V9K 2B3 ☎ (250) 752-6652

Sandwiched between the beach and the highway, St. Andrews is spotlessly clean and a true bargain. The proprietor, Miss Elizabeth Little, has been here since 1938, when the lodge was established and her family began building the little ocean-view cottages, which have names like Glen Morag and Glengarry. The lodge has small rooms with private baths, but the tiny one- and two-bedroom cottages (equipped with cable TV) are the best units—and all of the accommodations are reasonably priced, even during peak season. Unlike neighboring Parksville, Qualicum's beach offers decent swimming opportunities, even when the tide's out. A grocery store and a handful of restaurants are within walking distance.

Greystone Manor

4014 Haas Road (RR 6, Site 684, Comp 2), Courtenay, BC V9N 8H9
☎ (250) 338-1422

If you liked Quatna Manor (see earlier review), you'll be happy here. Mike and Mo Shipton emigrated from Bath and transplanted their love of English gardens

Dorm Stay

You can stay in a single room at Malaspina University College (750 4th St, Nanaimo; (250)754-6338) for as little as $15–$20 per night (it's less if you bring your own linens).

Strathcona Park Lodge

To enjoy breathtaking views of upper Campbell Lake and the surrounding peaks, and to take advantage of the area's boating, rock-climbing, and hiking opportunities, stay at the Strathcona Park Lodge in Campbell River; (250)286-8206. The lodge's hostel accommodations run about $20 per night (call first for availability). You might end up sharing a deluxe cabin with a group of people you've never met—but that's part of the fun.

into the spectacular 1½ acres surrounding one of the valley's oldest houses, built in 1918. Guests lounge on the front deck or, when the weather gets wet, by the sitting-room fire.

The Log Cabin, DeeKayTee Ranch
6301 Headquarters Road, Courtenay, BC V9N 7J3 ☎ (250) 337-5553

This little beauty is a real find! The Log Cabin is a new, cozy, light-colored cabin nestled in the trees on an 80-acre farm. It comfortably sleeps up to four people. Guests may play tennis on the ranch's court or have fun lending a hand with the farm animals. For more solitary pleasures, owners Dan and Maggie Thran can point you toward the Tsolum River swimming hole or some peaceful hiking trails. The $75-per-night rate (for two people) drops to $50 per night if you stay for two days. And who wouldn't?

Haig-Brown House
2250 Campbell River Road, Campbell River, BC V9W 4N7 ☎ (250) 286-6646

Haig-Brown House is one of Vancouver Island's top lodgings. This circa-1920 restored farmhouse, home of the late writer, conservationist, and celebrated fly fisher Roderick Haig-Brown, offers lots of character, an amiable, witty host, a riverfront setting, and a fine country breakfast. Manager/host Kevin Brown (no relation to Roderick) oversees the B&B, which is set on 2 acres of gardens and orchards.

Passage View Motel
517 Island Highway, Campbell River, BC V9W 2B9 ☎ (250) 286-1156

Tucked unobtrusively among a string of expensive highwayside resorts at the south end of town, the Passage View offers pleasant, colorful rooms with a view of Discovery Passage and Quadra Island. You can even access the beach via the small yard in back.

Pier House Bed & Breakfast
670 Island Highway, Campbell River, BC V9W 2C3 ☎ (250) 287-2943

Pier House stands at the entrance to Campbell River's famous fishing pier, where a few 30-pounders have been landed. Built in 1924, it's the oldest house in town and was the home of the region's first provincial police officer. Proprietors Peter Dwillies and Patricia Young have created a B&B that's a charming mix of old curiosity shop and museum. Borrow a tome from their floor-to-ceiling bookshelves or examine their many relics, which include an old short-wave radio. Breakfast is served on bone china while tunes are played on the old Victrola. No children, please.

Roberts Lake Resort

30 kilometers north of Campbell River (RR 1, Sayward, BC V0P 1R0)
☎ (250) 287-9421

Tucked inside remote Sayward Forest, this little resort is a good place to escape civilization (Campbell River and Sayward are 30 kilometers away on either side). Rent one of the five rustic cabins for about $50 per night, or take over the three-bedroom bunkhouse for $80 a night (if available, renting just one of the bunkhouse rooms costs only $40). Enjoy the wildlife, row a boat on desolate Roberts Lake, or visit the small museum featuring old logging equipment.

Joha Eagle View

Quathiaski Cove (PO Box 668), Quadra Island, BC V0P 1N0 ☎ (250) 285-2247

Joyce and Harold Johnson's low-lying house is in a residential area just minutes from the ferry dock (a bonus if you come over as a foot passenger for a night). It sits on the cove overlooking Discovery Passage (the backyard steps lead to the Johnsons' own dock), and you can watch the cruise ships and tugs with barge loads heading farther north. The two guest rooms offer brass beds, antique quilts, and stained-glass windows, and one unit even boasts an ocean view. Guests share the bathroom (and there's another half bath downstairs), the inviting living room is graced with a rock fireplace, and the broad, shade-dappled veranda overlooks the sea. A self-contained lower unit (minimum three-night stay) is $75 per night—a good deal for a family or group. If you're lucky, Joyce will be cooking pancakes with sautéed apples for breakfast. Be sure to ask her for tips on touring the island.

Blue Heron Bed and Breakfast

Potlatch Road, Cortes Island, BC V0P 1K0 ☎ (250) 935-6584

The Blue Heron is a charming waterfront property with three great attractions: deck chairs with a sunset view, Emilia Hansen's oatmeal pancakes with blackberry sauce, and a blissfully peaceful setting that's within earshot of the ocean's waves. The three guest rooms are in a separate wing with a private entrance; the most expensive unit (about $70) has an ocean view and a private bath. A short walk past the B&B's beach leads to a sandier beach.

Gulf Islands

The Gulf Islands, a 240-kilometer chain of small islands in the Strait of Georgia, are British Columbia's more remote version of Washington's San Juans. Similar in geography and character to their southern neighbors, the Gulf Islands also enjoy the same temperate weather and offer wonderful boating and cycling opportunities. Six main islands snug against the southeast coast of Vancouver Island; smaller ones sparkle in nearby waters. Eagles soar above the forests, deer graze on roadsides, and seals swim under kayaks and canoes. Mountainous terrain, clear water, quiet glens, and pebble-and-shell beaches are nature's other gifts to this enchanting archipelago.

Native culture, present at Montague Harbour on Galiano Island as long as 6,000 years ago, is still woven into the mystique of the Gulf Islands. Farmers have always been an integral part of local lore, too. The oldest farm in British Columbia is on Saltspring (the largest and most populated island). While the farms these days are mostly the realm of hobbyists, the landscape retains its idyllic, pastoral charm. Sheep meander over the well-kept meadows and through ancient orchards. Huge weathered barns lend a rustic element to all of the islands.

Islanders are a diverse lot. Artists are drawn to the stunning physical beauty of the area, and an active artist community enriches everyone: painters (world-famous wildlife artist Robert Bateman lives here); singers (Canadian folk institution Valdy calls Saltspring home); authors (where do we start?). Even the silversmith who makes the intricate trophies for the Queen's Plate, Canada's top horse race, plies his trade here.

Access

Ferries charge the car owner plenty, and if you are inclined to visit three or four islands, the bill for your car alone could easily set you back $85. Many people opt to just bike or walk onto the ferries (hitchhiking is safe and quite accepted on the islands, and ferry terminal parking fees are reasonable at 75 cents per hour, with a maximum of $8). **Biking** is a great way to get around, although hills and cracked roads demand that bikers be alert and in at least fair shape. Narrow roads and hairpin turns make for hazardous biking, so wear a helmet. Regardless of the mode you choose, access to the Gulf Islands is via BC Ferries. Ferries travel to the southern Gulf Islands from Tsawwassen, 20 minutes south of Vancouver, or from Swartz Bay, north of Victoria on Vancouver Island. Call BC Ferries for rates; (888)223-3779 (in British Columbia) or (250)386-3431.

Exploring

If you have time for only one Gulf Island, visit **Saltspring**. It is certainly the most developed, yet it manages to maintain much of its rural character. Sheep here barely outnumber artists and their flock of **galleries**. The best way to take in the island's art scene is to stop by ArtCraft, a summerlong art exhibition on display at Mahon Hall in Ganges. Saltspring holds a **Festival of the Performing Arts**, usually in July, where jazz, classical, bluegrass, country, and folk music is presented by local and international artists. Theater, dance, and comedy shows add to the festive atmosphere. For information, call the Saltspring Tourist Information Centre; (250)537-5252.

Every Saturday morning from April through October, on the waterfront in the center of Ganges at Centennial Park, a **farmers market** sells everything imaginable, from organic, homegrown produce and preserves to locally produced crafts, both fine and not-so-fine. The schlock factor has been tamed, if not completely eliminated, though the atmosphere remains disarmingly circuslike.

Ruckle Provincial Park, at the south end of the island, encompasses a farmhouse dating from the 1870s, complete with barns and sheds containing farm implements and knickknacks. Sheep still graze in the fields, and visitors can wander at will. Ten kilometers of hiking trails join Ruckle's farmland to the rocky seashore and beaches. Picnic tables and fire pits are provided.

Green, rural **North and South Pender Islands** are separated by a canal and united by a bridge. Pender has the most, and best, public beaches—and they're easier to access here than on the other islands. On South Pender, **Mount Norman Provincial Park**, the highest point on the Penders, is a wonderful hike. Old logging roads lead the way up, with a short but steep bit at the end of the 30-minute climb. A remarkable view of Bedwell Harbour and the San Juan Islands awaits at the summit. Near Magic Lake, North Pender's suburban-style residential development, you can practice your skills at a wilderness Frisbee park; enthusiasts and novice tossers alike will enjoy the free course. For a glimpse of the old days, visit North Pender's quaint Port Washington, with its general store, public wharf, and crafts center. Cottages, orchards, fences, and dense shrubbery add an Old English atmosphere. Even islanders think a visit is a must.

Saturna Island, the most isolated, and arguably the most beautiful, of the Gulf Islands, offers precious little in the way of commercial amenities. Its big attraction is its unspoiled natural splendor. The scenery is breathtaking, and hiking, biking, or kayaking richly reward the effort expended. **Winter Cove Marine Park** is the place to start exploring. Trails meander deep into the forest and along the exposed north edge of the island. Windswept trees hug the shale rock formations. Beachcombers and naturalists will have a heyday spying on the abundant wildlife that includes herons, seagulls, ducks, and seals. Picnic tables and fire pits are provided, and there's great swimming off the helicopter pad at high tide.

Mayne Island, at 11 square kilometers, is the perfect size for a day trip. Hike out to the grassy point of the Indian reservation, drop by the lighthouse, or stroll to the top of Mayne's mountain for a view of the Strait of Georgia, and you'll begin to discover what tiny Mayne is all about. Spend a day at the tranquil beach at Dinner Bay Park, with views of Navy Channel and Active Pass. All the amenities for an enjoyable picnic are here, including tables, a cookhouse, barbecue pits, running water, and restrooms. The **Mayne Museum**, at one time the local jail, gives visitors a taste of Gulf Island culture and history. Galleries display Indian artifacts documenting aboriginal life on the islands, a collection of tools and utensils used by white settlers, and relics from a nearby 1872 shipwreck.

Galiano Island is a secluded, narrow strip of lushly forested hills, 30 kilometers long. Services (clustered on the southern end) are not abundant. There's one gas station and a couple of grocery stores but no bank. No wonder, then, that **hiking and biking** are the main pastimes on Galiano. Mount Galiano and Mount Sutil provide hiking on logging roads and trails that lead to the summits of each, where views take in Active Pass, Saltspring Island, Mayne Island, the Pender Islands, and Vancouver Island. At the north end of the island, the 270-meter-high Narrow Bodega Ridge provides hikers with a breathtaking walk. One can easily spend hours on these trails, so pack a lunch and potables. Ask at the **tourist information booth** near the ferry terminal for detailed directions to any of the island's trails.

Galiano's **Montague Harbour Marine Provincial Park** is one of the most popular marine parks in British Columbia, and for good reason. White shells, driftwood, and sunbathers line the beaches at Montague in summer months. Hiking trails weave throughout the park. An underwater archaeological dig during the summer of 1991 found evidence of ancient native civilizations here. The interpretive center offers periodic lectures on local flora, fauna, and natural history. The first Saturday in August brings the much-anticipated **Galiano Fiesta**. Games of chance, Barterin' Bob, local arts, crafts, cooking, and a salmon barbecue make this the event to introduce neophytes to the pulse of the island. It's a guaranteed traditional good time for everyone.

Gabriola Island (20 minutes by ferry from Nanaimo; contact the ferry at (250)537-9921) has become a bedroom community for that nearby city. Even though it's easily accessible from Vancouver Island, it manages to remain fairly rustic. Gabriola Sands Provincial Park, on the north end of the island, has picnic tables, a play area, a large sports field, and twin sandy beaches in Pilot and Taylor Bays with views of the mainland. The highlight of the fine beach walks is the **Malaspina Gallery**, with its weird rock formations and caves carved by the sea. To get there, go to the end of Malaspina Drive, look for the beach access, turn left at the beach, and walk around the point.

Cheap Eats

The Flying Saucer Cafe

112 Hereford Avenue, Saltspring Island ☎ (250)537-0500

Tucked into a startlingly purple house, the Flying Saucer is quickly becoming an island favorite for good homemade vegetarian food at island-friendly prices.

Lamb Bake

Every year on July 1, Saturna Islanders put on a community fund raiser at Winter Cove Park. Those who want to join in the free festivities (or indulge in the lamb feed, for a nominal fee) are encouraged to come by boat but are welcomed even on wheels. For information, call the Saltspring Tourist Information Centre; (250)537-5252.

The decor is friendly-funky-artsy; ditto for the food. This is the perfect spot to curl up in a cozy armchair with a magazine or book (thoughtfully provided), a steaming mug of tea or cappuccino, and a generous, dense chunk of carrot cake. As a bonus, there's often a local musician (or two or three) on hand to make things lively after dark.

Moby's Marine Pub

120 Upper Ganges Road, Saltspring Island ☎ (250) 537-5559

There are pubs, and there are great pubs. Moby's falls into the latter category, with the tastiest, most imaginative pub menu on the islands. (Psst . . . don't miss the baked tomato soup or the lamb burger.) Expect lots of local color, with natives and visitors jostling for elbow room in this marina-side home-away-from-home. The rotating art exhibits and great views of Ganges Harbour are almost incidental to the lively atmosphere. All this and live music, too.

Rodrigos

2921 Fulford-Ganges Road, Saltspring Island ☎ (250) 653-9222

It's a toss-up whether Rodrigos is so popular because the food is great and inexpensive, or because it's so handy to the Fulford–Swartz Bay ferry terminal. Don't be dismayed by the greasy-spoon atmo—the Mexican-style food is tasty, portions are generous, and the company is colorful, lively, and friendly. Fresh-baked muffins and pastries are a notch or two above Mom's best efforts, and the cheese scones are especially memorable, best appreciated while waiting for an early-morning ferry.

The Salt Spring Roasting Company

109 McPhillips Avenue, Saltspring Island ☎ (250) 537-0826

For the best coffee on these (so far) Starbucks-free islands (not to mention the best people-watching on Saltspring) plus great pastries, sandwiches, and pizzas, you can't beat the Roasting Company in downtown Ganges, where coffee is roasted fresh on the premises each morning, doing wonders for the local air quality. Service tends to be cheerfully anarchical, and seating is limited and not particularly comfortable, but these are mere quibbles compared to the genuinely sterling quality of the brew and munchies.

Inn on Pender Island

4709 Canal Road, North Pender Island ☎ (800) 550-0172 or (250) 629-3353

Situated midisland, on 7 wooded acres adjacent to Prior Centennial Provincial Park, the Inn on Pender Island's dining room offers cordial, competent service and fare ranging from better-than-okay to hey-that's-quite-good! Though the inn's atmosphere may seem a bit stiff, the menu's tariff (pastas, pizzas, and steaks are its mainstays) is not.

The Stand
At the Otter Bay ferry landing, North Pender Island (no phone)

If you're hankering for something simple and fast, you just can't beat the aptly named Stand for hot dogs, sandwiches, and the biggest, juiciest, all-around best burgers going. Prices are budget-friendly, and if the alternative is waiting to chow down on BC Ferries' less-than-stellar food, there's no contest.

Lighthouse Pub
102 East Point Road, Saturna Island ☎ (250) 539-5725

For a casual nosh, head to the Lighthouse Pub, beside the ferry terminal, for lunch and hearty dinner specials. The food is so-so at best, but on Saturna, alternative dining opportunities are severely limited. While the atmosphere is a trifle rough around the edges, the setting—with its views of Lyle Harbour, home to an abundance of seals—is out-and-out gorgeous.

Saturna Lodge
130 Payne Road, Saturna Island ☎ (888) 539-8800 or (250) 539-2254

The best deal on Saturna—no, the best deal in the Gulf Islands—has to be the three-course, multiple-choice, prix-fixe dinner at the Saturna Lodge. While the rooms are pricey, dinner is a splurge that's well worth it at $20 a head (a trifle over budget, but life is short, the service and the food are elegant, and such affordable luxuries are rare. The menu changes daily, taking advantage of local seafood, Saturna lamb, and fresh organic produce. Warm weather brings outdoor seating on a deck overlooking the bay.

Springwater Lodge
400 Fernhill Road, Mayne Island ☎ (250) 539-5521

There are few options for cheap eats on Mayne Island, but for reliable inexpensive food you could do worse than to sink your teeth into a burger on the deck of the Springwater Lodge. Funky rusticity is the general theme of the decor here, but the setting—on the edge of a pretty, leafy little village—and the genial, low-key atmosphere make this an appealing choice.

Cafe Boheme
Corner of Montague Harbour and Clanton Roads, Galiano Island
☎ (250) 539-5392

New on Galiano, Cafe Boheme is an offshoot of the island's well-loved La Berengerie. Really nothing more elaborate than a few tables set in the garden when the weather permits (so far it's open only during July and August), this little outdoor bistro offers great, strictly vegetarian food, the best people-watching vantage point on the island, and prices that bring back change from a $20 bill. No credit cards.

Hummingbird Inn

47 Sturdies Bay Road, Galiano Island ☎ (250) 539-5472

Along with hearty pub food and reasonable prices, you get billiard tables, darts, and occasional live music in a rustic garden setting (one of the prettiest in the islands). The atmosphere is sociable year-round, but particularly so in the summer months, when backpackers and campers swell Galiano's population.

White Hart Pub

1 South Road, Gabriola Island ☎ (250) 247-8588

The White Hart, on the doorstep of the ferry landing, is a convenient place to grab a bite—either outdoors on the spacious deck, or inside amid the dark English-pub atmosphere. Expect standard pub fare with an emphasis on burgers and steaks. There's a pool table and a decent selection of beers, including a solid representation of microbrews.

Cheap Sleeps

Beachcomber Motel

770 Vesuvius Bay Road, Saltspring Island, BC V8K 1L6 ☎ (250) 537-5415

Okay, it's your basic motel—complete with 1950s-style furnishings and artwork. Still, it is clean, comfortable, and not without a certain charm. Set on a grassy knoll, the Beachcomber has a productive little orchard out front—from which, in season, guests are free to pick a fresh fruit snack or three. The real attraction here, though, is the location: upstairs rooms have splendid views over Sansum Narrows to Vancouver Island. Saltspring's best swimming beach is half a block away. Ditto for the ferry to Crofton. A block away is the Vesuvius Pub; avoid the food but grab a beer at the bar, head for the veranda, and take in the island's prettiest sunsets.

Cusheon Creek Hostel

640 Cusheon Lake Road, Saltspring Island, BC V8K 2C2 ☎ (250) 537-4149

This hostel rents very basic, clean, and comfortable accommodations in a variety of configurations. From its secluded wooded setting, you're just a short hike from Cusheon Lake and Beddis Beach for a choice of fresh- or saltwater swimming. With only a few neighboring sheep and goats to disturb the tranquillity, this is the height of rustic simplicity. Cusheon Creek is the only lodging in the Gulf Islands affiliated with the International Hostel Association, offering two dorms, a family room, and three tepees (sleeping platforms and mattresses included). For the young and agile, there is also a tree house that sleeps two, 6 meters above the ground. No outdoor cooking allowed, but there's a well-equipped kitchen and a living room with a wood-burning stove. Showers and washrooms are shared.

The Tides Inn

132 Lower Ganges Road, Saltspring Island, BC V8K 2S9 ☎ (250) 537-1097

Located in the center of Ganges, above one of the town's better restaurants, the Tides Inn is one of Saltspring's rare bargains. Except for glimpses of the harbor, there's not much of a view from the bedroom windows, but the rooms are charming and immaculate—with enough character to inspire rumors of a ghost. Bathrooms are shared. The inn is within walking distance of Moby's Marine Pub (see review in Cheap Eats) and several restaurants, galleries, and shops. While the village bustles during the day, nightlife is nonexistent, ensuring a peaceful night's rest.

Inn on Pender Island

4709 Canal Road, North Pender Island, BC V0N 2M0
☎ **(800) 550-0172 or (250) 629-3353**

There are fancier places on Pender, and certainly places with more character. There may even be one or two cheaper sleeps. But for its wooded location next to Prior Centennial Provincial Park, its clean, comfortable rooms (all with private bath), and a few amenities that go beyond the minimum, the Inn (think "better-than-average motel") gets our vote. Ten bucks added to the basic rate buys a larger room with a sofa or loveseat. Small pets are welcome. There's also a decent adjoining licensed restaurant and pizza bar (see review in Cheap Eats).

Breezy Bay Bed and Breakfast

131 Payne Road (PO Box 40), Saturna Island, BC V0N 2Y0 ☎ (250) 539-5957

For pure island character, Breezy Bay is hard to beat—a house set aside for guests in a communal farm setting. Nothing fancy, though a sense of history permeates the century-old building. A comfortable library with ancient furniture is open to guests, as is the spacious deck overlooking the lovely farmland.

Blue Vista Resort

563 Arbutus Road (RR 1, Box C19), Mayne Island, BC V0N 2J0
☎ **(250) 539-2463**

For something quieter than the Springwater (see next review), try the Blue Vista. Small cabins—some with wood stoves—surround a shaded courtyard with swings and things for little people. Cabins have kitchens (BYO groceries) and a porch—perfect for settling in with a good book. Picnic tables, barbecues, rowboats, and bicycles are provided. Ask about off-season discounts.

Springwater Lodge

400 Fernhill Road, Mayne Island, BC V0N 4J0 ☎ (250) 539-5521

Established in 1892, the Springwater is reportedly the oldest continually operated hotel in British Columbia. And it's also among the least expensive island lodging options, aside from sleeping under the stars (which merits considera-

Gulf Island Reservations

Tom and Ann Hennessy, who own Galiano Island's Sutil Lodge, provide a free booking service for B&Bs, inns, resorts, lodges, and cottages throughout the Gulf Islands: Canadian Gulf Islands B&B Reservation Service (637 Southwind Rd, Galiano Island, BC V0N 1P0; (250)539-5390). The Hennessys personally check out all their listings during the off season and make recommendations in all price ranges.

Camping

Provincial campgrounds are probably the best deals going on the islands. Most have running water, firewood, and separate areas for tent campers. To avoid the summer crunch, arrive early; only some of the campgrounds have spillover areas. No reservations are accepted, except for large groups; (800)689-9025 (closed in winter; opens March 1). Fees run between $6 and $10 per site. Parties of 15 to 50 should call (250)539-2115 to reserve sites in Ruckle Provincial Park on Saltspring, or Montague Harbour Marine Provincial Park on Galiano.

***Galiano Island—Montague Harbour Marine Provincial Park,** (250)391-2300: Along with the beaches, hiking, and educational opportunities, Montague has 32 wooded campsites just off the beach. Nearby is a marina with a seasonal store where you can purchase groceries and supplies. **Dionisio Point Provincial Park** has a few free camping spots but little in the way of amenities; access is by boat, foot, or bicycle only.*

***North Pender Island—Prior Centennial Provincial Park,** (250)391-2300: For those who don't mind camping but don't want to cook, the campground is convenient to a pub. There are 17 campsites.*

***Saltspring Island—Ruckle Provincial Park,** (250)391-2300: Ruckle offers 70 tent sites with picnic tables (the best are the waterfront sites). On weekends things can get tight, and on long weekends the place is crammed. It's far from any restaurant, so bring provisions. **Mouat Park** (no phone) is not far from Ganges. Its 15 wooded camping spots are great if you want access to the town's restaurants and nightlife or want to get an early start on the Saturday farmers market. Unfortunately, you also have to watch out for thieves here.*

tion on warm summer nights). The charmingly dilapidated lodge has six bedrooms. The bathrooms are old and shared, but for character, price, and friendliness quotient, it's a fine spot indeed. There are two duplex waterfront cabins, each with two bedrooms, kitchen, and bath. At night, local folksingers sometimes drop by and entertain the guests and island residents.

Cliff Pagoda Bed and Breakfast
2851 Montague Harbour Road, Galiano Island, BC V0N 1P0
☎ (250) 539-2260

The Oriental-style Cliff Pagoda, which looks as if it were plucked from Beijing's Forbidden City, stands out for its design, amenities, and breathtaking view of Montague Harbour and Park Island. Bicyclists may struggle up the long dirt driveway, but they're rewarded with bicycle racks. Rooms are small and bathrooms are shared, but with the large porch and hot tub, why stay in your room?

Haven by the Sea

240 Davis Road (RR 1, Site 9), Gabriola Island, BC V0R 1X0
☎ (250) 247-9211

This "haven" is neither exciting nor picturesque, but it is clean and comfortable and, with rooms (all with private baths) starting at $45, certainly affordable. Cabins with kitchenettes are decidedly more costly (about $85 a night). There's a television room and a sitting room, and the dining room serves up buffet-style breakfasts, lunches, and dinners at reasonable prices.

Surf Lodge

855 Berry Point Road (RR 1, Site 1, C17), Gabriola Island, BC V0R 1X0
☎ (250) 247-9231

This rustic wood and stone lodge is across from the beach on the northwest shore of Gabriola Island. You'll find a very relaxed, comfortable atmosphere, a great stone fireplace in the lodge's sitting room, a saltwater pool, and outdoor recreational facilities. Accommodations include rooms and cabins, some with kitchens. The lodge has a restaurant and a cocktail lounge.

Sunshine Coast

L ying in the rain shadow of Vancouver Island and its mountains, the Sunshine Coast has become a minor mecca for vacationing Vancouver denizens in search of the sun. Bordered by Howe Sound in the south and remote Desolation Sound in the north, the coast is dotted with lakes, and water sports abound. The modest towns of the Sunshine Coast are hardly attractions in themselves, but the community of Powell River, with its warm, protected waters and shipwreck remains, calls itself the diving capital of Canada. Canoes and kayaks are perfect alternatives to exploring on foot (or by motorboat), and the fishing is good nearly all year long. The area abounds with wildlife, from orcas slicing through the waters of Pender Harbour to eagles circling above the islands. Trails and logging roads offer adventures on terra firma.

The towns are perfectly good hubs for a series of day trips—perhaps to view the Skookumchuck Narrows, do some telemark skiing at Mount Elphinstone, or visit one of the many accessible provincial or marine parks. A drive between the seaside fishing villages winds along the forests and bays of the pretty Sunshine Coast Highway.

Exploring

As you progress north along the coast from Horseshoe Bay on Highway 101, the first town on the map is the fishing village of **Gibsons**, whose population swells in the summer. Stroll along the Gibsons Seawalk; then visit the set of Molly's Reach Cafe (647 School St, Gibsons; (604)886-9710), where the popular TV show *The Beachcombers* was shot for many years. You can also visit the Elphinstone Pioneer Museum, across from the post office (716 Winn Rd, Gibsons; (604)886-8232), which re-creates the turn-of-the-century office, bedroom, and kitchen of early settlers and includes photos of old Gibsons streetscapes,

a Native American dugout canoe, a double-ender fishing boat, and equipment from early local commercial ventures. In Gibsons you'll also find the spot on Gower Point where Captain George Vancouver landed in 1792. Stop by Ernie and Gwen's Drive-In (Hwy 101, Gibsons, (604)886-7813) for real milk shakes and burgers with all the fixings.

Farther north lies **Sechelt**, an artists' community where work is displayed at the Sunshine Coast Arts Centre (5714 Medusa St, Sechelt; (604)885-5412) and various galleries around town. The Sechelt Nation's cultural center, the House of Héwhîwus (5555 Hwy 101,

Sechelt; (604)885-2273), is home to the Tems Swiya Museum and the Raven's Cry Theater. Before crossing from Earls Cove over to Saltery Bay, take a 4-kilometer hike (via a brief detour to Egmont) to see the tides of three bodies of water rip through the Skookumchuck Narrows (see "Getting There and Back" tip). Most local businesses have tide tables.

Powell River is the location of one of the world's largest pulp and paper mills—MacMillan Bloedel's Powell River Division (6270 Yew St, Powell River; (604)483-3722), which employs about 2,000 people and offers **free mill tours** (reservations recommended) in the summer. It's a town where you really sense the power of industry, past and present: flagpoles were hewn from the surrounding tall trees at the turn of the century, fishing boats clang at the docks, and limestone is mined on Texada Island. For only a couple of bucks, you can get a glimpse of the town's past at the Powell River Historical Museum (4800 Marine Ave, Powell River; (604)485-2222), across from Willingdon Beach.

Over the years, this good-size mill town has achieved destination status on the Sunshine Coast because, although it's unassuming on land, underwater it's a diver's dream. Powell River attracts hun-

dreds of **scuba divers** to explore its shoreline and view *Mermaid*, reportedly the world's first underwater sculpture.

The best diving season is winter, believe it or not, when the reduced concentration of plankton increases underwater visibility. The Sunshine Coast Fitness and Sports Center dive shop (at Beach Garden Resort, 7074 Westminster Ave, Powell River; (604)485-6809) rents gear and offers guided diving charters with a few days' notice.

Consider renting a canoe and spending a few days exploring the **Powell Forest Canoe Route**, a great trip for families, with its 72 kilometers of paddling and 8 kilometers of portage on 12 lakes. Wolfson Creek Canoe Rentals (9537 Nassichuk Rd, Powell River; (604)487-1699) has information and sells and rents all the canoeing accessories you could ever need.

There are plenty of **fish** to be caught all along the coast and in the freshwater lakes. Charters are pricey, so try your luck on the eastern shore of Sechelt Inlet or at the public docks on Powell River. Gather **oysters and clams** from Porpoise Bay near Sechelt, on the beaches at Saltery Bay, or at Okeover, just south of Lund. The fishing wharves as well as the 13-kilometer hiking trail at Inland Lake (just outside of Powell River) are wheelchair accessible.

Getting There and Back

The pleasant 119-kilometer drive up the Sunshine Coast is interrupted by two spectacular ferry rides. First is the 40-minute ferry crossing from Horseshoe Bay (just west of West Vancouver) to Langdale. Then there's a 50-minute ride on the Earls Cove ferry from Sechelt Peninsula to Saltery Bay. One ferry ticket is good for two rides—either a round-trip passage on one ferry or a one-way ride on both. The ferries run about eight times daily. Call BC Ferries for the schedule; (888)223-3779 (in British Columbia) or (250)386-3431.

Instead of driving to Powell River and back, you might want to make a loop. At Powell River, cross over to Comox on Vancouver Island via the Queen of Sidney; (604)339-3310. Drive down the island's eastern coast and return to the mainland via BC Ferries from Nanaimo or Sidney. BC Ferries offers a CirclePac ticket for this loop route that can save you 25 percent off the regular fare.

Highway 101 ends—literally—in the water at **Lund**, and Desolation Sound is a mere boat ride away. But first, fortify yourself for any excursions with a delectable cinnamon roll from Nancy's Bakery (1436 Lund Hwy, Lund; (604)483-4180).

Cheap Eats

Howl at the Moon
450 Marine Drive, Gibsons ☎ **(604)886-8881**

If you board the ferry and find yourself hungry enough to howl, hold on till you get to Gibsons. Howl at the Moon frightens away those hunger pangs with Tex-Mex staples augmented by steaks, burgers, and six imaginative chicken dishes. Service is prompt and friendly, portions are generous, and the water view is almost as expansive as if you were back on the ferry.

Gumboot Garden
1057 Roberts Creek Road, Roberts Creek ☎ **(604)885-4216**

To find Gumboot Garden, just look for an old maroon house with a sign that says "Cafe." The menu is primarily Mexican. Try the Huevos Gumboot, a hearty breakfast dish that's served all day: eggs and black beans are piled on a tortilla layered with Jack cheese, green onions, and homemade salsa. The cooks use organic produce whenever possible. Breads and cheesecakes are baked daily at the Gumboot, too.

Ruby Lake Resort
Highway 101, Madeira Park ☎ **(604)883-2269**

An engaging family from Milan recently bought this resort, and the kitchen crew has been drawing accolades for its Northern Italian cuisine and fresh seafood. You'll get the most bang for your budget bucks by ordering the pasta plates. Be sure to arrive by 6pm to witness the nightly eagle feeding.

Cheap Sleeps

Bonniebrook Lodge
1532 Ocean Beach Esplanade (RR 4, Site 10, C34), Gibsons, BC V0N 1V0
☎ **(604)886-2887**

Located at Gower Point, this 1922 yellow clapboard lodge was remodeled by owners Karen and Philippe Lacoste. There are four spacious units, two with lovely vistas of the Strait of Georgia. A room with a view will cost a bit more, but it's worth the splurge. Breakfast is served at the elegant adjoining restaurant, Chez Philippe, and is included in the room rate.

Camping

*The Sunshine Coast is dotted with numerous scenic provincial parks,
some of which are accessible only by boat or floatplane, including Copeland Islands Marine
Park, north of Lund, and Princess Louisa Marine Park, site of the famous Chatterbox
Falls, on Princess Louisa Inlet, at the top of Jervis, 90 kilometers north of Skookumchuck
Narrows. Only two parks accept advance reservations for campsites; all other campsites
are available on a first-come, first-served basis. Approximately 40 percent of the 86 campsites at Porpoise Bay (at the south end of Sechelt Inlet) and the 42 campsites at Saltery
Bay (near the ferry terminal south of Powell River) may be reserved up to three months in
advance by calling Discover Camping, (800)689-9025. For general park information, call
the Garibaldi Sunshine Coast District Office, (604)898-3678.*

Cattanach Bed and Breakfast

RR 2, F18, C7, Roberts Creek, BC V0N 1V0 ☎ (604) 885-5444

Owners Barb and Ian Cattanach built this cozy two-room B&B on their 5-acre
plot of land. The inn offers a rock fireplace, a guest living room, and a wood-
burning stove. Guests share the bathroom. Be sure to ask Barb to make her
Fraser Valley blueberry pancakes for breakfast.

Sundowner Inn

**4339 Garden Bay Road (PO Box 113), Garden Bay, BC V0N 1S0
☎ (604) 883-9676**

Housed in a former hospital built in 1929, the Sundowner offers recently renovated, comfortably furnished rooms with a view of Garden Bay (off Pender Harbour). The rooms that share a bath are, of course, the least expensive, but even
the units with fireplaces are available at a reasonable rate. The Sundowner has a
restaurant, and occasionally theater productions are staged in the dining room.
The inn is closed in the winter.

Hampshire's Country Inn

RR 1, Fleury Road, Powell River, BC V8A 4Z2 ☎ (604) 487-9011

Situated about 10 kilometers south of Powell River on 5 grassy acres near
Malaspina Strait, this inn offers comfortable rooms complete with a private
bath, a TV, and a full breakfast. There's even a hot tub—an ideal place to
unwind after an evening stroll on the inn's private beach. Closed in the winter.

The Old Courthouse Inn

6243 Walnut Street, Powell River, BC V8A 4K4 ☎ (604) 483-4000

The historic courthouse in the Powell River Townsite has been converted into an
inviting, inexpensive, 10-room inn. Five rooms share bathrooms and are rented
by the night; the other five rooms have private baths (some also have views of
the strait) and are available for stays of a week or longer only. Zarzuela, the
inn's restaurant, serves Mediterranean-influenced seafood dishes.

Whistler & the Fraser River Canyon

Highway 99, running north from Vancouver to Whistler, is an adventure in itself. The aptly named Sea-to-Sky Highway hugs fir-covered mountains that tumble sharply into island-filled Howe Sound. The views are breathtaking. But don't get carried away—the curves of the road demand constant attention. Occasional delays are caused by rock slides and road work, and accidents are typically the result of too many people trying to escape the city (or get home to the city) too quickly. At Squamish, the highway climbs beyond Howe Sound into spectacular Garibaldi Provincial Park, crowned by the exploded volcanic remnant known as the Black Tusk.

Two hours north of Vancouver, the Whistler-Blackcomb ski resort offers some of the finest skiing in the country. The village (actually two cheek-by-jowl communities—Whistler Village and Blackcomb Resort) boasts a world-class reputation (and two world-class mountains). Here you'll find swank resorts, fine art galleries, and designer stores. In the winter the area is often booked to capacity with skiers, and in the summer it becomes a popular destination for those seeking mountain air. As usual, the best lodgings don't come cheap, but prices are drastically reduced in the summer, and they drop even more in the "shoulder" seasons. Trust us, you can stay—and play—at Whistler, even if the only car you own is a Volkswagen Rabbit.

Exploring

Just north of Horseshoe Bay, as you head up Highway 99 from Vancouver, turn right to **Furry Creek Golf & Country Club**; (604)896-2216. It's a spectacular and brutally tough new Robert Muir Graves–designed course that was forced to go public when it couldn't sell enough memberships (the original fee: $36,000!). Lucky you. A superb clubhouse overlooking the mountains is a big bonus for

Ski & Snowboard Festival

Whistler and Blackcomb are well-traveled venues on the competitive downhill racing and freestyle skiing circuits, but visitors have the most fun during the World Ski and Snowboard Festival each April. Virtually all of the competitive events here are aimed at recreational skiers and snowboarders, and there are many free concerts and events for kids, too. Perhaps the biggest draw is simply the value: lift tickets and accommodations cost about 40 percent less than in high season, at a time when snow conditions are quite reliable. Call (604)938-7595 for more details.

pay-as-you-play golfers. Also on the way to Whistler, on Highway 99N at Britannia Beach, is a funky roadside collection of former mining-company buildings that is now the **BC Museum of Mining**; (604)896-2233. Skiers stop for java at the 99er Restaurant (off Hwy 99N at Britannia Beach; (604)896-2497), where roadside coffee is still under a buck.

An hour north of Vancouver, you'll find the logging and rock-climbing town of **Squamish**. Four kilometers south of Squamish is the granitic monolith of the Stawamus Chief, one of the top 10 climbing areas in North America (a viewing pullout is on the east side of the road). Hikers can do the steep but technically easy "backside trail" starting from nearby Shannon Falls. Entry-level climbers favor the Smoke Bluffs, right at the entrance to downtown.

Six times the vertical drop of Niagara Falls, **Shannon Falls** is the fifth-largest waterfall in the world, plummeting 335 meters. It's a great spot for a picnic, though not terribly secluded when the tour buses roll in. Out in Howe Sound, wind surfers set sail at Squamish Spit, where the hot sun and summer breezes are tempered by the glacier-fed waters of the river. Fourteen kilometers north of Squamish at **Brackendale**, the Sunwolf Outdoor Centre, (604)898-1537, fronts the Cheakamus River at an ideal spot for rafting, kayaking, and fishing. In the winter, hundreds of bald eagles hunt the shorelines of the Cheakamus, Mamquam, and Squamish Rivers for spawning salmon.

Garibaldi Provincial Park boasts 400,000 acres of glacier-fed lakes, towering evergreens, and volcanic peaks stretching from Squamish to Pemberton, interrupted briefly by the village of Whistler. The park is cherished by avid hikers and skiers. Alpine cabins at Elfin Lake, Red Heather Meadows, and Garibaldi Lake are an easy day hike from the trailheads. Call Garibaldi/Squamish BC Parks for maps or trail suggestions; (604)898-3678.

Rated North America's number one ski resort by numerous ski and travel magazines, **Whistler** has also gained a reputation as a world-class year-round resort. In ski season, you'll hear plenty of American, European, and Japanese accents in the chair-lift lineups, along with those of the many Aussie lifties. The huge European-style resort is actually two communities: pedestrian-only **Whistler Village** and **Upper Village** (also known as **Blackcomb Resort**). A third village (where cars can park), **Village North**, is home to Market Place, which in turn is home to shops, cafes, a post office, and a liquor store. If you haven't been there recently, you'll hardly know your way around this boomtown. Intrawest, a premier resort developer, took over both mountains in 1997, and more than $35 million in enhancements are in the works; the developer promises to retain the distinct personalities of each mountain, though. Currently, the newest development in Village North is the Town Plaza, between Whistler Village and Market

Place. A smaller, less expensive "base" a few miles closer to Vancouver is the **Creekside** area (down at Whistler's original south side).

For an orientation and any information you need on skiing or other year-round activities, rentals, lodgings, or events, stop by the **Whistler Activity and Information Centre** in the village (4010 Whistler Way, (604)932-2394).

Frequent rain at lower elevations is Whistler's dirty little secret, but the broad roof-decks that hang over the elevated walkways were specifically designed so skiers and pedestrians would not get wet when they walked from hotel to mountain. And it works—even in the worst downpour the village is mobbed with people. In the heart of Whistler Village, check out the complex that houses the Hard Rock Cafe (Madonna's first gold LP is on display; Joplin, Hendrix, and Elvis are on the ceiling), Helly Hansen, a Starbucks coffee bar, and Mongolie Grill. One of Whistler's coolest (and most overlooked) nooks of commerce is **Function Junction**, home of the Whistler Brewing Company (1209 Alpha Lake Rd, Whistler, (604)932-6185). Drink a round of Whistler's own premium lager or Black Tusk Ale with the brewmaster. Tours are available Tuesday through Saturday.

At the **Whistler-Blackcomb ski area**, the stats tell the tale: average annual snowfall of over 11 meters (450 inches); vertical drop of over 1,500 meters (5,000 feet, the longest in North America) at each area; and 25 lifts (the largest high-speed lift system in North America, including three gondolas, seven quads, and six triples) to cover 200 runs, 3 glaciers, and 12 massive, high-alpine bowls. A good way for first-time visitors to learn about the two mountains is to attend the Thursday- or Sunday-night welcome and orientation at the Conference Centre; (604)932-2394.

If you want to ski two mountains in one day, ski Blackcomb first. At noon, ski to Whistler's gondola base, have lunch in the village, and then take the 15-minute gondola ride to the top. Summit to summit is 40 minutes. Nonskiers are welcome to go topside for the view and lunch (many resorts don't allow this).

Lift tickets are quite costly, but discount cards, multiday passes, and a plethora of other options are available. For information on ticket prices, rentals, and passes, call the main information

Real Four-Wheeling

You'll see more Jeep Cherokees, Land Rovers, and other sport utility vehicles in the parking lots around Whistler than you could ever imagine. And most of them will just stay there, on the pavement, shiny and new. Which is a shame, because the Coast Range and Fraser Canyon have some of the absolute best four-wheel driving experiences in the world, courtesy of the local forestry industry.

One road that can even be navigated by most cars in the warm months is the Hurley, which leads north off Highway 99 in Pemberton to the ghost towns of Gold Bridge, Bralorne, and Bradian. This steep yet well-graded road takes you over a mountain pass and into scenery that would not look out of place in Alaska. No kidding. The remains of the Pioneer Mine on Cadwallader Creek are worth checking out, as are the incredible wildflowers at McGillivray Pass. Road conditions and updates on logging operations (some roads are gated, but companies are required by law to provide a key) are available by calling the Squamish Forest District, (604)898-2100, which also publishes a map of roads, trails, campgrounds, and fishing lakes.

Whistler No-No's

Be sure to observe Whistler's many rules! Dogs must be kept on a leash, bicycling and skateboarding are verboten (though in-line skating is not), and there's even a no-swearing bylaw to keep up Whistler's image as Disneyland North. You can also forget that old ski-bum trick of parking your van in a lot and waking up in time for first tracks—overnight parking is prohibited during the winter months in both municipal lots and side streets because it hinders snow removal.

line, (800)766-0449 or (604)932-3434. For the snow report, call (604)932-4211. Discount tickets can also be purchased en route to the mountains at the Save-On store (in Squamish) and at 7-11 stores (in Squamish and Vancouver), but restrictions apply.

Biggest thrill for intermediates: riding up Whistler's steep **Peak Chair** knowing there's an easy way down the backside as well as an unforgettable view over the back of bowls, glaciers, and Black Tusk. Blackcomb's double black diamond (Canada's first) **Couloir Extreme** is still a badge-of-courage gulper. Advanced and expert skiers regularly sign up for adult camps (choices include moguls, masters, and women only; call (604)938-7720). The best ski tuning is at Summit Ski, (604)932-6225, in the Delta Hotel; the best boot refitting (reserve ahead) is by George McConkey at McCoo's; (604)932-2842.

Cross-country ski trails begin at the village edge and wind through the adjacent residential communities. A favorite trail leads out to Lost Lake. There's a warming hut at the trailhead ($6 fee) and lights for evening skiing, free after 4pm; for more details, call the Lost Lake Ticket Booth, (604)932-6436. A good pit stop along the way is the Chateau Whistler golf course's clubhouse, where you can usually have a beer-and-burger meal for less than $10; (604)938-8000. The ski trails are free on the other golf course (across Hwy 99 from Whistler).

At Whistler you can also try **paragliding**, **snowboarding**, **dogsledding**, or **heli-skiing** (if you can figure out a way to get

reduced prices on this, let us know), as well as **snowshoeing**, **snowmobiling**, and **sleigh rides**. One favorite cold-snap sport that won't cost you a thing (if you have your own skates) is **skating** on Alta Lake (check first to make sure the ice is safe). Call the Whistler Activity and Information Centre for information on all of the above.

If you're looking for sporting goods at bargain prices, shop at the Katmandu Outdoor General Store (111-4368 Main St in the Market Pavilion, Whistler; (604)932-6381), which sells more outdoor merchandise than any other store in Whistler. An adventure-skiing option is offered by Extremely Canadian, (604)938-9656, whose trio of guides takes skiers of all abilities off-piste.

Après-ski at the base of Blackcomb: enjoy leisurely patio viewing from Monk's Grill or the Chateau's Mallard Bar (great pasta snacks), or lively beer drinking at Merlin's. In the village, head for the Garibaldi Lift Co. and Longhorn. Later, try Buffalo Bill's, which usually has good and sometimes great live bands; Savage Beagle and Tommy Africa's attract younger crowds.

Whistler has done a lot to develop year-round recreation and is definitely worth checking out even when there's no snow on the ground. (In summer, though, you can go glacier skiing on Blackcomb from mid-June to early August.) **Mountain biking** in Whistler is as new and adventurous as skiing was 20 years ago. Novice riders stick to the paved Valley Trail or the wide cross-country trails near Lost Lake; both networks start right from the village. A guided descent of Whistler Mountain can be organized through Whistler Backroad Adventures; (604)932-3111. Solo riders can play around 8 kilometers of trails in the Whistler Mountain bike park. For the ultimate challenge, the 140-kilometer Sea-to-Sky Trail, running from Squamish to D'Arcy, is now a reality.

In-line skaters (the only wheels allowed in the town center), joggers, cyclists, pedestrians, and walkers somehow share the **Valley Trail**. Whistler's mostly paved foot-freeway runs from one end of the valley to the other—past all the lakes and golf courses.

There are plenty of sports at the five **lakes** in the surrounding valley. Fishing and swimming are best in the clear, not-too-cold Lost Lake. Others might opt for volleyball at Rainbow Lake; board sailing at Alta Lake (call Whistler Sailing for equipment in the summer, (604)932-SAIL); or canoeing, sailing, or riding pedal-boats (rentals available from Whistler Outdoor Experience Company, (604)932-3389). The Alta Lake free-form tree house will capture kids' imaginations. The area's best easy canoe trip is the meandering River of Golden Dreams, especially if you arrange for someone to pick you up at the other end (most rental companies will).

Families enjoy **Meadow Park**, home to a skating rink and swimming pool. For hockey fans, one great freebie is watching the Vancouver Canucks, (604)899-4600, go through their preseason training at Meadow Park in Whistler.

Golfers with gold credit cards can tee off at the scenic Arnold Palmer–designed Whistler Golf Club, the rugged, link-style Robert Trent Jones–designed Chateau Whistler golf course, or the new Nicklaus North and Big Sky clubs. Inquire about early-bird or twilight rates in order to get a discount. The Squamish Golf and Country Club in Garibaldi Highlands, (604)898-9521, provides a less expensive alternative too.

Hikes abound in the Whistler region. Both Whistler and Blackcomb Mountains provide summer access to the alpine via gondola or ski lifts. Families will love the wide pathway leading to Cheakamus Lake, while hikers looking for a more strenuous workout should cross the bridge over the Cheakamus River and head up the Helm Creek trail for Black Tusk and Panorama Ridge. Another good hike is up to Rainbow Lake, about an 18-kilometer round-trip journey. The best description of hiking trails in the Whistler area is provided in Jack Christie's *The Whistler Outdoors Guide*, available at tiny Armchair Books in Whistler Village (4205 Village Square, Whistler; (604)932-5557).

Two **horse outfitters** near Whistler offer day or overnight trips: Whistler Stables, (604)932-6623, and Whistler Outdoor Experience Company, near Pemberton, (604)932-3389.

Concerts occur daily in the village from June through September, with free **music festivals** featuring everything from classical and jazz to country and blues. In mid-August, catch the Vancouver Symphony on top of Whistler Mountain. For about $44 you can get a lift up (and down), admission to the concert, and a bale of hay to sit on. (BYO picnic; several of the delis in the village will prepare one for you in advance.) The **Farmers Market** is open Sundays at the base of Blackcomb throughout the summer. The year always ends with **Whistler First Night**, an outdoor, nonalcoholic family New Year's Eve celebration with entertainment (about $6 per person). Call or drop by the Whistler Activity and Information Centre for more event information.

North of Whistler is the no-glitz town of **Pemberton**, home to the Lil'wat people and the annual May (and sometimes September) Lillooet Lake Rodeo; (604)894-6507. Just outside of Pemberton, take a pleasant, flat, half-hour walk into dramatic Nairn Falls. One of the best day hikes in all of Sea-to-Sky country is the walk into Tenquille Lake; ask for directions at one of the gas stations or restaurants in town.

If you've got time on your hands, tour the circular route (Hwy 99, Hwy 12, and Trans-Canada 1) that passes through **Lillooet** and the **Fraser River Canyon**. It's one of the most scenic loops in British Columbia, winding past fields of cultivated ginseng and ranch mesas. The Fraser and Thompson Rivers descend from Lillooet and Ashcroft, respectively, to converge in Lytton, where they squeeze through the narrow walls of the Fraser River Canyon. British Columbia's mightiest river rushes through the canyon for 85 kilometers. You can get a good sense of the whirling rapids from the many roadside pullouts.

You'll have the most fun here on a hot summer day, when you can buy some wet thrills on a **raft trip**. The biggest fleet on the river is Kumsheen Raft Adventures Ltd. (Main Street, Lytton; (250)455-2296). Other companies include Fraser River Raft Expeditions, (800)363-RAFT or (604)863-2336, and River Rogues (at Spences Bridge, (888)231-RAFT or (604)452-2252). Downriver, from mid-April to mid-October, the popular Hell's Gate Airtram takes you across the boiling waters of the Fraser at the narrowest part of the gorge; it's located in Boston Bar, (250)867-9277. The river turns sharply west and calms down at **Hope**, 140 kilometers east of Vancouver. Keep your eye to the sky while passing through Hope; many sailplanes and hang gliders soar on the thermal updrafts in the nearby hills. Avoid the crowded freeway by taking Highway 7 from Harrison Lake back to Mission, and then cross back to Trans-Canada 1.

Cheap Eats

Howe Sound Brewing Company
37801 Cleveland Avenue, Squamish ☎ (604) 892-2603

There was a time when the notion of "dining in Squamish" would elicit a good belly laugh from just about any gastronome since, after all, this is a town that wears its Golden Arches on its sleeve. The Howe Sound Brewing Company is attempting to change all that with its great pub food and superb selection of microbrews that demonstrate just how mainstream this oft-forgotten part of the Pacific Northwest has become.

Auntie Em's Kitchen
129-4340 Lorimer Road, Whistler ☎ (604) 932-1163

Whistler has an abundance of delis and coffee shops, and indeed, these are just about the only affordable places to eat outside of the plethora of fast-food joints that have sprung up in the past five years. Small, cozy Auntie Em's (she's not in Kansas anymore) is tucked away in the Marketplace Mall and offers hearty breakfasts and healthy soups, salads, and sandwiches. So take that, Big Mac.

Gone Bakery & Soup Company
4205 Village Square, Whistler ☎ (604) 905-4663

After you've gone skiing, hiking, biking, or golfing, Kit Dickinson and partner/baker Bob Lorriman's Gone Bakery is a welcome spot for refueling. In the morning Bob bakes croissants and muffins, at lunch he whips up hearty soups with hot loaves of bread, and at night it's just desserts (be sure to indulge in the giant piece of chocolate cake—large enough for two). Gone's a great value.

Hoz's Creekside Cafe & Pub
2129 Lake Placid Road, Whistler ☎ (604) 932-4424

Hang with the locals at Hoz's Creekside. It's a friendly, casual, and happy neighborhood joint just around the corner from the train station in Whistler Creek. Families are welcome, and the bar menu is available until late at night. In a town with no shortage of pub fare, locals give Hoz's the nod for the best and biggest burger.

Mallard Bar (Chateau Whistler)
4599 Chateau Boulevard, Whistler ☎ (604) 938-8000

Okay, so Chateau Whistler is a Gold Card kind of place. But those on a budget can confidently stride into the hotel's Mallard Room, ease down into a plush loveseat by the huge river-rock fireplace, nurse a plate of nachos and a pint of Black Tusk Ale for an hour or so after skiing, and feel like the sultan of Oman. (You can ski way better than the sultan, anyway.)

Mondo Pizza
Village Marketplace, Whistler ☎ (604) 938-9554

When you're dining on a budget, there's always pizza. Mondo is a favorite stopover for Vancouver backpackers returning to the city after a weekend in the mountains. The pies arrive hot and huge from the brick oven, and you can save even more dough by checking for discount ads in *The Pique*, Whistler's weekly magazine. Mondo also has microbrews on tap, natch.

Mongolie Grill
201-4295 Blackcomb Way, Whistler ☎ (604) 938-9416

Select your combination of seafood, meat, and vegetables as well as one of the Mongolie's 18 sauces. The food is weighed and then cooked in a wok in front of your eyes. The prices are right, and the place is very kid-friendly.

South Side Deli
1202 Lake Placid Road, Whistler ☎ (604) 932-3368

The ingredients in the omelets at this local hangout are considerably more exotic than what you'll find at other British Columbia roadside breakfast joints. In addition, the produce is always fresh and the portions are generous. South Side's BELTCH (bacon, egg, lettuce, tomato, cheese, and ham) sandwich is legendary.

Thai One On
4557 Blackcomb Way, Whistler ☎ (604) 932-4822

Indeed, if you've "tied one on" already, you might have a hard time finding this place, tucked into a corner of Le Chamois in Blackcomb Village. But keep searching for it, because the Thai cuisine is respectable and, most importantly, reasonably priced. (You don't have to have pasta every night!)

Cheap Sleeps

Garibaldi Inn
38012 3rd Avenue, Squamish, BC V0N 3G0 ☎ (604) 892-5204

Slumbering in Squamish is not quite as nice (or expensive) as staying in Whistler, but at least getting to Whistler is quite easy from here. It's a 50-minute drive, or you can take the bus (Maverick Coach Lines, (604)255-1177) or train (BC Rail, (604)984-5246). Squamish has lots of reasonably priced lodgings, including the small 25-room Garibaldi. Nine of the inn's rooms even have kitchenettes, which might save you from blowing your wad in too many restaurants.

Sunwolf Outdoor Centre
70002 Government Road (PO Box 244), Brackendale, BC V0N 1H0
☎ (604) 898-1537

Sunwolf offers 10 recently refurbished guest cabins scattered along the Cheakamus River. Cabins boast hardwood floors, vaulted ceilings, four-poster beds, *and* a single day bed. Each has a gas fireplace and private bath; five offer kitchenettes. Whitewater rafting tours are offered in summer, eagle viewing in winter.

Brio Haus
3005 Brio Entrance (Brio), Whistler, BC V0N 1B3
☎ (800) 331-BRIO or (604) 932-3313

You get a lot for a little money at Brio Haus. Four people can rent the family room (with a king-size bed and two bunks), lounge in the deep Jacuzzi, sweat in the large sauna, cook dinner in the guest kitchen, watch a video on the VCR in the living room, and dry their wet ski clothes—what more could you ask for? Room rates jump up in the winter.

Chalet Beau Sejour
7414 Ambassador Crescent (PO Box 472), Whistler, BC V0N 1B0
☎ (604) 938-4966

After a big day of skiing, hosts Sue and Hal Stangel like to have a snack and a glass of *gluwein*—and that's what they provide for their guests around the big rock fireplace in their contemporary home in White Gold Estates. Sue can suggest lots of good, reasonably priced restaurants, but you're also welcome to have a pizza delivered to the chalet or buy deli fare and prepare your own lunch.

Fireside Lodge
2117 Nordic Drive (Nordic Estates), Whistler, BC V0N 1B2 ☎ (604) 932-4545

Don't be fooled by the lodge's boxy exterior or the tough-eyed manager, Marj Currie. We suspect she's the reason this big, comfortable lodge owned by the Power Mountain Ski Club (which opens it to nonmembers on a limited basis) is run so well and looks so great. Lots of families flock to this place. It has 12 private rooms, a dormitory that sleeps 31, and a large stone fireplace in an impressive living room. It's run on a cooperative basis: bring your own groceries, bedding, and towels, and do your own cooking and cleaning. Club members may make reservations as far in advance as they like, whereas nonmembers can't book a bed until 30 days before their stay.

Golden Dreams Bed and Breakfast

6412 Easy Street, Whistler, BC V4L 4L2 ☎ (800) 668-7055 or (604) 932-2667

Ann Myette-Spence's three-room B&B in the Whistler Cay subdivision is set up in such a way that guests seem to have their own separate apartment, away from Myette-Spence's busy family. Each room has its own theme: Oriental, Victorian, and Aztecan (the only unit with a private bath). The shared bathroom has a Jacuzzi. Ski conditions are often discussed at the breakfast table, and if Terry Spence is around, ask the former Canadian National Ski Team coach to wow you with tales of the World Cup circuit.

Rainbow Creek Bed and Breakfast

8243 Alpine Way (PO Box 1142), Whistler, BC V0N 1B0 ☎ (604) 932-7001

Almost taller than it is wide, this three-story log home is reminiscent of a terrific tree house. Inside, Heidi Lieberherr pulls out all the stops to make you comfortable. The B&B has three guest rooms (two with a private bath) and a spare fridge for storing your food. Enjoy a steaming cup of tea in the afternoon, and then stroll over to the new ice rink and swimming pool at Meadow Park.

Shoestring Lodge

7124 Nancy Greene Drive, Whistler, BC V0N 1B0 ☎ (604) 932-3338

Despite the lofty lift-ticket prices, Whistler's international clientele includes Gen-X and younger crowds who have lots of time on their hands and no visible means of financial support. They cram four to a room in the Shoestring Lodge, one of Whistler's oldest establishments (originally known as the Ski Boot Inn). If the walls could talk in the adjacent Boot Pub, the stories they could tell. . . . And with the paper-thin walls and floors at the Shoestring, noise travels fast from one room to the next. Oh, to be 21 and footloose.

11th Hour Lodgings

Sometimes it pays to make last-minute reservations. Of course, you risk not getting one at all, but you also might luck into a bargain room in the village, thanks to a cancellation or a slow day. Call Central Reservations, (800) 944-7853, and ask for their special deals; they change daily. If that doesn't work, call the Whistler Activity and Information Centre, (604) 932-2394, and request their list of private homes, condominiums, and less expensive private studios and dormitories. Also take a gander at the Saturday edition of the Vancouver Sun, *which lists extensive private rentals in its classified ad section.*

Southside Lodge

2101 Lake Placid Road (Whistler Creek), Whistler, BC V0N 1B0
☎ (604) 938-6477

Kitty-corner from the Whistler Creek quad, across from Union Station, and two floors above the Southside Deli (which has been known to crank up the music), the "lodge" is more like a back entrance to six low-key rooms with baths. It's primarily for the young at heart. And the longer you stay, the lower the rates; a bunk room sleeps four for about $80. The location is great—especially if you don't have wheels.

Stancliff House

3333 Panorama Ridge (Brio), Whistler, BC V0N 1B0 ☎ (604) 932-2393

If you want to know everything about Whistler, speak to Stancliff hosts Shirley and Stan Langtry. They're both well-informed and very involved locals who will make anyone's stay in Whistler a good one. They know where to direct families looking for an inexpensive meal, couples in search of romance, or guys looking for good suds on tap. Their three rooms are simple, and guests share the facilities and a large indoor hot tub. Be sure to try on those knit slippers—they're as warm as the fireplace upstairs.

Swiss Cottage Bed & Breakfast

7321 Fitzsimmons Drive (PO Box 1209), Whistler, BC V0N 1B0
☎ (604) 932-6062

White Gold Estates is turning into B&B heaven—and this cottage in a quiet cul-de-sac is one of its gems. Lost Lake trails are just outside the inn's door, a tennis court stands beyond the lawn, and the walk to Blackcomb is easy. Plus, by the time you step out from underneath the duvet onto the heated floor, Willy and Louise Gerig are whipping up eggs Benny or waffles for you in their large kitchen.

UBC AMS Whistler Lodge

2124 Nordic Drive, Whistler
(AMS at UBC, 6138 SUB Blvd, Vancouver, BC V6T IZI)
☎ (604) 932-6604 or (604) 822-5851 (reservations)

These club lodges are always a bargain, and UBC is no exception: $15 for UBC students, $23 for the rest of us (more on weekends). This 56-bed facility, managed by the Alma Mater Society of the University of British Columbia, definitely feels as though it caters toward students more than families, but it's open to everyone. Management is friendly. Beware the windowless rooms—they can be a bit frosty.

Whistler Hostel

5678 Alta Lake Road, Whistler, BC V0N 1B0 ☎ (604) 932-5492

Aside from being 15 minutes south of Whistler Village, this former fishing lodge has a great location on the west side of Alta Lake. If you arrive by train, you can get dropped off at the Whistler Hostel flag stop in the backyard, but if you're going to ski, you'll need a car or a big, friendly thumb. The no-shoes policy inside the hostel keeps the place clean and dry. There's a large living room with a wood-burning stove, an upright piano, and a well-used sauna and pool tables. In the summer, you can use the canoes for free. The eight bunk rooms (four bunks to a room) are upstairs, and one private double is available. The kitchen is shared. Whistler Hostel makes a primo base for windsurfing on Alta Lake.

The Log House B&B

1357 Elmwood (PO Box 699, General Delivery), Pemberton, BC V0N 2L0
☎ **(800) 894-6002 or (604) 894-6000**

This new, 5,000-square-foot log house looks slightly out of place on its residential street, but the space inside—and on the wraparound deck with a wraparound view—is wonderful. Irish-born Margaret and husband Bill Scott have a flair for design and hospitality. Each of the three very large guest rooms—with sleigh or poster beds—has its own TV, Jacuzzi, private bath, guest robes, mini-fridges, and comfy reading chairs. There's a hot tub outside. The location alone (about 20 minutes from Whistler) keeps the place affordable; and daily buses make ski travel a cinch.

Steelhead Inn

PO Box 100, Spences Bridge, BC V0K 2L0 ☎ **(250) 458-2398**

Historic Steelhead Inn, located on the Thompson River just off Trans-Canada 1, is one of the few notable lodgings along the Coast Mountain route. If you're feeling flush, fork over an extra $10 for one of the four rooms with a private bath, so you won't have to fight over the two potties shared by the eight units without. Owner Chazaq Ministeries offers reasonably priced dinners in the restaurant.

Okanagan Valley

The arid Okanagan Valley, splashed with lakes from the Canadian/U.S. border to Vernon at the north end of Okanagan Lake, is the favorite summer playground for western Canadians. Four lakes—Osoyoos (reportedly Canada's warmest freshwater lake), Skaha, Kalamalka, and the Okanagan—cover three-quarters of the length of the valley. The climate is Canada's driest, with only 10 inches of rain a year. No wonder waterlogged British Columbians and winter-weary Albertans make a yearly pilgrimage to its sun-soaked shores.

Laden with orchards, the valley is most striking in spring, when the fruit trees are in full bloom and the hillsides shimmer like green velvet. Autumn winemaking is a big event (western Canada's largest and best-attended wine festival is held here), and vineyards climb the hills above the orchards. Then winter comes, and the valley is quiet. The local climate is a powdery compromise between the chill of the Rockies and the slush of the Coast Mountains, and challenging ski slopes ring the valley.

Exploring

At the southernmost end of the Okanagan Valley, almost dipping into Washington, **Osoyoos** curiously bills itself as "the Spanish capital of Canada"—though no Spanish pioneers actually lived here. In 1975 the city realized it needed a facelift, observed that the Bavarian motif had been pre-empted by cities elsewhere, and decided to "go Spanish" by tacking up some fake red-tile roofs and matador billboards. View the valley splendor from atop Mount Kobau, just west of Osoyoos, off Kobau Road. Take the 2-kilometer Kobau Lookout Trail to the fire lookout, or hike the 5-kilometer Testalinden Trail. Bird-watchers shouldn't miss the Osoyoos Lake Ecological Reserve, located on the Inkaneep Indian Reserva-

tion south of town. A half hour west of Osoyoos is **Cathedral Provincial Park**, where azure lakes are framed by jagged peaks. Unusual rock formations make the area a fascinating place to hike.

Penticton takes full advantage of its dual lakefronts. The south end of town (essentially an unofficial summer amusement park, complete with go-cart tracks, amusement centers, miniature golf courses, water slides, and RV parks) touches the north shore of Skaha Lake. The north end of town sidles along the southern tip of Okanagan Lake. One of the most popular summer diversions is inner-tubing at a leisurely pace along the scenic river channel connecting the two lakes. Hydrophobes can cycle or in-line

Okanagan Skiing

Most experienced skiers prefer to walk to the lifts from their hotel in the morning, but it's a privilege that usually costs big bucks. Let's face it: The bargain beds are a drive away from the ski resorts. But the good news is that many in-town motels now offer free lift tickets to lure you to their beds. Check out the ski deals offered at lodgings in Kelowna, Penticton, and Vernon—then access some of the best (little-known) powder in North America.

Silver Star Mountain, east of Vernon, provides the best combination of downhill and cross-country skiing. The Klondike-style gaslight village is easy to navigate, and the mountain extends across two distinct faces; (250)542-0224.

East of Kelowna, **Big White** features 92 marked trails descending 765 vertical meters. Its location in the Monashee Range snowbelt makes artificial snow unnecessary. There's good cross-country skiing here, too; (250)765-3101.

Apex Resort, located west of Penticton, offers Okanagan's best expert runs. Its high-speed quad rises out of the Wild West theme village. Their Nordic Centre has track-set trails, and more trails can be accessed at Nickel Plate Lake, 5 kilometers south of Apex; (250)492-2880.

West of Osoyoos, there's more downhill skiing at **Mount Baldy**, usually one of the first mountains in the area to get blasted with snow; (604)498-2262.

---

skate on an adjacent pathway. On the fourth Sunday in August, the town is taken over by jocks of all ages (and their supporters), who come to town for the Ironman Canada Triathlon.

Summerland is another theme town, only these residents chose Tudor. Old Summerland is down on the water, but most of the town's businesses now thrive up on the hill. Swim at Antlers Beach Provincial Park, about 35 kilometers north of Summerland, where you'll find a great beach. In mid-September, walk up the easy trail to watch the spawning kokanee leap up Okanagan Falls. On the east side of Okanagan Lake, **Kelowna** is the largest and liveliest of the Okanagan cities, with some noisy nightlife, an attempt at culture (an art museum and summer theater), a growing range of continental and ethnic restaurants, a family regatta in July, and a free historical preserve at Father Pandosy's Mission, (250)860-8369, restored from the mid-1800s. The town even has its own version of the Loch Ness monster: Ogopogo. Turn

a blind eye to the urban sprawl along the main drag north of downtown, though.

At the Okanagan Valley's northern tip sits **Vernon**, the area's only city that isn't directly on a lake—though it's nestled between three of them. Kalamalka Lake boasts one of the Okanagan's prettiest beaches, at Jade Bay in nearby Coldstream. Its tropical hue is caused by the rich mineralization of the lake bed. **O'Keefe Historic Ranch**, 11 kilometers north of Vernon on Highway 97, is an original cattle ranch from the late 1800s. Now a museum, the compound retains most of its original buildings and equipment from that era. Tours run from May through October; (250)542-7868. You can get your morning java fix at Bean Scene (2923 30th Ave, Vernon; (250)558-1817).

The best time to purchase the Okanagan Valley's wonderful **fruit** is from mid-August through early September; however, beginning as early as late June the fruit starts ripening. Here's your harvest calendar: cherries (late June through mid-July), apricots (mid-July through mid-

August), peaches (mid-July through September), pears (August through September), apples (August through October), plums (September), and grapes (September through mid-October).

Just like Rodney Dangerfield, British Columbian winemakers used to get "no respect" from wine snobs and local folk alike. These days, however, they can hold their heads high; ever since British Columbia authorized estate and smaller "farmgate" **wineries**, many excellent small wineries have sprung up. Some of the best estate offerings come out of Gray Monk, 5 kilometers west of Winfield off Highway 97, (250)766-3168; Cedar Creek, 14 kilometers south of Kelowna in Okanagan Mission, (250)764-8866; Sumac Ridge, off Highway 97 just north of Summerland,

(250)494-0451; Hainle Vineyards, in Peachland, (250)767-2525; and Quail's Gate Vineyards, located between Westbank and Kelowna, (250)769-4451.

Other notable wineries worth a visit include Calona (1125 Richter St, Kelowna; (250)762-9144); Gehringer Brothers (4 kilometers south of Oliver, off Hwy 97 on Rd 8; (250)498-3537); St. Hubertus (on Lakeshore Rd in Kelowna; (250)764-7888); and Divino, (250)498-2784, and Okanagan Vineyards, (250)498-6663, both 5 kilometers south of Oliver off Highway 97. A chardonnay from Mission Hill Vineyards (south of Kelowna, off Boucherie Rd in Westbank; (250)768-7611) was recently named one of the world's best. Most wineries offer tastings and seasonal tours; call ahead for times and dates.

Cheap Eats

Campo Marina
Main Street, Osoyoos ☎ (250) 495-7650

Oddly enough, the two best (and most expensive) restaurants in this Spanish-style town are Italian (Campo Marina) and Greek (the Diamond restaurant). You won't find a dock at Campo Marina, but you will find superb pasta dishes at this intimate yet bustling little bistro. On hot summer nights, ask for a seat on the patio.

Hog's Breath Coffee Company
202 Main Street, Penticton ☎ (250) 493-7800

Local triathlete Mike Barrett competed in an Australian race that passed by a bar called the Hog's Breath Saloon. He liked the moniker so much that he gave the name to his own coffee bar in Penticton. Now the Hog's Breath is the unofficial hangout for triathletes from around the world on the day after the annual Ironman Canada Triathlon. So suck in your tummy and tuck into one of the special quiches, salads, and sandwiches that make this spot so popular with tourists and locals alike.

Theo's
687 Main Street, Penticton ☎ (250) 492-4019

The ever-popular Theo's boasts a series of sun-dappled covered patios—roofed with rough-sawn beams, floored with red tile, walled in white stucco—where you can munch on some excellent octopus or fried squid or a mighty moussaka or rabbit (from nearby Summerland).

Shaughnessy's Cove

12817 Lake Shore Drive, Summerland ☎ (250) 494-1212

Built as close to the water as the law allows, this restaurant offers everything from fish 'n' chips to pasta and steak, plus the house specialty known as Puff and Stuff—a seafood combo wrapped in puff pastry. If you're traveling to Shaughnessy's by boat, several slips are available at the nearby dock.

Chinese Laundry

5818 Beach Avenue, Peachland ☎ (250) 767-2722

Yes indeed, the Chinese Laundry had a previous life as a laundromat, and now it's a popular Chinese restaurant decorated with laundry-related antiques. Expect all the usual Cantonese favorites, including sweet-and-sour this and that as well as seafood-studded chow mein noodles. The Sunday buffet dinner is a good deal.

Fintry Queen

Foot of Bernard Avenue, Kelowna ☎ (250) 763-2780

The festive paddle wheeler *Fintry Queen* plies the waters of Okanagan Lake in search of Ogopogo, Kelowna's version of the Loch Ness monster. Younger customers might blanch at its kitschy appurtenances, but the grandparents will probably love it. The *Fintry*'s restaurant offers a mean smorgasbord. Cruise-only patrons should be aware that brown-bagging is not allowed. The *Fintry* stays put during the winter, and the restaurant is closed.

Hotel Eldorado

500 Cook Road, Kelowna ☎ (250) 763-7500

If you can afford to splurge a little, do it at an outdoor table on the porch of the Gatsbyesque Hotel Eldorado. The do-it-yourself pasta bar is a hit, especially when you wash down the noodles with a local Okanagan wine.

Cheap Sleeps

Avalon Motel

9106 Main Street (PO Box 92), Osoyoos, BC V0H 1V0 ☎ (250) 495-6334

The centrally located Avalon is just a short walk from the Lion's Park, Gyro Park, and Legion Beaches. Amiable owner Phil Elliott offers 12 guest rooms at reasonable rates. This older hotel is clean and comfortable and features full baths, cable TV, free coffee, and complimentary continental breakfast.

Inkaneep Resort

RR 2, Osoyoos, BC V0H 1V0 ☎ (250) 495-6353

This old resort's best attribute is its location on its own miniature peninsula: all 10 beach-level rooms face directly south (getting maximum sun) and are only minutes away from the water's edge. Most folks (some have been vacationing here for years) don't mind that the accommodations are a bit camplike, because they really come for the sun. In the summer all rooms are rented by the week only (and prices edge out of the budget range), but winter rates are a bargain.

Houseboating

Houseboating on 113-kilometer-long Lake Okanagan is a good three- to seven-day vacation plan for the entire family. Most houseboats sleep up to 10 and come equipped with everything from a microwave oven to a water slide. No previous boating experience is necessary. Contact Okanagan Boat Charters and Sailboats in Penticton at (250)492-5099. You can also explore the 1,600 kilometers of Shuswap Lake's spiderlike shoreline at the northern end of the Okanagan Valley. A seven-day houseboat trip will cost a tidy sum, but if you bring a bunch of friends to split the bill, it won't do too much damage to your pocketbook. Call Waterway Houseboats at (250)836-2505.

Lakeside Resort
RR 3, Site 6, Comp 5, Oliver, BC V6H 1T0 ☎ (250) 498-2177

It doesn't rain very often at the south end of the Okanagan, but when it does you'll be happy to be holed up in a cabana at the Lakeside Resort. Owner Paul Bouchard describes his cabanas as "condo camping"—there's a roof over your head, cold running water, and kitchen space, but you have to bring your own bedding and pots and pans. There is a flat fee for each cabana, which sleeps up to six people. Campsites and a 20-unit motel are available, too. The nearby beach on Tuc-el-Nuit Lake is one of the best in the Okanagan, plus it's jet-ski-free—whoopee!

Chute Lake Resort
797 Alexander Avenue, Penticton, BC V2A 1E6 ☎ (250) 493-3535

This rustic resort is a year-round base camp for folks who come to hike, fish, cross-country ski, and snowmobile, among other outdoor activities. In the summer the lake is clear, the trout are jumping, and the hiking is terrific. This is a rickety old BYO-bedding kind of place; most cabins have wood-burning stoves, but only two have running water. The lodge offers eight guest rooms with slanted floors, plug-in electric heaters, shower facilities, and an informal dining room. If you're a bicyclist, you'll love the incredible descent into the Okanagan Mission area, as well as riding across the trestle bridge on the old Kettle Valley rail bed.

Club Paradise Motel
1000 Lakeshore Drive, Penticton, BC V2A 1C1 ☎ (250) 493-8400

Just across the street from Okanagan Lake's sandy beaches stands the 11-room Club Paradise Motel. Some rooms have kitchenettes, and all have access to the indoor Jacuzzi. Picnic tables and barbecues are part of the deal, or you can dine indoors at Salty's Seafood in front of the motel.

Penticton Youth Hostel
464 Ellis Street, Penticton, BC V2A 4M2 ☎ (250) 492-3992

The Penticton Youth Hostel sets high standards, offering dorm rooms, family rooms, and private rooms, as well as communal dining facilities, a kitchen, a barbecue, a living room, and a coin-operated laundry. If it's summertime and you haven't reserved a space, keep your fingers crossed and show up early. Hostel members save about four bucks a night.

Camping

There's no shortage of camping in the Okanagan Valley, now that dozens of commercial sites have sprung up. The prime real estate, however, is within the two dozen provincial parks; most of their campgrounds are open April through October, though some are open year-round. During the peak season of July and August, several parks will take advance reservations. Listed below are some lakeside provincial parks with campsites. The sites at the first five parks can be reserved in advance; call Discover BC Camping at (800)689-9025, or contact the BC Parks regional office, located 11 kilometers north of Summerland on Highway 97 at Okanagan Lake Provincial Park; (250)494-6500.

Bear Creek Provincial Park *(9 kilometers west of Kelowna). Here you'll find kokanee spawning in Bear Creek in mid-September, great hikes in a cool canyon, and mountain whitefish in the lake.*

Fintry Provincial Park *(9 kilometers west of Kelowna). This park, adjacent to Bear Creek, is on an historic farm purchased in 1996 by BC Parks. There are more than 890 acres of parkland, including the Old Manor House, which will be restored and opened to the public someday.*

Ellison Provincial Park *(northeastern shore of Okanagan Lake, southwest of Vernon). Ellison offers good fishing, six archaeological sites, and an underwater park for scuba divers.*

Haynes Point Provincial Park *(2 kilometers south of Osoyoos). At Haynes you'll find good fishing for rainbow trout and bass, coveted lakefront campsites, and a campsite reservation system during the peak season.*

Okanagan Lake Provincial Park *(24 kilometers north of Penticton). The valley's biggest provincial park, Okanagan has sandy beaches, ponderosa pines, and sagebrush. Open year-round.*

Darke Lake Provincial Park *(18 kilometers northwest of Summerland). Darke Lake is known for ice fishing and skating in the winter, and rainbow and brook-trout fishing in the summer. Unfortunately, there are only five campsites. Open year-round.*

Inkaneep Provincial Park *(6 kilometers north of Oliver). The Okanagan River runs through the park, providing good fishing, bird-watching, and canoeing opportunities (as long as you don't mind carrying your canoe the short distance to the river). Open year-round.*

Mabel Lake Provincial Park *(76 kilometers northeast of Vernon). Located on the flanks of the Monashee Mountains, this park is a cool respite from the desert heat of the Okanagan Valley.*

Okanagan Falls Provincial Park *(in Okanagan Falls). Come here for sandy beaches and lots of little mammals.*

Vaseux Provincial Park *(25 kilometers south of Penticton). Vaseux boasts an excellent wildlife habitat, a spring and winter range of California bighorn sheep, fabulous bird watching, and great ice fishing and skating. Open year-round.*

Idabel Lake Resort

12000 Highway 33E, #4, Kelowna, BC V1P 4K4 ☎ (250) 765-9511

During the summer the Okanagan Valley can become stifling, and the exhaust from jet-skis and car traffic can be nauseating if there isn't a breeze to freshen the air. At times like these, heading for the mountains makes perfect sense, and Idabel Lake offers great fishing and surprisingly warm water for a mountain lake. It's also the perfect base camp for cycling or hiking on the abandoned Kettle Valley Railway line at Myra Canyon. The resort's "hot-tub suites" are luxurious but pricey; the outlying cottages are a better deal and sleep up to six. There are campsites here, too. Canoes and rowboats are complimentary for lodge and cabin guests. Bring your own food; kitchen facilities are available.

Sandalwood Inn

3377 Lakeshore Road, Kelowna, BC V1W 3S9 ☎ (250) 762-5300

Perfectly situated across from Boyce-Gyro Beach on Lake Okanagan, the Sandalwood Inn's units are quite a find, since most of the hotels along this popular strip charge almost twice as much. Guests have an easy bike ride to the vineyards of Summerhill, St. Hubertus, and Cedar Creek, and there's good swimming at nearby Bertram Creek Regional Park.

Blue Stream

4202 32nd Street, Vernon, BC V1T 5P4 ☎ (250) 545-2221

Blue Stream may be the smallest motel in town, but it dishes out the biggest banana splits at its creekside ice cream parlor. Located 6½ kilometers north of pretty Kalamalka Lake, the motel has 11 sparkling guest rooms, and you can even bring your small pet. Rates start at $35.

The Kootenays

The sparkling waterways of the Columbia and Kootenay Rivers divide the four dramatic mountain ranges of the Kootenays. The Columbia River widens into the glacial reserves of Upper and Lower Arrow Lakes, carving along the flanks of the remote and densely forested Monashees and the rugged Selkirks. Dividing the West and East Kootenays is the Kootenay River, which becomes the sparkling, 110-kilometer-long Kootenay Lake. The pinnacles of the Purcells rise from the eastern shore of the tranquil lake. Beyond, at the edge of Alberta, are the Rocky Mountains.

All in all, this is one of the most stirringly beautiful areas in British Columbia, with no fewer than 58 provincial parks, each graced with deep river valleys, shimmering alpine lakes, and noble granite peaks trimmed with spectacular glaciers that attract world-class mountaineers. Access to some of these natural wonders is quite a challenge in itself; adventurers must boat into the Valhallas, a spectacular wilderness on the virgin shoreline of Slocan Lake, hike into the peaks of the Purcell Wilderness Conservancy from the northeast shore of Kootenay Lake, or drive 45 kilometers on a gravel road to reach the edge of the massive sculpted peaks of the Bugaboos.

You don't need to climb the Kokanee Glacier to enjoy the splendor of this area, though. Many of the jagged peaks, crevassed glaciers, and flowered meadows are visible from the roads that wind up and down along Arrow, Slocan, and Kootenay Lakes. And plenty of civilization fills such towns as tiny Rossland, historic Nelson, Bavarian Kimberley, and alpine Invermere.

Exploring

At the southwestern edge of the Kootenays, the 1890s Gold Rush town of Rossland is undergoing a second boom—this one fueled by snow. **Red Mountain Resort Ski Area** (6 kilometers southwest of Rossland; (250)362-7384) is one of the more challenging ski areas in British Columbia, with runs so steep that some carry a "triple black diamond" designation. Despair not, faint of heart, there's a whole mountain of great intermediate skiing on Red's Paradise lift; for

Cheap(er) Ski Tickets

Most accommodations in Rossland get ski lift tickets at a reduced rate. So purchase your ticket from your innkeeper before you get to **Red Mountain** *and save about $5. Most of the locals have season passes, and if you're planning to ski more than 17 days this year, it might be worth your wallet to purchase one too. Or call Red Mountain Resort Ski Area, (250)362-7384, and ask if they're offering any special promotions.*

snow conditions and reservations, call (250)362-5500. For striders and skaters, Black Jack Cross-Country Ski Club, (250)362-5811, has cut over 40 kilometers of cross-country ski trails; about half are groomed on a regular basis. Backcountry skiers can buy a one-way ticket for the Granite Chairlift to access Record Ridge, Mount Kirkup, and Gray Mountain. Be sure to sign out with the ski patrol before you go. For local trail info, consult Val Ash at the Red Mountain Motel, (250)362-9000.

In the summer, the colorful turn-of-the-century main street of **Rossland** bustles with hikers bound for alpine lakes, mountain bikers en route to numerous trails, and slackers sipping cappuccino. Several trailheads for mountain-biking and hiking routes start on the fringe of downtown. Locals know many afternoon-length **bike rides**, such as the ones up Kootenay-Columbia, along the Smuggler's Loop (where bootleggers used to cross the border), and over the Dewdney Trail. But before heading off, check with your host or the ever-helpful Rossland Chamber of Commerce (2185 Columbia Ave, Rossland; (250)362-5666). Many of the most popular trails cross private property.

With so much focus on the outdoors, it's no wonder that a number of **sports stores** have opened up in the area. You can rent mountain bikes and cross-country skis at most of the outdoor shops (although the only place to rent downhill equipment is up at Red Mountain; (250)362-7700). In Rossland, you can rent mountain bikes at Powder Hound

Boutique (2040 Columbia Ave, Rossland; (250)362-5311) in the summer and at High Country Sport (Red Mountain Motel, Hwy 3B, Rossland; (250)362-9000), usually closed in summer but open the rest of the year. Rossland Bike and Board (1999 2nd Ave, Rossland; (250)362-7211) is run by "Bones" Bonnery, who offers great deals on used bikes and boards (his shop doubles as a snowboard store in winter). You can save a couple of bucks by renting down in Trail at Gerick Cycle and Sports (908 Rossland Ave, Trail; (250)364-1661).

If you need a break from the outdoors, try going underground: tour Rossland's fascinating **Le Roi Gold Mine**, Canada's only hard-rock gold mine open to the public. With 109 kilometers of tunnels underneath Red Mountain, it's not just another roadside attraction. Open May through September; (250)362-7722.

Nestled in a valley on the shore of Kootenay Lake, **Nelson** sprang up with a silver and gold mining boom in the late 1890s. About a decade ago, residents tore off the fake sheet-metal and plastic storefronts that proliferated in the '50s and '60s and restored the town's Victorian character. Over 350 heritage sites are listed in this small, picturesque city. In recent years, Nelson played a starring role in the films *Housekeeping* and *Roxanne*. Nelsonites are pleased with all the attention the movies brought them, but they wearily remind visitors that their town is a lot more than just a pretty stage set. From theatrical productions to wildlife lectures to nationally known folk-rock groups, there's almost always something

Nelson Artwalk

In July, August, and September the entire town turns into an art gallery, with artists' work exhibited in almost 20 shops, restaurants, and galleries. Maps of Artwalk Gallery Tours can be picked up all over town and at the Tourist Information Bureau (225 Hall St, Nelson; (250)352-3433), or contact Artwalk (PO Box 422, Nelson, BC V1L 5R2; (250)352-2402).

going on at Nelson's Capitol Theatre; (250)352-6363. For a calendar of weekly events in town, pick up a free copy of the *Kootenay Weekly Express.*

Many mountain lakes are too cold for **swimming**, but Kootenay Lake's West Arm offers a refreshing dip. Located just before the bridge on Highway 3A, Lakeside Park has a great beach and beautifully landscaped gardens (there's even a Dairy Queen across the street for a dip of another kind).

Wilderness recreation is all the rage in the Kootenays, especially in summer. The most popular local hike is up to an old miner's cabin called Slocan Chief Cabin in **Kokanee Glacier Provincial Park**. You can throw your sleeping bag on one of the bunks (mattresses provided), and cooking facilities are available for $10 a night. In winter, Slocan Chief is so popular that the price goes up an additional five bucks and accommodations are assigned by a lottery system. You need a group of 12 to reserve (money up front), and you must stay for the entire week; call (250)352-6363 for information. If the Battleship Glacier looming overhead looks familiar, it's because the mountains grace the label of the Kootenays' most famous beer, Kokanee Lager.

To the west lie the even more wild and majestic **Valhallas**. A nice, easy trail leads the way along the edge of Slocan Lake. Although some hikers arrive by boat, the easiest way to the alpine trail is to drive 44 kilometers on good gravel road to the trailhead of Drinnon Pass and Gwillim Lakes. Watch for the blue parks sign at Passmore on Highway 6, and follow the

arrows to the parking area. The trail to Gwillim Lakes is easy to follow and takes 3 hours (one way); once there, numerous alpine hiking options exist for experienced parties. Be aware that snow often lingers in the alpine basins until mid-July. For complete information on the trails in the Kootenays, contact the district office of BC Parks, (250)825-4421.

Mountain biking is illegal within the perimeters of the provincial parks, but myriad logging roads in the region await adventuresome pedalers. Find out more (and rent a bike if needed) from Cool Sport (737 Baker St, Nelson; (250)354-4674). You can obtain other outdoor gear (such as canoes and cross-country skis) from Snowpack (333 Baker St, Nelson; (250)352-6411).

Due to its high elevation, **Whitewater Ski Area**, 20 kilometers south of Nelson, gets prodigious dumps of snow, and the tree skiing attracts expert skiers from all over North America; (250)354-4944 or (250)352-7669 (24-hour snow report). Although "WH20" is smaller than nearby Red Mountain, few Nelson skiers would ever trade places. Cross-country ski trails begin at Apex Nordic Center, at the base of Whitewater's Mount Ymir. The warming hut is open for use all the time, and the trail fee is $5; contact the Nelson Nordic Ski Club, (250)354-4292 (snow report).

The Kootenays' beauty isn't all superficial. At **Cody Caves Provincial Park** near Ainsworth, you can discover a subterranean passage crammed with stalactites. The logging road (accessible from Hwy 31) is not suitable for low-clearance vehicles or those pulling trailers. Sixty kilometers north of Nelson, on the shore of Kootenay Lake, backed by Kokanee Glacier Provincial Park and face to face with the pyramid-shaped peaks of the Purcells, rests the town of **Kaslo**. Sitting in dry dock here is the SS *Moyie*, a vintage stern-wheeler and now a National Historic Site, which logged over 3 million kilometers in its 50-year service on Kootenay Lake.

Slocan Lake slices between Kokanee Glacier Provincial Park and the awe-inspiring Valhallas. Three towns perch on the western shore of the deep blue lake: Silverton, New Denver, and Rosebury. The recreational opportunities in **Silverton** include fishing and trail rides. You can rent canoes from the Silverton Resort, (250)358-7157, and outfit yourself for the trail at Mistaya Outfitting, (250)358-7787.

The peaceful community of **New Denver** is home to a memorial of an infamous chapter in Canadian history. During World War II, thousands of Japanese-Canadians were declared "enemy aliens" and sent to internment camps in the British Columbia Interior. The **Nikkei Internment Memorial Centre** (306 Josephine St, New Denver; (250)358-7288) was built as part of an historic redress settlement, and it's open for public viewing.

If your spirits need lifting after you visit this somber site, hop in your car and head for Sandon. From there, drive up **Idaho Mountain**. The view from Wildgoose Basin on the way up is not only stunning, it's one of the most colorful places in the province, courtesy of a brilliant carpet of alpine wildflowers that festoon the meadows in midsummer. The hike to the lookout, once used by the Forest service as a fire tower, is suitable for kids, but don't forget the bug juice.

Bubbling hot pools are common in the Kootenays. Don't miss **Ainsworth Hot Springs** (on Hwy 31 about 46 kilometers north of Nelson; (250)229-4212) where

for $6 you can explore a cave of piping-hot waist-deep water or swim in the slightly cooler pool (open 365 days a year). High atop the steep shores of Upper Arrow Lake (actually a very wide spot in the Columbia River) is the town of Nakusp; 12 kilometers up a dirt road north of town, you'll find Nakusp Hot Springs, a wilderness swimming pool.

North of Nelson in Balfour, take the **ferry** across Kootenay Lake. It's a pretty 40-minute trip one way and the world's longest free ferry ride. You may feel caught in a time warp if you follow Highway 3A to **Creston**. Kootenay Forge, (250)227-9466, is an authentic blacksmith shop where you can watch Kootenay artisans plying this forgotten trade. Perhaps the most bizarre sight on all of Kootenay Lake is the **Glass House**, 25 miles north of Creston on the shores of Kootenay Lake, built from a half-million empty square-shaped bottles of embalming fluid. The grounds are beautifully landscaped, and visitors are welcome May through October.

Ornithologists from all over Canada come to the **Creston Wildlife Interpretive Centre** (PO Box 640, Creston, BC V0B 1G0; (250)428-3259) to scope out the wetland habitat at the south end of Kootenay Lake. Watch for ospreys painstakingly building their nests on top of the pilings. Admission is free, and you can camp for a fee at nearby Summit Creek.

Over in the East Kootenays, Cranbrook is a stretch of strip malls and grocery chains, useful to locals but not inspiring as a tourist destination except for the **Canadian Museum of Rail Transportation** (1 Van Horne, Cranbrook; (250)489-3918), which documents the history of the former railroad hub of this corner of British Columbia. Take the 30-minute guided tour ($6.75 for adults, $2.80 for students, 65 cents for children under 6) through a railroad yard of elegantly restored Canadian Pacific Railway Trans-Canada passenger-train cars. After the tour, English tea and scones are available in the dining car (Sundays only in the winter). Those willing to forgo the guided tour can view the cars from the platform outside for a buck less.

In some ways, **Kimberley** is like other Bavarianesque towns, with its chalet-style storefronts flanking a downtown pedestrian mall (called the Bavarian Platzl). Taped accordion music flows from the sizable wooden gazebo that sits squarely in the middle of this three-block, brick-paved street. Kimberley has at least one unique attraction, though: Canada's **largest cuckoo clock**. For two bits, Happy Hans pops out of the clock window and yodels. The town offers a sprinkling of shops selling wood carvings, European crystal, and Austrian linens. Gardeners shouldn't miss the teahouse, greenhouse, and immaculately kept gardens on the grounds of Kimberley Hospital (260 4th Ave, Kimberley; (250)427-2215. In summer, take English-style tea at the teahouse.

At 1,110 meters, Kimberley (the highest incorporated city in Canada) boasts an alpine setting in which skiing dominates all other activities for nearly half the year. Appropriately, the Rocky Mountain summits that thrust skyward from across the valley are called The Steeples. Mark Creek gushes through downtown. Only a few kilometers up the hill from the Platzl, **Kimberley Ski Resort**, (800)667-0871 or (250)427-4881, has two triple chair lifts, a double, a T-bar, 35 mostly intermediate ski runs, and a stunning view of several mountain ranges in the vicinity. For snow reports, call (250)427-7332. Package deals are available through area hotels and motels; call the ski resort for a list of participating establishments. The Kimberley Nordic Club's 26 kilometers of cross-country ski trails, an easy walk from the downhill resort, are varied and groomed well into spring. About 3½ kilometers are lit for night skiing. Kimberley now maintains two 18-hole golf courses: Kimberley Golf Club, (250)427-

4161, and the newer Trickle Creek Golf Resort, (250)427-3389, just down the mountain from the ski area.

Fort Steele Heritage Town (9851 Hwy 93/95, Fort Steele; (250)489-3351) is a faithful re-creation of Fort Steele, an 1890s Gold Rush town that was named after an officer of the North-West Mounted Police who was hired to defuse tensions between natives and new settlers. Though it's open year-round, it's most fun during the hustle and bustle of the summer months. Admission is a very reasonable $10.75 for a family group, or $5.50 for adults.

Eighteen kilometers west of Invermere off Highway 95, the ski area at **Panorama Resort** (Toby Creek Rd, Invermere; (250)342-6941) features North America's second-highest vertical drop—1,220 meters (4,000 feet). You can walk to the lifts from Panorama's own village, a sprawling establishment in the Purcell Mountains that contains two hotels, numerous condos, two restaurants, a nightclub, and outdoor recreation aplenty. Eight well-maintained tennis courts, as well as horseback riding, hiking trails, and river rafting on Toby Creek, relieve the resort from dependence on the winter ski trade. But ski season is still the time to visit. The snow is a deep powder (World Cup competitions have been held here), and if nature doesn't dispense enough of it, machines will. The hotel rooms are the best deal at the resort, but you can find even less expensive lodgings in Invermere. Resort accommodations are never more than a 5-minute walk to the chair lifts. The cross-country trail network here is exceptional too.

Towering mountains rise all around **Revelstoke**, a town whose history is tied to the building of the Canadian Pacific Railway; learn more about it at the Revelstoke Railway Museum (719 Track St; (250)837-6060). The four-block-long downtown on MacKenzie Avenue makes a nice stroll; a map of a self-guided heritage walking tour is available at the Revelstoke Museum (315 W 1st St; (250)837-3067). The **Canyon Hotsprings**, (250)837-2420, 34 kilometers east of Revelstoke on Trans-Canada 1, feature a mineral-water hot pool and mineral-water swimming pool; open summers only.

Revelstoke serves as a base camp for some amazing ski runs in and around the **Albert Icefields**. Trouble is, you need a helicopter to get to them. We're not about to list all the heli-ski operations in this territory (though you might start with Selkirk Tangiers Helicopter Skiing Ltd., (250)837-5378), but we will tell you that there are some great alpine cabins in Glacier National Park near Rogers Pass, where snow falls almost daily in winter. The cabins are open year-round for well-equipped backcountry skiers; to reserve, call (250)837-5345 or Glacier National Park, (250)837-7500.

Cheap Eats

Elmer's Corner Cafe
1999 2nd Avenue, Rossland ☎ (250) 362-5266

For youthful energy and imaginative cross-cultural culinary adventure, try Elmer's, a fave of the under-30 set. The Thai noodle burrito is much better than it sounds, and soups are from-scratch, as are the homemade breads. The decor is light and bright, making this one of the prettiest spots in a town where "pretty" is in no short supply.

Flying Steamshovel Inn
2003 2nd Avenue, Rossland ☎ (250) 362-7323

The atmosphere is minimal in the pub, but the standard pub-style fare offers good value for the dollar, with all the expected burgers, sandwiches, pastas, and seafood, all under $10. An adjoining dining room opened just before press time, serving Mexican food.

Sunshine Cafe
2116 Columbia Avenue, Rossland ☎ (250) 362-7630

The little Sunshine Cafe remains this small town's favorite. Breakfast, lunch, and dinner fare is nothing fancy—just good, filling food that won't set you back by more than a few bucks. The decor isn't anything to write home about, but the people who live and work in Rossland hang out here, making it the best spot for getting in touch with the political and social sensibilities that drive this unique little town.

Book Garden Cafe
556 Josephine Street, Nelson ☎ (250) 352-1812

The patio garden of this pleasant little bookstore is a good place to stop for lunch or a midday snack. While away an hour with a good book or the Sunday paper in one hand, and a cup of java and a rosemary-scented scone in the other. The fare is fresh, imaginative, and geared to the budget-minded bookworm, with soups (the pear soup is terrific), sandwiches (try the eggplant), salads, and such daily specials as Thai-style fried rice.

The Glacier Gourmet
621 Vernon Street, Nelson ☎ (250) 354-4495

For light munchies you could do far worse than the Glacier Gourmet, situated at the corner of Vernon and Hall Streets. The food leans toward the pizza-by-the-slice end of the spectrum, with sandwiches and veggie rolls, pasta salads, and sweets rounding out the menu. No booze, but they stay open late for java junkies looking for an inexpensive place to hang.

Main Street Diner
616 Baker Street, Nelson ☎ (250) 354-4848

Satisfyingly good, unpretentious, and down-home comfortable, the diner is one of the most popular spots in town. Locals congregate for Canadian classics like steak and fries or fish 'n' chips, as well as such Mediterranean comfort foods as Greek salad, hummus, or souvlaki with warm pita bread.

The Outer Clove
536 Baker Street, Nelson ☎ (250) 354-1667

This trendy little spot is for those who hold to the wisdom that there is no such thing as too much garlic. The menu gets rave reviews for its wily ways with the odiferous lily. Everything here, from tapas to soup to dessert(!), is garlic-based. As an idea, this one-trick pony could be disastrous; thankfully, there's a skilled hand in the kitchen, and the results are a revelation. Especially yummy are the garlic-chip cookies and the garlic ice cream.

Hungry Wolf Cafe
Highway 6, Winlaw ☎ (250) 226-7355

It's worth the 45-kilometer drive to tiny Winlaw in the Slocan Valley to totally stuff yourself at the famous Hungry Wolf Cafe (formerly the equally famous Duck Stop). The eclectic menu ranges from an 8-ounce New York strip steak to pizzas, stir-fries, vegetarian fare, and the Woodstock Special (pesto pizza and a salad). While the food is exceptional, the decor is not. Still, the appeal is down-home country casual, and kids are made to feel not only comfortable but welcome.

Treehouse
419 Front Street, Kaslo ☎ (250) 353-2955

If you're looking for great cheap eats in Kaslo, do as the locals do and chow down at the Treehouse. This neglected-looking place has a surprisingly diverse menu that will satisfy and delight just about any appetite; selections range from Mexican to pastas to Asian-style stir-fries to better-than-average burgers and dogs.

Wild Rose Cafe
Highway 6 and Rosebury Loop Road, Rosebury ☎ (250) 358-7744

The Wild Rose Cafe just might be the best-kept secret in the Kootenays, but only because Rosebury (population 50), about 65 miles from Nelson, is so darned hard to find. Start looking just north of New Denver. Once you've found Rosebury, you'll have no problem finding the Wild Rose, which is on the only road through the village. The food is a tasty hybrid the owners have dubbed "Mexinadian." Vegetarians will appreciate a menu that acknowledges their needs. In the summer the cafe is open 5pm to 9pm Wednesday through

Sunday. After Labor Day, it's weekend evenings only until late October, when it closes until the following April.

Lord Minto

93 5th Avenue, Nakusp ☎ (250) 265-4033

The bustling Lord Minto, named after a paddle wheeler that once hauled supplies and passengers up and down Arrow Lake, serves up a little bit of just about everything, from the expected steaks and pastas to a juicy Greek burger with feta, onions, lettuce, and tomato. Nothing fancy, but the food is good and the prices are right.

Kootenay Rose Coffeehouse

129 N 10th Avenue, Creston ☎ (250) 428-7252

Be sure to stop for a steaming cup of java at the Kootenay Rose—the only coffeehouse east of Kelowna that roasts its own beans. But it's not just black gold that makes the grade here: the strictly vegetarian menu offers soups, salads, quiches, and lasagne to help keep the jitters at bay.

Snowdrift Cafe

110 Spokane Street, Kimberley ☎ (250) 427-2001

The sporting-crowd locals blow into the Snowdrift Cafe on the Platzl for vegetarian food to go along with their lattes and mochas—possibly the best coffee in the East Kootenays. The menu boasts wholesome whole-wheat breads, vegetarian chili, pizza, and fresh salads. For a hit of decadence, try the impressive desserts, especially any one of the many different cheesecakes.

Cheap Sleeps

Angela's

1520 Spokane Street (PO Box 944), Rossland, BC V0G 1Y0 ☎ (250) 362-7790

Angela is delightful, and if you can afford to pay full price you'll get the full treatment: a whopping breakfast, a fireplace in your room, and a soak in the hot tub. But even if you happen to be a poor Australian ski bum (or an American or Canadian one, for that matter), she can probably work something out, as there are always extra foamies around. There are two bedrooms in the apartment on the top floor, which is well stocked with food and kitchen equipment. Groups often take over the whole joint. Plead your case or bring something to barter, and as long as it's not a holiday, you may just get a very good deal. Open November through April (and "some summers," says Angela).

Red Shutter

Red Mountain Road (PO Box 742), Rossland, BC V0G 1Y0 ☎ (250) 362-5131

You don't walk to Red Mountain from here, you ski. Larry Williams and John Heintz have been running this slopeside bed and breakfast for over 20 years now, and they've got a good thing going. It's a comfy, kick-back kind of place, and summer rates are a moderate $56 per night, double occupancy. In winter, when Rossland is really jumping, prices leap to about $59 per person per night.

Scotsman Motel

Junction of Highway 3B and Highway 22
(PO Box 1071) Rossland, BC V0G 1Y0 ☎ (250) 362-7364

It may be plain as the proverbial Jane, but the Scotsman Motel has an outdoor hot tub that has cured a lot of sore muscles. All the rooms are the right price (some even have their own kitchens). There's also a multiroom suite that sleeps six and may just be the best per-person deal (off season) in Rossland.

The Alpine

1120 Hall Mines Road, Nelson, BC V1L 1G6 ☎ (250) 352-5501

The Alpine is the nicest little motel in town. The least expensive of the 30 rooms comes in at about $55. Splurge a bit more, and you can slide into a room with a Jacuzzi (they've all got complimentary coffee and coffeemakers). Families or ski-bum pals might consider the two-bedroom suite that's practically a small apartment, featuring a kitchenette with twin beds in one bedroom and a queen in the other.

The Dancing Bear Inn

171 Baker Street, Nelson, BC V1L 4H1 ☎ (250) 352-7573

The Dancing Bear Inn (formerly known as the Allen Hotel) is so pleasant and inexpensive, it's almost too good to be true. For 40 years the hotel was a boardinghouse that catered to miners and railway workers. Things changed drastically after the owners took a summer trip to Europe and, impressed with the quality of hostel accommodations there, decided to open a European-style hostel in Nelson. The decor is simple but tasteful, and the rooms are comfortable. Solo travelers may end up sharing a room with another guest, and everyone is free to use the communal kitchen and laundry facilities. There are reading and video libraries for guests, and even Internet access (for a small fee). A night's stay will cost $17 (IYH members) or $20 (nonmembers).

Heritage Inn Bed and Breakfast

422 Vernon Street, Nelson, BC V1L 4E5 ☎ (250) 352-5331

In 1897, the Hume brothers decided that Nelson (then a bustling town of 3,000) needed a first-class hotel—so they built one. In a recent remodel, the hardwood floors and fireplace in the bar were rediscovered. After a complete restoration, the spacious rooms ($64) have been decorated with floral prints, lace curtains, and four-poster beds. The Library Lounge is the most comfortable meeting place in town, and Taffy Jack's (a disco) and Mike's Place, with a big-screen TV, can be lively, especially on weekends. Room rates include breakfast.

Lemon Creek Lodge

Kennedy Road (PO Box 68), Slocan, BC V0G 2C0 ☎ (250) 355-2403

Located between Nelson and Slocan is the Lemon Creek Lodge: part lodge, part cabins, and part tent and RV sites. Sociable types should choose one of the 10 lodge rooms, where mingling is encouraged by reading nooks, oversize chairs, and family-style meals (there's a licensed restaurant on the premises). Cabins (with their own kitchens) are more private. If you don't like sharing your vacation with RVs, come in the winter, when cross-country skiing (right outside the front door) is routine. Owners Judy and Barry Derco can organize backcountry ski tours via snowmobiles or via mountain bikes in summer. Visit ghost towns, hot springs, and remote mountain lakes. You can even pan for gold. A room for two in the lodge will run $60, including breakfast.

Valhalla Lodge and Tipi Retreat

City Beach, Slocan, BC ☎ (250) 365-3226

The Slocan Valley has always been a hideaway for earth-loving types, and it's only natural that one of the most environmentally friendly resorts in the Kootenays would be located here. Dean and Lynda Carter will pick you up by boat in Slocan and take you directly to their retreat, located right on the beach where Kutenai natives fished and camped for centuries. There's canoeing, hiking, and just plain relaxing on one of the most beautiful lakes in British Columbia. In the winter (October through April), the Carters take down their tepees and relinquish their spot to Mother Nature. There's a two-night minimum ($59 per night—which includes the use of a canoe), and tepees sleep up to five people. Be sure to bring your own sleeping bags and food (kitchen facilities are available). Adult oriented and no pets, please.

Mountain Edge Resort Inn

930 Dogwood Drive (PO Box 98), Kimberley, BC V1A 2Y5
☎ (800) 525-6622 or (250) 427-5381

Though they're down the hill from the ski resort, these one-bedroom condos are still within a hardy walking distance of the lifts. Some units have views of the Rockies; all have a fireplace, TV, hideabed, and access to laundry facilities and sauna. Each condo has kitchen facilities (either a kitchenette or the full quid). Depending on the season (Christmas is the priciest), units range from $53 to $99.

Alpine Huts

Alpine Club of Canada (ACC), PO Box 8040, Canmore, AB T1W 2T8
☎ (403) 678-3200

Seventeen alpine huts are hidden away throughout the Kootenays and Rockies: standing at the corner of a wildflower meadow near Lake O'Hara, blanketed under meters of snow in Rogers Pass, or nested on a forested bench above Tokkum Creek. Access might require an easy 15-minute hike or a challenging 12-kilometer ski. Each hut is equipped with a Coleman stove, lantern, dishes, rudimentary kitchens, and extra foamies for sweet dreams. The huts sleep anywhere from 6 to 30 people and cost from $12 to $22 a night. ACC members get reservation priority and discounts.

Index

Nancy Leson is a Seattle-based restaurant critic, food writer, and travel guidebook editor who slung gourmet hash at some of the country's finest restaurants for nearly two decades before retiring her white blouse, black skirt, and apron to write about food. Her restaurant reviews appear twice-weekly in *The Seattle Times*, and her freelance work has appeared in the *Seattle Weekly, Northwest Palate, Bon Appetit, Town & Country, Bride's, TimeOut London*, and numerous other publications.

Northwest Budget Traveler

Report Form

Based on my personal experience, I wish to nominate the following restaurant or place of lodging as a Cheap Eat or Cheap Sleep; or confirm/correct/disagree with the current review.

_____

_____

_____

(Please include address and telephone number of establishment, if convenient.)

Report

Please describe food, service, style, comfort, value, date of visit, and other aspects of your experience; continue on another piece of paper if necessary.

_____

_____

_____

_____

_____

_____

_____

_____

_____

I am not concerned, directly or indirectly, with the management or ownership of this establishment.

_____
SIGNED

_____
ADDRESS

_____
PHONE   DATE

Please address to *Northwest Budget Traveler* and send to:
SASQUATCH BOOKS
615 Second Avenue, Suite 260
Seattle, WA 98104
Feel free to email feedback as well: books@sasquatchbooks.com